*Rebuilding a Low-Income
Housing Policy*

Rebuilding a Low-Income Housing Policy

RACHEL G. BRATT

 Temple University Press • Philadelphia

Temple University Press, Philadelphia 19122
Copyright © 1989 by Temple University. All rights reserved
Published 1989
Printed in the United States of America

The paper used in this publication meets the minimum requirements of
American National Standard for Information Sciences—Permanence of
Paper for Printed Library Materials, ANSI Z39.48-1984

Library of Congress Cataloging-in-Publication Data
Bratt, Rachel G., 1946–
    Rebuilding a low-income housing policy / Rachel G. Bratt.
      p.   cm.
    Bibliography: p. 361
    Includes index.
    ISBN 0-87722-595-8 (alk. paper) ·
    1. Public housing—United States.   2. Housing policy—United
States.   3. Public housing—United States—Case studies.   I. Title.
HD7288.78.U5B73 1989
363.5'8—dc 19   88-19016
                                                                          CIP

To my mother, Jennie Glass,
A true inspiration,
With so much love

Contents

Preface

IN THE early 1980s, when this book was begun, housing had fallen low on the federal agenda. The private housing market, in conjunction with housing certificates or vouchers, was viewed widely as the solution to the limited housing ills that the federal government was willing to acknowledge; negative images of public housing prevailed; nonprofit housing organizations were still somewhat anomalous; and no coherent alternative vision was being offered. In some ways, much has changed; in others, we are just about where we were at the beginning of the decade.

Much of the criticism of the housing status quo that stimulated me to write this book was also beginning to be formulated by other scholars and activists. By now, public housing is generally no longer viewed as a total failure, and the need for programs that add to the supply of affordable housing is more widely recognized.

One of the most dramatic shifts on the housing scene during the past decade has been the growing appreciation of the role of community-based housing organizations. Embraced by a group of newly formed, well-respected national organizations, such as the Enterprise Foundation and the Local Initiatives Support Corporation, and fueled by longer-standing work with nonprofits by the Neighborhood Reinvestment Corporation, community-based housing was given added recognition in 1988, both by the introduction of a bill in Congress to create a new housing-supply program targeted to these organizations and by the recommendations of the National Housing Task Force.

It has been exciting to have been a witness to, and perhaps a small part of, the developing critique of prevailing housing policies and to the growing enthusiasm for community-based housing. I hope this book will contribute to the continuing debate on—and even the resolution of—the housing problems of the poor.

Acknowledgments

SEVERAL colleagues provided detailed comments on various chapters. Thanks go to Emily Achtenberg, Chester Hartman, Langley Keyes, and Robert Whittlesey. Andrew Mott reviewed the entire manuscript and offered many useful suggestions. In addition, earlier versions of several chapters were critiqued by Phillip Clay, Judith Feins, Terry Lane, Peter Marcuse, Eugene Meehan, Ann Meyerson, Mary Nenno, Florence Roisman, Marvin Siflinger, and Eleanor White. Over the years, William Apgar generously provided a great deal of information, and Emily Achtenberg and Langley Keyes provided regular infusions of intellectual stimulation. In the course of this project, several dozen people were interviewed, whose input was critical in helping the book take form.

I owe a special thank-you to the students in the Department of Urban and Environmental Policy at Tufts University with whom several of the chapters are co-authored. Thomas M. Harden, Emily Morris, and Wendy Plotkin composed a memorable group of graduate students whose energy and enthusiasm for housing issues gave me an added boost in writing this book.

I am also indebted to my colleagues at Tufts for their support, particularly to Ken Geiser, Robert Hollister, and Richard Schramm. Ann Gerroir, Arville Grady, and Patricia Watson, who staff the department, provided assistance in innumerable ways, and I owe them my thanks. Susan Anderson expertly word-processed much of the manuscript.

Michael Ames and Mary Capouya of Temple University Press were a joy to work with. They provided me with many helpful suggestions and, from the outset, Michael's enthusiasm for this book was a major source of encouragement.

Finally, and always, there is my family. Loving thanks to my mother Jennie Glass and brother Leon Glass for helping me to get to this point in my life. And to my husband, Michael Bratt, and our children, Jeremy Bratt and Joanna Bratt, my deepest appreciation for all their love, devotion, patience, and support.

Part I

Introduction

1

Housing Problems and Current Responses

AFTER THE devastating reductions in direct housing subsidies during the early and mid-1980s, Congress recently has begun to direct some efforts toward low-income housing issues. A new tax credit for low-income housing was authorized in the Tax Reform Act of 1986; the Stewart B. McKinney Homeless Assistance Act of 1987 was passed, signaling the first new direct federal subsidy for housing in many years; and in the last hours of the 1987 legislative session a new Housing and Community Development Act was enacted. In addition, during 1988 a series of major task force reports on housing were released (Report by the National Housing Preservation Task Force, 1988; Report of the National Housing Task Force, 1988; Report of the National Low Income Housing Preservation Commission, 1988), and several innovative housing bills were introduced in Congress. Finally, after eight years of federal neglect, housing may be returning to the national agenda.

This prospect, however, must be tempered by the outcome of the 1988 presidential election. As a candidate, President George Bush indicated in the first televised debate on September 25, 1988, that the McKinney Act, in conjunction with the involvement of voluntary organizations—1000 points of light—would place us on the right track concerning the homeless. As for housing in general, he stated: "If we spend and spend and spend, that is going to wrap up the housing market and we'll go right back to the days of the misery index and malaise." These statements provide a good preview of the new administration's views on housing: a likely continuation of the policies of President Reagan.

On the other hand, President George Bush's support of the McKinney Act (although only a small part of the overall solution) and his appointment of Jack Kemp, who has voiced a concern for the homeless and the poor, as Secretary of the Department of Housing and Urban Development provide some reason for cautious optimism.

During the Reagan administration, between 1981 and 1988, the total new budget authority for low-income housing programs fell from $32 billion to less than $8 billion. This trend must be reversed, and the country should commit itself to rebuilding a low-income housing policy. Although the housing problem has changed since Franklin Roosevelt proclaimed that "one third of the nation is ill-housed," it has by no means disappeared. For most low-income people, and to a lesser extent for those with moderate incomes, housing still presents formidable problems. And these problems are disproportionately severe for people of color.

Those of us who are among the lucky hear about the housing crisis only through media descriptions of elderly people being forced to move because their building is being converted to condominiums, young couples moving in with parents because they cannot find an affordable apartment or house to buy, and the family with several children living in an old school bus in a junkyard—or, even worse, finding themselves among the growing ranks of the homeless. For people who are experiencing these travails, where to find shelter and how to pay for it present immediate and daily dilemmas.

These vignettes of housing problems are confirmed by statistical trends.

1. Hundreds of thousands of Americans are currently homeless, and the numbers are increasing. Some cities have reported a doubling in their homeless populations from one year to the next (see, for example, Hopper and Hamberg, 1986).
2. Since 1981, contract rents have increased 16 percent faster than the rate of inflation and are at their highest levels in more than two decades. At roughly the same time, from 1983 to 1987, the number of renter households with incomes below the poverty level increased from 7.2 million to 7.5 million (Apgar, 1988).
3. Only 28 percent (2.1 million) of all renter households with incomes at or below the poverty level (7.5 million) live in public or other subsidized housing (Apgar, 1988).
4. Almost 12 million lower-income renter households (64 percent) pay more than 30 percent of their income for rent (GAO, 1985a).
5. Projections of the gap between the total supply of low-rent units and households needing such housing have estimated 7.8 million units by the year 2003 (Clay, 1987).
6. The homeownership rate has gone down since 1986, with particularly sharp declines among young households (Apgar, 1988).

While many policymakers have acknowledged these trends for some time, housing for low-income people has not been a major concern of government for at least two decades; many might argue that it has never been a major concern.

This book looks at past federal multifamily housing production programs, explores their strengths and weaknesses, and analyzes a new strategy to provide housing—production, rehabilitation, management, or ownership by community-based organizations. It argues that the potential of a new housing policy built on empowering community groups and low-income households is compelling. Providing even more than much-needed shelter, community-based housing also can offer participants control over and security in their living environments—qualities that have been lacking in housing provided by the private, for-profit sector as well as previous subsidy programs. In addition, the new housing agenda being proposed here includes a revived public housing program and a reconceptualization of the role of the private for-profit sector in subsidized housing. Taken together, these initiatives would go a long way toward rebuilding a low-income housing policy.

In brief, the book has seven broad objectives:

1. To reaffirm the need for more low-cost housing and develop a rationale for rebuilding a low-income housing policy
2. To analyze what past federal multifamily housing subsidy programs have accomplished and how they have pointed the way to new policy initiatives
3. To understand the limitations of the traditional public–private partnership in housing and explore whether and under what circumstances partnerships are viable, particularly in relation to community-based housing
4. To review the role of the U.S. Department of Housing and Urban Development (HUD) in administering housing programs and recommend ways for future policy to be implemented
5. To assess the overall community-based housing strategy and understand the positive and negative attributes of this approach
6. To examine a model state system for supporting community-based housing and draw preliminary conclusions about its strengths and weaknesses, and its potential for replication by other states and at the national level
7. To outline a new low-income housing policy that builds on our knowledge of past programs and that will meet the needs of current and future citizens

The remainder of this chapter presents the rationale for rebuilding a low-income housing policy. Two specific questions provide the framework for this discussion: What is the nature of the current low-income housing problem, with a specific emphasis on low-income renters? What are the prevailing views about how these problems should be addressed?

Shifts in the Nature of the Housing Problem

Academics and housing analysts recognize four major aspects of the housing problem: affordability (ratio of housing costs to income), adequacy (including quality and overcrowding), neighborhood conditions, and availability. Over the past several decades, the nature of the country's housing problem has undergone some important transformations.

Traditionally, the phrase *housing problem* conjured up images of low-quality and overcrowded conditions that were principally the concern of low-income and minority people. By the late 1970s, however, a new aspect of the housing problem had become fixed in the American consciousness. The September 12, 1977, issue of *Time* magazine devoted its cover story to "Sky High Housing" costs and proclaimed that "outasight" prices were endangering the American dream of homeownership.

An affordability problem exists when shelter costs far exceed what people can pay, which is traditionally assumed to be about 25 percent of income.[1] Yet a substantial number of households have been paying more than this amount for decades. For example, in 1950 about 32 percent of all renters paid more than a quarter of their income for rent. By 1983, the proportion had risen to 58 percent (*Report of the President's Commission on Housing*, 1982; U.S. Bureau of the Census, 1983). Although some of this increase reflected decreasing incomes of the overall renter population and increases in quality of the rental stock, the cost of shelter has gone up faster than renter incomes (Apgar, 1988).

For renters considered to have very low incomes,[2] lack of sufficient income to pay for housing is even more problematic: 78 percent paid more than 30 percent of their income for rent in 1983. Particularly disturbing is that the trend is worsening: Between 1975 and 1983, the number of lower-income households (which includes the low- and very-low-income groups) with rent burdens in excess of 30 percent of income increased from 7.8 million (54 percent) to 11.9 million (64 percent) (GAO, 1985a).

Although affordability is a major concern for millions of people, low-quality housing also poses serious problems. In 1940, over 45 percent of all housing units lacked some or all plumbing, and 15 percent were dilapidated or needed major repairs. Over the past five decades, the situation has improved significantly, although the pace of this improvement has stalled since 1974; about 11.5 percent of all occupied dwelling units are still considered structurally inadequate (Apgar, 1985). Between 1974 and 1983, the number of renter households living in severely inadequate housing actually increased, from 3.6 million to 3.85 million (Apgar, 1985). And among various subgroups, such as blacks, Hispanics, very-low-income renters, and rural southern households, a higher-than-average incidence of inadequacy persists (GAO, 1985a; *Report of the President's Commission on Housing*, 1982).

An important aspect of overall housing quality is the condition of the neighborhood. In 1979, 73 percent of all renters rated their neighborhoods as deficient in one or more respects—for example, too much litter, noise or crime, streets needing lighting or repairs (U.S. Bureau of the Census, 1982). Moreover, as of 1983, one in twelve renters was living in units with boarded-up buildings on the same street. For renters earning less than $7000 per year, one in seven households lived in such units (U.S. Bureau of the Census, 1983).

Housing analysts generally agree that the affordability problem has worsened and that overall housing quality (including the incidence of overcrowding) has gotten better; there has been debate on whether the supply of low-cost housing is adequate. In 1979, the U.S. General Accounting Office (GAO) called rental housing "a national problem that needs immediate attention" and cited a lack of affordable rental units, particularly for lower-income and large families. Nevertheless, just two years later, HUD published a report that said the reverse: "There is no current nationwide shortage in the rental housing market" (1981, ii). While admitting that "there are adverse conditions for rental housing existing in some local areas," the report concluded that "rental housing is not currently in a crisis state on a national level" (1981, 3). This view was shared by several noted housing economists. For example, John Weicher asserted that "most if not all of [the demand for rental units] can be met by the private market" (1981, 98). Ira Lowry claimed that he was

> unable to find persuasive evidence of a general shortage of rental housing, even in cities such as Los Angeles where public concern is intense. It is more accurate to say that in many places renters are

unable to find dwellings of the size and quality they have come to prefer at rents they are accustomed to paying. (1981, 35) [3]

The debate over rental housing shortages became so confusing that one highly respected economist, Anthony Downs, seemingly all at the same time predicted a significant shortfall, denied that it could actually persist, and admitted that it could take the market "some time" before adjustments would take place. He stated:

> *Predicted shortfalls in rental housing construction cannot actually persist.* If the number of households demanding rental units exceeds the number of units available at some moment, competition among the demanders will drive up prices until equilibrium is reached. That will occur when some demanders drop out because they cannot afford the increased prices and more suppliers offer units for rent at those prices. Eventually the number of units supplied, and relative prices will stabilize. *Such adjustments do not occur instantaneously, however. The rental market can be in disequilibrium for some time while they are taking place.* (Downs, 1983, 127; italics added)

In a more straightforward way, other housing analysts have shown that the supply and demand of rental units have been out of phase and that the disparities are getting worse. For example, George Sternlieb and James Hughes (1981), using data from the *Annual Housing Survey*, found that

> more than a million units, which in 1973 rented for less than $150 a month, literally disappeared from the total housing inventory [in 1977]. . . . Low rent housing units are literally being removed, and the potential renter, who can only afford low rent, finds the inventory available to him or her shrinking markedly. (Sternlieb and Hughes, 1981, 111–112)

Also citing *Annual Housing Survey* data (which had been compiled by the Low Income Housing Information Service), Rolf Goetze pointed out that there either was "a 'deficit' of at least 2.8 million affordable rentals, or . . . that millions of lower income tenants must have been spending well over one-quarter of their income on housing in 1978" (1983, 16). And while he did not make specific predictions about the future, he did add, "Surely this situation has worsened" (1983, 37).

Perhaps the clearest statement on the seriousness of the availability problem was made by Cushing Dolbeare, former president of the National Low Income Housing Coalition. Based on 1980 census data, she estimated that for very-low-income renter households, a gap of 1.2 million units existed between the number of such households and the number of rental units available at rents representing 30 percent of their incomes (Dolbeare, 1983). And, as noted earlier, this gap has been predicted to increase dramatically by the turn of the century. Indeed, even the President's Commission on Housing admitted that "an increase in the stock of adequate housing may be needed . . . particularly in markets where the stock of lower-priced housing may be physically inadequate" (1982, 26).

Rhetoric aside, data generated in many locales, as well as the observations and experiences of many renters, point in the direction of serious shortages of rental housing. In Boston, New York, San Francisco, and many other large cities, the rental vacancy rate, particularly for low-rent and moderately priced units, is well below 5 percent, the generally accepted minimum needed to support household mobility (Hartman, 1983; Liebert, 1983). Although alarming, even these vacancy rate data do not tell the whole story. Also critical is whether available units are located in the right places, affordable to those who need shelter, and of the right size. Moreover, even when vacant units and needy households match, the possibility that discrimination will limit access still poses very real problems (Feins and Bratt, 1983; Hartman, 1983).

A decline in the household formation rate has been predicted for the rest of the century (Apgar, 1988), but lowered demand will not necessarily translate into adequate supply. Unless units are actually available to those in need of shelter, supply still will be inadequate. And according to economist William Apgar, this is the situation. There is a mismatch between available units and what lower-income people can afford, and "with the number of poor people increasing, the supply of inexpensive housing is not nearly keeping up."[4]

The scarcity of low-cost rental housing is poignantly demonstrated whenever subsidized units are advertised for rent. Over the past few years, in Boston, we have seen thousands of people apply for apartments in each newly built subsidized development, which may contain only 100–200 units. As one observer put it, "This is the reality of all those statistics about the housing shortage" (Taylor, 1981).

The increase in homelessness places the controversy over housing shortages in human, rather than statistical, terms. Available units, to the extent they exist, are often in the wrong places, unaffordable, or otherwise not accessible to the already homeless and those soon to be in need of housing.

According to Anthony Downs, homelessness probably is viewed as an unfortunate side effect of what happens when the housing market is in disequilibrium. Based on his predictions, other likely results of market imbalances include people being willing to accept lower-quality units; owners of rental property being able to get higher rents for marginal-quality units; and people spending larger proportions of income on rent, as rents increase faster than house purchase prices and prices in general. Finally, unwanted doubling up and household mergers are likely to occur more frequently as a result of economic constraints (Downs, 1983). Thus, even according to Downs, the technical term *market imbalances* can cause highly untechnical housing problems.

The debate in the early 1980s over rental housing shortages subsided by the end of the decade. But whether there was and is a *national* rental housing crisis (as suggested by the GAO and many housing advocates and analysts) or not (as argued by HUD and some economists), there is compelling evidence that many local markets have severe shortages of adequate low-cost rental housing and that these shortages will persist.

The Scarcity of Low-Rent Housing: What Should Be Done?

What, if anything, should be done about the lack of low-rent housing? Using Downs's terminology, should the market be helped to reach an equilibrium? Should any action be taken to alleviate problematic situations that are likely to occur while the market is trying to adjust itself? At one extreme, the answer seems to be no or not very much. For example, citing a "lack of evidence of housing market failure," Frank de Leeuw stated that "the rental 'crisis,' such as it is, does not warrant any special rental housing market remedies" (1981, 64). And although Anthony Downs saw the need for new construction of rental housing under certain limited circumstances and recommended grants or low-interest loans for rehabilitating and building a small number of new public housing units, these recommendations were viewed as relatively low priorities (1983).

Rolf Goetze has also acknowledged the need for some government involvement, but he advocates the use of incentives to encourage existing owners of rental housing to maintain their buildings. In any case, Goetze foresees that much of the impact of the future crunch in rental housing will have to be borne by individual households: "If the rental inventory will expand so little, how will people be housed? More densely than before—and the adjustment could be painful whenever realities are judged against housing expectations of the 1970s" (Goetze, 1983, 87). In short, "tenant expectations must adjust" (Goetze, 1983, 60). Downs has even recommended that we reconceptualize the meaning of the nation's housing goal, first articulated in the Housing Act of 1949: "A decent home and suitable living environment for every American family." His reasoning:

> Given the Reagan administration's drive to reduce federal non-defense spending, the realization of the [nation's housing] goal is not likely to be feasible soon. Hence this goal must be regarded primarily as an aspiration, not as a guarantee that individual families can use to demand publicly financed fulfillment of their "rights" to decent housing and a suitable environment. (Downs, 1983, 131)

Reinforcing the view that significant government intervention in housing is not called for, the *Report of the President's Commission on Housing* (1982) proclaimed that "the genius of the market economy, freed of the distortions forced by government housing policies and regulations . . . can provide for housing far better than Federal programs" (p. xvii).[5] Yet, in an apparently contradictory statement, the same report noted that "the private market has been unwilling or unable to house many of the families [who live in public housing], including many single-parent, minority, and large families" (p. 31). What, then, did the commission really recommend? On the one hand, it argued that major restrictions imposed on the private market have thwarted its ability to provide housing for low-income people. On the other hand, it conceded that the unassisted private housing market cannot provide the needed housing. This conflict is important to an understanding of the present conservative nonpolicy toward housing.

Even before the reductions in government spending for housing under the Reagan administration, many housing analysts and policymakers began to advocate a switch in government housing policy. Citing a multiplicity of defects with the long-standing subsidized housing production programs, and pointing to the burgeoning affordability problem, there was a general retreat from the status quo.

In abandoning subsidized production programs, many began to support a new kind of program that increases effective demand.

Direct cash vouchers or housing allowances that enable lower-income households to rent units on the private market have been proposed and supported by a host of academics and housing analysts, including even those who advocate little or no government intervention, such as the President's Commission on Housing (also see Aaron, 1972; Downs, 1983; Solomon, 1974). This strategy also has been translated into public policy. The Section 8 Existing Housing program, created in 1974, provides certificates to low-income households, thereby enabling them to afford an apartment in the private rental market. In addition, the Housing and Urban–Rural Recovery Act of 1983 authorized a slightly different housing voucher program.

Some of the enthusiasm for direct cash payments on behalf of low-income renters comes from the results of the Experimental Housing Allowance Program (EHAP). Authorized by Congress in 1970, EHAP tested how a housing allowance program could be administered and what impact it would have on both housing consumers and the local rental housing market. Although housing allowances seem to have some advantages over production programs, in view of the shortage of rental units it is important to ascertain whether allowances would help to increase the supply of housing. The concluding report on EHAP stated the findings on this issue very simply: "EHAP appears to have had no measurable effect on new construction" (HUD, 1980a, 53–54).

To remedy this, and to help overcome what the *Report of the President's Commission on Housing* called "local housing supply problems" (1982, 28), the commission recommended that new construction be added as an eligible activity of the Community Development Block Grant (CDBG) program and that a specific Housing Component of CDBG be created. Although these proposals were never implemented, some commissioners were fearful that even these measures would have been inadequate: "Without effective federal priorities for and constraints on the use of Housing Component funds . . . the needs of . . . [minority and large] households would not be met and . . . the Commission would fail to recommend any kind of realistic program to add to the supply of housing for those with the most critical housing problems in areas where the private sector simply cannot respond" (1982, 30). The fears of these commissioners notwithstanding, throughout the Reagan administration HUD held to its position that "there is simply *no* justification for a national rental production program" (Demery, 1987).

In the forefront of criticizing the lack of federal policies to deal with the inadequate supply of housing, and taking exception to prevailing views of what to do about our housing problems, is an articulate group of progressive housing analysts. Rather than accept that tenants should lower their expectations and that government involvement should decrease, they see the need for a significantly expanded public role in housing.

Toward the end of the 1980s, this view began to be embraced by a broad spectrum of housing advocates and congressional leaders. In the Housing and Community Development Act of 1987, Congress articulated an alarming view of housing needs and acknowledged federal responsibility to respond to the problem. The act stated that

> recent reductions in Federal assistance have contributed to a deepening housing crisis for low- and moderate-income families [and that] the tragedy of homelessness in urban and suburban communities across the Nation, involving a record number of people, dramatically demonstrates the lack of affordable residential shelter, and people living on the economic margins of our society . . . have few available alternatives for shelter.[6]

Based on this finding, the purpose of the act is

> to reaffirm the principle that decent and affordable shelter is a basic necessity, and the general welfare of the Nation and the health and living standards of its people *require the addition of new housing units to remedy a serious shortage of housing units for all Americans, particularly for persons of low and moderate income.* (Italics added.)[7]

Despite the strong language of the legislation, new housing production received only modest funding authorizations. For fiscal year 1988, $481 million was authorized for public housing and $1.682 billion for housing for the elderly and handicapped. An additional $25 million was earmarked for a new low-income homeownership program, known as Nehemiah Housing Opportunity Grants, although only limited funding has been appropriated.

While some lawmakers may have been influenced by how progressives described the housing problem and the responsibility of government, few would likely subscribe to the left's analysis of why these problems exist. According to Chester Hartman, a leading progressive housing advocate, the housing crisis is a direct outcome of our economic system—"the failure of incomes to keep up with housing costs . . . the over-reliance on credit for building and buying housing, and . . . the workings of the profit system as it manifests itself in all phases of housing development, ownership, trading, and management" (Hartman, 1983, 8). Solutions, he argues, entail the provision of substantial government resources and "removing as much of the housing system as possible from the profit-maximization drive, and basing it instead on development mechanisms that have as their central motor provision of decent, affordable housing service rather than the extraction of profits" (Hartman, 1983, 9).

This book is in basic agreement with the left's analysis of our housing problems and what should be done to solve them. Yet, in advocating a progressive view of housing, the left's argument has been vulnerable to criticism. Before a proposal to expand the government's role in housing can be taken seriously, the widespread negative images about public housing must be explained. It is difficult to argue that public ownership and management of housing is the answer as long as conventional images about the nation's major experiment with this approach persist.

Ideas for rebuilding a low-income housing policy must also be informed by the experiences of subsidy programs that have relied on private, for-profit developers. In view of the popularity of public–private partnerships, it is important to understand how this approach compares to the public housing program and what conflicts arise when for-profit sponsors provide housing that is supposed to have clear public-purpose objectives.

In addition, in advancing a revived federal commitment to low-income housing, we need to propose new ideas and strategies. Much of this book is devoted to such a new approach: production, rehabilitation, management or ownership of housing by community-based and resident groups. Although this is referred to as a "new strategy," nonprofit organizations already have sponsored thousands of units of privately owned subsidized housing. But they have done so in the absence of a coordinated system of supports and subsidies; as a result, these efforts have been incidental to low-income housing production by private, for-profit developers or local housing authorities. Nevertheless, there is strong evidence that the community-based approach can produce solid achievements and warrants careful consideration as a potential housing strategy.

The accomplishments of community-based housing groups to date can be viewed in one of two ways: (1) as rare, anomalous occurrences that show how "the system" can be manipulated at the margin to produce decent, affordable housing, but that have little transferability and applicability to a broad array of circumstances; or (2) as a demonstration for how community- and tenant-owned housing could operate on a wide scale, supported by public programs. This book is concerned with exploring the latter perspective.

It is important to mention briefly what this book does not cover. First, a comprehensive housing policy would also need to address such issues as homeownership affordability for middle-class and young households; availability and cost of mortgage credit and the roles of financial institutions and federal financial regulatory agencies; utility of housing market controls; and incentives to private owners of unsubsidized rental housing to maintain their units. Although each area clearly merits a place in an overall housing agenda, this book has a different focus.

Second, this book does not specifically address the unique housing needs of various subgroups, such as the elderly and handicapped, and the homeless, and it discusses only briefly the needs of single women with children (Chapter 13). Nevertheless, the recommendations offered here would have an impact on all these groups, since they constitute a significant portion of the population in need of housing assistance. This book does not single out the homeless, for example, since their long-term housing needs are virtually identical to other low-income persons in need of affordable shelter. The only real difference is that the homeless need immediate short-term shelter, as well as available social service programs. But if this country embarked on rebuilding a low-income housing policy, the need for emergency shelters would be minimal, and *homelessness* would disappear from our contemporary vocabulary, since would-be homeless families would be immediately placed into permanent housing.

Third, while recommendations for changes in policy are detailed, no attempt has been made to estimate the cost of the proposed programs or to present the alternative financing mechanisms that could be employed.

Chapter 2, which completes the first section of the book, describes federal multifamily subsidized housing production programs in operation since 1937 and discusses criteria used in previous housing evaluations. It argues that a need exists to broaden the way in which housing policy is assessed to include important qualitative measures, such as the extent to which the programs affect psychological well-being and provide opportunities for empowerment. After briefly examining the role of citizens in federal community development initiatives, it also argues that housing programs will be best able to meet consumer needs through community-based strategies.

The second section of the book analyzes the multifamily housing subsidy programs and examines HUD's role as the implementer of federal housing policy. Chapters 3 and 4 evaluate the relative merits of the traditional federally subsidized multifamily strategies: the public housing program and the publicly subsidized, privately owned multifamily housing programs. In addition to focusing on an assessment of these approaches, each chapter presents a historical overview that includes an analysis of interest groups involved and political and economic forces that helped shape the various programs.

Chapter 5 consists of a case study of a policy debate that took place in Massachusetts. This debate is important because it reveals some clear conflicts between private owners of subsidized housing and public goals, and because it raises questions about the utility of traditional public–private partnerships in housing.

The last two chapters in this section, Chapters 6 and 7, focus on HUD's historical and contemporary roles in implementing low-income housing programs. For the latter, a case study examines HUD's property-disposition policies.

Part III is devoted to a study of the past, present, and future of community-based housing. Chapter 8 examines community-based housing programs that have been initiated, evaluates the strengths and weaknesses of the overall strategy, and articulates ways in which this approach improves on the two traditional mechanisms for increasing the supply of low-rent housing, discussed in Chapters 3 and 4.

Chapter 9 presents a case study of a community-based development organization in Holyoke, Massachusetts, and focuses on the challenges it faces both in terms of general economic trends and the local political environment. Chapter 10 continues the examination of community-based groups by looking at a series of dilemmas they are likely to encounter and presenting case studies of two groups that faced one of these difficult issues.

Chapter 11 analyzes the Massachusetts state programs that have evolved into a unique support system for community-based housing. The Massachusetts experience is instructive because it serves as an important example of how the public sector can provide "top-down" supports to "bottom-up" community-based housing initiatives. Chapter 12 presents a final case study, of the Boston Housing Partnership (BHP), a new program that institutionalizes some significant public and private supports for community-based housing.

The last chapter focuses on a series of recommendations for rebuilding a low-income housing policy and discusses some of the issues involved in enacting and implementing a national program to support community-based housing.

Concluding Note

A highly respected housing economist, Wallace Smith, introduced a 1983 collection of articles, *Housing in America*, by questioning whether what he termed our "general good standard of housing" was "due to reliance on market decision making, or . . . because we have —until recently at any rate—employed public policy to good effect in harnessing market forces"? He continued, "Like it or not, we are engaged in a nationwide experiment to shed light on that question by terminating major elements of public involvement; by the end of the decade we will probably have a better understanding of whether past governmental involvement has been beneficial or harmful" (Smith, 1983, 13).

Indeed, I believe we have now learned through hard experience what the curtailment of federal funding for housing has meant. This book charts a viable new direction for housing policy based on an evaluation of past programs and an analysis of innovative alternatives. I hope that this will be helpful in launching new programs in an administration that is supportive to housing and other needs of the poor. Until then, new ideas are still needed as states and cities continue to grapple with severe housing problems.

Implicit in the new agenda being proposed is that housing should be viewed as a fundamental right, that consumer needs should come before those of other actors in the housing system, and that since housing is a central focus of people's lives, subsidized programs must have resident input and control as key features. When a renewed commitment is made to housing, these ideas should be an important part of the debate.

2

Housing Programs and Housing Evaluations

A CENTRAL theme of this book is that housing policy in the United States should have, as its primary objective, meeting the shelter needs of the poor. In addition, it should be sensitive to the sociological and psychological meanings of housing in people's lives and should incorporate ways to enhance emotional well-being. Having shown in Chapter 1 that additional low-income housing is necessary, in this chapter I present the major housing production strategies that have been pursued; examine the contributions and limitations of previous evaluations of housing programs; argue that there is a need to broaden the criteria customarily used in these evaluations to include the intangible impacts of housing; explain why these impacts of housing programs have received little attention; review the traditional role of citizens in community development programs; and conclude that if citizens are more involved in the design, implementation, and management of housing and community development programs, there is a much greater chance that their needs will be served.

Major Housing Production Strategies

This book assumes that the private market will not produce the needed low-income housing without public incentives and that there is a clear need for the public sector to play a major role. Four ways in which the public sector has attempted to produce or stimulate the construction of housing are by providing supports to financial institutions, through tax incentives, by regulating the private market, and through direct subsidies for production.

Supports to Financial Institutions

Since the Great Depression, the federal government has actively supported private financial institutions, both as a way to ensure their long-term viability and to stimulate the production of housing. The first major production-oriented support program for financial institutions was provided through the Federal Housing Administration (FHA). Created in 1934, the FHA insured homeowners' rehabilitation loans and mortgages on newly purchased or constructed homes. At the time, financial institutions were reeling from the high rate of foreclosure brought on by the depression, and the FHA gave them a renewed confidence in mortgage lending. With FHA insurance, financial institutions were willing once again to lend, with the guarantee that most of the loaned funds could be recouped from the FHA in the event of foreclosure. And with the knowledge that newly built homes could be sold because attractive financing was available, builders became willing to get back into construction, which in turn stimulated the overall economy.

A second key financial support to help a depression-wary financial community, the Federal National Mortgage Association (FNMA, pronounced "Fannie May"), addressed another common fear of lenders—the need for quick liquidity. FNMA was created in 1938 to purchase FHA-insured loans from financial institutions in the event that they needed or wanted to convert these long-term, nonliquid assets into cash. Although FNMA was not used extensively in its early days, it did provide an important backup to financial institutions and contributed to their willingness to provide the needed funds for homebuilding.

In 1961, FNMA became the financing vehicle for a new subsidized multifamily housing development program, known as the Section 221(d)(3) program, to be discussed below. Seven years later, FNMA's functions were divided between market-oriented activities and those that gave special assistance to low-income housing programs. The former were placed under the control of a newly organized private corporation, retaining the FNMA name; the latter were given to a new public agency, known as the Government National Mortgage Association (GNMA, or "Ginnie Mae"). Through a program known as the FNMA-GNMA Tandem Plan, federally subsidized multifamily housing developments were able to obtain mortgage financing at attractive rates.

A third agency to support what is known as "secondary mortgage market" activities, that is, the buying and selling of mortgage loans after the loan has been originated by a lender, is the Federal Home Loan Mortgage Corporation (FHLMC, or "Freddie Mac"). FHLMC was created in 1970 specifically to serve as a secondary mortgage market facility for financial institutions regulated by the Federal

Home Loan Bank System, typically Federal Savings and Loan Associations.

Despite the success of the financial support agencies in bolstering the economy in the 1930s, and in enhancing the flow and availability of mortgage credit since then, the agencies have neither been geared to nor have they had a major impact on stimulating the production of low-income housing. Without tax incentives and direct subsidies, to be discussed below, supports to financial institutions would not have produced much low-income housing on their own. In general, this kind of approach represents a shallower form of subsidy than other production strategies.

Tax Incentives

Without tax incentives, the private sector would probably never have been a major producer of federally subsidized housing. During the 1960s and until the passage of the Tax Reform Act of 1986, Internal Revenue Service (IRS) regulations provided lucrative incentives for investment in subsidized housing. By "depreciating" the housing, developers could either use those tax losses to shelter income from other sources or could sell shares in the development to outside investors, thereby reaping large profits through a process known as *syndication*. (For more information on how tax incentives operate in low-income housing programs, see Chapter 5.)

Although the 1986 legislation made housing tax shelters much less attractive, it did include a new low-income tax credit. There are many reasons why tax incentives are both an attractive and a problematic option. On the positive side, tax incentives have proven that they achieve what they are supposed to achieve: production of housing. Also, because tax losses are not as clearly identified as expenditures as are direct appropriations, they are politically a more palatable mechanism for funding housing. Finally, because these subsidies depend on private investment decisions, administrative costs are probably lower than in direct subsidy programs.

There are also some serious criticisms of tax incentives as a vehicle for producing low-income housing. As discussed in Chapter 5, when the ability to make a profit fuels the investment in low-income housing, it is not surprising that conflicts between private developers, on the one hand, and the public sector and tenants, on the other, arise. In addition, using the tax system to produce low-income housing can be viewed as inequitable, since very large financial benefits accrue to those who are least in need of assistance. Although this allegedly is done to benefit the recipients of the housing, the lost taxes could theoretically be used directly to assist those in the greatest need. Also, the large profits enjoyed by private investors end up being a major factor in the overall cost of producing subsidized housing through the tax system. As discussed in Chapter 3, direct capital grants are generally a cheaper way of producing low-cost housing than subsidies channeled through the tax system. Finally through this mechanism Congress gives up some degree of control over the appropriations process. Because it is hard to assign an exact price tag to tax write-offs, it is difficult to carry out a full and fair evaluation of the tax subsidy approach, both with reference to what is produced and in comparison to other low-income housing strategies.

Regulating the Private Market

Tax incentives are obviously enormously popular among private-sector investors; the reverse is true for programs that regulate the activities of private actors in the housing market. Most such regulations limit what can be done with, or what can be charged for, housing. The two most common such regulations are ordinances concerning rent control and condominium conversion. Neither produces housing. Two additional strategies that do result in new units have been used on a limited basis in various parts of the country.

Inclusionary zoning ordinances and linkage take advantage of "hot" housing and commercial development markets to produce affordable housing. In locales where inclusionary zoning is in effect, a developer must set aside a certain percentage of the housing units to be built or rehabilitated for low- or moderate-income households. Although the developer will either take a loss on these units or reduce his profits, he is willing to do so in exchange for the necessary permits or to increase the density of his development.

Linkage is a mechanism whereby a developer of a downtown property either contributes a fixed percentage of the development cost to a fund set aside for affordable housing or agrees to build a certain number of such units in residential neighborhoods. Again, developers agree to this arrangement because it is viewed as a cost of doing business in a particular locale in which, it is assumed, the marketplace can withstand the surcharge. Despite the effectiveness of these two strategies, they have the potential to produce a limited number of units and they can only be used in areas that are in a boom stage of growth. (For more information see Advisory Group, 1983; Mallach, 1984; Metropolitan Area Planning Council, 1986.)

Direct Subsidies for Production

The largest production programs by far rely on direct subsidies. Within this category, two broad federal policies have been used to increase the supply of low-rent housing: production and ownership by the public sector, and private housing production and ownership with public incentives.

Public Sector Production and Ownership. The public housing program, created by the U.S. Housing Act of 1937, is the major mechanism through which production and ownership of housing are achieved by the public sector. Traditionally, local housing authorities (LHAs) raised capital to construct low-income housing by floating tax-exempt bonds that were purchased by private investors. The federal government contracted to pay the principal and interest on these notes over a forty-year period. This subsidy mechanism was replaced by a capital grant approach, authorized in the Housing and Community Development Act of 1987 (see Chapter 3). In 1969, Congress enacted the first of several operating subsidies to protect tenants from rising maintenance and energy costs. Over the past fifty years, over 1.3 million units of public housing have been built, with most of the construction taking place before 1970.

The much smaller military housing program, with a total of about 450,000 units, is generally not viewed as a form of public housing. With complete financing and ownership by the federal government, however, it is appropriate to place it in this category. Military housing is built on or near military bases in areas where the local market is unable to meet the housing needs of military personnel and their families. The actual construction and operating costs are funded through lump-sum congressional appropriations; as a result, there is no long-term debt financing (Hartman and Stone, 1986).

To the extent that there is a popular image of military housing, it is certainly positive or, at least, without major opponents or critics. As discussed in Chapter 3, the opposite is true of the conventional public housing program, which has had a stormy history and is saddled with a generally negative reputation.

Private Housing Production and Ownership with Public Incentives. In 1959, the first in a series of programs that provided financial incentives to private builders of multifamily housing was enacted. *Section 202* provided low-interest direct government loans to nonprofit sponsors of housing for the elderly. *Section 221(d)(3)*, enacted in 1961, authorized the federal government, through the Federal National Morgage Association, to purchase mortgages at below-market interest rates (BMIR) of 3 percent. For-profit or nonprofit developers were eligible to participate; the low-interest loans were translated into lowered rents that accommodated moderate-income households. *The Rent Supplement program,* by far the smallest of the subsidy programs, was created in 1965 and was almost a blueprint for the Section 8 program. Tenants paid 25 percent of their income for rent; the federal government paid the private landlord the difference between this amount and economic rent levels. The rent supplement program was frequently used in conjunction with the Section 221(d)(3) or Section 236 programs. *Section 236,* enacted in 1968, also authorized interest-rate subsidies. But instead of the public financing mechanism of the Section 221(d)(3) program, the Section 236 subsidy went toward lowering the interest rate on mortgages provided by private financial institutions to as low as 1 percent. *The Section 8 New Construction and Substantial Rehabilitation Program,* enacted in 1974, replaced the Section 236 program. Under Section 8, developers constructed new or substantially rehabilitated rental units for low-income people. Tenants pay 30 percent[1] of their income for rent with the difference between this amount and HUD-established "fair market rents" supplied as a subsidy by the government. Under the Reagan administration, this program came to a halt. Other components of Section 8—the Section 8 Existing Housing program and the Moderate Rehabilitation program—provide similar subsidies for households renting existing and moderately rehabilitated units on the private market and are still operational.

Almost 6000 federally subsidized housing projects were built through the Section 221(d)(3) and Section 236 programs, representing over 600,000 units of housing. Section 202 and the Section 8 New Construction and Substantial Rehabilitation program and the Section 8 Moderate Rehabilitation program contributed over 100,000, almost 800,000, and over 300,000 units respectively. Finally, the Rent Supplement program contributed some 29,000 units (Achtenberg, 1989; Council of Large Public Housing Authorities, 1986; Demery, 1987; HUD, 1978a, 1980b).

Section 202 has had the least tumultuous history of all the private multifamily subsidized housing programs and has had the longest lifespan. Except for a nine-year hiatus, between 1968 and 1977, when the Section 236 program assumed the production of housing for the elderly, the Section 202 program has been operational since 1959.

This compares to seven years for the Section 221(d)(3) program, eight years for the Section 236 program, and about ten years for the Section 8 New Construction and Substantial Rehabilitation program. Although the Section 202 program was significantly weakened during the Reagan administration, it nevertheless, managed to survive. (For more information on the production programs mentioned in this section, see Chapters 4 and 8.)

In view of the number and variety of housing programs, as well as the years they have been in existence, it would be reasonable enough to expect a fairly substantial literature on housing evaluations. However, the housing economist Henry Aaron has gone on record as stating that "the lack of solid information on housing programs, some of which have been in existence for decades, is appalling" (quoted in HUD, 1980a, 1). Nevertheless, several analysts, Aaron included, have produced some useful evaluations of federal housing subsidy programs.

Contributions and Limitations of Housing Evaluations

Overall, the kinds of questions asked and the measures used in housing evaluations have had a quantitative focus. The following are some of the most frequently raised questions in evaluations of multifamily housing programs performed in the 1970s and 1980s. References to important works that address these questions are also included.

1. How much does the program cost the federal government in both direct and indirect expenditures, per subsidized household (Aaron, 1972; GAO, 1978, 1980; Urban Systems Research and Engineering, 1982; Wallace et al., 1981)?
2. What percentage of the eligible population has been served (Aaron, 1972; GAO, 1980; Solomon, 1974; Wallace et al., 1981)?
3. What percentage of the subsidy dollars is channeled to those who are in the greatest need, as opposed to households with lesser need or to administrative costs (Solomon, 1974)?
4. How has the program been administered in terms of adequacy of underwriting, processing applications, and so on (HUD, 1972)?
5. What is the racial composition of program participants, and how does the program influence patterns of racial segregation (GAO, 1978; Wallace et al., 1981)?
6. Within the privately owned subsidized stock, what is the rate of default and foreclosure (GAO, 1978)?
7. What percentage of the subsidized stock is in need of repairs, and how

much would it cost to bring the entire stock up to certain specified standards (Abt Associates, 1988; Jones et al., 1979; Perkins and Will, 1980)?

8. How do benefits to tenants compare to costs borne by the public sector (Aaron, 1972; Solomon, 1974; Wallace et al., 1981)?
9. What impact have the subsidy programs had on employment and local property taxes (Solomon, 1974)?
10. What impact do housing programs that intervene in private market operations, such as rent control, have on various kinds of housing market activity, such as rates of abandonment and levels of investment (Marcuse, 1981; Sternlieb, 1972)?

Based on the above questions, the following set of criteria has been adapted for the present assessment of the public housing program and other multifamily subsidized housing programs:

1. Characteristics of tenants and tenant perceptions
2. Physical characteristics, condition, and design of developments
3. Management of developments
4. Accessibility of developments
5. Impact on racial integration
6. Costs to the federal government
7. Financial viability of developments
8. Ability to accommodate the neediest households

Despite the usefulness of these measures, they do not tell the whole story about a given set of housing programs. First, they do not address whether the housing program is able to provide shelter affordable to low-income households over the long term. Thus, an additional criterion should be added:

9. Extent to which the housing program demonstrates a long-term commitment to the goal of providing decent, affordable housing

Second, a major problem with these criteria is that they largely look at quantitative measures, thereby neglecting crucial variables that are not quantifiable. This is a problem facing all public and social policy evaluators. For example, an intervention in an educational curriculum is easier to measure in terms of test scores than in terms of how the child *feels* about the new program, or about himself or herself, or whether the initiative has produced changes in other aspects of the child's life. Similarly, medical interventions are readily measured in terms of days in the hospital, costs of treatment, and lost days of work; they are less easy to assess in terms of patient morale and impact on family members.

By neglecting to factor in costs and benefits that are not amenable to number values, it has been easy to make critical mistakes in the housing area. For example, although the negative effects on residents displaced from urban renewal areas may not have been considered terribly important, the initial decision to undertake urban renewal programs failed to consider the human costs involved. And, as demonstrated in studies by Fried (1963) and Gans (1962), these costs can be substantial. Treating people as people, not as chess pawns that can be easily moved from place to place or inert subjects in social programs—and, indeed, not simply as objects to be housed—is the crucial ingredient missing from nearly all housing evaluations.

A Need to Broaden Housing Evaluation Criteria

Housing is fundamental to how people live and how they feel about themselves. It is logical, therefore, that the house is both an extension of oneself and a reflection of one's position in life. Despite, or perhaps because of, the obvious relationship between housing and emotional well-being, research in this area is sparse and somewhat contradictory.

One of the most important, although inconclusive, studies on the social effects of housing was done in Baltimore in 1962 by Wilner et al. The researchers followed two sets of families over time—one that had moved into public housing and another that had stayed in slum housing. Very little difference was found between the two groups in terms of incidence of illness, level of aspirations, and school performance of children. The families in public housing did have significantly more interactions with their new neighbors, however.

In 1963, Alvin Schorr reviewed the available research on the effects of housing. In contrast to Wilner, he boldly concluded:

> The type of housing occupied influences health, behavior and attitude, particularly if the housing is desperately inadequate. . . . Housing, even when it is minimally adequate, appears to influence family and social relationships. . . . [Specifically,] the following effects may spring from poor housing: a perception of one's self that leads to pessimism and passivity, stress to which the individual cannot adapt, poor health, and a state of dissatisfaction. (P. 31)

Much of the research on the impact of housing on people's lives is based on experiences in Third World countries. For example, Healy (1971) investigated the impact of rehousing a group of workers in Mexico in terms of their productivity on the job, health, and absenteeism. Short-term productivity was found to increase after rehousing, although health-clinic visits remained the same and, somewhat surprisingly, absenteeism from work increased.

Interestingly enough, a large portion of the work in this area looks at the specific impact of "self-help"—the act of using one's own labor and resources to build one's housing. This research not only describes the importance of housing in people's lives but also underscores the benefits to individuals of being involved in the provision and maintenance of their housing. The argument is thoroughly logical: Given the central role of housing, it is apparent that the more people feel they are in control, the more likely they will feel overall contentment with their lives. These studies also have important implications for community-based housing. A central feature of self-help housing, individual control, is also a critical ingredient of the community-based housing strategy.

Burns and Shoup (1981) looked at resident satisfaction and housing investment behavior at several housing projects in El Salvador. The group that relocated into houses they built and owned themselves demonstrated greater satisfaction than a group whose housing was upgraded without any community organization or participation in the process, and without the group's attaining homeownership. In addition, owners were more likely to invest in the upgrading of their homes.

Another study by Burns (1983), also based in El Salvador, surveyed residents who had participated in a self-help housebuilding project. Focusing specifically on attitudinal changes, Burns concluded:

> As a consequence of their involvement, participants showed increased solidarity within their communities. In their view the potency of smaller, more immediate groups such as neighbourhood associations grew at the expense of more abstract agents of change. Just as power became more immediate, matters of the moment at least temporarily assumed precedence over the events in an abstract future.
>
> In contrast to studies depicting life in conventional public housing (e.g., Rainwater, 1970), these project participants gained identities through exercising initiative and, in so doing, realising the intrinsic worth of self-expression through taking active part in designing, building, and managing their projects. (P. 309)

One of the most passionate advocates for individual autonomy over housing is John F. C. Turner. Basing his observations largely on field work in Peru and Mexico, he has stated: "What matters in housing is what it *does* for people rather than what it *is*. [This] leads to the *principle of self-government in housing*. Only when housing is determined by households and local institutions and the enterprises that they control, can the requisite variety in dwelling environments be achieved" (Turner, 1976, 108).[2]

Self-help has also been used in the United States, although to a far lesser extent than abroad. The most comprehensive evaluation of self-help housing in this country was completed in 1969 by the Organization for Social and Technical Innovation (OSTI), under contract to HUD. Researchers defined self-help as "participation by an *individual* in any or all phases of the process regarding his own dwelling, with the primary intention being to reduce the amount of external assistance required for the completion of the process" (p. 9). Although the report cautions that self-help is not the right approach in all circumstances, it suggests that it can produce some far-reaching social benefits.

> The moderate income family with aspirations for higher status consolidates its upward mobility. . . . The capable but disadvantaged minority family [will establish] . . . itself in the wider society. . . . The family incapacitated by prolonged unemployment discovers or rediscovers hope and opportunity. . . . The indigenous and unambitious self-helper consolidates his independence and improves his condition. . . . The aspiring but extremely poor independent self-helper realizes his own opportunities and consolidates his improved status. (Pp. 104–111)

Some of the most convincing evidence on the link between housing and one's sense of self is anecdotal. The OSTI study provided numerous examples of how involvement with a self-help project seemed to change people's lives. One man "declared, spontaneously, that it was the sense of achievement gained through building his own house that led to his promotions and the tripling of his income in less than 15 years." The report continued, "Whether this is entirely true or not, the fact that he says so is in itself significant." Further evidence of the apparently extraordinary effects of self-help comes from the case of two men who became civil rights leaders after completing their houses, although they had never assumed such roles before (OSTI, 1969, 105–106).

An elated Philadelphia squatter who obtained legal ownership of her home stated: "Words can't explain how I feel. We have plenty of room. We're happy. If people were allowed to get a home to fix up, something that's theirs, there wouldn't be so much vandalism. Housing is the main issue for everyone and I won't forget how it was before" (quoted in Hartman et al., 1982, 69).

According to Barbara Ward, an expert on human settlements:

> The policy of encouraging home ownership can be used effectively to help poorer citizens. It does more than simply provide them with secure shelter. Even deeper needs are at issue here. It has been said of the poorest citizens, sadly but with too much truth, that they are "the people whose plans never work out." . . . [They] feel utterly powerless in the face of a system which, private or public, seems simply to push them around. . . . Perhaps the fundamental point in tenants organizing themselves for action is not simply to get themselves their own homes. It is the very act of organization . . . self-organization can be the creative answer. It turns the flow of authority back to the citizen, however impoverished. It can be the beginning of a plan that actually works out. (1976, 116)

Rental housing can invoke similar feelings (see also Chapter 8). A public housing resident in a scattered-site unit owned by a suburban housing authority stated:

> Before we moved into the public housing, I didn't even realize how much the kids were being affected. But as soon as we got settled into the new house and the kids started going to their new school, the change was enormous. They were able to concentrate better and they started doing much better in their school work. Since I didn't have to worry anymore about where I was going to live, I could focus on getting a good job. Before I got into the public housing, I realized that I just couldn't look for a job and look for a house at the same time. I had to do one thing at a time, and the house came first.[3]

Further evidence that housing is intimately related to one's sense of self comes from research on slum residents' perceptions of their dwellings. Citing a survey of people living in El Fanguito, Puerto Rico, known, before it was cleared, as "the largest slum in the world," Schorr noted that "many residents neglected to mention it when researchers asked them to name a slum" (1963, 8–9). Similarly, Stokes (1962) made the distinction between "slums of hope" and "slums of despair." Elaborating on this concept, Peattie (1969) stated:

> A typical "slum of despair" is the urban "gray area" in which once-good housing is being occupied by poor people and in which it is said that "the neighborhood is going down." The shacks of the hopeful entrants into the urban economy are typical "slums of hope"; their

occupants are people who feel that they are going up. It is not the
housing which makes the difference; it is the thrust of the social
forces affecting its residents or, at any rate, the way they perceive
those social forces. (Pp. 20–21)

Is there a contradiction between the two preceding arguments:
that housing has an important impact on people's lives and that even
the worst slums may not be perceived as poor housing by their occupants? I think not. The latter observation demonstrates that the link
between housing and sense of self works both ways. It is not just the
housing that has its impact on the individual, but the social context
in which the housing is experienced can essentially blind occupants
to the objectively low quality of their housing.

In addition to housing's close linkage to individual needs and perceptions, housing is also intertwined with community and societal
concerns. The quality of housing in a neighborhood is often viewed
as a quick way of assessing a community. Also, whether the majority
of the area's residents are homeowners or renters has been linked to
neighborhood stability and level of maintenance (Sternlieb, 1966).

But research on the impact of housing on the community is
sparse. The massive evaluation of housing programs done by HUD in
1973, which followed President Nixon's moratorium on subsidized
housing, made reference to this issue, but only cited studies on how
subsidized housing affects property values.

A particularly thoughtful view of what improved housing means
for the individual and the community comes from an analysis of
socialist Vienna's housing policies in the 1920s:

> The real contribution of Red Vienna's housing policies lies, I believe,
> in an aspect of housing policy to which it is difficult to give a name—
> in part because we are so little used to considering it a "real" aspect
> of housing. "Fairness" or "equity" are perhaps the closest to general
> terms for what is referred to here. "Symbolic" might also be appro-
> priate, except that it suggests appearance rather than reality, and this
> aspect of housing was a very real part of a real social rearrangement
> to the benefit of working people in Vienna. "Democratic" might be
> the best word, if it is clear that substantive democracy, not merely
> a set of formal procedures, is meant. It was what the city's housing
> policy *said* to the people of Vienna about their lives, their roles in
> society, the respect to which they were entitled and the importance
> of their welfare, their ultimate control over their own conditions of
> life, that made the difference—even if they could not at the particular
> time provide for themselves the ultimate level of housing which they

wanted and believed they would eventually obtain. (Marcuse, 1986, 578–579)

The idea that seems best to capture the essence of what housing can and should provide its occupants is a sense of personal empowerment and control over their living environments. In addition, the benefits of housing to the community should be assessed in terms of ability to stabilize the neighborhood, achieve upgrading without displacement, or both. Thus, this book argues that housing evaluations should include two additional criteria:

1. Potential for enhancing the well-being of individuals and contributing to a sense of empowerment and control
2. Potential for producing social and community benefits, particularly in terms of neighborhood stability and upgrading without displacement

It is important to recognize the difficulty of measuring the impact of improved housing on the individual and the community. For example, how can you tell if individuals have been empowered or if neighborhood improvements are due to the housing?

A study of mutual housing, a type of community-based housing discussed in Chapter 8, made an initial attempt at measuring the impact of changes in a housing situation on people's lives at one point in time after the move (Bratt, 1988). But it would be more desirable to obtain a series of measurements before the move, immediately after the move, and several years later; psychological tests on residents' self-image; incidences of divorces, separations, and so on; improvements in job and school situations; and increases in household income. Empowerment and control over one's life also may be inferred by several of the measures cited in the text above, particularly improvements in job and school situations and involvement in community-building activities. Also, information on such indices could be gathered for residents of one kind of development, such as one operated by a community-based housing organization, and compared to responses from residents living in another development type, such as conventionally owned and managed housing.[4]

Clear indicators of improvements at the neighborhood level are probably even more elusive than those one might use for measuring personal impacts. A 1973 HUD study pointed out the problem:

[It] is . . . necessary to show that the improved conditions result from better housing and not from other factors. This is not an easy causal relationship to prove or disprove. The improved conditions in one section of a community may result from the characteristics of the families drawn to subsidized housing. In that event, the improved housing may merely lead to the transfer of conditions from one location to another in a community. Similarly, the improved conditions may result from other factors, such as improved police protection, better health care, or community services other than housing. (Pp. 4–33)

A recent evaluation of the Local Initiatives Support Corporation devoted a section to "Neighborhood Effects" of community development work done with their support. After conceding the general difficulty of assessing these effects, the researchers pointed out that the unique characteristics of each neighborhood needs to be considered in such an evaluation.

The impacts of community development activities must be evaluated with . . . differences clearly in mind, because the types of changes that signal improvement vary with neighborhood type. In a badly deteriorated setting, a decline in the number of abandoned buildings can signal that the worst is over. In a rapidly gentrifying area, merely maintaining the existence of low-income housing units may be an important accomplishment. (Vidal et al., 1986, V–2)

The researchers further state that in the most devastated areas, signs of neighborhood improvement include, in addition to reduced levels of abandonment by owners, reduced vacancy rates, increased property prices at city auctions, the availability of property insurance and mortgage financing, an increase in consumer-oriented commercial establishments, and improvements in neighborhood facilities. For neighborhoods that are economically troubled and declining, but still viable, signs of improvement include stabilized real estate values, investment by current residents in their property, increased sales and sales tax revenues recorded by commercial establishments with an increase in the number and kinds of businesses, and, again, increased availability of insurance and financing. In areas that are economically troubled but with enough revitalization to make them subject to gentrification, positive effects on the community include stabilizing rising housing prices, an increase in availability of and support for affordable housing, and an increase in the variety of retail services (Vidal et al., 1986, V–2, 3).

This suggests that it may, indeed, be feasible to measure neighborhood effects of housing programs. Although it may never be possible to say that housing was the only contributor to change, powerful correlations may still be observed.

The present evaluation underscores the importance of assessing both the individual and the social impacts of housing programs. But the scope of this book does not include the measurement of individual or social impacts through data collection. Instead, this book emphasizes that these areas are of critical importance in providing thorough evaluations of housing programs, that more research in these areas is both desirable and feasible, and that, on a theoretical level, some programs seem far better than others when measured against these criteria.

Multiple Goals of Housing Programs: Why Human Impacts Receive Little Attention

In view of the importance of including individual and social impacts of housing in program evaluations and the relative absence of such material in evaluations, we can question why the omission has occurred. In addition to the difficulty of measuring these effects, it may be that analysts have generally overlooked the more human side of housing because housing policy in this country has emphasized a host of political and economic objectives. The provision of housing, as a human need, has not been the driving force. Thus it follows that if providing housing and serving the poor have not been the central objectives, then assessing how well the recipients are housed, in the fullest sense of the word, would have merited little attention.

Many housing analysts have concluded that this country's housing policies have been created to meet a multiplicity of goals. For example, making the argument that the slum clearance movement of the late nineteenth and early twentieth centuries was aimed at benefiting society in general, rather than slum dwellers, Lawrence Friedman has stated:

> Throughout American history . . . men have frequently advanced solutions to urban housing problems which meet external difficulties only. The law has emphasized fire prevention, sanitation, minimum standards of building and maintenance, and outright demolition of the slums. These are ways of protecting society from contamination rising out of the slums. The pathology of this . . . approach is its tendency to disregard the problems of people who live in the slums. (1968, 12)

One of this country's most significant housing initiatives, the Federal Housing Administration, (FHA) mentioned earlier, has been cited more for its role in helping the failing economy, the sluggish construction industry, and the depressed financial institutions than as a way of providing housing. According to John Dean, an early writer on the subject:

> The favorable attitudes of those testifying at the hearings before the Senate Committee which handled the FHA legislation indicate whose bread was to be buttered by the passage of the act (i.e., lumbermen, building trade representatives, real estate men, building materials suppliers, and bankers all spoke with enthusiasm for the FHA). (1945, 48)

Similarly, Nathaniel Keith, a former FHA official, stated:

> While the establishment of the FHA mortgage insurance program had some reform aspects from the standpoint of correcting the mortgage abuses of the Twenties, it was primarily sold politically as a program to unfreeze the home building industry and thereby stimulate employment and the economy. (1973, 24)

Finally, Miles Colean, author of a 1940s book, *American Housing*, summed up the results of FHA's multiple goals:

> The new measures had far-reaching implications and were for the most part intended to be of indefinite duration, but they were enacted when emergency conditions prevailed and had an emergency point of view. Each new housing bill was advocated as a means of stimulating the durable goods industries or putting men to work. Housing thus was looked upon as a remedy for general economic ills rather than a problem in itself. This confusion of objectives has hindered the coordinated development of Federal housing policy. (1944, 261–262)

Concerning the overall emphasis of housing policies through the early 1960s, the urban planner Charles Abrams concluded: "The economic motivation had been the dominant ingredient in Federal housing recipes from the inception and the stated ideal of better housing for everybody had simply supplied the sweetening" (1965, 85).

The multigoal nature of federal housing policies has been acknowledged by staff reports of Democratic and Republican presidents. In 1968, the *Report of the President's Committee on Urban Housing*, appointed by President Johnson, stated: "Housing programs have been enacted for a variety of purposes—to create jobs, to clear slums, to improve the tax base of central cities, and to help the poor" (p. 53). Five years later, a report based on President Nixon's National Housing Policy Review noted:

The multiple goals are perhaps the greatest reason for the prolifera-
tion and the confused state of housing law and housing programs.
Many housing laws have assigned to individual housing programs
the awesome job of achieving higher or stable housing production,
higher wages for construction workers, equal opportunity, urban
renewal and a higher quality environment—while at the same time
taking care to protect the consumer and further the free enterprise
system and all this without unbalancing the Federal budget and not
upsetting public opinion. (HUD, 1973, 1–37)

The construction industry, financial institutions, and private real
estate developers have formed powerful lobbying groups to ensure
that the private sector's interest in maintaining and increasing profits
has been well tended to by the federal government (see, e.g., Checkoway, 1980). The human side of housing has been neither a major
goal of housing programs nor a part of housing evaluations. An important question is: How can the needs of consumers be elevated
to a more important position? One immediate response would be:
by eliminating the multiple and sometimes conflicting objectives of
federal housing programs. But while housing advocates should work
toward policies that are more focused on consumer than on industry
needs, it is also critical that housing programs involve citizens more
closely in the processes of policy development, implementation, and
evaluation.

Citizen Participation

During the 1960s, the phrase *citizen participation* was in good currency. It would be convenient to argue that the move to include
citizens in planning and development projects grew out of a sudden
recognition that consumer needs should be the dominant goal of public policy and therefore it would make sense to involve citizens in the
process. Instead, citizen participation was the federal government's
response both to the growing grass-roots mobilization associated primarily with the civil rights movement and to the protests that had
sprung up in opposition to the first wave of urban renewal programs.
Thus, it is likely that the major factor behind citizen participation was
the government's desire to channel protests in the streets into more
comfortable and controllable discussions at the negotiating table.

In this context, citizen participation refers to a "top–down" initiative, that is, government devises the rules and terms for citizen
input. This can be distinguished from a "bottom–up" form of par-

ticipation, in which citizens decide how and for what purposes to become involved. The latter is synonymous with a grass-roots organizing strategy.

Within the academic community, a wide range of views on citizen participation have been articulated. Some accept both the top–down and bottom–up forms as legitimate participation (Langton, 1978); others are critical of the top–down approach, but the reasons vary widely. Some, such as Perlman (1978) and Gittell (1980), see top–down participation as not yielding true benefits to citizens or redistributing resources; others, such as Wilson (1966), argue against top–down participation because those most closely involved or affected by a plan or policy cannot be objective.

In the political arena, there has been little debate on the relative merits of top–down and bottom–up citizen participation. Instead, the issue has revolved around the amount and kind of top–down participation that should be required: Democrats have traditionally mandated more, while Republicans have mandated less. As a political issue, the question of how much top–down participation is desirable may have appeal, but as a practical matter, it may be more or less irrelevant.

As discussed in the following section, studies of federal programs that included specific citizen participation requirements generally reveal minimal real or lasting gains for residents. The federal community development initiatives provide good examples of the limitations of such top–down participation. By examining the way in which citizen participation was approached in each of these programs, a better understanding of the top–down approach should emerge. For purposes of the larger study, this analysis is important for two reasons. First, by demonstrating that top–down citizen involvement provides limited or no benefits for the participants, we have further support for a community-based housing strategy. Second, it serves as a backdrop for a key question considered in the final chapter: Is it possible for resident groups that organize themselves in a bottom–up way to acquire resources through top–down channels and still retain the best features of the grass-roots initiative? Or is it more likely that once federal resources are provided, the more typical features of top–down federally proscribed citizen participation initiatives will prevail?

The Role of Citizens in Community Development Programs

There have been three major federal programs aimed at revitalizing cities. A fourth, the War on Poverty, was not a HUD-implemented community development program, but it is being included here because it had a substantial impact on federal thinking concerning community development and revealed a great deal about the role of citizens in that process. As one team of researchers noted, this legislation "contributed to a necessary and desirable change in public attitudes concerning the role of poor people in civic affairs" (Lipsky et al., 1971, 898).

Urban Renewal

Enacted as part of the Housing Act of 1949, the Urban Renewal program was aimed at the renewal or redevelopment of slum or blighted areas through land acquisition, tenant relocation, site clearance and preparation, and disposition of the land to new developers. The federal government provided capital grants that were used to write down the cost of this process, thereby making redevelopment economically feasible.

Five years after the Urban Renewal program was launched, citizen participation was included, for the first time, as a prerequisite for a locality to receive federal funds. The Workable Program requirement of the Housing Act of 1954 requested, among other things, that the local government include citizens in the entire program. Despite this stipulation, citizen participation was never taken very seriously in the Urban Renewal program. For example, Richard Cole (1974) stated that "committees formed in accordance with [the Workable Program] requirement have blue-ribbon panels appointed by the mayor or planning staff and largely ignore residents of the project area" (p. 12). Similarly, a survey of renewal directors in the ninety-one cities that had approved workable programs as of July 31, 1956, disclosed that "the residents of project areas . . . seem to be relatively uninvolved" in Urban Renewal and that citizen representation on renewal committees is "almost totally absent" (cited in Wilson, 1966, 417).

Sherry Arnstein (1969) observed that the form of citizen participation commonly associated with the Urban Renewal program could be labeled as one of "manipulation."

In the name of citizen participation, people are placed on rubber-stamp advisory committees or advisory boards for the express purpose of "educating" them or engineering their support. Instead of genuine citizen participation, . . . [this manipulation] signifies the distortion of participation into a public relations vehicle by power-holders.

This illusory form of "participation" initially came into vogue with urban renewal when the socially elite were invited by city housing officials to serve on Citizen Advisory Committees. . . .

At meetings of the Citizen Advisory Committees, it was the officials who educated, persuaded, and advised the citizens, not the reverse. Federal guidelines for the renewal programs legitimized the manipulative agenda by emphasizing the terms "information gathering," "public relations," and "support" as the explicit functions of the committees. (P. 218)

Herbert Gans's vivid account of the destruction of Boston's West End provides the classic example of what Urban Renewal meant to many low-income people and neighborhoods that were planned *for*, not *with*. Citing a lack of information provided to residents of the renewal area, Gans (1962) summed up the extent to which citizens, including community leaders, were excluded from the process:

The truth was, that for a group unaccustomed to organizational activity, saving the West End was an overwhelming, and perhaps impossible, task. Indeed, there was relatively little the [Save the West End] Committee could do. The decision to redevelop the West End had been made early in the decade, and it had received the blessings of the city's decisive business leaders and politicians. The West End's local politicians all opposed the redevelopment, but were powerless against the unanimity of those who favored it. (Pp. 339–340)

In short, Rossi and Dentler (1961) concluded that "the maximum role to be played by a citizen participation movement in urban renewal is primarily a passive one" (p. 287).

Local renewal directors and chief executives were not the only ones who resisted the idea of including residents in the planning process. There was also an influential group of academics who voiced pessimism about the whole notion of citizen participation in Urban Renewal. For example, James Q. Wilson, professor of government at Harvard, had this to say:

"Planning with people" assumes on the part of the people involved a willingness and a capacity to engage in a collaborative search for the common good. The willingness is obviously almost never present when the persons involved will be severely penalized by having their homes and neighborhoods destroyed through wholesale clearance. . . .

If we decide to try to obtain the consent of those neighborhoods selected for renewal we had better prepare ourselves for a drastic reevaluation of the potential impact of that program. Adjusting the goals of renewal to the demands of the lower classes means, among other things, substantially reducing the prospects for assembling sufficiently large tracts of cleared land to make feasible the construction of dwelling units attractive to the middle-class suburbanite whom the city is anxious to woo back into its taxing jurisdiction. This, in turn, means that the central city may have to abandon the goal of recolonizing itself with a tax-paying, culture-loving, free-spending middle class and be content instead with serving as a slightly dilapidated way-station in which lower-income and minority groups find shelter and a minimal level of public services while working toward the day when they, too, can move out to a better life. (1966, 418)

Hence, to Wilson, participation by those affected by urban renewal plans could not be trusted, since their views could never be objective. The needs of local neighborhood people are seen as something apart from the "common good." And if one were to try to accommodate the demands of low-income residents, large-scale renewal would be infeasible, and the city would be relegated to a permanent position of inferiority and undesirability.

This argument gives a clear sense of what the citizen participation movement was up against. Wilson's views, highly respected in government circles, legitimized the notion that citizens' concerns were simply not relevant to the massive task of redevelopment.

The weak role played by residents had serious implications for hundreds of thousands of low-income and minority people who lost their homes as a result of Urban Renewal. As Scott Greer succinctly stated in 1965, "At a cost of more than $3 billion the Urban Renewal Agency has succeeded in materially reducing the supply of low-cost housing in American cities" (p. 1). In 1971, the statistics on demolitions compared to new construction of low- and moderate-income housing were still grim: More than twice as many units were removed as were added, and of those newly built units, only about one half were for low- and moderate-income households (Congressional Research Service, 1973, 56).

In 1974, Urban Renewal was terminated as a separate categorical program and became an eligible activity under the Community Development Block Grant program, to be discussed below. But the program left an important legacy; as the first federally funded community development initiative, it created an official citizen participation process, but did not guarantee that resident views, to the extent that they were even heard, would be incorporated into the final plans. Urban Renewal became an important backdrop for future controversies between elected officials and frustrated residents.

The War on Poverty

By the 1960s, citizens were no longer willing to be silent observers in revitalization programs. Moreover, the War on Poverty declared by President Johnson took a far more aggressive approach to the issue of citizen participation. Title II of the Economic Opportunity Act of 1964, which allocated funds to urban and rural community action programs, challenged local communities to create long-range plans for attacking poverty by utilizing all public and private resources available. But, above all, the poor were to be given the opportunity to help themselves (Marris and Rein, 1967, 113).

Following the precedent set by social action programs funded by the Ford Foundation and President Kennedy's Committee on Juvenile Delinquency and Youth Crime, the poverty program viewed the problems facing the poor less as the result of individual pathology and more the result of complex social and environmental forces. The remedy included two broad strategies: providing services that the poor usually were unable to obtain, such as vocational training; and developing mechanisms to enable the poor to become better organized and politically more powerful. In short, the Economic Opportunity Act was aimed at reducing poverty or its causes "through developing employment opportunities, improving human performance, motivation and productivity, or bettering the conditions under which people live, learn and work." The community action program was to be organized by a public or private nonprofit agency and "developed, conducted, and administered with the maximum feasible participation of the residents of the areas and members of the groups served" (quoted in Marris and Rein, 1967, 210).

There was an important conflict in the poverty program: The program was committed to encourage citizen participation, yet its designers were convinced that only the mayors were in a strong enough position to coordinate the resources necessary to implement a comprehensive attack on poverty. Marris and Rein (1967) expressed the dilemma this way:

> From whom were the projects to take their lead, elected government or those they served? . . . What *was* the maximum feasible participation of the poor in an endeavour that was also to include [numerous public and private actors] . . . The Office of Economic Opportunity . . . began to insist that it meant effective representation, and encouraged the idea that the residents of poor neighbourhoods should themselves elect a majority of the project's board. And this was more than the mayors of most American cities could willingly accept. (Pp. 215–217)

As a result of the ambiguity in the program's objectives concerning citizen participation, many different models of resident involvement emerged, models ranging from very low to high levels of control. Similar to many urban renewal programs, manipulation was also a common form of nonparticipation in many community action programs. According to Sherry Arnstein, the Community Action Agencies (CAAs) created "neighborhood councils" or "neighborhood advisory groups" that frequently had no legitimate function or power. Instead, they were used to demonstrate that local residents were involved with the program, although it may not have been discussed with "the people" or may have been described in only the most general terms (Arnstein, 1969, 218).

At the other end of the participation spectrum, some community action councils were controlled by a majority of local residents and had genuine powers. Arnstein (1969) has noted that "in some cities, CAAs have issued subcontracts to resident dominated groups to plan and/or operate one or more decentralized neighborhood program components like a multipurpose service center or a Headstart program" (p. 223).

Did it make a difference whether or not citizens controlled the local community action agency? According to political scientists Lineberry and Sharkansky (1971), what little evidence is available to answer this question points to greater effectiveness of those programs that had politically independent and activist-oriented community action boards:

> [In one study] the more effective programs were relatively autonomous and free from political intervention by local officials; they were program, rather than patronage, oriented; and they were led by sophisticated boards with real political power. [A second study] . . .

concluded that the most effective [antipoverty programs] emphasized community organization and mobilization of the poor. (P. 255)

In addition to demonstrating that citizen participation could produce beneficial results in a programmatic context, the poverty programs also served to open new lines of communication between residents and city bureaucracies, bringing new participants into the urban political arena:

> At the least, the various strategies of citizen participation in the late 1960s had the effect of creating a voluble neighborhood voice able to articulate complaints about public services and the unresponsiveness of service bureaucracies. This neighborhood voice, in turn, had the effect of establishing a dialogue between citizen and city agencies— a dialogue that had deteriorated progressively since the heyday of the machine and the ward heeler. (Yates, 1977, 51)

According to Frances Piven and Richard Cloward (1971), one of the most significant ways that citizen participants in the War on Poverty found a voice for themselves was by forming the National Welfare Rights Organization, a group that represented the interests of welfare recipients. In this way, a top–down citizen participation movement stimulated a bottom–up initiative. But on a more cynical and critical note, Daniel Patrick Moynihan, in his landmark work on the War on Poverty era, stated: "At the risk of oversimplification, it might be said that the CAPs [Community Action Programs] most closely controlled by City Hall were disappointing, and that the ones most antagonistic were destroyed" (Moynihan, 1969, 131).

Thus, despite some benefits, most observers have concluded that all was far from well with the citizen participation approach mandated in the poverty program. The advocacy interests of residents often were deflected as people got caught up in the act of participating. And, as mentioned above, few local chief executives were willing to give up enough power to allow citizens a high level of control. Finally, although communication may have been improved, it was not always meaningful or productive.

> Interaction between citizens and city government typically evolved into a ritualized game of shadowboxing in which the political energies created by community action were largely consumed by the constant sparring with government. The shadowboxing game, as played in government, was a closed and hollow one. Instead of producing administrative efforts to deal with fundamental problems of service delivery, this game channeled administrative energy into the business

of defending the government by dodging or parrying community demands and protests. (Yates, 1977, 52)

Moreover, for many community people expected to "participate," there was a realization that their own needs would be best served by landing a job with the community action program, not merely by being a provider of citizen input or a student in a training program. This view was characterized in a novel by Tom Wolfe (1970):

> Brothers from down the hall like Dudley got down to the heart of the poverty program very rapidly. It took them no time at all to see that the poverty program's big projects, like manpower training, in which you would get some job counseling and some training so you would be able to apply for a job in the bank or on the assembly line—everybody with a brain in his head knew that this was the usual bureaucratic shuck. . . . Everybody but the most hopeless lames knew that the only job you wanted out of the poverty program was a job *in* the program itself. Get on the payroll, that was the idea. (Pp. 167–168)

Citizen participation in the poverty program was always a confusing issue. In view of this experience, HUD was reluctant to place a strong emphasis on community control when it came to implementing the Model Cities program. As Sherry Arnstein (1969) observed: "Policymakers at HUD were determined to return the genie of citizen power to the bottle from which it had escaped (in a few cities) as a result of the provision stipulating 'maximum feasible participation' in poverty programs" (p. 220). It is not surprising that the Model Cities program emerged as a more clearly defined mayor's program.

Model Cities

With perhaps the loftiest goals of any of the community development initiatives, the 1966 Model Cities program was aimed at alleviating the most serious physical and social problems of the most troubled sections of cities within a mere five-year period. A key goal of Model Cities was to coordinate the array of federal programs targeted to urban areas that had proliferated during the early 1960s. This focus marked the first major attempt to rationalize and centralize a locality's community development efforts.

Setting the stage for the increasing interest in block grant funding, the Model Cities program attempted to reverse the way in which the federal government had been providing aid to the cities, with each problem always being addressed with a single weapon. "Programs operated side by side—usually indifferent to one another, failing, in general, to treat problems in an integrated manner. No means existed for coordinating the impact of programs" (Congressional Research Service, 1973, 172). There was little opposition to the Model Cities program's emphasis on coordination. But how this was to be achieved—whether through strong mayoral control or significant resident involvement—stimulated a debate reminiscent of the controversies surrounding the War on Poverty program.

At the outset, HUD officials placed control of Model Cities in the hands of the local chief executive. Initial requirements for citizen participation were vague, urging cities to provide residents with a "meaningful role" in policymaking and encouraging a "flow of communication" between residents and Model Cities staff (quoted in Frieden and Kaplan, 1975, 74). In short, although not giving much clarity to the term, Model Cities sought "widespread citizen participation."

At the program's outset, citizens often played minimal roles. According to Lipsky et al. (1971), most local Model Cities applications were prepared by mayors' offices with little or no resident input. In addition, citizens were invariably excluded from the designation of a city's model neighborhood and were not consulted about how participation would actually be achieved (Lipsky et al., 1971, 901).

As HUD became aware of the lack of citizen involvement, a few officials, notably Sherry Arnstein, chief staff adviser on citizen participation, became outspoken critics of HUD's loosely defined citizen participation requirements and lobbied for a more explicit and stronger role for residents of Model Cities neighborhoods. But Ralph Taylor, assistant secretary of HUD in charge of the Model Cities program, clarified the agency's views about the lesser role of citizens:

> In the Model Cities program, the responsibility for marshalling the public and private forces through political leadership, is placed on the Chief Executive of local government.
>
> Citizen participation works best when, despite the rhetoric of control, citizen and city government negotiate a sharing of power that permits the people of the neighborhood to participate effectively in determining the use of the resources that affect the quality of life in the neighborhood.
>
> In this partnership, the city is clearly the dominant partner . . . this does not mean the partners should not negotiate out rights and obligations that clarify their respective roles. (Quoted in Frieden and Kaplan, 1975, 79)

Thus, although Model Cities was firmly under the control of City Hall, HUD, under the Johnson administration, was willing to allow local chief executives to accommodate local residents as they saw fit.

Within a few months after Richard Nixon took office, there was a shift in this conceptualization of citizen participation in Model Cities. With the vote of confidence going even more strongly to the mayor's office, Nixon's HUD was critical of compromises that may have been reached between the chief executive and citizen groups. The agency was concerned lest too much power be given away; more than ever, control over the Model Cities program rested with local government.

In view of this orientation, it is not surprising that assessments of the role of citizens in Model Cities programs were extremely negative. A private consultant's report noted:

> In practically no Model Cities structure does citizen participation mean truly shared decision-making, such that citizens might view themselves as "the partners in this program."
>
> By and large, people are once again being planned *for*. In most situations the major planning decisions are being made by CDA [local Model Cities agency] staff and approved in a formalistic way by policy boards. (Quoted in Arnstein, 1969, 221)

Similar to the War on Poverty program, Model Cities left a wealth of experiences around the citizen participation issue. While HUD may have tried to relegate citizens to less important positions, the potential of citizen participation was clearly recognized. In a handful of communities, resident control of Model Cities programs demonstrated how people could play much more decisive roles than those advocated by HUD (see, e.g., Arnstein, 1969). Probably the most important lesson that can be drawn from the Model Cities experience was summed up by Sherry Arnstein:

> In most cases where power has come to be shared it was *taken by the citizens*, not given by the city. There is nothing new about that process. Since those who have power normally want to hang onto it, historically it has had to be wrested by the powerless rather than proffered by the powerful. (1969, p. 222)

The Model Cities program brings into focus some critical questions concerning federally mandated citizen participation: Can top–down invitations or requirements for resident involvement ever amount to more than tokenism? Is it not true that "community development," almost by definition, has to be interwoven with a bottom–up effort? The logic of a grass-roots, neighborhood-based approach to community development clearly emerged during the Model Cities era.

In large part because of some strong support within HUD and by the National League of Cities and the U.S. Conference of Mayors, President Nixon allowed the Model Cities program to continue during the early years of his administration. By the middle of 1972, however, plans were being made to fold it into the soon-to-be-enacted Community Development Block Grant program.

Community Development Block Grant (CDBG)

The Housing and Community Development Act of 1974 authorized a new federal block grant to local jurisdictions to assist them with their community development activities. Emerging as part of President Nixon's New Federalism, CDBG allowed local governments to set their own priorities and create their own solutions to problems. Folded into this program were seven categorical programs, including Urban Renewal and Model Cities. Key goals of CDBG were to rationalize and simplify the funding process for community development programs and to place control of the federal grant squarely in the hands of the local chief executive.

Since the start of the CDBG program, there have been considerable fluctuations in the mandated role of citizens. At the outset, citizen participation requirements were minimal. Local chief executives needed only to provide "satisfactory assurances" that citizens (1) had been given adequate information about the amount of funds available and the kinds of activities permitted; (2) had an opportunity to present their views on community development and housing needs at public hearings; and (3) had an "adequate opportunity" to participate in the development of the CDBG application. Clarifying the fairly limited expectations concerning the role of citizens, the legislation continued: "But no part of this paragraph shall be construed to restrict the responsibility and authority of the applicant for the development of the application and execution of its Community Development Program." [5] In short, the program belonged to local elected officials.

As citizens became more familiar with the CDBG requirements, they slowly became more involved in the decision-making process. This trend was bolstered by amendments to the Housing Act enacted in 1977 that, in fact, were stimulated by pressure from community groups. The new requirements mandated that local communities develop a written citizen participation plan, that residents be given the opportunity to comment on past CDBG performance, and that groups representing low- and moderate-income people be asked to present proposals for CDBG funding.

Paralleling the increasing attempt to include citizens in the CDBG program, efforts were being made to target CDBG funds better to low- and moderate-income people. The original 1974 act had a built-in conflict. On the one hand, applicants were required to give "maximum feasible priority" to activities aimed at benefiting low- or moderate-income families or at preventing or eliminating slums or blight. On the other hand, funds could also be used for other urgent community development needs.

Not surprisingly, in the first few years of the program, "urgent needs" often took priority over programs for low-income people. By the fourth year of the program's operation, however, a study of a sample of locales indicated that low- and moderate-income people were the beneficiaries of almost two-thirds of the allocations (62 percent) compared to a little more than half (54 percent) in the first year (Dommel et al., 1980, 161). This trend in part reflected the shift from the Ford to the Carter administration. Early in President Carter's term, HUD made clear that at least 75 percent of each jurisdiction's funds were to be targeted to low- and moderate-income groups (Dommel et al., 1980).

Steps toward increasing the role of citizens and requiring the targeting of funds to benefit lower-income groups were short-lived. Shortly after President Reagan took office, the Omnibus Budget Reconciliation Act (1981) was enacted. Cities could now hold only one public hearing (instead of two), and the formal application, in which justifications for each program had to be included, was replaced by the requirement of a simple statement of the community's objectives and the proposed use of funds. Following this, HUD issued regulations that advised communities to place an equal emphasis on the three goals of the original legislation. Projects addressing "urgent needs" and the prevention or elimination of slums and blight were to have an equal value with those benefiting low- and moderate-income people. In the Housing and Urban–Rural Recovery Act of 1983, Congress reversed this directive and revived the philosophy of the Carter administration, declaring that the primary objective of the CDBG program was to benefit low- and moderate-income people.

Not less than 51 percent of the total CDBG appropriation was to be used to benefit low- and moderate-income households. In addition, the 1983 legislation strengthened requirements for citizens to participate in the allocation of CDBG funds. It called for local jurisdictions to prepare and follow a written citizen participation plan that provided citizens with an opportunity to participate in the development of the CDBG application, and it directed the scheduling of hearings (notice the plural) at times and locations that would permit broad participation.

The Housing and Community Development Act of 1987 further refined the targeting and citizen participation requirements. Specifically, it called for at least 60 percent of CDBG funds to be used to benefit low- and moderate-income people and reinforced the mandate for citizen participation, particularly by those with low and moderate incomes. In addition, the act directed local jurisdictions to provide technical assistance to groups representing low- and moderate-income people who request such assistance in developing their proposals.

As intended by Congress, the CDBG program always has been under strong mayoral control. Based on a study of the first six years of the program's operation, the chief executive was found to be a leading actor in no less than thirty-seven of fifty sample locales (74 percent) and was, in most years, a leading actor in forty-two of these locales (84 percent). Citizens were never leading actors in more than ten of the fifty locales (20 percent) and, in one year, were leading actors in only six locales (14 percent) (Dommel et al., 1982).

During the first six years of the CDBG program, formal advisory structures and neighborhood-based groups were the most prevalent forms of citizen participation. In the sixth year, each of these two forms was dominant in about half the fifty locales studied by Dommel et al. In a subsample of ten large cities, however, Dommel et al. (1983, 58) found that neighborhood groups were a more important vehicle for enabling citizens to participate than advisory committees. Nevertheless, the mere presence of such groups did not guarantee that they would be influential in helping choose the specific programs to be funded. Similar to earlier federal community development programs, there was a wide range of power wielded by citizen organizations.

Citizen effectiveness in the CDBG program appears to be influenced by the extent to which local officials are supportive of citizen input and are willing to form coalitions with citizen groups. Although residents sometimes have assumed a confrontational posture or formed coalitions among themselves, "the more general pattern has been for citizen groups to become linked with a governmental participant as the means of gaining influence in decisions" (Dommel et al., 1982, 58).

Thus, in the CDBG program, mayors have been in key positions of power. To the extent that citizens have managed to be heard, usually this has been achieved through the good graces of the local chief executive's office. The overall results of the CDBG program have been predictable: It generally has not disturbed the racial and socioeconomic mix of a community, has maintained the status quo, and often has been used as a substitute for local revenues (Dommel et al., 1982, 119).

Based on this review of citizen participation in the federal community development programs, it seems clear that where participation is mandated from above, citizen needs are not the primary focus of public programs, and a real sharing of power and individual and community empowerment are virtually guaranteed not to take place. While it is still important for public programs to offer individuals opportunities to express their views, top–down participation should certainly not be the only form of citizen involvement. In addition, more opportunities and supports for bottom–up participation should be provided, as discussed in Part III. The importance of housing in people's lives and the apparent impact of housing on behavior and attitudes contribute to a persuasive argument that housing *for* the poor should *include* the poor in as many phases of the process as possible.

Before we examine the community-based housing strategy, we evaluate in Part II the major multifamily housing programs and analyze the role of HUD as implementer of federal low-income housing programs.

Part II

Traditional Federally Subsidized
Multifamily Housing Programs

3

The Public Housing Program

THERE is a widespread belief in this country that the public sector is unable to build or manage decent housing. Rhetoric describing public housing developments as vertical ghettos, pictures of notorious projects such as Pruitt-Igoe in St. Louis being demolished, and news reports detailing the financial plight of many large housing authorities have reinforced this notion.

These images persist despite the growing interest in clarifying the record of the public housing program (Bratt, 1985a, 1986a; Connerly, 1986; Council of Large Public Housing Authorities, 1986; Genung, 1971; *Journal of Housing*, 1973; Matulef, 1987; Meehan, 1975, 1979; Rabushka and Weissert, 1977; Stegman, 1988; Struyk, 1980). This interest has no doubt been fueled by an increased awareness of the housing problem, frustration with the newer public–private partnership programs (to be discussed in Chapter 4), and a sense that the federal government, sooner or later, will look to past housing programs as models for future policies.

As the nation's oldest and largest multifamily subsidized housing program, public housing has a special place in the history of U.S. housing programs. The purpose of this chapter is to examine the record of public housing in providing decent, affordable housing to low-income people. In other words, is the conventional wisdom of most policy analysts, journalists, and the general public accurate? (See box on pages 54–55.)

The first part of this chapter presents the historical context of the public housing program and underscores how some of its chief difficulties arose from the intense opposition to the concept of public ownership of housing. The second part examines the record of public housing, using available information. The last part of the chapter raises some policy questions concerning the future of public housing.

Out of the Poor House

No single image has ever captured the welfare state's failure to help poor Americans quite like pictures of the demolition of St. Louis's Pruitt-Igoe public housing project in the 1970s only a few years after it was built. President Reagan's Privatization Commission has just endorsed several ideas that could prevent future Pruitt-Igoes, if anyone in Washington is listening.

The bipartisan Commission, which announced its findings last Friday, spent six months sifting through evidence and listening to testimony. What it discovered is what anecdotal evidence has already suggested—federal housing policy hasn't done very much to help the poor. Though the U.S. government has spent tens of billions of dollars to build public housing, the expense of new housing means that federal policy is what John Weicher of the American Enterprise Institute has called a "lottery." About a quarter of America's low-income people win big by receiving a large housing subsidy. The rest get little or nothing.

What's more, government-aided housing projects tend to segregate Americans into made-in-Washington ghettos, where social pathologies such as drug abuse and gangs often abound. Parents who might like to move away to protect their children, or to where jobs are more plentiful are virtually stuck. Because government bureaucrats who live elsewhere "manage" the

properties, residents also have little incentive or capability either to maintain their homes or improve their neighborhoods. The housing often deteriorates until it has to be destroyed, as the Commission says Newark, N.J., is now preparing to do to nearly a third of its public housing.

Instead of this social warehousing, the Commission endorses ideas that would both cost less and give the poor more dignity and independence. Rental subsidies in the form of vouchers would allow the government to help more families and to give them greater say in where and how they want to live. Selling public units at a discount to tenants would give the poor the same stake most Americans have in maintaining their homes. And in the case of large public projects, where sales to tenants might not be practical, greater resident self-management would encourage greater resident pride and upkeep.

It's true enough that policy reforms alone won't solve all of America's housing problems. In many big public housing projects simply surviving amid all the crime may be the largest problem. And the Commission's report recognizes the damage done by rent control and zoning laws that limit the incentive and ability to build any new low-cost housing. Commission Chairman David Linowes, a Democrat, points out that the average housing vacancy rate in the U.S. is now about 8%, one of the highest rates in years, while in cities with rent control such as New York it is closer to 2% or 3%.

Still, the Commission's report is a breath of fresh air in a city that, even in the Reagan years, still thinks government meddling is the answer to every social problem. A few of these ideas have been tried on a small scale in recent years, but too many in Congress and the bureaucracy still oppose any idea that might mean a loss of their control, and thus their power. They'd rather have people coming back for federal alms to stay in the poor house. Why not for once try something new?

From the *Wall Street Journal*, March 24, 1988

Public Housing—A Historical Overview

The country's first major subsidized housing program was not enacted until the need for better housing could be coupled with another national objective: the need to reduce unemployment resulting from the Great Depression. Section 1 of the Housing Act of 1937 made clear the dual objectives of the legislation: "to alleviate present and recurring unemployment and to remedy the unsafe and insanitary housing conditions and the acute shortage of decent, safe, and sanitary dwellings for families of low income."[1] Although the need to stimulate the economy was key to creation of the program, other forces determined its shape.

Probably the major factor that contributed to the form of the public housing program was the extent of the opposition to it. Although the 1937 Housing Act held out the promise of jobs and apartments for the "deserving poor," there were still many dissenters. President Roosevelt himself had to be coaxed; a large-scale public housing program had not been part of the first phase of the New Deal (Friedman, 1968). Organized opposition came from several interest groups, such as the U.S. Chamber of Commerce and the U.S. Savings and Loan League. Also in the forefront of the opposition was the National Association of Real Estate Boards, whose president summarized the views of the private homebuilding industry as follows:

> Housing should remain a matter of private enterprise and private ownership. It is contrary to the genius of the American people and the ideals they have established that government become landlord to its citizens. . . . There is sound logic in the continuance of the practice under which those who have initiative and the will to save acquire

> better living facilities and yield their former quarters at modest rents
> to the group below. (Quoted in Keith, 1973, 33)

Within Congress, conservative members labeled public housing a socialist program and opposed it on the grounds that it would put the government in competition with private property (Friedman, 1968; Keith, 1973).

Largely as a concession to the private housing industry, the public housing legislation included an "equivalent elimination" provision requiring local housing authorities to eliminate a substandard or unsafe dwelling unit for each new unit of public housing built. Public housing could replace inadequate units, but it was not to increase the overall supply of housing, since doing so could drive down rents in the private housing market.

The argument that public housing should not interfere with the private market logically led to the view that public housing should be clearly differentiated. This had important implications, for example, for its physical design: Public housing, with its austere appearance, is usually easily distinguished from the overall housing stock.[2]

The early public housing program was short-lived. World War II interrupted all non-war-related programs, and public housing construction fell victim to defense needs. Because thousands of units were in the "pipeline" before the war, however, it was not until 1944 that production virtually stopped (see Table 1). Before the program was reactivated by the 1949 Housing Act, the real estate lobby launched an all-out attack on public housing. The familiar cry of socialism and the warning that public housing would destroy the private building industry were heard again. President Truman, a supporter of the program, responded with this pointed counterattack:

> I have been shocked in recent days at the extraordinary propaganda
> campaign that has been unleashed against this bill [Housing Act of
> 1949] by the real estate lobby. I do not recall ever having witnessed a
> more deliberate campaign of misrepresentation and distortion against
> legislation of such crucial importance to the public welfare. The
> propaganda of the real estate lobby consistently misrepresents what
> will be the actual effect of the bill, and consistently distorts the facts
> of the housing situation in the country. (Quoted in Keith, 1973, 96)

Ultimately, proponents of public housing prevailed, but the legislative intent was clear: Public housing was to serve only those people who could not compete for housing on the private market. Private interest groups were willing to tolerate public housing as long as it was explicitly serving a different consumer.

TABLE 1
PUBLIC HOUSING COMPLETIONS, 1939–1987

Year	Units	Year	Units
1939	4,960	1964	24,488
1940	34,308	1965	30,769
1941	61,065	1966	31,483
1942	36,172	1967	38,756
1943	24,296	1968	72,638
1944	3,269	1969	78,003
1945	3,080	1970	73,723
1946	1,925	1971	91,539
1947	466	1972	58,590
1948	1,348	1973	52,791
1949	547	1974	43,928
1950	1,255	1975	24,514
1951	10,246	1976	6,862
1952	58,258	1977	6,229
1953	58,214	1978	10,295
1954	44,293	1979	44,019
1955	20,899	1980	15,109
1956	11,993	1981	33,631
1957	10,513	1982	28,529
1958	15,472	1983	27,876
1959	21,939	1984	24,092
1960	16,401	1985	19,267
1961	20,965	1986	15,464
1962	28,682	1987	10,415
1963	27,327		

Sources: The Report of the President's Committee on Urban Housing, 1968, 61; HUD 1980b, 204; and *The 1989 Low Income Housing Budget,* Special Memorandum, Low Income Housing Service, April 1988.

But not all low-income people were eligible for a public housing unit. From the program's inception, it was aimed at providing housing only for the deserving, temporarily poor—the "submerged middle class" (Friedman, 1968). The program therefore targeted those who could not find decent, affordable housing on the private market, but not the so-called unworthy poor and those with no means to pay rent.

The expectation that tenants should pay their own way expressed itself in the formula the federal government devised for financing public housing. Tenant rents were to cover all operating expenses, exclusive of debt service. Only the principal and interest on bonds, which were floated by the local authorities to construct the buildings, were paid by the federal government, through annual contribution contracts. Thus the federal government covered the long-term debt financing, while ownership and management were vested in local public agencies. This arrangement worked well during the early years of the program.

After World War II, however, the country's demographic picture began to shift, and so did the population served by public housing. As Federal Housing Administration (FHA) and Veterans Administration (VA) mortgage insurance and guarantee programs became available to vast numbers of new home buyers, and as the interstate highway system took form, most of the submerged middle-class residents of public housing surfaced, to assume full-fledged suburban middle-class status. As a further concession to the private construction industry, the 1949 Housing Act limited public housing to very-low-income people by requiring that the highest rents be 20 percent lower than the lowest prevailing rents for decent housing in the private market, and by authorizing the eviction of above-income families (Kolodny, 1979; National Center for Housing Management, n.d.). Publicly provided housing thus was now to be available only to the very poor. Once public housing was reactivated and could no longer claim to be a depression-stimulated support for the temporarily poor, it became clearly defined as permanent housing for people who were more or less separated from society's mainstream.

As a result of these postwar changes, vacated units were quickly occupied by a new group of tenants, many of whom had very low incomes and multiple problems. The large housing authorities of the Midwest and Northeast also began to accommodate black migrants from the South. In addition, displacees from urban renewal and highway programs, the majority of whom were members of minorities, were given priority for public housing units. By 1978, over 60 percent of the residents of public housing were minority-group members (HUD, 1980), whereas from 1944 to 1951 nonwhite families represented between 26 and 39 percent of all public housing tenants (Fisher, 1959).

By the 1960s, serious problems with the financing formula had surfaced. Inflation was having an increasing impact on operating costs, while rental income remained static. Starting in 1961, the Public Housing Administration (later merged into HUD) made the first in a series of attempts to alleviate this problem by authorizing additional subsidies up to $120 per year for each elderly household. Within a few years, these subsidies were also provided in behalf of handicapped, displaced, large, and very-low-income families (Kolodny, 1979).

During the 1970s, the overall problems facing public housing worsened. Inflation continued to boost operating expenses, and many buildings that were, by then, twenty or more years old, began to show signs of aging and a need for major repairs. At the same time, rental revenues were either declining or, at best, not keeping up with expenses.

In an effort to insulate tenants from having to make up operating cost shortfalls, Senator Edward Brooke (R-Mass.) sponsored legislation (known as the Brooke Amendments, 1969–1971) that capped rentals at 25 percent of income and provided additional operating subsidies. Between 1969 and 1972, operating subsidies nationally rose from $12.6 million to $102.8 million (Sherwood and March, 1983). Between 1971 and 1982, operating subsidies jumped more than tenfold, to $1.3 billion (U.S. Congressional Budget Office, 1983). And for fiscal years 1988 and 1989, the Housing and Community Development Act of 1987 authorized a total of more than $3 billion, with an appropriation of $1.45 billion for FY 1988.

Since 1975, operating subsidies have been provided through a mechanism known as the Performance Funding System (PFS). Funding levels under the PFS are set by examining the costs of a sample of housing authorities considered to be well managed and then using these costs to determine reasonable expenses for all authorities. One of the major criticisms of the PFS is that operating subsidies are based on past funding levels of well-managed authorities and do not take into account the actual cost of providing an adequate level of management services (Stegman, 1988; Struyk, 1980; U.S. Congressional Budget Office, 1983).

Thus the original funding formula, by excluding funds for operating and maintenance costs, undermined the public housing program. Despite the assistance provided by operating subsidies, many repair problems worsened to such an extent that very large sums of money were needed to remedy the most physically dilapidated projects. Altogether, the current modernization program, called the Comprehensive Improvement Assistance Program, and its predecessors received $7.9 billion from 1975 to 1986. During the middle years of the Reagan administration, funding declined considerably, with only $707 million expended in 1986, down from $1.26 billion in 1983 (Stegman, 1988). With the passage of the Housing and Community Development Act of 1987, the modernization program received a major boost, with an appropriation of $1.7 billion.

The highly polarized nature of the debate surrounding the 1937 Housing Act also helped shape the administrative structure of the public housing program. Administration was to be decentralized, and participation by localities was to be voluntary. According to Lawrence Friedman, "For legal[3] and political reasons and to disarm conservative opposition, a decentralized program was desirable. Local initiative would govern as much as possible; states and communities would be allowed to opt out if they wished" (1968, 105).

This meant that decisions about public housing—whether to build it and where to locate it—would be made by local officials, who would be under significant pressure from their constituents. The decentralized structure also eliminated the potential for the federal government either to enforce more progressive policies or override local decisions.

The right of local communities not to participate in the public housing program guaranteed that within metropolitan areas, public housing would be most prevalent in large cities. As a result, low-income people, already lacking housing options, were to be restricted still further; the choice to move to the suburbs usually was not available to them. Local control over the program meant that little or no public housing was built in more affluent areas.[4]

As the program evolved, accommodating increasing numbers of blacks and other minorities, local control over public housing contributed to patterns of racial segregation with white areas effectively keeping out blacks. Large cities, with large minority populations, also served a high percentage of minorities in their public housing developments. As of 1976, 83 percent of public housing tenants in twenty large cities were members of minorities, compared to 61 percent for the overall public housing population (Kolodny, 1979; Struyk, 1980).

Thus, opposition by the private homebuilding industry, maintenance and operating fund shortfalls, and class and racial segregation have continuously plagued the public housing program. As early as the 1950s, some of public housing's most ardent supporters began to lose heart. Catherine Bauer Wurster, one of the key proponents from the 1930s, bemoaned "The Dreary Deadlock of Public Housing" and commented that "after more than two decades, [public housing] still drags along in a kind of a limbo, continuously controversial, not dead but never more than half alive" (1957, 140).

The uncertainty and controversy that have always surrounded the public housing program are reflected in the sporadic rates of public housing production. Between 1939 and 1943, 160,801 public housing units were made available for occupancy, with 61,000 units completed in 1941 alone. In the postwar years, production reached over 58,000 units in both 1952 and 1953 (Table 1).[5] During the late 1960s, as concern about urban unrest mounted, there was a sharp increase in public housing production compared to earlier in the decade. Following enactment of the Housing and Urban Development Act of 1968, in which Congress set a private and public production goal of 26 million new or substantially rehabilitated units over the following decade, including 6 million for low- and moderate-income households, public housing completions reached an all-time high; over 91,000 units were completed in 1971. Rather than signal a renewed commitment to public housing, however, the high levels of construction were short-lived. In 1973, President Nixon called a halt to all federally subsidized housing programs. Since then, the program has limped along, with the full impact of the moratorium being felt from 1976 to 1978. With very little new money appropriated during the 1980s, production declined, once the projects that had been in the pipeline during the Carter administration were completed.

The history of public housing not only reveals how several key forces and decisions shaped the program but also reflects how the federal government has changed its thinking about its role in subsidizing housing for low-income people. Although the public housing program started out with management and ownership resting solely with the local public housing authority, as the program came under attack in the mid-1960s, the private sector was looked to as a way to rescue it.

The Section 23 program was authorized in 1965. Known as the leased-housing program, it served as a prototype for the housing allowance idea and enabled low-income families to rent units in privately owned housing. The housing authority entered into long-term contracts with landlords and paid the difference between the unit's market rent and a proportion of the tenant's income. Over 100,000 units were financed through this program before it was superseded by the Section 8 Existing Housing program in 1974.

The "turnkey" form of public housing also was introduced in 1965. Under this program, a developer entered into a contract with a local housing authority to construct a project. The developer then sold the project (or "turned the key" over) to the housing authority at the stipulated price. Since 1965, about one-third of all new public housing projects have been built by the turnkey method, but it is unclear whether it has reduced either the time or costs of development or improved quality (Kolodny, 1979; Meehan, 1979). From the developers' viewpoint, the turnkey program was enormously popular. In 1968, the president of the National Association of Home Builders suggested that new public housing authorizations be directed primarily at that program. Calling it "the first attempt in the 30-year history of public housing to use, for the lowest income brackets, the tremendous resources and productive capacity of the private homebuilding industry," he cited the turnkey program for exemplifying "the proper role of Government in helping private industry to expand into areas not attainable without such help" (U.S. Senate, 1968, 293).

In addition to these changes in the public housing program, other subsidized housing programs were including a new role for the private sector. As discussed in Chapters 2 and 4, in 1959 private entrepreneurs were given their first opportunity to produce subsidized housing. The Section 202 program enacted in that year provided direct below-market interest-rate loans to private nonprofit sponsors of housing for the elderly. The Section 221(d)(3), Section 236, and Section 8 programs, enacted in 1961, 1968, and 1974, also invited sponsorship of multifamily subsidized housing by private, for-profit groups.

Thus, while the early history of the public housing program was characterized by staunch opposition by the private sector, over the past two decades private interest groups have evolved into active supporters of most housing subsidy programs. Although they are still opposed to conventional public housing, they are certain to show support for government programs explicitly geared to stimulating the homebuilding industry and providing new investment opportunities.

Public housing currently provides housing to about 4 million people and its 1.3 million units represent almost 1.5 percent of the nation's overall housing stock and about 5 percent of the rental stock. An evaluation of public housing requires a clear image of the projects and who lives in them. Public housing projects have often been characterized as large, dilapidated old high-rises in central cities, inaccessible to public services and shopping, and occupied mostly by minority, single-parent, welfare households with many children who generally are dissatisfied with their accommodations. To what extent does the conventional image of public housing residents and the developments match reality? To what extent is the generally negative view of public housing accurate? This evaluation includes the criteria outlined in Chapter 2.

Public Housing: Image versus Reality
Characteristics of Tenants and Tenant Perceptions

Popular perceptions concerning public housing tenants turn out to be relatively accurate. Although there is some disparity on the demographics of public housing tenants, depending on the source, the following provides a general picture. A majority of residents are nonwhite, with estimates ranging from 62 to 86 percent. White residents tend to be much older than nonwhites, with the latter generally having at least two children. Over three-quarters of all public housing households are headed by single adults, usually an elderly person living alone or a single parent with children. Finally, more than half of all public housing tenants depend on welfare for their incomes (Citizens Housing and Planning Association, 1986; Kolodny, 1979; Matulef, 1987).

Interesting data on resident perceptions of public housing come from three studies of local housing authorities.[6] In the first study, Meehan (1975) analyzed why households moved away from St. Louis housing authority projects between 1954 and 1969. He found that while some discontent was clearly evident, with about 20 percent finding better alternatives, nearly half of the moves were precipitated by reasons that had nothing to do with dissatisfaction with the projects. Meehan concluded:

> The point that emerges most strongly from an examination of the tenants in the public housing program . . . is that conventional public housing, for all its inadequacies and faults, served a real and important human need that would not otherwise have been served. Had the alternative been significantly superior, the occupants would have voted with their feet and done so willingly and openly, recording their dissatisfaction for all to see. (1975, 135)

Despite the overall willingness of tenants to stay, Meehan was quick to point out that all was far from well with the projects.

> The conditions by the end of the 1960s were deplorable in most cases and unspeakable in some. . . . What is impressive is the extent to which the population was willing to live in such generally unappetizing facilities. . . . The need of the population should be kept separate and distinct from the failure or success of any particular attempt to cope with it. The fact of the need for cheap and decent housing is the evidence that justifies continued efforts to provide it. (1975, 136)

In a second study, researchers interviewed almost 2000 Wilmington, Delaware, public housing residents to ascertain their views on the quality of life in the projects and solicit ideas for improving management. Other than expressing concerns for personal safety and a desire for more police protection, tenants, by and large, did not complain about housing problems:

> Even as the image of public housing steadily deteriorates and its few remaining supporters speak in softer tones, tenants keep clamoring to get in.
>
> Is it not ironical that people should want to move into this housing of last resort? And that people in public housing don't want to leave? Even some tenants who can afford better alternatives in the private housing market don't want to go. Every year public housing authorities have to evict people who exceed the income limitations of the program but who would stay if permitted. We have, in short, a paradox: nobody likes public housing except the people who live there and those who want to get in. (Rabushka and Weissert, 1977, xvi)

The study found that the overwhelming majority of tenants do not accept the tarnished image of public housing: Only 12 percent of the total sample reported that they were ashamed to be living in public housing. Elderly tenants were even more favorably disposed than family respondents; only one in forty was ashamed to be living there. Concerning adequacy of the housing units and quality of housing authority management, more than 60 percent of tenant family heads and over 90 percent of elderly tenants reported no problems.

In a third study, 530 residents of Boston's public housing developments were interviewed. Despite the fact that the Boston Housing Authority has been seriously troubled and several projects have received adverse publicity, more than two-thirds of the respondents reported they were either very satisfied (32 percent) or somewhat satisfied (35 percent) with the condition of their housing (Boston Housing Authority, 1983).[7]

Additional information about general levels of satisfaction of public housing tenants comes from a survey of residents at ten public housing developments in various parts of the country. According to Francescato et al. (1979), more than twice as many residents indicated they were satisfied (56 percent) as were dissatisfied (24 percent) with where they lived; 20 percent indicated that they were neither satisfied nor dissatisfied.

Thus, while conventional wisdom assumes low satisfaction levels among public housing tenants, the surveys cited here make clear that the majority of residents report positive feelings about their housing.

Physical Characteristics, Condition, and Design

Despite its concentration in large cities, public housing is still far more dispersed than many believe. Almost two-thirds of all public housing units are administered by the 2775 housing authorities that operate fewer than 6500 units; the 22 largest public housing authorities administer the remaining one-third of the units (U.S. Congressional Budget Office, 1983). In addition, most public housing developments (54 percent) are relatively small, having fewer than 200 units; most family public housing units (75 percent) are in low-rise buildings (four or fewer storeys); only 7 percent of all family public housing projects are both high-rise and have more than 200 units; and as of 1980, public housing projects were, on average, seventeen years old (Perkins and Will and the Ehrenkrantz Group, 1980).

Concerning the condition and design of public housing, the available evidence is mixed: Public housing, overall, is not in bad physical shape, but its design has been justifiably subject to criticism. Based on a sample of nearly 700 public housing projects, Jones et al. (1979) concluded that less than 4 percent of all projects were in bad or very bad condition. Projects in good or average condition were also rated as "troubled" if they were reported to have five or more other significant problems. Altogether, Jones et al. found that only 7 percent of all public housing projects, accounting for 15 percent of all public housing units, were troubled. A second study found an even lower problem rate. Perkins and Will and the Ehrenkrantz Group (1980) studied a national sample of 350 public housing projects and concluded:

> The vast majority of the housing stock is in good condition. While some of it is not attractive, these units appear to successfully comply with the MPS [minimum property standards] physical standards. Rehabilitation is required largely due to the aging of structures and systems, to the normal wear and tear of building components, minor vandalism and changes in state and local codes. A sound and adequately funded routine maintenance program as well as routine modernization is needed to improve upon and preserve the generally good condition of public housing. (P. 13)

Perkins and Will and the Ehrenkrantz Group found that a small number of projects exhibited "chronic problems." A chronic-problem project was defined as one requiring in excess of $2500 per unit to correct violations of basic health and safety standards and bring the building up to minimum property standards. According to the study, only 6 percent of all projects, containing 7 percent of all public housing units, exhibited chronic problems.[8]

Although Perkins and Will and the Ehrenkrantz Group provided estimates to repair the public housing stock, the most recent projections of improvement costs come from a 1988 study conducted by Abt Associates under contract to HUD. They have calculated that about $22.2 billion will be needed, including $9.3 billion to repair or replace existing architectural, mechanical, and electrical systems. The remaining $12.9 billion would be used to upgrade and modernize the public housing stock (Bain et al., 1988).

Included in the above estimates is the cost of repairs and modernization for a segment of the public housing stock that may be too distressed to fix. The current number of units in projects that are not economically or socially viable ranges from a HUD estimate of 73,000 with another 95,000 that could fall into this category (HUD, 1988) to an estimate by the Council of Large Public Housing Authorities of some 138,000 units that are facing serious difficulties (Council of Large Public Housing Authorities, 1988).

Jones et al. examined the extent to which projects with stereotypical characteristics—large, old, urban, and family (as opposed to elderly)—were likely to be troubled. They found that almost three out of four projects with these attributes were untroubled, although projects with these characteristics were three times more likely to be troubled than were other public housing projects. Perkins and Will and the Ehrenkrantz Group further found that most of the chronic-problem projects were not large, high-rise projects but small, low-rise family projects: 62 percent of the chronic-problem projects were small, family, low-rise; only 9 percent were large, family, high-rise.[9]

Further evidence that high-rise public housing can provide decent shelter comes from New York City. The housing authority in that city administers over 174,000 units[10]—more than 10 percent of the nation's public housing stock—and has a reputation for having one of the best public housing programs in the country, boasting a very low vacancy rate and long waiting lists.

To summarize, the conventional wisdom of what constitutes a physically bad project is not borne out by the evidence: Most stereotypical projects do not exhibit severe problems. Although projects with stereotypical characteristics present problems more frequently than the rest of the public housing stock, they represent only a small percentage of all public housing developments.

To what extent has the overall poor design of public housing contributed to creating troubled projects? Jones et al. (1979) report that site and design factors are among the most significant variables. Sixty-three percent of troubled projects were reported to be adversely affected by project design and site deficiencies (e.g., project size and lack of defensible space—space under the control and surveillance of the residents), compared to only 4 percent of untroubled projects.

As discussed earlier, the design of public housing, in large part, was shaped by the private sector's insistence that it not be competitive with private housing. Public housing administrators, furthermore, continually tried to prove that public housing could make do with less. Writing about the first twenty-five years of the public housing program, Albert Mayer, a noted architect, stated:

> Housing officials, federal and local, have . . . been excessively on the defense. They have sought to escape attack by being undeniably vir-tuous, and penurious, and inoffensive, practicing stark economies, squeezing down space, minimizing community facilities, eliminating anything that could be thought of as "glamorizing." . . . As a mat-ter of fact, there was a great competition to achieve virtue. It was a source of pride to the authority that discovered closet doors could be eliminated. Thus such housing officials sold the birthright of pub-lic housing, producing the dullest stuff imaginable . . . and getting exactly the same opposition and vituperation anyway. (Quoted in Kolodny, 1979, 20)

By going along with the notion that public housing should pro-vide only minimal accommodations, administrators may have given the opposition its greatest ammunition. Indeed, many public housing projects, overly modest and austere, did evolve into bad housing. The public sector's quest to provide no-frills housing, combined with the private sector's unrelenting demand that public housing be different from the rest of the housing stock, undermined the notion that public housing could also be attractive housing.

Management

Management has a significant impact on the quality of public housing. Since the 1960s, inadequate management has been cited as a serious deficiency of many large housing authorities. Problems have revolved around two broad issues: financial mismanagement, and inadequate or insensitive handling of tenant-related matters.

The inspector general of HUD found that of the 134 largest public housing authorities, 30 were financially troubled. (HUD considers a housing authority financially troubled if it fails to maintain adequate operating reserve funds.) Although these housing authorities represent only 1 percent of all housing authorities, together they administer 23 percent of the units in the entire conventional public housing program (HUD, 1983). Another study by HUD's inspector general cited public housing authorities for intentionally underestimating income in order to get additional subsidies (HUD, 1984). The Council of Large Public Housing Authorities refuted many of the findings from the inspector general's second report, however, charging that it did not seek explanations for observed problems and preferred "to create an impression of willful PHA [public housing authority] wrongdoing for political and media purposes" (Sherman and Sherwood, 1984, 5).

In addition to financial matters, housing authorities are in charge of a wide range of activities that place them in close contact with tenants, such as rent collection, eviction, and routine maintenance and repair. For some housing authorities, fulfilling these basic tasks has been problematic. For example, before being placed in receivership, the Boston Housing Authority's poor maintenance created grim conditions in many developments. Disruptive tenants were seldom evicted and repairs went undone, with employees often doing no work at all. And because of political patronage, the housing authority became a deeply entrenched and isolated haven for the politically faithful.

According to the former court-appointed receiver of the Boston Housing Authority, the housing authority neither protected the tenants nor maintained the buildings:

> Ultimately, the withdrawal of institutional supports destroys any sense of cooperative capacity among residents, destroys any sense of community. Each family becomes an isolated fearful unit. Poverty has already impressed on them a sense of powerlessness—now the violence that consumes the community and frightens and humiliates them daily gives final proof of their impotence.
> . . . and the most savage thing is—having walked away from the poor, then everybody says (the media most of all) look at how those scum live. Isn't it foul how poor people live? . . . It's as classic a case of blaming the victim as I know. (Spence, 1981, 44)

Short of such overt negligence on the part of some housing authorities, insensitivity to tenant needs by housing authority officials and managers also has been documented. A nationwide survey of public housing authority commissioners by Hartman and Carr (1969) found a prevalence of antagonistic and negative feelings toward public housing families. According to the researchers, this "can lead only to conflict between tenants and management and probably serves to reduce the effectiveness of public housing as a supportive experience for poor families" (p. 17). A key reason why commissioners were not sympathetic to their clients might have been the substantial difference in socioeconomic status between the two groups. In contrast to the public housing population, commissioners were often middle- or upper-income white males who were well-educated businessmen and professionals. Hartman and Levi (1973) concluded that

> it is likely that at least some of the tension in public housing today derives directly from wide disparities in race and class between the managers and the tenants. Managers are likely to feel more responsible and responsive to the housing authority, their professional colleagues, and to the middle-class public than to their present clientele. (P. 135)

Over the years, HUD has instituted a series of programs to encourage better management procedures. Overall, the results of these initiatives have been mixed. Some of the programs were not fully implemented or evaluated, while others were only one-shot efforts (Kolodny, 1979; Struyk, 1980). One of the most significant efforts to upgrade management was the National Tenant Management demonstration, a program modeled after tenant management corporations in St. Louis and several other cities. Although the record of tenant management has been encouraging, as discussed in more detail in Chapter 6, HUD has not strongly advocated this approach. According to the National Housing Law Project, HUD's regulations concerning the role of public housing authorities in fostering tenant participation and the contracting with tenant management corporations to perform certain management functions

> provide no meaningful rights or obligations. The Introductory Comments to the regulations note that nothing in the rules indicates that tenant recommendations are to be anything but advisory and that any advocated tenant management arrangements are purely at the discretion of the PHA. In fact, there is not even a requirement that a PHA must recognize an established tenant organization. (National Housing Law Project, 1987, 102)

Until passage of the Housing and Community Development Act of 1987, HUD did not offer any programs to local housing authorities to support the creation of tenant management corporations. With the passage of this act, Congress authorized HUD to spend some $5 million in fiscal years 1988 and 1989, with no more than $100,000 to be expended for the development of each new resident management corporation. Although this is a significant step, it is of such a small scale that tenant management will not, at least at this point, become a dominant feature of local housing authorities' operations. (For reasons why local housing authority commissioners and managers have been resistant to the idea of tenant management, see Hartman and Carr, 1969; Hartman and Levi, 1973.)

Accessibility

The image of public housing as inaccessible to public services and other facilities is frequently accurate. Because public housing in many large cities was developed quite late in their stage of development, much of the best land was often already built upon. In addition, public housing development costs had to fall within prescribed limits, which also put pressure on local housing authorities to acquire the cheapest land available, usually in less desirable locations. But the most important factor contributing to the location of public housing relates to a key administrative aspect of the program discussed earlier, the power of local governments to determine the location of developments. Opposition to proposed projects was usually vehement, and as a result, projects tended to be located less in existing neighborhoods than in more out-of-the-way areas. Local city councilors and chief executives were reluctant to antagonize community residents. Therefore, the easiest and most expedient solution often was to build public housing in areas where no one lived or wanted to live. Boston's notorious Columbia Point public housing project was located on the site of the former city dump.

Impact on Racial Integration

Public housing has not furthered the goal of racial integration. In addition to the program's decentralized administrative structure, which gave local housing authorities the freedom to discriminate at will, segregation in public housing was also the policy of the federal government during the early years of the program. The Neighborhood Composition Rule, formulated by Secretary of the Interior Harold Ickes, stated that housing projects should not alter the racial character of their surrounding neighborhoods (Meyerson and Banfield, 1955). Although housing authorities were permitted to offer units to whites and blacks on an "open occupancy" basis, most authorities chose to provide "separate but equal" housing (U.S. Commission on Civil Rights, 1975).

As a result of these policies, the earliest public housing projects were built for occupancy either by whites or by blacks. Bowly (1978) has described how, in Chicago, two of the first public housing projects were in white areas and were rented exclusively to white tenants; another early project was built for blacks only. Similarly, the original plan for Pruitt-Igoe in St. Louis was for two segregated projects, Pruitt for blacks and Igoe, across the street, for whites (Rainwater, 1970). Segregation patterns in Boston's public housing were also finely drawn. In 1940, the first project to accept blacks was completely segregated. The second project open to blacks had specific buildings earmarked "the colored section" (Pynoos, 1974).

New York, in 1939, led the states in barring discrimination in public housing. Massachusetts was next, in 1948, followed by Connecticut and Wisconsin in 1949. By 1961, three years before Congress enacted Title VI of the Civil Rights Act of 1964, which prohibited discrimination in all federally assisted housing, thirty-two states operated public housing on an open-occupancy basis (U.S. Commission on Civil Rights, 1975). In these areas, some inroads were made to reduce segregation in public housing. In 1960, 55 percent of the 886 projects located in communities with open-occupancy laws had mixed-occupancy patterns. But many of these projects had only a few minority families living in predominantly white projects, and vice versa (U.S. Commission on Civil Rights, 1975). For example, despite the early enactment of a fair housing law in Massachusetts, Boston's public housing stock was still highly segregated in 1960.

> 13 of 25 projects were more than 96 percent white; of these, 7 were exclusively occupied by whites. Of the 1,733 Negro families in 15 federally aided projects, 98.6 percent were in 7 projects, two of which were entirely black. Discrimination was even more evident in the ten state aided projects—3.6 percent of 3,675 units were occupied by Negroes. Of these, 122 Negro families were concentrated in 4 projects, one of which was entirely Negro. That the pattern of segregation was neither accidental nor a matter of location is vividly evidenced by two projects across the street from each other—Mission Hill is 100 percent white while Mission Hill Extension is 80 percent Negro. (Hipshman, 1967, 29)

Discriminatory practices persisted in many cities. In a landmark court case, *Gautreaux* v. *Hills*, plaintiffs successfully argued that the Chicago Housing Authority and HUD had carried out tenant assignments and site-selection procedures along racial lines (Peroff et al., 1979). Following almost a decade of litigation in various courts, including the U.S. Supreme Court (which decided the case in 1976), tenants in, and applicants to, Chicago public housing were invited to participate in a demonstration program that enabled them to move to private housing, using Section 8 certificates, anywhere within the Chicago metropolitan area.

Notwithstanding this effort and other changes in HUD site-selection procedures, years of discriminatory practices have had their effect. At present, public housing, particularly family public housing, is still often segregated. In many cities, such as Boston, predominantly white projects and predominantly black projects may be only a few blocks from one another.

As mentioned earlier, the decentralized operation of the program and the option of locales not to participate meant that a wide spectrum of cities and towns within a given metropolitan area would not be under the jurisdiction of a single housing authority. This has substantially reduced the accessibility of suburban and nonmetropolitan public housing to inner-city applicants, most of whom are minority.

It is important to emphasize that in its racially segregating policies, the public housing program was operating within the norms of society. Discrimination in the private market was standard procedure, and public housing did nothing to challenge the system.

Costs to the Federal Government

The costs of the public housing program have been examined by housing analysts in two major ways. Comparisons have been made, on the one hand, with direct income supplements and the Section 8 Existing Housing program and, on the other, with other subsidized new construction programs. As is discussed below, only the second comparison is legitimate. The first is really a comparison between "apples and oranges" (Hartman, 1983)—programs that subsidize household incomes or rents in existing houses versus a program that actually builds and creates new housing. But despite the shortcomings of this comparison, it is important to include it here because it has been a major argument used against the public housing program.

Public Housing, Income Supplements, and the Section 8 Existing Housing Program. The costs of building new public housing have been compared to the costs of providing income supplements, which are similar to cash vouchers. One of the most influential early studies was performed by Eugene Smolensky (1968), who concluded: "Economic considerations alone suggest that the most efficient scheme is to give those families now eligible for public housing a cash subsidy, which the recipient can spend as he wishes so long as he lives in standard housing" (p. 99).

This finding helped stimulate a whole generation of analyses of the benefits and costs of public housing in comparison to other subsidy mechanisms. Within a few years, many other economists had published studies that pointed to the greater benefits of a direct cash subsidy or a housing allowance program. For example, both Aaron (1972) and Muth (1973) concluded that excessive costs of public housing, compounded by the inequity of relatively few low-income households receiving large benefits, warranted a shift in federal housing policy to an income-supplement strategy.

Solomon (1974) continued this critique of the conventional public housing program, comparing it with the Section 23 leased-housing program, which, it was argued, most resembled a housing allowance or income strategy. He concluded that the public housing program provided "disproportionately large benefits" to each subsidized household. According to Solomon:

> If the goal of national housing policy were simply to provide a maximum improvement in the housing conditions of a few poor housholds (the small percentage of those actually receiving government assistance) without regard to equity and cost factors, a reliance on new construction would indeed be a satisfactory policy. But, given both the scarcity of federal resources in relation to overall need and the large number of eligible families receiving no assistance, any definitive judgment regarding program alternatives must also consider their equitableness, cost effectiveness, and political acceptability. (Pp. 69–70)

This kind of analysis confirmed the conventional wisdom about subsidized housing. The growing frustration over the alleged high costs and other problems associated with the subsidized construction programs resulted in a series of experiments, starting in 1970, to test the housing allowance concept, as well as the enactment of the Section 8 Existing Housing program in 1974. Both initiatives generated further research, which continued to make the already well established and not surprising point that in the short run new construction costs more than simply supplying subsidies for existing housing.

Mayo et al. (1980) compared the per unit cost of public housing, the Section 23 leased-housing program, Section 236 (with and without rent supplements), and housing allowances. They estimated that the total annual per unit cost for new public housing or Section 236 was 82 percent higher than the per unit cost for housing allowances. Similarly, the Section 23 program was much less costly than the new construction programs. This point was again made by Wallace et al. (1981) in a study of the Section 8 New Construction and Existing Housing programs. For equivalent subsidy dollars, roughly twice as many households were able to attain decent housing through the Existing Housing program as through the New Construction program.

Equity is also cited as a major reason for opposing public housing and the other subsidized production programs in favor of income supplements. For example, the *Report of the President's Commission on Housing* (1982) pointed out that past housing programs were not equitable "because they provide a few fortunate tenants very high quality housing at a price less than their neighbors pay for lower-quality housing" (p. 3). Yet its own housing allowance proposal was open to similar criticism: The commission did not recommend that it be an entitlement program. Thus, as long as budgetary constraints preclude all eligible households from receiving benefits, any housing program is certain to have inequities.

Those who wave the banner of equity when assessing the subsidized production programs appear to have a misplaced sense of social justice: The benefits of the nation's largest housing subsidy are enjoyed by households far more affluent than public housing tenants. All homeowners, regardless of income, are entitled to deduct mortgage interest as well as property tax payments from their income for federal tax purposes. The result is that about $40 billion in tax revenues are currently being lost to the federal government, with this amount expected to increase to over $50 billion by 1993 (U.S. Congress, 1988). Even more alarming is that the beneficiaries of this subsidy are those in the upper-income groups. Barry Zigas, executive secretary of the Low Income Housing Information Service, has calculated that about two-thirds of the total homeowners' subsidy is received by those earning over $50,000 a year (Low Income Housing Information Service, 1988a). In the aggregate, less than 30 percent of the total housing subsidy—which includes tax deductions as well as direct outlays for low-income housing programs—is received by households earning less than $30,000 a year; only 16 percent is received by those earning less than $10,000 (Low Income Housing Information Service, 1988b). Thus, "large" benefits to public housing tenants are not nearly as large as the savings enjoyed by upper-income households.

The public housing program also has been compared to the Section 8 Existing Housing program by examining the cost of operating existing public housing developments with the cost of subsidizing low-income families in existing private units under the Section 8 program. According to the *Report of the President's Commission on Housing* (1982), the direct costs of operating public housing are no higher than providing a Section 8 subsidy to a family living in existing housing. The national average of the cost of operating existing public housing, as a percentage of Section 8 Existing Housing program costs, is 93–100 percent (*Report of the President's Commission on Housing, 1982*). Further, a 1981 report prepared for the President's Housing Commission by HUD's Office of Policy Development and Research indicated that "average public housing costs were about $1,600 per unit in 1979, as opposed to Abt's[11] estimate of $1,560 for Section 8 Existing for the same period. Keeping in mind that Section 8 Existing has smaller average household and bedroom sizes, the net outlay cost of public housing was lower than that of Section 8."[12]

It seems clear that, at worst, the cost of operating existing public housing developments is on a par with the costs of the Section 8 Existing Housing program. Meehan (1979) showed that two older public housing developments in St. Louis actually cost about 30 to 40 percent less to operate than Section 23 leased housing. Even the *Report of the President's Commission on Housing* (1982) concluded: "While Federal costs [of public housing] have risen, the average cost is not out of line with private rental housing" (p. 32).

Public Housing and Other Subsidized New Construction Housing Programs. A more legitimate assessment of the costs of the production programs is between the programs themselves. There is a considerable amount of disagreement, however, on the costs of public housing compared with both the Section 8 New Construction and Section 236 programs. Mayo et al. (1980) found that public housing and Section 236 had almost identical construction costs. In contrast, the General Accounting Office (GAO) concluded: "For units of the same quality, public housing is the least costly alternative over a 20-year subsidy life and it results in housing projects which are likely to provide service for much longer than privately owned Section 8 units" (1980, 113; see also U.S. Congressional Research Service, 1976).

Additional contradictory findings emerged from a third study, completed in 1982 for HUD. Using actual program data rather than the hypothetical estimates used in the GAO study, Urban Systems Research and Engineering (1982) found that the total per unit development cost for conventional public housing was as much as $10,000 more than for other subsidized new construction programs. The Section 8 New Construction program demonstrated consistently lower subsidy costs than the public housing program, with savings ranging from about $300 to almost $2000 per year.[13] Some of the higher costs of public housing resulted from the construction of larger units, higher land and site development costs, and more costly structures, such as high-rise elevator buildings or very-low-density projects. This discrepancy is, in itself, an important finding. It underscores the fact that empirical studies to date have not controlled for a host of variables and that without such controls, a clear comparison of the subsidy mechanisms used in public housing and other new construction programs is impossible.

The most recent theoretical attempt to compare costs of different kinds of housing subsidies was performed by me in collaboration with Housing Economics, Inc., under contract to the Neighborhood Reinvestment Corporation (Bratt, 1988). Mutual housing, which ideally relies on a 95 percent up-front capital grant, was compared to such programs as Section 8 New Construction, Section 236, and the public housing program, using both traditional debt financing and the newly authorized capital grant method of financing (to be discussed later in this chapter).

The discounted cost of producing a unit of housing whose original construction cost is $68,669 (the 1988 cost for a new unit of public housing) was found to be more expensive using the traditional public housing financing mechanism than for the Section 236 program, the Section 8 New Construction program, or the capital grant financing mechanism recently instituted for public housing. Nevertheless, the latter three programs were all within $7500 of one another, not including operating costs for the public housing program (Bratt, 1988, figure 3.2 and Appendix II, table 2).

Although the Section 236 and Section 8 programs emerged as slightly less expensive in this analysis, it is important to point out that calculations for these programs assumed pre-1986 tax incentives and post-1986 tax rates. (For further discussion on the 1986 tax changes pertaining to housing, see Chapter 5.) Therefore, the specific program characteristics used in the comparison neither existed in the past (since they operated only when pre-1986 tax rates applied) nor do they currently exist (since these programs are no longer funded).

Thus it is uncertain whether they would at present provide sufficient incentives to private developers actually to produce the housing.

Another component of the cost issue relates to who owns the housing when the subsidy period terminates. As discussed in Chapter 4, privately owned subsidized housing is earmarked for low–moderate income occupancy for limited periods of time. In contrast, local public housing authorities own public housing in perpetuity.

The residual value of the housing at the end of the "use restriction" period must be calculated into the total costs of each subsidy program. Private for-profit developers using the Section 236 and Section 8 programs may remove the housing from the affordable stock at the end of the use-restriction period. As a result, the government may need to replace an old affordable unit whose use restriction has expired with a new unit of equal value, acquired some fifteen or more years into the future. This could add an undiscounted cost to such programs of between $51,469 and $106,521 per unit. In discounted dollars, the increased cost to the federal government is between $13,995 and $28,964 (Bratt, 1988, Appendix II, table 25). If such replacement costs are added into the base costs of the programs, public housing and other programs that will not be removed from the stock of subsidized housing emerge as highly cost effective.

The issue of costs can be summarized as follows. First, although this chapter has argued that the comparison is not a fair one because, in the case of public housing, new units are built, and in the housing allowance programs they are not, it is less costly to subsidize a household through the Section 8 Existing Housing program than to subsidize the *construction* of a new unit of public housing. Second, the cost of subsidizing households in *existing* public housing units is no higher than the cost of subsidizing households in *existing* private units through the Section 8 program. Third, although no definitive conclusions can be drawn about the present cost of building new public housing in comparison to the other types of subsidized housing programs that have been utilized in the past, public housing does emerge in a relatively positive position.

Financial Viability

As discussed earlier, a 1983 HUD report disclosed that over one-fifth of the 134 largest housing authorities are financially troubled. Nevertheless, the vast majority of public housing developments and units appear to be financially sound. Beyond this, three relevant questions pertain to the financial viability of public housing. They relate to whether the program provides adequate funding to operate the buildings, to upgrade the buildings as modernization or other improvements are needed, and to salvage seriously distressed developments.

It will be recalled that the public housing funding formula guaranteed annual federal contributions to pay off the principal and interest on bonds floated by local housing authorities to raise the capital to build the housing. By the 1960s, many projects faced serious financial difficulties when operating costs outstripped the ability of housing authorities to raise sufficient revenues through rental payments. While appropriations for public housing operating subsidies came long after they were needed and have often been insufficient, they were significantly better than the meager operating subsidies appropriated for the Section 221(d)(3) and 236 programs. Thus, although public housing has always faced financial constraints and difficulties, Congress has ultimately accepted responsibility for the basic operation of the program.

Funding to modernize and substantially upgrade public housing developments has been forthcoming since the early 1980s. Similar to operating subsidies, however, modernization funds have been both insufficient and long in coming. Despite these inadequacies, Congress *has* appropriated enough money to improve thousands of public housing units and preserve them for low-income tenants for many additional years.

In a relatively few instances, local housing authorities have abandoned seriously distressed projects. Some notable examples are Pruitt-Igoe in St. Louis, Columbia Point in Boston, and America Park in Lynn, Massachusetts. In each of these cases, however, inadequate funding to upgrade the buildings was probably not the major reason for abandoning the low-income projects. Instead, poor location and long-standing social problems may have precluded the continuation of those particular low-income developments.

In summary, the vast majority of public housing developments are financially viable. Although operating subsidies and modernization funds have often been "too little" or "too late," they have managed to keep the vast majority of projects running.

Ability to Accommodate the Neediest

Public housing is the only multifamily subsidy program that is targeted to, and serves, a very-low-income population. In addition, more than half of public housing tenants are families and a majority are nonwhite.

In contrast, as discussed in Chapter 4, both the Section 221(d)(3) and 236 programs were aimed at a slightly higher-income group; the Section 8 program, with similar income guidelines to public housing, has served only a portion of the public housing clientele. Thus, among the major housing subsidy programs, public housing emerges as the only alternative for millions of poor people, particularly those in large families, single-parent households, and minorities.[14]

Long-term Commitment to Housing

The public housing program includes a forty-year federal commitment to provide low-rent housing. In addition, as discussed above, most of the stock of public housing is financially viable because of the federal government's commitment to the program. This commitment was reinforced by the Housing and Community Development Act of 1987 (discussed below), which attempts to safeguard the existing stock of public housing by requiring the replacement of any units that have been demolished or otherwise disposed.

On the negative side, the need for this provision was prompted by Reagan administration moves to privatize the public housing stock, thereby jeopardizing the availability of this housing to future generations of low-income households (*Federal Register*, 1984; see Report of the *President's Commission on Housing*, 1982). In addition, some local housing authorities have been less than supportive of public housing, for they have watched surrounding neighborhoods rise in value as gentrification has occurred or as proximity to downtown business districts has made the land occupied by public housing extremely valuable (see, e.g., GAO, 1986).

Despite these shortcomings, the federal government has been far more committed to the long-term maintenance of public housing than to other subsidized housing programs (discussed in Chapter 4).

Enhancing Individual Well-Being and Producing Social Benefits

It is not surprising that information on how the public housing program measures on enhancing individual well-being and producing social benefits is lacking. As mentioned in Chapter 2, these criteria have generally been omitted from housing evaluations. It is probably safe to conclude, however, that public housing per se has not often led to individual empowerment.

There are some notable exceptions, such as tenant organizations that have evolved to protect tenant interests, tenant management corporations, and tenant-initiated lawsuits brought against local housing authorities for violating health or building codes. Unfortunately, empowerment in all these cases is the end result of negative situations, ones that may have already exacted a high personal toll from the tenants.

Public Housing: Future Policy

There is no question that public housing has made a considerable contribution to addressing the low-income housing problem in this country. Millions of low-income families have been provided with decent, affordable units with which the great majority of tenants appear to be satisfied. Moreover, the majority of public housing developments have been reported to be in good condition. But public housing also has been disappointing. It has not promoted racial integration and, often, the designs of the buildings have been bleak, accessibility has been poor, and management has been a problem. Yet, as the preceding review has demonstrated, many of public housing's failings have reflected persistent opposition by private-sector critics who, from the program's inception, attempted to kill the program. While public housing cannot and should not be "let off the hook," particularly regarding problems with racial integration and management, these problems are correctible and do not reflect inherent flaws in the basic concept of the public housing program.

In view of the real achievements of public housing, why do completely negative stereotypes persist? First, some of the most problem-laden projects are clustered in large cities and are readily observable to many people. The vast numbers of successful projects are more dispersed; often they are in small cities and towns. The reality that a handful of projects are in serious difficulty may have created the myth that all public housing has failed. Second, the notion that public housing has been a failure is certainly what many interest groups want to believe and propound. Public ownership of housing is still not a popular concept, and a successful program that bypasses the private homebuilding industry would be just as unwelcome among the private sector today as it was when the program was enacted. Third, the media have tended to cover the failures within the public housing stock to a far greater degree than they have depicted the successes.

Beyond the preceding attempt to clarify the actual accomplishments of public housing, two broad questions need to be addressed: To what extent is the program a fair test of public ownership of housing? And what should be the future direction for public housing?

A Test of Public Ownership?

The public housing program was never given a fair chance at success. Opposition by the real estate lobby continually undermined the program, and the private sector's insistence that public housing not be competitive with market housing virtually assured that public housing would be not only different but less desirable. In addition, the funding formula provided inadequate operating reserves, which led to maintenance and repair deficiencies. Eugene Meehan (1983) has stated:

> The public housing program, effectively if not deliberately, was designed to fail. The design remained unchanged long past the time when minor modifications might have produced a genuine test of the principle of public ownership and operation of low-income housing. Public housing was not tested and found wanting; it was condemned without trial. Of course, a genuine test might also have revealed public housing's failure. The point is, the test was not made. (P. 75)

When problems in the public housing program became evident, there was a major push toward privatization, instead of trying to improve the public-ownership approach. The major "innovations" in public housing that occurred in the late 1960s all embraced an expanded role for the private sector. The leased-housing program depended on private landlords, and the turnkey program depended on private developers. Meehan (1979) has questioned the thinking behind this shift toward a greater reliance on the private sector:

> Why a transfer of control over development or operations from a public employee to a private entrepreneur was expected to lead to significant improvements in performance is uncertain. Some proponents of privatization simply opposed public ownership on ideological grounds and took the "failure" of public housing as evidence favorable to their position. Others accepted the popular belief in the superiority of private enterprise (as opposed to the intrinsic evil of public ownership). In most cases, supporters of privatization apparently had only the vaguest notion of how and why it would improve the housing program. (P. 136)

According to Meehan, privatization was a costly error, and

> the assumption that privatization was justified because public ownership had been tried and found wanting was grossly mistaken. . . . The poor quality and performance of some of the conventional develop-

ments were no more a simple function of public ownership than the poor performance and quality of some recent turnkey developments were a simple function of private development. (1979, 205–206)

As mentioned above, many of the difficulties experienced by the public housing program stemmed from the continued opposition it faced, given its highly controversial nature in a "free enterprise" system. But the issue remains that it is the only major federal housing program involving government ownership. This concept, although admittedly difficult to investigate within an environment committed to ensuring failure (or, at least the appearance of failure), still awaits a fair evaluation.

Future Directions for Public Housing

Although we know that most public housing has provided relatively decent, low-rent shelter in the past, policymakers are confronted with two questions: What should be done with the existing stock of public housing? And should new public housing be produced?

Concerning the first question, the threat to the existing stock of public housing dates back to the mid-1970s. Since 1974, HUD has had the power to sell public housing units to tenants, although, through the end of 1983, HUD had authorized only 1731 such sales (Stegman, 1988). During the mid-1980s, under the Reagan administration, interest in selling public housing units to tenants was fueled by the expansion of England's public housing sales program under Prime Minister Margaret Thatcher (see, e.g., Schifferes, 1986).

In 1985, HUD launched the Public Housing Ownership Demonstration program, which authorized seventeen local housing authorities to transfer 1290 public housing units to tenants. As of late 1987, less than 10 percent of the total had been transferred to resident owners (Stegman, 1988). In addition, the Housing and Community Development Act of 1987 established a new program whereby public housing tenants can purchase units from resident management corporations that acquire the development from the local housing authority. Although this program requires that a new unit of public housing be provided for each unit removed from the public housing stock, there is no specific funding for such replacements.

The answer to the first question is clear. The existing stock of public housing represents a scarce and invaluable resource that must be protected and supported. Efforts to privatize, demolish, or convert the existing stock should generally be opposed. Key exceptions are the relatively small number of seriously distressed projects for which even substantial repairs and modernization would not remedy the multiple problems. Dealing with these special problem projects, either through demolition or substantial modification, is an important component of a new public housing agenda (Stegman, 1988). For the vast majority of projects, resources and supports should be made available to ensure that public housing remains a viable option for needy households.

The Housing and Community Development Act of 1987 embraces this view in Section 121, which requires local housing authorities to make provisions to satisfy the extra demand for low-rent housing created by a demolition or disposition action on a one-to-one basis. The legislative intent of this section is to

> assure that the demolition or disposition of public housing units does not occur unless the project is obsolete due to its physical condition, location, or other factors which make it unusable for housing *and* no reasonable modifications, such as rehabilitation, are feasible to return the project to useful life. Given the desperate need for affordable housing for lower income families, care must be taken not to sell or demolish these units unless no way can be devised to make the units livable. (U.S. House of Representatives, Committee on Banking, Finance and Urban Affairs, 1987, 25)

As with any legislation, there can be a large gap between rhetoric and implementation. Only time will tell whether the goals of Congress to preserve public housing will be fulfilled.

Concerning the second question, funding for new public housing was authorized at the level of $481 million in the Housing and Community Development Act of 1987. Appropriations in FY 1988 for this amount, however, will translate only into about 7000 new units of public housing, including 2000 units of Indian Housing (National Housing Law Project, 1988). Although it is a positive step to have funding for public housing development—the first in many years—this sum is minuscule in comparison to the overall need for affordable shelter.

Thus the answer to the second question, although more complex, calls for the development of a significant new and revised public housing program. Such a program would optimally include "up-front" capital grants for the construction or rehabilitation of buildings, and adequate operating subsidies and modernization allocations. Calling "up-front" financing an "endowment grant," the Congressional Budget Office in 1981 identified this as "optimal because it is higher in efficiency, relatively short term in federal involvement, and comparatively certain in budgetary impact, compared to the other devices" (Neighborhood Reinvestment Corporation, 1985, 23). Although this approach is particularly attractive to policy analysts who advocate significant federal involvement in housing, it has been pointed out that

> ample precedent exists for direct capital grant financing of housing in our society, including a substantial portion of the 450,000 units of family housing built by the armed forces for military personnel and their families. Construction, modernization, and maintenance of these units has been funded largely through direct Congressional appropriations to the Defense Department budget. Another example is FmHA's [Farmer's Home Administration] Section 514/516 program, which has been successful in producing low-cost rural housing. (Institute for Policy Studies' Working Group on Housing, 1987, 43)

After fifty years of federal financing of public housing through tax-exempt financing, with the interest and principal on the bonds paid by the federal government (the Annual Contributions Contract), the Housing and Community Development Act of 1987 included a new provision, Section 112(a)(2), which authorizes direct capital grants for the development of public and Indian housing. The House Committee on Banking, Finance, and Urban Affairs offered several reasons why this action was needed. First, the tax-exempt status of public housing notes was called into question by 1984 federal tax amendments: as a result, HUD was forced to suspend the sale of these notes until the IRS ruled on whether they satisfied various requirements of the tax code. By September 1984, the IRS had not provided such guidance, so no new public housing notes were issued, and HUD turned to another "very cumbersome and awkward method of funding the pipeline for public housing" (U.S. House of Representatives, Committee on Banking, Finance, and Urban Affairs, 1987, 15). Second, and quite simply, the committee acknowledged that capital grants were a cheaper subsidy mechanism. Specifically, the capital grant method "calls for much less budget authority because [it] provides for federal grants . . . 'up front' rather than providing annual direct outlays and tax expenditures over the long period of time needed to retire the tax-exempt bonds" (p. 15).

Any new public housing program also should supply funding

to support tenant management corporations, as well as pay special attention to design, siting, neighborhood amenities, and the need for social service programs (see Chapter 13).

Finally, a new public housing program should be geared to providing nonstigmatizing, community-building, and individual-empowering environments. Although this may be a tall order, it is a feasible one. Unless policymakers and legislators are convinced that new public housing will be significantly better than past public housing —even though the images may be erroneous—it will be difficult politically to get a major new program enacted.

In the meantime, a great deal more needs to be learned about what makes a problem project or even a problem housing authority. Research is needed on why some housing authorities have been successful, while others have failed. Similarly, we know very little about why some projects in a given city are virtually trouble-free, while others, often only a few blocks away, are public disgraces.

Public housing presents a compelling case: The demand for low-rent housing is acute in many areas, and the public housing program alleviates a pressing need. Public housing has not failed; if anything, it can claim an impressive success. Despite opposition to the program and unrelenting efforts by the private sector to sabotage it, public housing, over the past five decades, has provided shelter for millions of poor households.

4

Publicly Subsidized Private Housing

MIDWAY THROUGH President Reagan's first term, a senior White House staff member addressed a group of academics and policymakers attending a HUD-sponsored conference, "Neighborhood Action in an Era of Fiscal Austerity." As the talk progressed, the message became clear: "Don't look to the federal government for help in solving neighborhood problems." This came as no surprise. What caused a murmur in the crowd, and an outright sense of shock, was how the speaker justified his position. He pointed with pride to the accomplishments of several community-based groups that had made steps toward alleviating their housing and community development problems. These organizations were paraded as models of how communities can do it "on their own." What the speaker neglected to mention was the numerous federal programs that had supported these organizations. Was the speaker simply misinformed, or did the distortion reflect a more pervasive effort by the Reagan administration to rewrite history to suit its perspective? Unfortunately, this does not seem to have been an isolated instance.

Another example of a glaring distortion is the way in which Reagan's *Report of the President's Commission on Housing* represented the historical involvement of the private sector with federal housing programs. The commission virtually ignored the substantial participation of the private sector in the past and argued that earlier approaches "reflected a common belief that all problems would be solved if only the government would set the right goals and enforce the right policies" (*Report of the President's Commission on Housing*, 1982, xvii). Stating that the Commission on Housing was established "to help chart a new path for the rest of this century," the report went on to assert that the private market is better able to provide housing than federal programs are.

A more accurate introduction to the commission's report might have detailed how and why the private sector became involved with subsidized housing over the prior two decades and might have questioned both what was right and what was wrong about this approach. In addition, it might have noted that if the private market had provided the needed housing for low-income people in the first place, the federal government might not have gotten involved at all.[1] By only minimally acknowledging the substantial amount of experience we have with public–private housing ventures,[2] the commission was free to unleash a full measure of its ideological bias: "Much of what needs to be done . . . cannot be the doing of the Federal government" (1982, xviii).

Far from being able to depend on the private sector to solve the nation's low-income housing problems, we know that private homebuilders, real estate brokers, and financial institutions have not met the housing needs of low-income households (see Chapter 1). Moreover, their involvement with federal subsidy programs has been mixed. On the one hand, they have assisted in the production or rehabilitation of some 1.5 million units of housing. On the other hand, as pointed out in Chapter 3, they were opposed to the conventional public housing program (in which they had no role), and their opposition created some serious obstacles for that program.

This chapter reviews the historical role of the private sector in federally subsidized multifamily housing programs. It then assesses the record of these programs, using many of the criteria used in evaluating the public housing program. The next chapter presents an in-depth case study of how the goals of private owners of subsidized housing conflict with public objectives.

Federal Housing Policy and the Private Sector: From the 1930s to the 1980s

Implementation of federal housing policy has always been heavily dependent on the private sector. Even in the 1930s, when government involvement was at its peak, private firms were integrally involved with most publicly supported programs. For example, the Federal Housing Administration (FHA) relied on private builders and private mortgage lenders to construct and finance housing, while the government provided mortgage insurance. In addition, the overhauling of the nation's financial institutions through the creation of the Federal Home Loan Bank System (1932) and the Federal Reserve System (1913) provided federal supports to private operations. Even the public housing program, in which there was no direct involvement by private developers, involved private investors in the purchase of housing authority bonds.

In 1949, Congress articulated a new role for the private sector in federally subsidized housing programs. Contained in the housing act of that year was a new national housing goal—"the realization as soon as feasible of the goal of a decent home and a suitable living environment for every American family"—that was to be attained by involving the private sector: "Private enterprise shall be encouraged to serve as large a part of the total need as it can; governmental assistance shall be utilized where feasible to enable private enterprise to serve more of the total need."[3] Despite this language, a role for the private sector in producing subsidized housing was not legislated until ten years later. But beginning in 1959, the private sector has been prominent in federal housing subsidy programs.

The Section 202 program was enacted as part of the Housing Act of 1959 to provide "independent living" for elderly and handicapped individuals. Three years earlier, Congress had enacted a special FHA insurance program for the elderly, Section 207. That program's market interest rate, however, combined with a forty-year amortization period, created rents considered "too high for most elderly couples and individuals" (U.S. House of Representatives, 1959, 326). The Section 207 program stimulated little activity. Between 1956 and 1959, there were applications for only thirty-two projects, totaling 4500 units; only one project, with 140 units, was completed. According to the secretary of the AFL-CIO's Housing Committee, the program was "virtually a complete failure" (U.S. House of Representatives, 1959, 326). The Section 202 program was to fill an important void: It was targeted to people whose incomes were too high for conventional public housing, but too low to afford an unsubsidized unit in the private rental market, with or without FHA insurance.

Modeled, in part, after the College Housing Program enacted in 1950, the Section 202 program also provided direct government loans, payable in up to fifty years, at about a 3 percent interest rate. Yet Section 202 was a path-breaking program in a number of important ways. Section 202 had the distinction of being the first subsidized housing program to utilize private owners, as opposed to local housing authorities. In addition, it was the first (and only) housing program to limit sponsorship to a wide array of nonprofit organizations. (In the College Housing Program, only one type of sponsor—college or university—was eligible.) Finally, the Section 202 program expanded the relatively new way of providing a housing subsidy, through low-interest direct government loans. (The government is able to offer below-market interest rates on loans it makes itself because the cost of borrowing for the federal government is less than the borrowing rates for private lenders.) This lowered interest rate, combined with an amortization period ten years longer than usual, reduced rentals below those charged under the earlier Section 207 program.

But the innovative aspects of Section 202 produced a considerable amount of concern while the bill was being debated. Although Section 202 was to be the opening wedge for private, for-profit developers to become involved with subsidized housing, the homebuilders did not know this at the time. Opposing the House version of the bill, which stipulated that government loans would be made available only to nonprofit corporations, the National Association of Home Builders (NAHB) went on record as supporting the Senate version of the bill, which would have permitted sponsorship of the elderly housing by for-profit entities and which relied on private funds insured by the FHA. During hearings before the House of Representatives in 1959, the NAHB tersely summarized its views:

> We believe that the history of housing legislation in this country has conclusively demonstrated that a workable program using private financing and the enterprise and resourcefulness of the building industry operating in a profit-and-loss economy will produce greater results more quickly than a program depending on Federal appropriations. (U.S. House of Representatives, 1959, 463)

Despite builders' opposition, the House version prevailed. Although for-profit developers would not be permitted to sponsor subsidized housing for two more years, a new and important precedent was set with the enactment of the Section 202 program: Subsidized housing was no longer the exclusive domain of the public sector.

But the direct-loan provisions of Section 202 did not sit well with the Eisenhower administration. Testifying against the proposed program, the administrator of the Housing and Home Finance Agency (the forerunner of HUD) stated:

> The administration believes that this direct Federal loan program would involve an unnecessary and undesirable use of Federal funds. It would compete with private enterprise and would have the effect of smothering the growing private interest in serving this field. . . . The $200 million loan fund provided for by this title is so small in relation

to the need that it would be only the beginning of a vast flow of
Federal funds which would be needed for this purpose, once private
initiative is discouraged. (U.S. House of Representatives, 1959, 40)

Partly because direct loans were considered major budgetary outlays, the early Section 202 program was quite small. Between 1959
and 1968, 335 projects, containing 45,275 units, were developed,
mostly through new construction. On average, then, only about 37
new projects were added to the inventory each year (HUD, 1979).

During the 1960 presidential campaign, housing was a strong
partisan issue, with the Democratic platform articulating a need for
direct government involvement and more low-rent public housing.
In contrast, the Republican platform made no reference to public
housing or to other programs for the poor (Keith, 1973).

The campaign promises of the new Kennedy administration were
quickly transformed into a legislative package. The urgency stemmed
from an economic downturn and the particularly difficult situation
facing the construction industry. Always hard hit by recessions and
tight-money policies, new private housing starts fell 18 percent between 1959 and 1960. Unemployment in the construction industry
outstripped all other major industries, with one out of every six
construction workers out of work (Keith, 1973). Testifying before
Congress in 1961 on the proposed housing legislation, the NAHB
president stated: "We have been concerned, as you know, about the
health of the homebuilding industry. The volume of housing that
was built in 1960 was not nearly adequate in this country. . . . We
think that a stimulated housing industry can be helpful in assuring
economic stability" (U.S. House of Representatives, 1961, 486).

NAHB agreed that many aspects of the legislation would help
stimulate homebuilding. But it questioned provisions relating to
housing production for lower-income families by private nonprofit
or for-profit sponsors, financed through below-market-interest Federal National Mortgage Association (FNMA) special assistance funds
and insured by the FHA. Asserting that "it might not be a sound
idea," NAHB argued that the proposed section (221(d)(3)) would
be "putting a welfare-type program into FHA," thereby threatening
its bulging insurance reserves (U.S. House of Representatives, 1961,
488–489). But, careful not to come out against the program, the
NAHB indicated that it was still being studied.

By 1965, the NAHB had made up its mind about the 221(d)(3)
program. Although it recommended changes to "expand its usefulness," the program was considered totally acceptable and its exten-

sion was endorsed (U.S. Senate, 1965, 389–391). Specifically concerning the housing legislation of 1965, NAHB's president spoke in favor of the proposed Rent Supplement program, which was to provide additional rental subsidies for low-income households living in FHA-insured multifamily housing:

> If . . . rent assistance is provided to truly needy or disadvantaged tenants, the productive capacity of the private homebuilding industry can—for the first time—be applied on a broad front to build for families of lower income. . . . Given the same advantages available to public housing, we can and will produce more and better housing for low-income families. We can and will do it quicker than can be done by the publicly financed and owned housing. We can and will do it at less cost to the Federal and local governments. And it can be done without the serious disadvantages now recognized by even the most ardent public housers. (U.S. Senate, 1965, 391)

The position of the NAHB was clear: Publicly owned housing was viewed as the wrong approach, while public subsidies to the private sector were now strongly supported. Senator Paul Douglas responded to NAHB's statement with a commendation for its position on housing assistance for the poor and a reminder that the organization had not always been as prohousing. As it turned out, the homebuilders' support was crucial for the enactment of the legislation: The rent-supplement program passed the House by only six votes. A member of Chairman Wright Patman's Banking and Currency Committee staff noted: "We just couldn't have done it without the homebuilders" (quoted in Lilley, 1973, 36).

In addition to the Rent Supplement program, homebuilders were given two opportunities to become involved with government-subsidized housing programs. As problems with the conventional public housing program surfaced during the 1960s, there was a major push to involve the private sector. The line of thinking was straightforward: Ownership and management by government are problematic, and so private participation automatically would be better. As mentioned in Chapter 3, although there was a lack of clarity about why privatization was preferable, two variants of the conventional public housing program, both of which included substantial roles for the private sector, were implemented in 1965: the leased-housing program and the turnkey program.

By the late 1960s, the private sector was a full-fledged partner in subsidized housing activities; it would have been unthinkable for any new subsidized housing legislation to exclude it. President Johnson's

Committee on Urban Housing underscored the importance of the private sector in housing programs:

> The nation has been slow to realize that private industry in many cases is an efficient vehicle for achieving social goals . . . some programs still make too little use of the talents of private entrepreneurs. . . . One of the basic lessons of the history of Federal housing programs seems to be that the programs which work best—such as the FHA mortgage insurance programs—are those that channel the forces of existing economic institutions into productive areas. This approach has proved to be better than wholly ignoring existing institutions and starting afresh outside the prevailing market system. Reliance on market forces should be increased in the future.[4] (*Report of the President's Committee on Urban Housing*, 1968, 54)

The Housing and Urban Development Act of 1968 presented an attractive package to private homebuilding and real estate interests. Most important were the Section 235 and 236 programs, which provided subsidies to reduce the costs for homeowners and renters. In both programs, production, financing, and ownership rested with the private sector. Public support for the programs came through payments made to private lenders to reduce the effective interest rate on the mortgage loan to as low as 1 percent, thereby lowering monthly costs. The Section 236 program replaced both the Section 202 and 221(d)(3) programs as the new multifamily housing subsidy mechanism for the elderly as well as family households.

The Housing and Urban Development Act of 1968 also reaffirmed the 1949 housing goal and declared that the newly authorized housing programs should be carried out with "the fullest practicable utilization of the resources and capabilities of private enterprise."[5]

This message was warmly greeted by the organized homebuilding and real estate industries, which were outspoken in their support for the new subsidy programs. The president of the National Association of Real Estate Boards (NAREB) gave what Senator Proxmire called a "ringing endorsement" of the 1968 legislation (U.S. Senate, 1968, 261), and the president of the NAHB testified: "We are fully in accord with the sense of urgency as expressed by the recommended legislation. . . . We think the pending bill . . . goes far in seeking to effect profound changes in the development of housing and its financing patterns" (U.S. Senate, 1968, 298). But he continued with a less straightforward message:

> [There is] an imperative need to remove some of the impediments to unleashing the vigor and capacity of private enterprise. Only if the

homebuilding industry is strong and healthy can it be encouraged
and adapted into production for income levels presently not fully
served. This simple truism has not always been fully appreciated.
(U.S. Senate, 1968, 289)

The NAHB's "simple truism" was really not that simple. What impediments stood in the way of the private sector unleashing its "vigor
and capacity" to provide more low-income housing on its own? And
was it the government's responsibility to make the homebuilding industry "strong and healthy"? Vagueness aside, rhetoric like this was
common during the 1968 housing hearings.

Despite the central role for the private sector in the 1968 legislation, the homebuilders were still uncompromising when it came
to conventional public housing. The NAHB proposed that *all* new
authorizations for public housing be directed primarily toward the
turnkey program. Calling it "the first attempt in the 30-year history
of public housing to use, for the lowest income brackets, the tremendous resources and productive capacity of the private homebuilding
industry," the NAHB cited the turnkey program for being an example
of "the proper role of Government in helping private industry to
expand into areas not attainable without such help" (U.S. Senate,
1968, 293).

By the early 1970s, problems with all housing subsidy programs
were being acknowledged (Downs, 1972; HUD, 1973). Escalating
maintenance costs, particularly for heating fuel, put serious financial
strains on many multifamily developments, whether publicly or
privately owned. In the case of public housing, operating subsidies,
although often inadequate, were appropriated. But for thousands of
privately owned subsidized developments—Section 221(d)(3) and
Section 236—operating cost overruns drove owners to default on
their mortgage payments. Yet the subsidy program that received
the most notoriety was the Section 235 homeownership program.
Shoddy construction, unscrupulous real estate brokers, outright dis-
honesty on the part of some FHA appraisers, poor bank underwriting, often by mortgage companies, and uncounseled and unprepared
first-time buyers of homes combined to undermine the program and
produce a high foreclosure rate (see, e.g., U.S. House of Representatives, 1972a, 1972b).

In response to problems such as these, President Nixon, in early
1973, called a moratorium on all federal housing subsidy programs.
Although problems with housing programs made them an easy target, the moratorium was also consistent with President Nixon's over-

all budget-cutting strategy as he started his second term. Following a period of evaluation, and based on early findings from the Experimental Housing Allowance Program, a new federal direction took shape. Future emphasis was to be placed on subsidizing low-income households in existing units through rental certificates (see Chapters 1 and 3). The Section 8 Existing Housing program was authorized by the Housing and Community Development Act of 1974, thereby creating the first large-scale housing-allowance program. With the program dependent on privately owned units, private landlords could be guaranteed rent payments by negotiating multiyear leases with local housing authorities. The homebuilders also turned out to be winners in the 1974 legislation. Despite the groundswell of support for the housing-allowance approach and the general dissatisfaction with the subsidized new construction programs, it is a testimony to the power of the homebuilding industry that the Section 8 program also included a New Construction and Substantial Rehabilitation component. At the same time, the Section 202 program was reactivated, to be used in conjunction with the Section 8 program.

Although the homebuilders were enormously successful in carving out an impressive role for themselves in the federal housing subsidy programs, the Reagan administration turned its back on support for the traditional public–private partnership, reversing several decades of fostering it. Public support for subsidized housing was viewed with disfavor and, as pointed out at the beginning of this chapter, federal officials denied the prominence of the private sector in past housing programs. Yet facts and history speak for themselves: For over twenty-five years, the private, for-profit sector has been directly involved in federal housing subsidy programs.

Much less aggregated information is available concerning the publicly subsidized, privately owned stock of multifamily housing than about the public housing program. The relative lack of data makes both an evaluation of this production strategy and a comparison with the public housing program difficult to accomplish. Specifically, almost no information for two criteria used in Chapter 3—accessibility[6] and management—is available. Moreover, since "costs to the federal government" of the public housing program, discussed in Chapter 3, presented a comparison with the subsidized new construction programs, this criterion is not included in this chapter. Information pertaining to the other criteria are presented and provide a good picture of experiences with the Section 221(d)(3), Section 236, and Section 8 programs.

Publicly Subsidized Private Housing: An Assessment

Characteristics of Tenants and Tenant Perceptions

Both the Section 221(d)(3) and Section 236 programs were designed to serve a slightly higher-income population than the public housing program. For example, in 1975, 60 percent of Section 236 households had incomes between $5000 and $10,000, while 71 percent of the tenants in public housing had incomes under $10,000. Further, while half of the households in Section 236 housing had adjusted incomes that were less than 50 percent of the median national income for all U.S. households, 87 percent of public housing tenants had incomes below this amount (GAO, 1978, 39–40).

In comparison to public housing, Section 236 households were less likely to be elderly, more likely to have one or more member employed, more likely to be smaller in terms of family size, more likely to have a male present in the house, and less likely to be minority members (GAO, 1978, 40–45).

The Section 8 New Construction program has also served a population that is dissimilar to the public housing tenantry, although both groups have very low incomes. For example, the New Construction program provides assistance primarily to the elderly, whites, women, and single persons (Wallace et al., 1981, 73; see also GAO, 1980).

Information on levels of satisfaction among residents in subsidized housing programs—including Section 221(d)(3) and 236, but not Section 8—comes primarily from a study by Francescato et al. (1979). Interviews with tenants at twenty-seven developments indicated that 62 percent were satisfied or very satisfied with their housing, while only about 20 percent were dissatisfied. A considerably higher percentage (97 percent) of tenants in a sample of new Section 8 developments rated their units as either excellent or good (Wallace et al., 1981). A third study, much smaller in scope, included interviews with thirty-five tenants in three new Section 221(d)(3) developments, both before and after their moves. Questions relating to space, design, safety, quietness, and childrearing features of the housing evoked a response of "like it better after the move" by at least 83 percent of the respondents. These results were compared to the responses of a sample of twenty-four movers into public housing: although this group also reported greater satisfaction after the move, the levels were somewhat higher among those moving into Section 221(d)(3) units (Feagin, Tilly, and Williams, 1972). Thus, similar to the responses of tenants in public housing, reported in Chapter 3, residents in publicly subsidized, privately owned developments seem to be quite satisfied with their housing.

Physical Characteristics, Condition, and Design

Very little information is available on physical characteristics of these developments. A recent HUD report, which included a study of all HUD/FHA-insured multifamily developments, not just those receiving subsidies (which is the focus of this chapter), summarized the inventory as being predominantly garden apartments or row houses (only 25 percent were high-rise buildings) having an average of 116 units per property. Slightly over half of the properties were located in central cities, 26 percent in suburbs, and 20 percent in nonmetropolitan areas (Hodes et al., 1987, 9).

A study of the Section 236 program provided no quantitative information on the quality of the developments and simply said that it was "probably good" and that researchers had "found only an occasional reference to poor quality" (GAO, 1978, 34). A report on the Section 8 program found that the buildings more frequently have certain amenities than do Section 236 projects (Urban Systems Research and Engineering, 1982). In fact, the Section 8 New Construction program has been criticized for providing such a good-quality unit that the cost has turned out to be "too high" (*Report of the President's Commission on Housing*, 1982).

Finally, the HUD study cited above disclosed that almost 80 percent of the properties, which include some 5600 developments, are in good physical condition and need only moderate levels of nonroutine repairs (Hodes et al., 1987).

Impact on Racial Integration

Information is sparse on the impact of subsidized multifamily housing developments on promoting racial integration. Yet a few studies do exist. A 1972 HUD study of the Section 236 program in the Washington, D.C., metropolitan area revealed that the program did not reduce the concentration of minorities in the central city; in fact, the proportion of blacks living in subsidized developments was consistently higher than for the census tract as a whole. In the suburbs, however, the program did serve to promote racial balance (cited in HUD, 1973a). A study on the Section 8 New Construction program reported that black households were able to move into neighborhoods with significantly lower minority populations (Wallace et al., 1981).

Another way of assessing the racial impact of the housing pro-

grams is to examine the likelihood that an eligible minority household will have access to a publicly supported unit. Although a majority of public housing units are occupied by minorities, about the
same proportion of white and black households have had access to
Section 236 housing (GAO, 1978). In contrast, minorities seem to
have had less access to new Section 8 housing, occupying only 15
percent of these units while accounting for 35 percent of the eligible
population (Wallace et al., 1981).

Financial Viability

There is enormous variation in the financial viability of subsidized multifamily housing developments. During the 1970s, dramatic
increases in energy and other operating costs of virtually all multifamily housing far outpaced the ability of tenants to pay. As discussed
in Chapter 3, the public housing program managed to bridge this
gap by receiving substantial operating subsidies. In contrast, many
Section 221(d)(3) and 236 projects were thrown into a financial tailspin. A 1977 study released by the Boston HUD office indicated that
operating costs in these projects had risen 68 percent since 1970,
while median family incomes had increased by only 28 percent. As
shown in Table 2, more than one-quarter of all the subsidized multifamily projects have encountered some form of financial difficulty,
with HUD holding the mortgages of projects, owning the projects, or
having sold the projects.

One can easily place the blame for the financial problems of
subsidized developments on rapidly increasing costs, but it is more
appropriate to view the financial record of the publicly subsidized
multifamily programs as the result of inadequacies in the programs
themselves. Probably the most significant flaws were incentives for
developers to underestimate operating costs, lack of a requirement
that adequate funds be set aside to deal with unforeseen expenses,
and a subsidy formula that did not increase when additional resources were needed (Boston Redevelopment Authority and HUD,
1973; GAO, 1978; HUD, 1973, 1978b). According to Emily Achtenberg, a Boston housing consultant, there were other major problems
with the Section 236 program:

> The original mortgagees earned their one-time placement fees and
> passed their fully insured loans on to permanent lenders, avoiding
> exposure for faulty feasibility decisions. FHA, under pressure to
> produce in order to comply with the National Housing Goals and
> resistant to its new social welfare role, routinely approved loans with

TABLE 2
STATUS OF FEDERALLY SUBSIDIZED AND
INSURED MULTIFAMILY HOUSING

	Projects	Units
Currently insured		
Section 236	3425	383,462
Section 221d3 BMIR	939	113,122
Rent Supplement	228	15,559
Total	4592	512,143
Percentage	72.92	74.41
HUD-HELD		
Section 236	448	49,506
Section 221d3 BMIR	244	36,440
Rent Supplement	40	2,285
Total	732	88,231
Percentage	11.62	12.82
HUD-owned		
All	45	6405
Percentage	0.71	0.93
HUD-sold		
All	831	65,445
Percentage	13.20	9.51
Status unknown		
All	97	16,014
Percentage	1.54	2.33
Ever insured		
Section 236	4240	464,483
Section 221d3 BMIR	1590	191,120
Rent Supplement	467	32,635
Total	6297	688,238
Percentage	100.00	100.00

Source: Emily Paradise Achtenberg, "Subsidized Housing at Risk: The Social Costs of Private Ownership," in *Housing Issues of the 1990s*, ed. Sara Rosenberg and Chester Hartman (Praeger Publishers, a division of Greenwood Press, Inc., New York). Copyright © 1989 by Praeger Publishers. Used with permission.

little scrutiny. As a result, many projects were infeasible from the start. (Achtenberg, 1989)

When utility costs skyrocketed in the early 1970s as a result of the oil crisis, owners of subsidized housing were faced with several difficult options in trying to meet increased operating expenses: raise rents, decrease maintenance and management services, cut into profits, or default on mortgage payments. Whatever strategies owners chose, the "bottom line" on these programs has been a high rate of default and foreclosure.

The 1987 HUD study performed by Hodes et al. found that 35 percent of HUD's insured properties (which includes nonsubsidized properties, as well as the subsidized developments that are the subject of this chapter) appear to have inadequate financial resources to meet their needs. Many subsidized properties have deteriorated and some have even ceased to be available to low- and moderate-income people, either because owners abandoned the buildings, rendering them uninhabitable, or because they were resold to investors who stopped maintaining the low- and moderate-income character of the developments. As discussed below, how HUD should deal with these problem-laden projects has been a question of congressional and public interest.

Since the late 1970s, two variations on the Section 8 program have come to be used for financially distressed Section 221(d)(3) and Section 236 developments. The Section 8 Loan Management Set Aside program, which is tied to specific projects, has helped alleviate tenants' rent burdens. Although not officially considered an operating subsidy, it essentially helps owners raise additional operating revenues. Another variant of Section 8, known as the Property Disposition program, has been used for projects that have been foreclosed or are being disposed of by HUD.

A final form of assistance for financially distressed properties was the Flexible Subsidy program. Grants or loans, payable on resale of the property, were made to finance repairs or pay off operating deficits. But this program cannot be used to cover normal operating expenses in nondistressed projects and is somewhat comparable to the public housing modernization program. Appropriations for the Flexible Subsidy have been far less than for the modernization program, and during the Reagan administration, virtually no new funding was made available. Funding has been limited to the recycling of extra income generated from so-called over-income—tenants for whom 30 percent of income is greater than the basic rent charged for the Section 221(d)(3) or 236 units.

Because the subsidy formula of the Section 8 New Construction and Substantial Rehabilitation programs includes increases for operating expenses, these programs seem financially sound. For example, a survey of subsidized developments financed through state housing finance programs in thirty-five states found virtually no delinquencies in Section 8 projects (Nuveen Research Comment, 1984). If HUD fair-market rentals do not keep pace with costs, however, defaults will likely result.

Ability to Accommodate the Neediest

As mentioned earlier, tenants in Section 221(d)(3) and 236 developments had somewhat higher incomes than public housing residents. This reflected the programs' goals to assist moderate-income households. Also, while the Section 8 New Construction program targeted a very-low-income population, minorities, large families, and single-parent households are less likely to live in this type of housing than in a public housing unit.

Long-term Commitment to Housing

Congress has been somewhat ambivalent about its commitment to the privately owned, publicly subsidized stock of multifamily housing. Unlike the public housing program, where the public-sector role is irrefutable, with other programs the question of who is responsible for financial difficulties surfaces. Since the developments are privately owned, one could argue that the owners have the responsibility of bailing out financially distressed projects. Yet it can also be argued that since HUD provides a subsidy, as well as the mortgage insurance, responsibility rests with the government.

This confusion has caused significant problems for the stock of privately owned subsidized housing and, as a result, for tenants of these developments. For example, HUD's refusal to implement the limited emergency operating subsidy program for troubled Section 236 projects was based on its "long-held belief that the government was not responsible for this housing after it was built, except to pay an insurance claim and, if necessary, dispose of the property" (U.S. Senate, 1980, 70). Furthermore, the Section 8 Loan Management Set Asides were both slow in coming and not actually recognized as operating subsidies.

A more recent conflict in HUD's commitment to the subsidized housing stock and the overall goal of providing decent quality, affordable housing has surfaced with HUD's policies toward the disposition of its foreclosed inventory. Under the Reagan administration, HUD systematically overlooked the congressional mandate to preserve this housing for low- and moderate-income people and chose to ignore certain property-disposition procedures designed to protect tenants in subsidized developments (see Achtenberg, 1989; Johnson and the National Housing Law Project, 1985; U.S. House of Representatives, 1983a, 1983b, 1983c; see also Chapter 7).

Before passage of the Tax Reform Act of 1986 (to be discussed more fully in Chapter 5), when the tax code provided significant incentives for the private, for-profit sector to develop subsidized housing, tax law sometimes operated at cross-purposes with the goal of producing decent, affordable housing. Specifically, provisions concerning depreciation (see Chapter 5) encouraged a change of ownership after ten to fifteen years, thereby threatening the viability of the projects. This conflict was recognized as early as 1972. In testimony before the U.S. Senate, the comptroller general stated:

> Incentives [including income tax shelters] provided to profit-motivated organizations to invest in Section 236 projects are sufficient to initially attract a substantial number of prospective sponsors but do not appear adequate to encourage long-term ownership of projects. . . . The incentives are available to project owners regardless of how well or how poorly they manage a project. . . . HUD stated that the incentives have influenced significantly the motivation of profit-motivated owners and that there appears to be little incentive to continue ownership after the initial 10-year period. (Staats, 1972, 14–15)

While tax benefits for private owners diminished after ten years, their inability to prepay mortgages before the twentieth year locks them into their properties for that length of time. After twenty years, HUD allows owners to prepay mortgages; if they do so, both the use restriction and the federal subsidy are terminated. Owners are then relieved of the requirement to rent units to low- or moderate-income households, thereby ending their lock-in period. At that time, owners can sell their buildings, convert them to condominiums, or rent them at market rents to higher-income tenants. This problem of "expiring use restrictions" has caused a great deal of concern in recent years as developments built during the 1960s have become eligible for mortgage prepayment. In the Housing and Community Development Act of 1987, Congress estimated that a potential existed for over 330,000 units of Section 221(d)(3) and 236 housing to be lost as a result of the termination of low-income affordability restrictions by the year 2002 (see also Clay, 1987). In addition, before the end of the decade, several hundred thousand units that have received Loan Management Set Asides will lose this funding because of expiring contracts, thereby making the developments less financially viable. Finally, owners of almost 500,000 units of Section 8 housing will be entitled to opt out of their obligation to rent to low-income tenants by the year 2002 (*Report of the National Low Income Housing Preservation Commission*, 1988).

In view of these alarming predictions, Congress enacted the Emergency Low Income Housing Preservation Act of 1987 as part of the Housing and Community Development Act of 1987. Its purpose is "to preserve and retain to the maximum extent practicable as housing affordable to low income families or persons those privately owned dwelling units that were produced for such purpose with Federal assistance; [and] to minimize the involuntary displacement of tenants currently residing in such housing."

The act stipulates that a private owner planning to prepay his mortgage must file a notice of intent with the secretary of HUD; among other things, the notice details the effect on existing tenants and on the supply of housing affordable to low-income people in the community. Further, a plan that involves termination of the low-income affordability restriction can be approved only if tenants will not be harmed or displaced from such action and if the supply of affordable units in the local area is adequate. In order to maximize the opportunity to protect tenants and the stock of affordable housing, HUD may offer the private owner a series of financial incentives.

Since no funding is available to help transfer the housing from private ownership to public or nonprofit ownership, however, and since owners appear to be unable to prepay under the new law without safeguarding both tenants and the stock of affordable housing, owners may be caught in a no-win situation.

From the point of view of housing advocates, while the act provides some short-term protections and reduces the threat of expiring use restrictions, it is not a panacea. First, the law protects only those projects that are eligible to prepay between 1988 and 1990. Second, rents could increase substantially even with the law. And, third, owners of subsidized developments have already begun to protest the situation in the courts, arguing that it deprives them of their rights to their property, according to their original regulatory agreements with HUD. Thus, depending on the outcome of the litigation, the act could be thrown out in the courts.

Although the 1987 act provides some important protections, its passage was hardly guaranteed and was enacted only in the closing hours of the 1987 legislative session. In fact, HUD was one of the opponents of the act.

Some of the problems with subsidy programs may be alleviated with this new law, but the basic question whether such public–private partnership programs are the optimum production strategy should be answered in the negative. Chapter 5 continues this argument by presenting a case study in which the public's interest in subsidized housing is shown to be in clear conflict with the needs and objectives of private, for-profit developers.

In contrast to the several ways in which the subsidy programs, either structurally or by implementation, conflict with public-purpose goals, the public housing program has been built around a forty-year commitment to provide low-rent housing. Although this commitment could change and, as mentioned in Chapter 3, may be somewhat less strong in view of the continuing federal interest in public housing sales, the government's traditional role vis-à-vis public housing has been far more consumer oriented than toward the privately owned stock of subsidized housing.

Enhancing Individual Well-Being and Producing Social Benefits

Similar to the public housing program, virtually no data are available for the individual well-being and social benefit criteria for the privately owned stock of subsidized housing.[7] Again, empowerment, where it has occurred, has usually come about from a tenant-organized protest action against the private landlord or HUD. With the recent concern over expiring-use restrictions, there have been instances of tenant groups organizing to protect their right to stay in their homes. Although empowerment has been one of the likely results, it was certainly not an anticipated goal of the subsidy programs.

While a lack of systematic data has hampered analysis of the privately owned, publicly subsidized multifamily housing programs and the comparison of these programs with public housing, we can summarize the results as follows: Both types of programs provide better-quality housing, with tenants more satisfied with their units, than is widely believed. Yet both types of programs probably do little to alter patterns of racial segregation. Nevertheless, because the public housing program has included a long-term federal commitment to affordable housing, because it seems to be no more costly than programs that engage the private sector, and because it is not laden with the conflicting goals of the private subsidy programs, it emerges as the most viable of past approaches to producing affordable housing.

5

Private versus Public Goals:
Conflicting Interests in Resyndication

UNTIL the mid-1960s, the U.S. homebuilding industry adamantly opposed subsidized housing programs, particularly the public housing program, which the industry saw as a threat to private enterprise and often called "socialistic" (Friedman, 1968). In creating mortgage subsidy programs for low-cost housing, however, Congress carved out a new role for private developers and homebuilders. In addition, when problems surfaced in the public housing program, the federal government made significant efforts to involve the private sector instead of trying to improve the public ownership approach (see Chapters 3 and 4).

Most of the important innovations in public housing of the mid-1960s embraced an expanded role for the private sector. By the end of the decade, it was unthinkable that any new housing program could appear on the federal agenda without a central role for for-profit developers. The Housing and Urban Development Act of 1968, with its ambitious production goals, attested to that burgeoning public–private partnership. Although the outcomes of the 1968 act were mixed at best (see Chapter 6 and Downs, 1972; HUD, 1973a), the basic question whether the private sector should be participating in housing subsidy programs has been little examined. (For two notable exceptions, see Achtenberg, 1989; Meehan, 1979.)

This question may have been of only academic interest through most of the 1980s, but there are recent signs that the housing needs of the poor finally may be capturing federal attention (see Chapter 1). Moreover, as states and cities continue to grapple with housing problems, we need to understand the strengths and limitations of various production approaches.

This chapter looks at one example of the public–private partnership in housing—the use of tax incentives to induce private participation in subsidy programs—and investigates the problems that arise from conflicting public and private goals for those programs. It is not particularly surprising that tax incentives generate conflict between public goals and private interests in subsidized housing programs. Tax incentives were designed primarily to benefit (and thereby attract) private, for-profit interests; the goal of producing and maintaining a long-term supply of decent, low-rent housing certainly is not a central goal for private real estate developers.

During the Reagan administration, tax incentives in subsidized housing development became more important than ever, as direct funding for new construction or substantial rehabilitation of public and subsidized housing was curtailed. Without tax incentives, production of federally supported low-cost housing would virtually have stopped. Although the specific form of tax incentive for low-cost housing was changed under the Tax Reform Act of 1986, tax incentives still are the most important federal approach for stimulating the private production of low-cost housing.

In view of the dependence of housing programs on the tax system, we need a clear understanding of the fundamental problems inherent in using tax incentives to induce private developers and investors to produce and maintain a public good: subsidized housing for low-income households. Analyzing this conflict should help policymakers judge the appropriateness of various ways of subsidizing housing.

This chapter sets the background for an analysis by describing how past and existing tax incentives for subsidized housing operate. It then outlines an example of the conflict created by the tax incentive approach and describes how the conflict was resolved. The case study comes from the Massachusetts experience in formulating a statewide policy to guide resyndication of subsidized housing. The concluding section presents recommendations based on the Massachusetts example and argues that a new form of public–private partnership is needed that can better meet public objectives. At the same time, direct housing programs that have the primary goal of housing the poor must be supported, and the long-espoused goal of decent housing for all must be reaffirmed as the dominant ingredient of federal housing policy.

Tax Incentives for Subsidized Housing

There was no mystery about the private sector's shift from opposition to support of federal subsidy programs (with the exception of public housing) in the 1960s. The new subsidy programs, unlike the conventional public housing program, provided substantial opportunities for profit. Before passage of the Tax Reform Act of 1986, tax incentives for low-income housing emerged from the following set of relationships: All rental property, including privately owned subsidized housing, generated huge losses for tax purposes because owners could depreciate their property on paper, and these losses could be used to offset ordinary income. Owners of large real estate developments usually sold interests in the property through a process known as *syndication*; the form of ownership was usually a limited partnership. This allowed wealthy investors to share in the financial benefits generated by investment property. *Resyndication* is a subsequent sale of interests in the property.

The most lucrative forms of depreciation were those that created the highest tax losses in the early years of ownership. One such accelerated method of depreciation, known as *200 percent declining balance,* commonly was used by initial owners of subsidized housing developments. Before passage of the Economic Recovery Tax Act of 1981 (ERTA), subsequent owners were restricted to less-profitable forms of depreciation, but ERTA allowed subsequent owners also to use the accelerated method of depreciation. Moreover, the act permitted all owners of rental housing to depreciate the cost of the property over a much shorter period—nineteen years for nonsubsidized rental housing and fifteen years for subsidized rental housing, instead of about thirty years. Together, these changes in the tax code greatly enhanced the profitability of housing developments for all owners, but the greatest shift probably was in the new attractiveness of becoming a *second* owner of a subsidized development.[1]

Using the 200 percent declining balance method, the amount of depreciation drops between the twelfth and fifteenth years to the extent that projects often begin to yield net incomes instead of losses. The point at which a project stops losing money for tax purposes and starts showing a profit is known as the *tax crossover point.* Before ERTA, owners might have wanted to sell their properties at the crossover point,[2] but usually had little opportunity to do so. The combined effect of ERTA allowing second owners to take advantage of the 200 percent declining balance form of depreciation and substantially reducing the depreciation period was that the sale of a subsidized development, and the resyndication that could go with it, became an extremely lucrative option for both sellers and new owners.[3]

All this has changed since passage of the Tax Reform Act of 1986. In general, investment in residential property is now much less attractive, and resyndication, made enormously attractive by ERTA, now has considerably fewer advantages for investors. First, the highest tax rate is reduced to 28 percent (although a 5 percent surtax is imposed on some taxpayers, producing an effective marginal rate of 33 percent) from 50 percent, thereby decreasing the value of all deductions, including depreciation from residential property. Second, the depreciation period is increased to 27.5 years, from 19 years for conventional residential property and 15 years for subsidized housing. This makes annual depreciation deductions considerably less valuable. In addition, the requirement that straight-line, rather than accelerated, depreciation schedules be used further reduces the benefits that traditionally have been generated from owning residential property. Third, the new tax law restricts the ability of individuals to shelter earned and portfolio income (e.g., income from dividends or interest) with passive losses, such as those resulting from real estate, including depreciation. In general, limited (nonactive) partners can use depreciation deductions only to the extent that they offset liability on income that results from real estate—cash flow or the gains on the sale of a rental property.[4] Unused depreciation deductions can be saved, however, and can be used to offset taxes on ordinary income in the year in which the investor sells his interest in the property. Fourth, a new, three-year, low-income rental housing tax-credit program was added to the tax code. (Whether Congress will extend the tax credit beyond 1989 is still uncertain.) A tax credit is subtracted from the amount of taxes due after the income tax has been calculated. Each dollar of tax credit is generally worth a dollar in the taxpayer's pocket; a deduction is worth a fraction of a dollar, depending on the taxpayer's marginal tax rate. Similar to the sale of depreciation benefits to wealthy investors, these tax credits are sold by owners of low-income developments to limited partners in exchange for equity contributions. The total amount of tax credit associated with a building is based on a fixed percentage of certain costs of development or acquisition. Depending on the housing (e.g., new construction, rehab, or acquisition of an existing building, and whether or not the development has received a federal subsidy), the tax credit for each year of a ten-year period will vary from 4 to 9 percent. Despite the recent changes in the tax code, the case example presented here reflects the set of incentives included in ERTA, before the 1986 tax reform legislation.

Also, the case studied took place before passage of the Housing and Community Development Act of 1987, which makes it more difficult for private owners of subsidized housing to remove units from the low-rent stock (see Chapter 4). As discussed in Chapter 4, an important distinguishing feature of subsidized housing is the use restriction attached to it—the requirement that occupancy be maintained for low-income households for a specified period. The use restriction is twenty years for developments owned by limited partnerships not additionally subsidized under the Rent Supplement or Flexible Subsidy programs and up to forty years for developments receiving these subsidies. Projects owned by nonprofit sponsors are restricted for low-income occupancy for forty years (Johnson and the National Housing Law Project, 1985, 23).[5]

The number of years that a development had to be available to low-income people had a significant bearing on how attractive a given syndication or resyndication deal was likely to be: The shorter the use restriction, the more lucrative the investment. First, once a use restriction expired, the owner was completely free to convert the property to a more profitable use, such as higher-rent units or condominiums. Second, the length of the use restriction affected the amount of capital the owner could raise through syndication during the early years of the project. As the length of the use restriction increased, a project's appraised value dropped, and the amount that could be raised through syndication declined.

For a ten-year-old property with a twenty-year use restriction and good future market potential, resyndication might have been extremely attractive to both sellers and buyers. The opportunity to sell the development for a good price could enable sellers to realize substantial gains and cover their tax liabilities. For new buyers, a potential windfall from the project's future conversion and sale, as well as the depreciation laws under ERTA, could combine to make an extremely attractive investment. If the same property had a forty-year use restriction, it would have been significantly less attractive to a potential buyer, since it would have been considerably longer before the property could be converted to more lucrative use. From the point of view of the tenants, or of the state or federal regulatory agency with an interest in the development, resyndication could provide an infusion of capital for repairs or for bolstering reserve funds.

In Massachusetts, a heated controversy arose between private developers and tenant advocates concerning what kind of resyndication policy the state's housing finance agency should adopt. The conflict revolved around three issues: (1) whether and by how much the use restriction would be reduced; (2) what protections developers would provide to tenants after the use restriction expired; and (3) how much money would be invested to maintain or upgrade the development. In this case, the tenants' goals were virtually the same as the public's goals: to keep the housing affordable to low-income households as long as possible; to protect tenants as fully as possible from displacement after the expiration of the use restriction; and to ensure that the resyndication would allocate adequate funds for the physical and financial needs of the development.

Although the specifics of the case study presented here are unique to its locale, the general issue of who gets what in a disposition deal pertains to hundreds of thousands of units of subsidized housing across the country. Developments built through the Section 221(d)(3) and Section 236 programs are quickly reaching the point where tax benefits are running out, and owners may be considering various disposition alternatives.

Privately owned, publicly subsidized housing is an important national resource. How resyndication policies are structured has a significant bearing on whether, for how long, in what condition, and at what long-term risks to tenant security this housing will continue to serve low- and moderate-income households. Even if resyndication disappeared as an issue, largely because the 1986 tax act has made resyndication much more difficult, the study still would have importance. The Massachusetts resyndication debate sheds light on fundamental problems associated with publicly subsidized housing programs being implemented by private, for-profit developers.

The Massachusetts Housing Finance Agency: A Case Study

The Massachusetts Housing Finance Agency (MHFA) began operations in 1970. As of June 30, 1988, it had provided loans totaling over $2.5 billion for the construction and permanent financing of more than 65,000 rental units and over $928 million in mortgage loans to more than 18,000 Massachusetts households (MHFA, 1988). Between 1984, when the resyndication policy was debated, and 1989, about half of MHFA's total portfolio was expected to reach the tax crossover point, making these units attractive prospects for ownership transfers. Like most developments receiving Section 236 or Section 8 subsidies, the vast majority of MHFA-financed projects are owned by limited partnerships; fewer than 5 percent are owned by nonprofit sponsors. (That does not include the numerous projects in which a nonprofit sponsor is a general or co-general partner in a limited partnership arrangement.) Any change of ownership requires consent of the MHFA as the mortgagee.

Against the backdrop of ERTA's new incentives for transferring ownership of subsidized housing, as well as MHFA's maturing portfolio, agency officials perceived a need to adopt a formal policy to guide resyndications. The agency's director, Marvin Siflinger, who moved to MHFA from the top position in HUD's Boston area office, felt that need particularly strongly. Siflinger was sensitive to the high foreclosure rate that had plagued the HUD inventory of subsidized multifamily housing in Boston and was determined to avoid a similar situation in MHFA's housing. Because the agency could require that the proceeds from new investment in the resyndication be used to assist projects in financial difficulty or provide capital improvements, Siflinger was eager for a resyndication policy. But he and other staff members also were aware that a 1982 audit by HUD's inspector general had criticized HUD policies toward resyndication for failing to require adequate funds for repairs.[6]

The problem was how to provide incentives to the private sector and sufficient funds to ensure project viability, and at the same time to guarantee that tenants would not be displaced. To help find a solution, Siflinger asked the agency's Multifamily Advisory Committee for recommendations on a resyndication policy. This committee, appointed by the governor, is mainly composed of representatives from the real estate development and academic communities. At the time of the deliberations on resyndication, there were fourteen advisory committee members, including two inactive members. Of the twelve active members, three—an academic, a nonprofit housing developer, and a tenant in an MHFA development who also was a member of the state's tenant advocacy group, the Massachusetts Tenants Organization (MTO)—constituted the protenant faction.[7]

By the end of the committee's first meeting on resyndication, it was clear that a difference of opinion existed between those who worked in the private, for-profit community and those allied with tenant (public) interests. During several months of debate, each side drafted and redrafted recommendations. Although a spirit of compromise permeated the discussions, the two sides approached the main issues from fundamentally different philosophies. Specifically, developers emphasized the importance of reducing the use-restriction period in exchange for capital contributions to the development. Tenant advocates focused on the need to maximize the length of the use-restriction period, while making sure that tenants would receive substantial protections on its expiration (see Table 3).

The Developers' Position

Citing a difference of opinion with tenant advocates on several key points, advisory committee members associated with the development community articulated their final recommendations (Kuehn and Finch, 1984). First, the amount of time that a development would be restricted to low-income use (whether currently subject to a twenty-year or forty-year use restriction)[8] would be a minimum of nine additional years from the time of resyndication. (Thus, if a development with a forty-year use restriction was resyndicated at the end of the fifteenth year, the use restriction would terminate nine years thereafter, or at the end of the twenty-fourth year, instead of at the end of the fortieth year.) At the end of that time, an owner planning to convert his property to condominiums or cooperatives would be required to give all low- and moderate-income, elderly, and handicapped tenants four years' notice and to make adequate relocation housing available; any unit that tenants voluntarily vacated before the four years were up could be converted immediately. If, after nine years, the owner decided to maintain the building as rental property, the leases of all tenants would be extended from year to year. For the first two years after the nine-year period, no rent increase greater than that of the Consumer Price Index (or another appropriate index) would be permitted.

Second, the developers proposed that a "reasonable" plan be provided to protect all tenants after the expiration of the use restriction, especially tenants with lower incomes.[9] In the developers' view, the public goal of providing decent and affordable housing would be served as long as the resyndication provided an infusion of capital to sustain the low- and moderate-income housing in the short run (e.g., less than ten years), even if it meant a reduction in the length of the use restriction.

Third, requirements for "reasonable" tenant protections, as well as infusion of capital, would be fulfilled if at least $2500 per unit from resyndication proceeds were pledged for project purposes. These

TABLE 3
COMPARISON OF POSITIONS ON RESYNDICATION:
DEVELOPERS, TENANT ADVOCATES, AND MASSACHUSETTS
HOUSING FINANCE AGENCY (MHFA)

	Developers	Tenant advocates	MHFA
Restriction to low-income use	—9 years, plus 4-year notification period	—Minimum of 15 years	—10 years, plus 4-year notification period
		—Projects under 40-year use restrictions would have to be maintained for low-income use for at least 25 years after resyndication	—Projects for which there would be a reduction in the use restriction would have to be maintained for low-income use for at least 22 years, in addition to the 4-year notification period
Protections for tenants	—Reasonable plan to protect all tenants when use restriction expires	—New owners required to offer assurance of continued benefit to low- and moderate-income households after expiration of use restriction, including making their best effort to maintain a maximum number of units for low- and moderate-income use	—At the end of the 10-year use restriction, owners would offer tenants the opportunity to buy the development for conversion to a limited-equity cooperative or for nonprofit ownership at a 25% discount
		—Tenant review process	—Tenant review process
		—Funds provided to tenants to enable them to hire technical consultants to represent their interests in the resyndication process	
		—Disbursement of funds to seller only after project-related expenses have been made	
		—Relocation benefits to tenants to be paid from syndication proceeds	—Relocation benefits ranging from $750 to $4000 per household; only tenants in

TABLE 3
Continued

			developments whose use restrictions are reduced are eligible to receive the maximum amount; all others to receive $750 to $1000
		—Emergency fund for project or tenant needs	
Financial investment	—$2500 per unit either to solve physical or financial problems or to provide tenant benefits after expiration of use restriction	—$2500 per unit to solve physical or financial needs of the project; Tenant benefits in addition to this amount	—$600 per unit for developments whose use restrictions are being extended (an extension in the use restriction could occur in the case of projects with original 20-year restriction periods that are being resyndicated after their 15th year)
			—$1500 per unit for developments whose use restrictions are being reduced; tenant benefits in addition to this amount

funds could be used to remedy physical or financial problems of the property or to relocate tenants who might be displaced when the use restriction expired.

The developers' final recommendations stipulated a substantial minimum expenditure per unit and acknowledged the need for tenant protections more explicitly than they had done earlier. But they did not change their original stance on the duration of the use restriction (see Finch, 1984; Kuehn and Finch, 1984).

The Tenants' Position

The few tenant advocates on the MHFA advisory committee managed to present a forceful counterposition. To offer the tenants' case as effectively as possible, the Massachusetts Tenants Organization (MTO) representative on the committee helped MTO negotiate a small grant from a foundation to hire an independent expert. With the assistance of Boston housing consultant Emily Achtenberg, MTO became an important, although *ex officio,* actor in the negotiations. On the three key points, the tenant advocates' views differed substantially from those of the developers.

First, the tenant advocates opposed any reduction in the use restriction and did not view an improvement in physical conditions as adequate compensation. "It is not in the tenants' interest to live in a better environment for 8–10 more years and then be faced with displacement due to condo conversion" (Massachusetts Tenants Organization, 1984a). According to the MTO, a reduction in the use restriction would be warranted only if

> the project has a compelling and immediate need for these funds and compensating public benefits are provided to enhance project viability, protect tenants, and facilitate continued use of the housing as a low and moderate income resource beyond the term of the (reduced) lock-in period. If this option is not feasible, in our view, the Commonwealth will be obligated to provide the necessary funds to enable these developments to remain as viable, affordable housing for low and moderate income families for the term originally committed. (Massachusetts Tenants Organization, 1984b, 10)

The tenants' final position on the use restriction was that it should be in effect for all developments for a minimum of fifteen years after resyndication. The use restriction would be twenty-five years for any project with a forty-year original use restriction, unless the MHFA determined that the need for low-rent housing in the area was no longer acute.

Second, and not surprisingly, the MTO proposed significantly stronger and more detailed tenant protections than the developers did. It stipulated that, in any development in which the use restriction was reduced, the new purchaser should provide a plan assuring continued availability of low- and moderate-income tenant housing after the use restriction expired. No reduction in the use restriction would be approved unless the protections provided reasonable security for low- and moderate-income tenants (Massachusetts Tenants Organization, 1984c). The required package of protections would be extensive:

1. The owner would have to demonstrate that he had made his best effort to facilitate the purchase or continued rental of the maximum num-

ber of units in the development by low- and moderate-income tenant households, consistent with his private financial interests.

2. Tenants would have an opportunity to review and comment on all aspects of the proposed resyndication that affected the current and future viability of the housing as a low- and moderate-income resource.
3. A portion of the resyndication proceeds would be provided to hire consultants to represent tenants' interests in the resyndication process.
4. Another portion of the proceeds would be set aside for relocation benefits equal to those required for tenants displaced by public action under state law (reasonable moving expenses, a $200 dislocation allowance, and a $4000 replacement housing payment).
5. A fund would be established out of the resyndication proceeds to cover current or projected operating shortfalls and to alleviate financial hardships for low- and moderate-income tenants who were paying a disproportionate share of their incomes for rent (Massachusetts Tenants Organization, 1984c).

The third point on which the tenant advocates differed from the developers was whether tenant-relocation costs could be counted toward the expenditures required on the project after resyndication. Like the developers, tenant advocates proposed that a minimum of $2500 per unit go to physical and financial needs of the project, but they added that tenant-relocation costs would be *in addition to* the $2500 for project improvements. Moreover, the tenant advocates wanted a timing stipulation on all these expenditures. In their view, the main reason for approving a resyndication in the first place, and for reducing the length of the use restriction, would be that the development required at least $2500 per unit for physical and financial needs that could not be met through other means. The tenants' position was that payments made by new investors after resyndication should be disbursed to the previous owner or to others with an interest in the developments only after the MHFA had determined that its loan and the management of the property were in good standing and that the required physical, financial, and relocation expenditures had been made.

The Resyndication Policy

After several months of debate between developers and tenant advocates, MHFA took its stand. The agency adopted a compromise policy that called for spending at least $1500 per unit on the physical and financial needs of developments whose use restrictions were being reduced and $600 per unit for those whose use restrictions were being extended (e.g., a fifteen-year-old project with a twenty-year use restriction). The MTO's recommendation that a separate relocation payment be made to displaced tenants found its way into the final policy. Only tenants in assisted units whose development was undergoing a reduction in the use restriction, however, would be eligible for payments the size of those advocated by the MTO (about $4000). Displaced elderly, handicapped, or low- to moderate-income tenants in other developments would receive $1000; all other tenants would receive $750.

On balance, both tenants and developers won points. The tenants got minimum dollar investments and relocation benefits, although not as much as they had requested. The recommendations for the minimum period that a development would be restricted to use as low- and moderate-income housing favored the developers. The developers had proposed a nine-year minimum: the tenants had asked for a fifteen-year minimum. The agency decided on a ten-year use restriction from the date of resyndication plus a four-year notification period. It recommended that projects whose use restrictions were to be reduced would have to be maintained for low-income use for a total of at least twenty-two years—a protection similar to, but not as restrictive, as the one proposed by the tenants.

MHFA's policy included several valuable tenant protections besides the relocation benefits discussed. At the end of the ten-year use restriction, owners would offer tenants the opportunity to purchase the development (for conversion to limited-equity cooperative or nonprofit rental housing) at a discount of at least 25 percent of the appraised value of the property. If the tenants' association did not purchase the property, and if the development was to be converted to cooperatives and condominiums, individual tenants would have the right of first refusal to purchase their units at a discounted price.

Some other significant tenant protections were missing from the agency's final policy. For example, tenants would be included in the MHFA review process, but funds for technical assistance were not set aside. Further, the agency did not recommend that a separate fund be established to alleviate financial hardships for low- and moderate-income tenants who were paying disproportionate shares of their income for rent.

Although the MHFA proposal went a long way toward balancing the reduction in the use restriction with significant tenant benefits and protections, the MHFA policy lacked much of the strong language of the tenant advocates' proposal. Nowhere in the policy did the agency state that a reduction in the use restriction should be approved only if there was a compelling need for an infusion of funds and if the public benefit was greater with resyndication than without it. The distinction is an important one: The tenant advocates saw resyndication as a last resort to rescue a faltering property; MHFA viewed it as an option for a wider range of developments with varying financial and repair needs.

Conclusions and Policy Implications

On one level, the Massachusetts resyndication case is a good example of a negotiated settlement between diverse interests. Members of the advisory committee articulated and debated key issues and were able to reach a consensus. A particularly important aspect of the process was that both developers and tenant advocates demonstrated that they had come to understand one another's main concerns. The significant changes in the developers' original proposal reflected a compromise with the tenants' position. Tenants, for their part, acknowledged that a reduction in the use restriction was necessary to encourage private-sector participation.

Yet the MTO was left wondering whether it had conceded too much and had been too agreeable in accepting MHFA's final plan. Nevertheless, the MTO was aware that if they had not been involved, the agency's policy might have been much closer to the developers' original proposal. In that instance, they reasoned, the resyndication policy would have been detrimental to the public goal of maintaining a good stock of subsidized housing. The developers, too, wondered if they had compromised too much. Several developers on the advisory committee reported that colleagues in the Boston community thought the recommendations were too protenant.

Beyond this initial view of the case study, the formulation of the Massachusetts resyndication policy underscores the limitations of this type of public–private partnership in housing. At the outset of this chapter, I indicated that it is not surprising that tax incentives to develop subsidized housing generate conflicts between public goals and private interests. Yet the message that public and private needs are not identical is often ignored in policy debates and decisions. The carefully argued and clear-cut positions that emerged during the resyndication discussions present a sharp view of the conflicting program needs that arise between the profit aims of private developers and the public's objectives for subsidized housing. The conflict brings into focus several issues for policymakers concerned with developing low-income housing programs.

First, use restrictions that require occupancy by low-income households only for limited periods of time generally are not in the public's best interest. There are many indications that housing needs among low-income households are likely to continue well into the future. As long as these tight conditions prevail, it is problematic to fund programs with use-restriction periods that expire after fifteen or twenty years.

This recommendation is at odds with at least two recent subsidy programs for low-income housing. The Massachusetts State Housing Assistance for Rental Production program, enacted in 1983, requires that developers using this program set aside no fewer than 25 percent of the units constructed for low-income households for fifteen years.[10] The new low-income housing tax credit, created by the Tax Reform Act of 1986, also requires low-income occupancy for a fifteen-year period.[11] In both cases, many low-income housing advocates have argued that "it's better than nothing" to have some new low-income housing, even if it may last for only a short term. This position admits that a public–private partnership for subsidized housing does not meet public goals perfectly, but sees conflicts as having a chance of being resolved once they surface.

Other low-income housing advocates take a more critical view of programs that provide significant incentives to the private sector and a relatively low level of public benefit. They argue that this type of public–private partnership in low-income housing is seriously flawed and should be abandoned altogether. Why pander to private interests that seek to maximize profits when doing so does not meet public objectives perfectly?

Rather than accept the defects of public–private partnerships or simply reject the view that they can have a positive impact, my second recommendation is for several new kinds of partnerships, which are discussed more fully in Chapters 12 and 13. One new partnership would allow for-profit developers a front-end profit only, as well as more honestly address the built-in conflicts and devise specific ways for resolving them as an integral part of the program. For example, as long as it is advantageous for developers to participate in subsidized housing programs only if the use-restriction period is limited, then it is important to incorporate in the original partnership agreement measures to safeguard the long-term viability of the housing for low-income use as well as tenant protections. Once tax benefits expire, the housing can be sold either to a nonprofit community-based housing organization or to the tenants and then converted to a limited-equity cooperative. Obviously, the program would need to include a subsidy to buy out the owner at market rates, or it would have to structure the partnership so that the development is sold at a substantially reduced rate at the end of the use-restriction period, in exchange for the tax benefits enjoyed during this time.

As discussed in Chapter 12, the Boston Housing Partnership has used some innovative mechanisms to safeguard the housing that it is helping to develop for long-term use by low-income households. However, structuring these arrangements is complex, and the Internal Revenue Service provides the final word on their legality.

Third, public incentives offered to private developers, whether through the tax system, as interest rate subsidies, or by some other means, should be as consistent with public goals as possible. For example, the old depreciation laws that allowed investors to take big write-offs in the early years of ownership created the tax crossover point, referred to earlier. This, in turn, either discouraged continued investment (to try to recoup the loss in tax benefits) or encouraged sale of the building, neither of which is in the public's best interests. Instead, the new public–private partnership could include incentives that would maximize the public benefit. Rather than encourage disinvestment or sale, incentives could be structured so that they would provide rewards for long-term management, cost containment, and overall good maintenance and repair. Along with this positive approach, negative sanctions could be included for inadequate performance on any of these criteria.

Fourth, and as discussed more fully in Chapter 13, federal and state governments must be more prepared to fund subsidized housing to the extent necessary to provide this much-needed resource. There are no cheap solutions. For example, the case study reveals that MHFA officials were particularly interested in resyndication because it was the only way to raise the capital needed to assist developments in financial difficulties or those requiring significant repairs. This was an unfortunate situation because it reduced the agency's ability to carry out its mission optimally. If adequate public funding had been available for distressed MHFA developments, the agency would not have been forced to consider reducing the use-restriction periods. It is unrealistic to think that a public agency can fully represent the public's interest as long as it is dependent on private funds. The availability of public funding to construct and rehabilitate housing, as well as to assist projects with special difficulties, is a critical component of any coherent housing program.

Fifth, Congress should authorize an in-depth study of the advisability of using tax incentives for producing low-income housing. For the past two decades, private involvement in housing subsidy programs has been achieved primarily through incentives provided by the tax code. With the passage of the Tax Reform Act of 1986, however, private investment in all housing, including low-income housing, is much reduced. Although the low-income tax credit supports some production of affordable housing, delays by the secretary of the treasury in issuing regulations severely reduced the program's effectiveness in 1987, the first year in which the program was in operation.

For the long term, it is not clear whether tax incentives will, or should, be available as a means for stimulating the production of low-income housing. There are compelling arguments on both sides. On the one hand, the need for removing tax loopholes is widely acknowledged. The fact that thousands of individuals with six- and seven-digit incomes manage to reduce or, in some instances, eliminate their tax liabilities is infuriating to taxpayers of more modest means. Certainly, write-offs for investment in low-income housing are one cause of inequities in the tax system.

On the other hand, in the absence of new direct appropriations and without tax incentives for low-income housing, production will be nonexistent. Isn't the housing that gets produced through tax incentives more critical to the poor and homeless than either the intangible goal of equity in taxation or the conflicts that will certainly arise as the result of imperfections in conventional public–private partnership?

Another aspect of the tax-shelter debate vis-à-vis low-income housing relates to how these write-offs compare to other loopholes. For example, the homeowners' tax deduction, discussed in Chapter 4, is a subsidy enjoyed disproportionately by upper-income taxpayers. Moreover, the loss of revenues to the U.S. Treasury from this deduction is almost ten times greater than the cost for investor deductions for *all* rental housing, not just low-income housing (Dolbeare, 1986). Tax incentives for low-income housing are relatively insignificant compared to other loopholes that remain immune from congressional action.

In conclusion, the Massachusetts case underscores the complexity of the conflicts that can arise when public needs depend on private actions. Although new forms of public–private partnerships may soften these conflicts, this book argues that it is more advantageous to develop programs aimed more explicitly and directly at providing decent, affordable housing over long periods of time. Such strategies are explored in Part III.

6

HUD and Low-Income Housing Programs

CENTRAL TO any discussion and policy recommendations about a future low-income housing policy is an understanding of the role that the key agency responsible for implementing federal housing programs has played. Created in 1965, the Department of Housing and Urban Development (HUD) has been plagued with criticism for mismanagement and a lack of consumer orientation.

The history of HUD's involvement with housing programs also underscores the problem discussed in Chapter 5: the difficulty of achieving public objectives through participation of the private, for-profit sector. A generous assessment of HUD's role vis-à-vis the consumer might place the blame for its problems on this dual mandate. A more critical assessment might attribute its lack of concern for consumer needs on negligence or incompetence. Whatever the reason, HUD's problems cast considerable doubt on the advisability and, indeed, capability of the agency, in its present form, to administer low-income housing programs.

A Historical View of HUD

Before 1965, housing and urban renewal programs were administered by separate agencies, such as the Federal Housing Administration (FHA), the U.S. Housing Authority, and the Urban Renewal Administration. As early as 1942, President Roosevelt saw the need to consolidate all federal housing functions in a single unit, the National Housing Agency (NHA). After the war, NHA received congressional approval and was made a permanent agency. In 1947, NHA was replaced by the Housing and Home Finance Agency (HHFA). Despite these efforts at coordination, each of the individual housing agencies acted more or less autonomously.

Housing was a key issue in the presidential campaign of 1960.

121

Speaking directly to the need to coordinate all federal housing activities, the Democratic platform promised to "give the city dweller a voice at the cabinet table by bringing together within a single Department programs concerned with urban and metropolitan problems" (quoted in Keith, 1973, 137). But President Kennedy's inability to secure congressional approval of a new, cabinet-level department was but one example of his overall difficulty in launching the "New Frontier." Although President Johnson continued Kennedy's request for a new department, only after Johnson's landslide victory in 1964 did Congress finally support this proposal. In January 1966, Johnson nominated Robert Weaver, the former head of the HHFA, as the first secretary of the new Department of Housing and Urban Development, thereby making him the first black to head a cabinet-level department.

The early years of HUD were filled with high hopes, energy, and expectations. New appointments included several liberal intellectuals, such as the MIT political scientist Robert Wood and the Harvard Law School professor Charles Haar. A "we can do anything" attitude was exemplified by the Model Cities program, HUD's first major initiative. Not only did Model Cities attempt to rectify a wide range of urban ills, but it hoped to achieve its goals in a mere five years, using federal resources intended for far fewer locales than were ultimately funded. Despite the concrete disappointments of the Model Cities program, the period marked one of HUD's finest hours in terms of enthusiasm for its overall mission. Many HUD employees seemed to embrace President Johnson's goals for the new agency: to improve the quality of life for low-income urban dwellers and increase the stock of low- and moderate-cost housing. But there were deep-seated problems in carrying out these objectives.

The problems came to a head when old-time FHA personnel were asked to embrace the new inner-city, low-income orientation of HUD. It was one thing to hire staff to implement new programs such as Model Cities; it was another story when old staff members were asked to change long-entrenched patterns of behavior and biases. HUD's implementation of the new programs embodied in the Housing and Urban Development Act of 1968 revealed significant weaknesses in the agency's ability to deal with the thorny issues of low-income, inner-city housing. HUD's record during the late 1960s and early 1970s is examined following a critique of the early FHA.

The FHA and HUD's Nonconsumer Orientation

The FHA has always been the backbone of HUD. As the oldest and largest section of the agency, the FHA's attitude and orientation, not surprisingly, greatly affected HUD initiatives. As mentioned in Chapter 2, the FHA was one of President Roosevelt's New Deal programs formed to boost the nation out of the Great Depression. With residential foreclosures mounting, lending institutions depleted of funds and unable or unwilling to provide new mortgages, and the construction industry stagnant, the FHA was set up to guarantee lenders repayment of losses due to foreclosure. With the reduced risk, institutions began to lend again, and homebuilders regained confidence that new homes would find a ready market with the attractive financing offered by the FHA. In a real sense, the FHA primed the pump of the postdepression housing and mortgage-lending industries.

Referring to the FHA's record between 1934 and the late 1960s, a long-time FHA official proudly wrote:

> FHA's achievements, during 35 years of public service without cost to the taxpayer, were enormous. Its influence was far-reaching.
> Every American family who had bought a home with 20 percent or less downpayment and financed the balance with a long-term, level payment mortgage was, directly or indirectly, the beneficiary of FHA. Homeownership during those 35 years had increased from about 45 percent to about 65 percent of American families.
> FHA's financial record was enviable. It had reserves of $1.5 billion, accumulated from net earnings after payment of expenses and losses. It had repaid, with interest, the capital that the Treasury had advanced to get it started, a total of about $86 million. It had paid about $200 million to home purchasers as partial return of premiums under the mutuality feature of its legislation. (Bazan, 1974, 5)

But there was also a significant "down side" to the FHA's early record. With New Deal and congressional goals for the FHA directed at stimulating the construction industry and safeguarding financial institutions, the FHA was destined to grow into an industry-oriented, rather than consumer-oriented, agency. The FHA created a wide range of problems, both for consumers who participated in its programs and for those who were systematically excluded.

Problems with Early FHA Programs

Following its legislative mandate, the FHA undertook its mission with a fervor rarely seen in public agencies. Launching a publicity campaign that could rival the most successful commercial advertising ventures, thousands of people joined the FHA home-improvement and purchase programs. The intensity of the "own your own home" movement, which gained momentum during the early 1930s, prompted one writer to warn that "every prospective home buyer should be immunized with an antitoxin against the blah-blah of own-your-own-home campaigns" (Stein, 1932, 90).

John Dean, a noted mid-1940s critic of the FHA campaign, urged that families buying houses ask themselves: "Just what is it we expect to get out of owning this home?" Instead, "American families are encouraged to bypass this kind of reflective consideration of home ownership and to step boldly ahead" (Dean, 1945, 18). Further, Dean wrote:

> It may be urged that criticism of the activities of those merchandising houses is captious, because they are simply engaging in normal business practices. But since the purchase of a home represents the largest single purchase a family ever makes and since a house and lot represent a highly complex choice, the rightness or wrongness of which colors a family's future for years, the delivery of the conditions of promotion and sale over to ballyhoo by interested groups of sellers . . . is a questionable social policy. (1945, 39)

It did not take long for some of the problems Dean predicted to surface. A series of congressional hearings between the 1940s and 1960s pointed to problems that the FHA and, later, the Veterans Administration (VA) were causing for house buyers.[1] These problems in large part reflected the FHA's industry orientation and its "let the buyer beware" attitude toward consumers.

For example, in 1955, the Senate Committee on Banking and Currency issued a report that disclosed abuses in the FHA's Title I program—insurance for lenders on loans used to rehabilitate existing homes. The hearings confirmed early fears that many families would be duped into undertaking home repairs because of the publicity campaign and without understanding their obligations. In addition, the 1955 investigation exposed what was to be a recurrent theme in FHA/VA programs: exploitation by private businessmen. The chairman of the Senate committee explained the problem:

> The act [Title I] permits a homeowner to make repairs without making any downpayment to the contractor and permits the contractor to discount the homeowner's note at a bank with an FHA guaranty. Over the years "suede-shoe salesmen" and "dynamiters"

whose ranks have included racketeers and gangsters have infiltrated this business. They have used fraudulent and deceptive sales practices on thousands of homeowners.

In the belief that home repairs of substantial value would cost them little or nothing, many homeowners have signed contracts which they did not read or understand. After obtaining work which was either unsatisfactory or worthless, these homeowners found that a bank held their note for a substantial sum of money and that under the law they had no defense to the payment of the note, in spite of the frauds practiced upon them. The testimony shows that many lending institutions were, at a minimum, careless in accepting notes from questionable dealers and thereby encouraged these fraudulent practices. Most home repair contractors are both honest and reliable. But the laxity in the administration of the Title I program enabled dishonest people to make illicit profits from owners of small homes who perhaps could least afford the losses. (U.S. Senate, 1955, 5)

The accuracy with which this statement predicted the problems that plagued the FHA home programs of the 1960s and 1970s is incredible and alarming: poor HUD–FHA administration, the tendency of even ethical private actors to renege on basic responsibilities in a risk-free situation, and the opportunity for a few disreputable characters to exploit FHA programs.

The FHA's unwillingness to protect buyers of houses by guaranteeing the quality of their houses was revealed during hearings held by the Subcommittee on Housing of the House Committee on Banking and Currency in 1952. Many consumers thought FHA approval meant that the government approved the overall condition of a house. In fact, approval meant only that the property was worth the amount being advanced by the lender and that FHA insurance would cover this sum in the event of foreclosure. The subcommittee's mission was

to determine to what extent the insurance or guaranty of . . . loans . . . has been granted in the case of housing which is defective with respect to construction, drainage, sanitary conditions, and other features, and to what extent the practices and procedures followed by any such agency or department, and any acts of omission or commission of officers or employees thereof, have facilitated or made possible the insuring or guaranteeing of loans for defective housing. (U.S. House of Representatives, 1952, 1)

In almost a thousand pages of hearings, investigating nine cities, the subcommittee heard testimony charging the FHA and VA with faulty inspection procedures. According to witnesses, this led to situations in which large numbers of people bought FHA-insured and VA-guaranteed houses that had significant defects.

One of the worst aspects of this problem was the sense of deception experienced by people who believed that their houses were guaranteed by the insuring agency and therefore were approved by the government. A Utah congresswoman described a problem-laden FHA single-family housing project in her home state.

> When the homeowners looked around for someone to hold responsible for failure of the heating units, there was no one to help them. FHA had no authority to finance any such adjustments. It could not put pressure on the building corporation because that corporation no longer existed. The homeowners could not appeal to the corporation for the same reason. . . . The project clearly shows that actually the home buyers have no legal protection. If FHA falls down on its part of the job, or if the builders go bankrupt, then the purchaser is the goat. (U.S. House of Representatives, 1952, 80)

Further making clear the FHA's responsibility (or lack thereof) to mortgagors, a New York congressman stated that "the government did not guarantee . . . that the home would be in good condition . . . there has been a misconception of the idea. . . . the government never approved the building. All it says is that the loans are guaranteed to the builder or to the bank" (U.S. House of Representatives, 1952, 163).

In response to this confusion, FHA personnel made attempts to clarify the meaning of FHA insurance. For example, the New Jersey district director of the FHA testified that he had "requested discontinuance of a sign in front of a builder's operation, where it says, FHA approved. Because the FHA does not approve. It passes on the eligibility for insurance only" (U.S. House of Representatives, 1952, 125). Nevertheless, such instructions were slow to be enforced, and whatever else the FHA did to try to remedy the misunderstanding, the identical problem arose nearly twenty years later.

The FHA's Exclusionary Practices

In addition to causing problems for some participants in FHA programs, until the mid-1960s the FHA consistently excluded minority and lower-income families and certain inner-city areas from FHA eligibility.

Following the traditional pattern of mortgage lending, the FHA paid considerable attention to the quality of the neighborhood in which the property to be insured was located. Through an eight-point Location Rating Scale, the notion that good location must include certain social, racial, and economic characteristics became a written law of mortgage-lending practice. Section 929 of the FHA underwriting manual of 1938 stipulated that the "varying social characteristics of neighborhood occupants must be carefully considered and incorporated into the rating" (Federal Housing Administration, 1938). And Section 937 articulated the importance of racial and social homogeneity:

> Areas surrounding a location [to be insured] are investigated to determine whether incompatible racial and social groups are present, for the purpose of making a prediction regarding the probability of the location being invaded by such groups. If a neighborhood is to retain stability, it is necessary that properties shall continue to be occupied by the *same* social and racial classes. A change in social and racial occupancy generally contributes to instability and a decline in values. (Federal Housing Administration, 1938)

In addition to espousing racial homogeneity, which, for the most part, meant no insurance for minority families, the FHA manual defined the practice that has since been termed *redlining*. Section 911 stated that

> the first step in making Established Ratings of Locations is to determine ineligible or caution areas. The central downtown area can usually be outlined and considered as ineligible. However, such downtown reject areas must be outlined with the greatest care in order to avoid unfair decisions in connection with application for mortgage insurance covering properties which lie within such borders. Central reject areas include slum and blighted areas as well as the central business and commercial sections of the city. (Federal Housing Administration, 1938)

Charles Abrams pointed out the continuing role that the early FHA policies played in discriminating against minority families and shaping two housing markets, one for whites and one for blacks.

> A government offering such bounty to builders and lenders could have required compliance with a nondiscrimination policy. Or the agency could at least have pursued a course of evasion, or hidden behind the screen of local autonomy. Instead, the FHA adopted a racial policy that could well have been culled from the Nuremberg laws. From its inception FHA set itself up as the protector of the all-

> white neighborhood. It sent its agents into the field to keep Negroes
> and other minorities from buying homes in white neighborhoods.
> It exerted pressure against builders who dared to build for minori-
> ties, and against lenders willing to lend on mortgages. (Abrams,
> 1955, 229)

Thus, with the FHA taking a firm discriminatory stance, the unavailability of mortgages for minorities and for certain areas became
well-entrenched tenets of mortgage-lending practice.

By 1949, the FHA had dropped all references to "inharmonious
racial groups" or "areas threatened by minority infiltrations." Nevertheless, Abrams noted:

> The damage had been done. It was more serious than most realize.
> It was the first time in our national history that a federal agency
> had openly exhorted segregation. . . . The evil that FHA did was of
> a peculiarly enduring character. Thousands of racially segregated
> neighborhoods were built, millions of people re-assorted on the basis
> of race, color, or class, the differences built in, in neighborhoods from
> coast to coast. (Abrams, 1955, 234)

The FHA continued to be an extremely conservative force in mortgage lending until the mid-1960s. The Section 203(b) program, the
standard home mortgage insurance program of the FHA, provided
that "no mortgage shall be accepted for insurance . . . unless the
Secretary finds that the project with respect to which the mortgage
is executed, is economically sound" (U.S. House of Representatives,
1972b, 51). According to the Committee on Government Operations,
this policy enabled the FHA "to avoid the risks of mortgages on properties in declining inner-city neighborhoods, or of mortgagors whose
income was considered too low to assure loan repayments without
excessive risk" (U.S. House of Representatives, 1972b, 51).

The first relaxation in the FHA's "economic soundness" criterion
occurred in 1954 with the passage of the 221(d)(2) program. This
program, which was aimed at providing mortgage insurance for low-
and moderate-income families and displaced families (i.e., by Urban
Renewal and other public actions), introduced the notion that properties must meet the less-stringent requirement of "acceptable risk."

Yet, in 1965–1966, only 38 percent of FHA's insurance activity
was inside central cities; 62 percent was outside (U.S. House of Representatives, 1974, 159–160). Thus, even slower to disappear from
FHA policy than the racial restrictions were the FHA's antiurban
prejudices. Not until 1966 did the FHA begin to insure properties

in older urban areas. In the text of the Demonstration Cities and Metropolitan Development Act of 1966 (Model Cities), a more explicit exemption from the "economic soundness" criterion of Section 203 was articulated by Congress. HUD was specifically directed to insure mortgages in areas threatened by rioting or other civil disorders and to give "due consideration to the need for providing adequate housing for families of low and moderate income in such areas" (U.S. House of Representatives, 1972b, 52).

But in spite of this new mandate, the response of the FHA was sluggish. In 1968, *The Report of the National Commission on Urban Problems* clearly described the prevailing nature of the FHA home insurance program and its impact on neighborhood decline:

> The experience of members of the Commission and others convinced us that up until the Summer of 1967, FHA almost never insured mortgages on homes in slum districts, and did so very seldom in the "gray areas" which surrounded them. Even middle-class residential districts in central cities were suspect, since there was always the prospect that they, too, might turn as Negroes and poor whites continued to pour into the cities, and as middle and upper-middle income whites continued to move out.
>
> The result was a general, even if unwritten agreement between lending institutions and FHA that most of the areas inside the central cities did not have a favorable economic future, and that their property values were likely to decline. . . .
>
> Redlining by insurers weakened still further the ability of the slums to obtain loan capital with which to improve existing housing or to construct new units.
>
> There was evidence of a tacit agreement among all groups— lending institutions, fire insurance companies, and FHA—to block off certain areas of cities within "red lines," and not to loan or insure within them. The net result, of course, was that the slums and the areas surrounding them went downhill farther and faster than before. (P. 100)

By the early 1970s, FHA lending patterns had changed to include older urban areas. In sharp contrast to the 1965–1966 insurance patterns, in 1973, 34 percent of FHA insurance activity was outside central cities; 66 percent was inside (U.S. House of Representatives, 1974, 100).

Consistent with the FHA's early antiurban practices, the agency excluded lower-income families from participation in its programs and dealt almost exclusively with middle-income house buyers. Until the 1960s, there was little difference between the kinds of people who participated in the FHA and conventional housing finance systems. While enabling families to become owners with minimal downpayments and on lenient terms, the FHA still had strict guidelines that dictated the income levels needed to support ownership.

In fact, data collected during the 1950s indicated that families purchasing houses with FHA insurance had even higher incomes than those buying houses through conventional financing (Break and Guttentag et al., 1963; Ratcliff et al., 1957; Saulnier et al., 1958).

Taking into account the FHA's exclusionary practices, the National Commission on Urban Problems concluded:

> The main weakness of FHA from a social point of view has not been in what it has done, but in what it has failed to do—in its relative neglect of the inner cities and of the poor, and especially Negro poor. Believing firmly that the poor were bad credit risks and that the presence of Negroes tended to lower real estate values, FHA has generally regarded loans to such groups as "economically unsound." Until recently, therefore, FHA benefits have been confined almost exclusively to the middle class, and primarily only to the middle section of the middle class. The poor and those on the fringes of poverty have been almost completely excluded. (*Report of the National Commission on Urban Problems*, 1968, 100)

Summing up the FHA's early record—through exclusion, lack of good management practices, and inadequate consumer safeguards and education—the early FHA caused many problems for consumers. But despite the nonconsumer orientation, with the scale always tipped against the consumer and toward the interests of real estate, building, and mortgage-lending institutions, the great majority of participants in FHA programs seemed to have fared adequately, if not admirably. The FHA is generally considered to have been extremely successful between 1934 and 1969. Taking no risks, either real or perceived, the FHA was able to maintain its proindustry orientation and still manage to assist vast numbers of house buyers.

After 1968, however, Congress opened the way for a totally new consumer to enter the house-purchasing process. Families with lower incomes, many of whom bought older, inner-city properties, were, for the first time, able to purchase homes with FHA insurance. Unfortunately, HUD was not prepared for these new customers, and the FHA's long-standing anticonsumer outlook dominated the department's overall management style. In this much-higher-risk environment, HUD's disregard for consumer needs could no longer be covered over by an otherwise successful record.

HUD and Homeownership for the Poor

HUD's performance implementing the homeownership programs legislated by the Housing and Urban Development Act of 1968 earned it a large measure of notoriety. The act put in place the most sweeping set of programs aimed at making homeownership affordable and available to thousands of previously excluded households. Indeed, there was something for almost everyone—"the good, the bad, and the ugly." The "good" lower-income family could purchase a house with a subsidy through the Section 235 program, which reduced the homeowner's interest on a mortgage loan to as low as 1 percent; the "bad" credit risk might be eligible to obtain a mortgage through the Section 237 program; and the "ugly," or older, sections of cities became officially eligible for FHA insurance with the Section 223(e) program.

Before enactment of the 1968 legislation, a vigorous debate ensued about the desirability of HUD's being in charge of the new homeownership programs. In 1967, Senator Charles Percy (R-Ill.) proposed a "homeownership for the poor" program and suggested the creation of a new, semiprivate agency, the National Home Ownership Foundation (NHOF). Through various political maneuvers, the Johnson administration managed to kill the Percy proposal and, with it, the plan for a new agency.

In presenting the 1968 legislation to Congress, HUD Secretary Weaver was questioned by Senator Percy about the omission of NHOF from the administration's homeownership package. Weaver claimed that he "found great difficulty . . . in discovering what the Foundation [was] to do and what its functions [were] to be" (U.S. Senate, 1968, 53). Further, he stated: "I have read the legislation. I have read the report of the Committee, and I have still not been able to find out the role that it plays or its basic rationale, and for that reason, I have not included it in the recommendation" (U.S. Senate, 1968, 53).

An astute critic suggested another, more plausible, reason why the NHOF was omitted from Secretary Weaver's recommendation:

> some of the principles . . . were a threat to HUD as an organization because the program was designed to circumvent HUD. Although the HUD Secretary would be on the board of the NHOF, he would

> have no firm control. . . . By competing with HUD and being semi-
> private, NHOF was seen as a threat to HUD's purported raison d'etre
> —efficient and coordinated exercise of federal influence to aid the
> rational development of urban areas. (Carnegie, 1970)

Thus HUD, which was still establishing itself as a cabinet-level department, was strongly opposed to competition.

Many senators and representatives disagreed with Secretary Weaver and saw the need for a new agency with a clear social mandate. Trying to revive Percy's original NHOF of 1967, Senator Edward Brooke (R-Mass.) proposed the creation of a separate division in HUD to administer the "socially oriented low- and moderate-income housing programs which would otherwise be administered by FHA" (U.S. Senate, 1968, 126). The need for a "Moderate Housing Division" was based on Brooke's perceptions of the FHA's inability to change its operations. Senator Brooke stated that the administration's proposals

> authorize FHA to take the risk of going into the ghetto. But I would
> point out to the committee that the Commissioner of FHA has himself
> been unable to persuade his people that FHA must enter the ghetto
> area.
>
> A 1965 directive to the regional offices [FHA] noted a "hesitancy
> on the part of insuring offices to make FHA programs available in
> older neighborhoods"; a July 1967 directive made the same point
> in identical language, while at the Directors Conference in October
> the Commissioner again repeated: "We have got to recognize that
> stimulating a flow of mortgage funds to the inner city . . . is an FHA
> mission of the highest priority."
>
> It is not an easy matter to change longstanding policies. It is still
> more difficult to ask that the old policy be applied in some cases
> and the new one in others. It is especially hard when administrators
> accustomed to the old ways are obliged to depart from their familiar
> practices.
>
> Surely the prospects that this system will succeed are slim. The
> different nature of low and moderate income housing programs
> demands that they be administered separately. The urgency of the
> Nation's need for this housing demands that the programs be given
> priority. I believe this can be achieved most sensibly and effectively
> through a Moderate Housing Division. (U.S. Senate, 1968, 128–129)

Moreover,

> The Government is really going into a new business when it goes into
> low and moderate income housing . . . philosophically FHA has just
> not been attuned to such a program. They have done excellent work

in the job that they were created to do but now government moves into social purpose legislation . . . into the ghettos, into the social areas.

The criteria are different. The procedures are different. And even though Commissioner Brownstein has attempted, and I think unquestionably in good faith, to move low- and moderate-income housing, the personnel that he has just are not attuned to doing it. . . . If we are really going to have a low- and moderate-income housing bill, we need new personnel who are attuned to doing exactly this job. (U.S. Senate, 1968, 131)

Many others, including businessmen, politicians, newsmen, and academics, also saw the need for a new organization with the special mandate to tend to the needs of lower-income house buyers. Pinpointing why he felt that the FHA could not do the job, George Sternlieb noted that the FHA's mandate had been narrower than the goals of the proposed legislation.

If we attempt to add to it [the FHA], the responsibility for facilitating the housing of the poor and lower moderate incomed, we can only water down its capacity to deal with the groups with which it has been very successful, while still inhibiting the development of facilitating activity for those less fortunate.

I think that the FHA has been criticized for not doing things which it in turn simply was never given the primary responsibility and mandate for. The mechanisms of the FHA are reasonably adequate to deal with middle income new construction mortgage guarantees; we can only impair its effectiveness if we continue to link this activity with the quite different activity of providing essential inputs into the financing of housing for the poor. (U.S. Senate, 1968, 143)

This view must have been based, in part, on some of Sternlieb's observations concerning the difficulty that FHA Commissioner Brownstein was having in trying to persuade FHA personnel to redirect some of their efforts to inner-city housing. Echoing Brooke's comments, Sternlieb noted:

I have had the privilege of reading some of Commissioner Brownstein's—I was going to say "encyclicals" to his parish heads, if you will. They are as strong, as from the heart, as the strongest housing person could ask for. They are as earnest and as solid. They are wonderful documents.

The mere redundancy of them indicates on the other hand that, somehow or other, we are hitting mattresses in there.

If I saw one of them I wouldn't think so. And if I had seen maybe two or three of them I would think he's just giving a reminder. But those things come out, you know, like the monthly mail. (U.S. Senate, 1968, 142)

The committee chairman, John Sparkman (D-Ala.), responding to Sternlieb's observations, added his own:

I notice some of the personnel of FHA, when they get these encyclicals as Dr. Sternlieb speaks of it, throw them away. They are interested in promotions and what not. And their records have been built on the basis of the number of cases that they have been able to work on which have been successful.

In other words, they are always avoiding these risks, and they don't want to take anything that looks like a risk because they don't want to have any failures on their record. It has become quite a thing in FHA. You just don't proceed up the ladder if you have had several cases that exhibit failures. . . .

People who have been working with this in mind as a paramount concern are not apt to take on any social-purpose cases and certainly not apt to take on anything which is below the economic risk that they had in the first instance, and this is no matter how many encyclicals are received by them. (U.S. Senate, 1968, 142)

In the midst of these attacks, FHA Commissioner Brownstein was making a desperate effort to maintain the strength of the FHA, already weakened as a result of its repositioning within HUD. He argued that his staff would be capable of abandoning its middle-class orientation and administering the new socially oriented programs. In an impassioned speech at an FHA Directors and Underwriters Conference, Brownstein told his staff that he had faith that they could adapt to the requirements of the new social legislation.

I suppose that it has come to your attention that there are some who say FHA cannot do this new job. There are those who believe FHA is too wedded to the split-level house for middle-class residents of suburban subdivision to be interested in, or capable of, mounting a massive effort to help private enterprise house families of low and moderate income. It is also believed that FHA has no interest in the inner city—that we, like most private lenders, redline large segments of the central city—where the housing needs are greatest and the problems most pressing. There are others who say that FHA has lost its drive, that it is too cautious and too bogged down in inflexible rules, immovable procedures and tortuous redtape to mobilize itself and private enterprise to do the job which must be done. . . . There are people today who are urging that this job be taken away from FHA and be given to a new organization in the Department or somewhere else.

I do not agree with these sentiments, and I will tell you why. First, FHA personnel have the skills to do the job that must be done. We have the experience, and the organization. It would take time and be difficult to create a substitute of the same size and competence. . . . Second, . . . FHA has already gone some distance in the direction of turning its programs and its talents to the inner city and to providing housing for low- and moderate-income families. . . . Third, I have faith that FHA, as an organization, can make the additional changes in attitude and action needed to accelerate the job we have already begun. (U.S. Senate, 1968, 309)

In his concluding comments, Brownstein spelled out what would happen to the FHA and its employees if it failed to respond to the needs of the inner city and low-moderate income families. What comes through clearly from Brownstein's statement is his desperate desire to see the FHA survive the threat of the creation of a new organization to administer the socially oriented programs.

Just as surely as you are sitting here today, if FHA fails to respond effectively and affirmatively to this challenge, if FHA fails to produce the results needed, then no longer will FHA be looked at as our Nation's housing agency and the need and justification for its continuation may very well be the central theme. Undoubtedly alternative organizations will be developed because the need is too great and too critical to leave a void.

I have given a number of reasons why I believe FHA must mount a major effort to accelerate and expand use of our programs which serve families of low- and moderate-income and revive and rebuild the inner city. Let me give you one more reason. You should work at this task as though your job depended on it, because it may. (U.S. Senate, 1968, 312)

Implementation of the 1968 Programs

Commissioner Brownstein's threats notwithstanding, shortly after the new homeownership programs got under way, HUD was cited for a host of poor management practices, such as inadequate property appraisals, faulty inspections, and weak oversight of lenders in charge of processing and servicing FHA-insured mortgages, particularly mortgage companies (also see Chapter 8).

With HUD/FHA playing the key role in appraising property under its homeownership programs, including the Section 235 program, the agency was in a critical position regarding consumer needs. Obviously, if a property is overvalued, a homeowner will have a difficult time recouping his investment on resale. As early as December 1970, the House Committee on Banking and Currency issued a report and recommendations, *Investigation and Hearing of Abuses in Federal Low- and Moderate-Income Housing Programs*. Basing its findings on experiences with Section 235 programs in ten cities across the country, the committee disclosed numerous instances of poor HUD/FHA practices that resulted in appraisals "inflated by several thousands of dollars above the true value of the home" (U.S. House of Representatives, 1970, 1). It was not uncommon, for example, to find that a house sold with FHA insurance under the 235 program was, only a month or two earlier, bought for half the price of the appraised value.

Soon after the problems with the 235 program were reported nationwide, Congress began to focus attention on Detroit, a city particularly hard hit by abuses and mismanagement in the HUD/FHA home insurance programs. In a June 1972 report issued by the House Committee on Government Operations, several problems in valuation procedures were cited, such as insufficient staff and the resulting reliance on part-time appraisers, who often had conflicts of interest regarding the properties they were appraising.

Repeating the problems of the 1950s, HUD's implementation of the 1968 homeownership programs left much room for criticism about its role in inspecting property to be insured. On the one hand, HUD handbooks explicitly stated that HUD did not warrant the condition of the property (HUD, Office of Audit, 1973, 5–17). On the other hand, the property was supposed to meet an array of "acceptability standards"—including minimum property standards—(HUD, Office of Audit, 1973, 5–3 to 5–5), and the HUD/FHA appraiser was responsible for detailing conditions that had to be satisfied before issuance of the insurance certificate.

Unfortunately, various reports issued in the early 1970s disclosed that faulty inspections by HUD/FHA were frequent. One such report disclosed that numerous new and existing Section 235 homes had severe defects.

> The staff found cases of families who have become disappointed owners of houses which will not even come close to lasting the life of the mortgage. In existing Section 235 housing the most common deficiencies are faulty plumbing, leaky basements, leaky roofs, cracked plaster, faulty or inadequate wiring, rotten wood in floors, staircases, ceilings, porches, lack of insulation, faulty heating units, and the like. . . . The staff also examined two Section 235 new con-

struction projects in Everett, Washington, and Elmwood, Missouri. In these two cases, in the staff's opinion the construction is of such poor quality and the cost so questionable that the projects can best be described as "instant slums." (U.S. House of Representatives, 1970, 3)

Similar to the appraisal situation, early disclosures of HUD's inadequate inspection procedures did not seem greatly to alter HUD's operations. Audits carried out in 1971 and 1973 disclosed many defects in homes insured by HUD/FHA.

Additional evidence pointing to major defects in FHA-insured houses was gathered by OSTI, a nonprofit consulting firm under contract to HUD. A survey of more than 500 purchasers of Section 235 houses in ten cities revealed that a staggering 56 percent reported major problems with their houses at the time of purchase. OSTI (1974) concluded: "That large number of . . . families purchased housing in inadequate condition—even with FHA property screening and appraisal—is a serious indication of how poorly the federal lower-income ownership programs function in the consumer's interests in this respect" (p. 180).

This, as well as mounds of other data, pointed to a substantial case against HUD/FHA for questionable inspection procedures. According to a spokesperson for the Wayne County Neighborhood Legal Services in Detroit, HUD/FHA flagrantly disobeyed the law:

The Federal Housing Administration has, in many instances, failed to abide by the clear requirements of Federal law. One section of the National Housing Act which governs both sections 221(d)(2) and 235 housing requires, and I quote: "To be eligible for insurance under this section a mortgage shall . . . be secured by property on which there is located a dwelling . . . meeting the requirements of all state laws, or local ordinances or regulations relating to the safety, zoning or otherwise, which may be applicable thereto." In hundreds of cases the Department of Housing and Urban Development has quite simply ignored this rather clear expression of Federal law. Congress foresaw the problem and expressed its desire that only dwellings meeting all applicable codes should be insured. Somehow, in the face of this mandatory directive HUD continues to claim that it has no duty to inspect homes to determine if they meet local codes. How HUD can take this position despite the clear wording of the statute is beyond me. (U.S. House of Representatives, 1971, 113)

Not surprisingly, buyers of houses generally assumed that if the government inspected the house, it was adequate, at the least. A government audit team reported that the mortgagor had no way of learning "the extent of responsibility, if any, which HUD assume[d] in connection with the condition of a house involved in an insured mortgage transaction" (HUD, 1971, 55). Further,

> Many mortgagors told us that a seller, broker or salesman had represented the house to be free of significant defects, as evidenced by a completed or to-be-made inspection and appraisal by HUD; however, many mortgagors informed us and our inspections confirmed the existence of defects that should have been corrected before the sale was closed. Even when no such overt or implied representations are made, the unsophisticated mortgagor could mistakenly assume that he can rely on HUD to insure detection and correction of defects. If data were furnished to prospective home buyers to explain the function of the HUD appraisal and the risks inherent in the purchase of a house, many unfortunate misunderstandings usually at the expense of the buyer might be avoided. (HUD, 1971, 55)

HUD's protestations that it was not responsible for the condition of the houses it insured were all the more absurd in view of Section 518(b), enacted as part of the Housing and Urban Development Act of 1970. This section authorized the secretary of HUD to "make expenditures to correct, or to compensate the owner for structural or other defects which seriously affect the use and livability of any single family dwelling which is covered by a mortgage insured under Section 235."[2] In order for the owner to receive compensation, the property must have been at least a year old at the time it was insured, the claim must have been filed within a year from the date the property was insured, and "the defect is one that existed on the date of the issuance of the insurance commitment and is one that a proper inspection could reasonably expect to disclose."[3] Through January 1975, HUD had paid a total of $7,626,426 in claims to 9896 Section 235 homeowners; the average claim was $770.[4]

Probably the most depressing aspect of the homeownership programs was the high foreclosure rate. The chairman of the House Legal and Monetary Affairs Subcommittee reported: "During the first three months of 1973 . . . HUD had acquired almost as many homes due to foreclosure as in the first twenty years of its history" (U.S. House of Representatives, 1973, 32). Unfortunately, HUD did not play an active role in assisting homeowners in default, thereby trying to help them avoid foreclosure. Its unwillingness to supervise mortgage lenders aggressively and advocate on behalf of homeowners is another important example of HUD's nonconsumer orientation.

Mortgage companies are the dominant lenders in FHA programs

and have the major responsibility for processing mortgage applications. In conventional mortgage lending, where the lender assumes the risk, both the value of the property and creditworthiness of the borrower are carefully assessed. But with the FHA assuming the risk as the insurer and with a secondary mortgage market that enables mortgage companies, as well as other lenders, to achieve rapid and full liquidity, the FHA system of home finance grew into a virtually risk-free operation for mortgage companies. This may not have caused problems if HUD had been willing or able to assume the risk, inherent in its role of mortgage insurer, and to carefully oversee all phases of the mortgage-lending process. But HUD repeatedly failed to assume responsibility, and the consumer was left at a considerable disadvantage (see Bratt, 1976).

Specifically concerning the default situation, HUD issued handbooks for mortgage lenders servicing FHA-insured loans, detailing a variety of methods to assist borrowers in catching up with their payments. These guidelines were not enforced, however, and mortgage lenders usually bypassed HUD's suggested relief measures. In testimony before the Senate Subcommittee on Antitrust and Monopoly in 1972, a legal services attorney lay the blame squarely on HUD: "If the FHA tells the bank to give forbearance relief and to allow a certain homeowner to make deferred payments on his mortgage . . . then they [the banks] will go along. I think the main way to attack the problem is through the FHA" (U.S. Senate, 1972, 122).

In short, the agency provided no positive incentives for mortgage lenders to grant relief, there were no negative sanctions imposed if relief was not granted, and, most remarkably, there were actually positive incentives for mortgage lenders not to grant relief and to foreclose quickly (see Bratt, 1976).

During the spring and summer of 1975, HUD officials not only began acknowledging mortgage abuses and noncompliance with HUD guidelines but also began to take steps toward correcting the problems. HUD's actions were, to a large extent, prompted by the pressure of citizen groups, such as the National Training and Information Center in Chicago, and Congress. In addition, several court cases revolved around mortgage lenders' unwillingness to follow HUD's guidelines related to default. In one such case, *Johnnie D. Brown v. Lynn and Mortgage Associates*, the secretary of HUD was named as a co-defendant along with the mortgage company. The district court judge specifically faulted HUD for catering to mortgage companies rather than low-income homeowners. Moreover,

> Contrary to its statutory obligation, HUD has forced foreclosures
> rather than taking action to prevent them. . . . If HUD had con-
> sciously and deliberately set out to frustrate the Congressional pur-
> pose and sabotage the program [Section 235] it could have hardly
> done so more effectively—short of simply refusing to carry it out.
> (Will, 1974)

In the wake of these criticisms, HUD launched several initiatives
to improve the monitoring of mortgagees, as well as its other administrative functions. But two clichés seem to typify HUD's actions
toward remedying well-documented deficiencies in its operation:
"too little, too late" and "pulling teeth." For example, a 1976 report
by the House Committee on Government Operations criticized HUD
for its "seeming unwillingness in the past to take corrective action.
. . . Recommendations for improvement . . . often have not been
given the attention they deserve. Consequently, reports critical of
HUD seem to have a quality of timeliness even when they are several
years old" (U.S. House of Representatives, 1976, 4, 7).

There is no single reason that can account for HUD's difficulties
and its slow pace in correcting the serious problems that faced the
agency in the late 1960s and early 1970s. In addition to its long-
standing proindustry orientation, discussed earlier, several reasons
have been proposed, such as the late 1960s reorganization of HUD
(Bazan, 1974; U.S. House of Representatives, 1976, 4); inadequate
staffing (U.S. House of Representatives, 1972, 22–24, and 1976, 13–
14); and fraud and abuses by some HUD personnel (*Housing and
Development Reporter*, 1975, 1185).

Two additional explanations warrant closer examination: confusion over whether HUD's mandate was to insure a large number of
loans or to insure quality loans; and difficulties in dealing with new
kinds of properties and house buyers.

Quantity versus Quality.   In order to reach the housing goal set by
Congress in 1949—"a decent home and a suitable living environment
for every American family"—in 1968 both President Johnson and
Congress asked for the construction or substantial rehabilitation of
26 million housing units in the next ten years. Thus, the FHA's long-
standing production orientation was reinforced.

Commissioner Brownstein, in an October 1967 speech before
HUD/FHA area office directors, emphasized the need for field offices
to insure a large volume of mortgages:

> I want you to go looking for applications. I want you to know that applications involving the inner city, rehabilitation, BMIR and rent supplements are the first things your staff should work on, not the last. . . . You will also hear more discussion of my recent field letter eliminating the requirement for a finding of economic soundness in riot or riot-prone areas of the city. This has the effect of making our programs available everywhere in the city. (U.S. Senate, 1968, 310)

Yet, almost in the same breath, Brownstein added some caveats, making clear that standards were still in force and that the quality of the property should not be overlooked.

> Risks are inherent in an insurance program (otherwise there would be no justification or need for insurance); that since the vast majority of the Congress as well as the executive branch expect us to carry out the mission (of assisting and encouraging private enterprise to house low- and moderate-income families, and to revive the inner city) . . . then they must expect us willingly to take the risks inherent in such a mission.
>
> This does not by any means require the elimination of prudence and common sense. . . . I want us to develop and support projects which give reasonable promise of improving the housing conditions of low- and moderate-income families, and improving the inner city. . . . A project should be rejected if it does not appear to give reasonable promise of accomplishing these objectives. It should not be rejected simply because it involves poor people, or because it is in a portion of the city you have been accustomed to rejecting or red-lining for old-fashioned, arbitrary reasons. (U.S. Senate, 1968, 311)

Unfortunately, Brownstein's plea for maintaining standards was not heeded. Instead, the message that many of the area personnel took back to their offices was the quantitative goal; the need and desire for "decent housing" got lost in the rush to swell production figures.

Reflecting on the 1968 housing goal and the way in which HUD responded to it, an audit report stated:

> The entire field structure was tending to emphasize production of new housing units and processing of appraisals on used houses to the degree that too little emphasis was being placed on the quality of the units produced or appraised. Although the need for more and better housing is great, production and appraisals must be measured in terms of the quality of the end products as well as in terms of the number of housing units provided, both new and used.
>
> Throughout the country we have been informed, both formally

and informally, that the word was out from the Central Office to "produce units." (HUD, 1973, 8–9)

By early 1972, HUD Secretary George Romney acknowledged the need to focus attention on insuring quality mortgages; his official stance stressed quality over high production levels. In testimony before the House Legal and Monetary Affairs Subcommittee, he stated: "Above all, we will insist on quality production and have instructed area and insuring offices to restrict their processing and supervision to what can be done on a quality basis—even if that means reduction of total production levels from 1971 highs" (U.S. House of Representatives, 1972a, 303).

Yet, by 1972, much of the damage had been done. For the previous four years, high production levels had been the focus of HUD policy. Romney's call for a return to insuring only quality mortgages had the ring of a "Monday morning quarterback."

In spite of Romney's admission that the quality of mortgages insured had been slipping, he nevertheless tried to place the blame on Congress for a faulty legislative mandate. In rebutting these charges, Senator John Sparkman, chairman of the Senate Banking and Currency Committee, stated:

> To keep the record straight, there was never any Congressional intent to authorize local FHA offices to insure substandard housing or to accept as mortgagors the poor whose financial condition did not justify homeownership. The strong language in the 1968 Housing Act and subsequent administrative rulings were intended to eliminate "redlining" in older declining urban areas, but not to blanket in as insurable risks all units in such areas regardless of their condition or otherwise insurable qualifications. (U.S. House of Representatives, 1971, 56)

It is not surprising that field office staff were confused about how to reach the dual goals of achieving a high volume of production while maintaining prudent insuring practices. As a result, vast numbers of ill-prepared or financially weak families purchased houses they could not afford, and numerous properties approved for FHA insurance were of very poor quality.

Dealing with New Buyers and Different Properties.   HUD administrators, in charge of carrying out the Housing and Urban Development Act of 1968, clearly wanted HUD/FHA to become the housing agency responsible for lower-income families and inner-city areas, as well as the familiar suburban middle class. Even if a major motivation for trying to adopt a new social orientation was self-interest, the desire to avoid competition with another housing agency, HUD personnel seemed aware of the challenge. Yet it was extremely difficult for old-timers to shift their thinking and adapt their procedures to suit the new mortgagors and properties.

Confirming some of the worst fears of many of the witnesses at the 1968 hearings, an audit of the Section 235 program observed:

> With the advent of subsidized housing programs . . . many of the personnel carrying out programs have not sufficiently adjusted their thinking and attitudes to encompass the Department's new programs. . . . While we recognize that the buyer must always share the responsibility for the selection and purchase of his home, we believe that intensified efforts are required to dispel remaining vestiges of the "caveat emptor" philosophy and to more effectively implement current Departmental policy objectives. (HUD, 1971, 8)

While many long-time HUD/FHA personnel had a great deal of difficulty accepting the social goals of the FHA insurance programs, and resented the drastic change in orientation, many young employees on the HUD staff, not the FHA staff, openly accepted the ideals of the department. This view was expressed by a young housing counselor/community services adviser from the Phoenix HUD insuring office: "There is a real split in our office. Some of us work for HUD and others—the old timers—still work for FHA."[5]

Whether or not HUD employees believed in the new socially oriented programs, they were expected to carry out the mandate of both the President and Congress. Talking about the new, unsophisticated mortgagors and their special needs, a representative of the General Accounting Office noted that

> the group of people that you are dealing with in subsidized housing programs have never owned a home before. Many of them, or most of them, are not aware of the type of defects they might run into, and when they see defects they do not necessarily realize their significance. . . . In order to make the program work you are going to have to deal with these people in a different manner than you deal with the people in your regular unsubsidized FHA programs. (U.S. Congress, 1972, 29)

But in HUD's attempt to carry out its mandate and reverse the exclusionary policies and redlining practices of the pre-1968 era, many HUD personnel seemed to lose sight of the fact that some people, for one reason or another, should probably not be homeowners. Representative Benjamin Blackburn (R-Ga.), during hearings of the Subcommittee on Priorities and Economy in Government, went so far as to state that *the* cause of problems with lower-income homeownership programs was that program participants were not suitable for homeownership. He stated:

> The problem is that we have been putting families into homes who have no sense of responsibility of ownership and that is where the problem has been, and that is the intrinsic problem in the program. . . . Can we not conclude that there are some people who do not have the sense of responsibility or the economic income to own a home? (U.S. Congress, 1973, 41–42)

Although Representative Blackburn's comments were one-sided and ignored the myriad other reasons why the lower-income homeownership programs encountered so much difficulty, an important dilemma—a "damned if you do and damned if you don't" situation —arises from this discussion.

If, indeed, some people are not capable of being homeowners, how can HUD and mortgage lenders determine who should and who should not own a house without being overly lenient or overly strict? Thus, since the post-1968 homeownership programs have been faulted for laxity in underwriting and appraising, and the pre-1968 programs have been faulted for conservatism and discrimination, is it possible to administer a program fairly—allowing participation by those who can own, yet barring participation by those who clearly cannot? This question has not been adequately answered.

HUD's experiment in promoting "homeownership for the poor" lasted only five years. In January 1973, President Nixon's moratorium on housing programs halted the operation of the Section 235 program. Although a revised and much reduced Section 235 limped back on to the federal agenda a few years later, there has only recently been federal interest in a new homeownership initiative, in the form of the Nehemiah program, enacted as part of the Housing and Community Development Act of 1987. Prior to its passage, however, Nehemiah was the subject of considerable congressional debate and has received only very modest funding (see also Chapter 8). Thus, to conclude, the policy of homeownership for low-moderate income families has not yet been given a full and fair test at the national level, since the numerous ways in which HUD's operations worked at cross-purposes with consumer needs precluded such a test.

Was this an isolated instance of HUD's not acting in the consumer's interest? Unfortunately, the answer is no. The following chapter details how HUD has dealt with a complex problem that has seriously affected tenants' needs in the 1980s.

7

HUD's Property Disposition Policies and the Granite Properties

EMILY J. MORRIS, co-author

PARALLELING the homeownership initiatives enacted in 1968, Congress passed new legislation authorizing the production and rehabilitation of low-rent multifamily housing, particularly in urban areas (see Chapters 2 and 4). Over the following years, numerous problems arose, and by the early 1980s about one-quarter of the total inventory of subsidized housing was in mortgage default. (See Table 2, p. 98.) Under the Reagan administration, HUD's stated policy for handling foreclosed properties was to auction them to the highest bidder as quickly as possible, often without any commitment to maintaining the housing for long-term low- or moderate-income occupancy.

Thus the promise of the HUD multifamily projects of the 1960s and early 1970s have culminated in a two-pronged set of disappointments. First, as discussed in Chapter 4, many low-income renters of subsidized units have been confronted with possible displacement from their homes because of expiring-use restrictions. Second, auctioning developments to the highest bidder has meant that projects can be reprivatized, with the potential for ultimately being removed from the inventory of subsidized housing—a significant public loss.

The history of one package of properties illustrates this evolution of HUD policy from publicly supported development to reprivatization. Over half of the 2000 Section 221(d)(3) properties rehabilitated through the Boston Urban Rehabilitation Program, or BURP (discussed in Chapter 12), and an additional 800 Rent Supplement units, were rehabilitated by one developer, Maurice Simon. These 1800 units are known as the Granite Properties. By the mid-1970s, half these units were in default, and conditions looked bleak. Problems included faulty wiring, peeling plaster, lack of adequate heat and plumbing, and leaking roofs. At the time, The Greater Boston Legal Services became involved, representing tenants in civil suits against Simon.

This case study begins at the point when HUD was faced with the problem of how to handle the Granite Properties once it assumed control in 1982 as "mortgagee in possession," a stage that precedes foreclosure. The overriding question is this: To what extent did HUD act to represent the public interest (i.e., the rights of the tenants to a decent living environment and the public investment in the housing)?

Management of the Granite Properties

Once HUD took possession of the Granite Properties, it became responsible for the operation of the buildings. Unfortunately, HUD was as bad a manager as Simon. In 1982, Granite Properties tenants again went to court. As a result of that suit, HUD agreed to pay $3 million, or about $1300 per apartment, for repairs, a major victory, although hardly adequate given the extent of deterioration (Gibbs, 1985, 25).

In 1983, Congressman Barney Frank (D-Mass.), chairman of a subcommittee of the Committee on Government Operations, convened hearings on "HUD Multifamily Repair and Foreclosure Policies." Representatives from subsidized developments in the Northeast and Midwest testified regarding problems encountered in dealing with HUD. The Granite Properties was a focus of the investigation.

In addition to highlighting the poor physical condition of the buildings, the attorney for the Granite Properties pointed to HUD's questionable policies concerning repairs, best expressed in two memoranda. The "Winn Memorandum," issued by HUD Assistant Secretary Philip D. Winn in November 1981, directed the agency to make only those "repairs needed on an emergency basis to protect life, health, and safety" (quoted in U.S. House of Representatives, 1983b, 81). All other repairs were to be made by a subsequent purchaser. A second memorandum directed the Boston HUD area office to authorize any repair on the Granite Properties necessary to achieve minimum conditions of habitability. This standard did not require that properties be brought into compliance with the local housing code (U.S. House of Representatives, 1983b, 69).

While the hearings were being held, Greater Boston Legal Services, the tenants, and a local black developer, Denis Blackett, were negotiating with HUD to purchase the Granite Properties through a Transfer of Physical Assets (TPA). A TPA is a method of transferring ownership in which the new owner assumes the original mortgage. HUD makes approval of the TPA contingent on a cash contribution by the new owner to meet the project's physical and financial needs. Funds are often raised through resyndication (see Chapter 5).

Although the TPA was ostensibly intended to benefit tenants, TPAs have often provided investors with a financially attractive means of disposing of burned-out tax shelters. Additionally, for financially troubled property like Granite, TPAs have frequently bailed out the former owner who retains a share of the property's residual value in conjunction with the transfer. As for tenant benefits, HUD has estimated that only 20 percent of syndication proceeds are reinvested in capital improvements for the project. Thus, use of the tax code by for-profit housing sponsors has served primarily private owners and investors, not the tenants or the projects (Achtenberg, 1989).

Despite these drawbacks, in this instance the tenants favored the TPA approach. They felt that Blackett was a known entity and would be easier to work with than the amorphous HUD bureaucracy.[1] Moreover, a transfer would shorten the period of interim management by HUD.

In an unusual request for a TPA, Blackett asked that HUD either provide sufficient Section 8 Moderate Rehab subsidies to allow him to finance repairs or make the needed repairs a condition of sale. HUD's response was that these subsidies were not available and that it would not make the repairs. Here was a Catch 22: The purchase would not be economically feasible without repairs, but it was HUD policy not to do significant repairs. HUD wanted the purchaser to make the repairs, yet the prospective buyer was unwilling to purchase the properties until either repairs were made or Section 8 subsidies were committed. Congressman Frank pinpointed the inconsistency: "They are not going to repair it until they can sell it. They are not going to sell it until they repair it, which means everyone is going to be here forever" (U.S. House of Representatives, 1983b, 94).

Not only was HUD unable or unwilling to agree to the developer's request for subsidies, but HUD claimed that it was not at fault because the subsidies were not available; blame lay in the budget passed by the Reagan administration and Congress. An incredulous Congressman Frank questioned this blatant denial of responsibility: "Has HUD seceded from the administration? Have they become part of the United Nations? HUD people [have indicated that] it was part of the administration's doing and not theirs?" (U.S. House of Representatives 1983b, 94).

Indeed, HUD under the Reagan administration continually disregarded the need for subsidies to deal with financially distressed properties, consistently requesting an inadequate level of support. This casts a further shadow on its attempt to disclaim responsibility for inadequate subsidies.

In early 1984, HUD rejected the TPA to Denis Blackett. At about the same time, in response to an ongoing lawsuit, HUD agreed to make an additional $8 million in repairs (Gibbs, 1985, 25). Shortly thereafter, HUD announced its intention to foreclose on the Granite Properties.

Meanwhile, a local group of concerned government officials, businesspeople, legal advocates, and community activists joined forces in reaction to the Reagan administration's policies concerning the disposition of defaulted properties. In 1983, Massachusetts's Community Economic Development Assistance Corporation (CEDAC) (see Chapter 11) convened a Task Force on HUD Distressed Properties. At that time, over 4500 units were slated for disposition. Granite Properties constituted about 40 percent of these units.

HUD's Multifamily Property Disposition Policy

Members of the task force had good reason to be worried. HUD's handling of its foreclosed inventory of insured and subsidized properties presented a disturbing story. If national policies prevailed in Boston, a significant number of affordable units would be lost, and low-income housing needs would be exacerbated in an already tight and expensive market.

HUD's policies were fueled by three broad sets of interests: to protect the federal financial interest in the properties, to minimize further outlays of funds, and to minimize the federal government's long-term obligation to the properties by transferring ownership to the private sector wherever feasible. In fact, HUD's third concern was thought to be a means to the other two: It was believed that privatization would cut costs, losses, or both.

This desire was particularly strong as a result of the costly but relatively effective disposition policy used by HUD during the Carter administration. During the late 1970s, 93 percent of the projects sold by HUD had a project-based subsidy attached. In addition, the Section 8 Loan Management and Property Disposition programs were expanded, and Flexible Subsidies were introduced in the form of no-interest grants or loans (see Chapter 4). By the end of the Carter years, these procedures became the focus of criticism, with Senator Proxmire (D-Wisc.) charging HUD with mismanagement and with using the mortgage insurance fund as a "back door entitlement" (GAO, 1979b, i).

It was also assumed that privatization would protect the tenants and properties by placing them under more capable management: private, profit-motivated owners. But probably most important, privatization was consistent with the Reagan philosophy: In virtually all areas, including housing, the private sector can perform better than the public sector, which should play as small a role as possible.

Several key actions taken by HUD under the Reagan administration exemplified the drive toward privatizing as much of the subsidized housing stock as possible: subversion of the intent of the Housing and Community Development Act of 1978; failure to implement the Multifamily Mortgage Foreclosure Act; disposition by high-bid auction; and adherence to policies that effectively precluded participation by nonprofit and tenant groups. These policies and procedures have resulted in significant financial costs to the public and often devastating social costs to the tenants. Taken together, they tell an important story about the way in which HUD has turned its back on the public interest and provide a backdrop for understanding the problems facing the Granite Properties.

The Housing and Community Development Act of 1978

In 1978, Congress passed Section 203 of the Housing and Community Development Act to deal specifically with disposition policy for subsidized HUD-owned properties. The statute required that HUD manage and dispose of properties it owned in a manner that protects the financial interest of the federal government and is "less costly," while preserving the low- and moderate-income character of the housing. The secretary of HUD was authorized to balance these competing goals, but the accompanying Senate report tempered the discretion given the secretary. It made clear that the committee's principal goal was to preserve the existing stock of multifamily housing as both decent and affordable to low- and moderate-income families (U.S. House of Representatives, 1983c, 10).

In 1979, HUD published an interim rule to implement Section 203. The rule required HUD, after conferring with the tenants, to develop a detailed disposition analysis for each project it owned. The department then was to determine whether the project would be sold with federal subsidies, a decision that was obviously critical for maintaining the affordability of the housing stock. For subsidized projects, HUD was automatically to provide Section 8 project-based subsidies for a term of fifteen or twenty years. For unsubsidized projects (e.g., only insured by HUD), HUD was also to attach project-based subsidies when there was a need for low- and moderate-income housing in the community. Such a need was presumed unless HUD made and supported a finding to the contrary (U.S. House of Representatives, 1983c, 10).

Section 203 represented a socially responsible approach to the problem of financially distressed projects. But it applied only to projects already foreclosed on and purchased by HUD at the foreclosure sale.

According to traditional HUD bidding procedures, HUD was authorized to bid up to 90 percent of the outstanding mortgage indebtedness plus foreclosure costs. If a private party bid a price higher than the statutory maximum, HUD avoided actually taking ownership of the property. In avoiding ownership, HUD was not obligated to follow the regulations implementing the Housing and Community Development Act of 1978. The law did not require the subsequent purchaser to "operate the property in accordance with the terms of the program and the Regulatory Agreement in effect prior to foreclosure" (Johnson and the National Low Income Housing Coalition, et al., 1985, 290). In other words, the new purchaser was under no obligation to limit occupancy to low- and moderate-income tenants.

To increase its chance of being outbid, HUD altered its previous bidding procedures. Rather than submit the statutory maximum, HUD submitted the appraised fair-market value, which in cases of extreme deterioration can be substantially lower than 90 percent of outstanding indebtedness. From this price, HUD also subtracted approximately $2000 per unit, to account for its savings on the cost of holding the unit for six months if HUD were to assume ownership.

This method of deriving a bid price was specifically intended to reduce the likelihood that HUD would become the owner of subsidized properties at foreclosure sales. In HUD's words, the purpose of formulating an adjusted price of the property, which "will in most cases be significantly less than the 90 percent of outstanding debt HUD has traditionally bid, [is] to reduce the number of projects HUD acquires through foreclosure" (quoted in U.S. House of Representatives, 1983c, 16). As of November 1983, HUD was outbid on all eight projects in which it used this new procedure.

Although the reduced bid helped fulfill the goal of privatizing the subsidized stock, it did not protect the federal government's financial interest in the housing. First, although the bid supposedly represented a more accurate fair-market value, the successful bids on all eight projects cited above exceeded the HUD bid by an average of $240,000. This indicated that HUD's bid underestimated fair-market value and resulted in a loss to the government (U.S. House of Representatives, 1983c, 16).

Second, the reduced bid failed to account for the effect that tax-shelter benefits have on the value of the property. As discussed in Chapter 5, the Economic Recovery Tax Act of 1981 provided particularly lucrative incentives for private owners of existing subsidized housing. These incentives constituted a major reason why profit-motivated parties were interested in purchasing distressed properties. HUD failed to consider this in determining the value of the housing, and "the clear intent [was] to lose the property and avoid its responsibility to preserve the existing stock" (U.S. House of Representatives, 1983c, 17).

When Section 203 was enacted, apparently nobody foresaw the problem. The possibility that private developers might want to outbid HUD for some financially distressed properties because market forces made them attractive investments was simply not anticipated. The Multifamily Mortgage Foreclosure Act, enacted in 1981, included important safeguards that attempted to close the loophole in Section 203.

The Multifamily Mortgage Foreclosure Act (MMFA)

Generally, the Multifamily Mortgage Foreclosure Act (MMFA) authorized HUD to use an optional nonjudicial and expeditious foreclosure process. Congress found that long periods to complete foreclosure of defaulted mortgages led to deteriorated conditions in most of the properties and necessitated substantial management and expenditures.

MMFA also clarified HUD procedures for properties that HUD

never technically owned because a private party outbid HUD at the foreclosure sale. MMFA stipulated that if the property was to be sold at foreclosure to a purchaser other than HUD, the secretary was to be given some discretion in determining the property's use. MMFA instructed the secretary to require that the new purchaser maintain it under the terms of the original program if the project was 50 percent or more occupied. If the project was less than 50 percent occupied, the secretary would use discretion in enforcing this requirement. The legislative intent was made clear in the conference report accompanying the statute. The provision is "intended to assure wherever possible and practicable that the multifamily programs be preserved as low- or moderate-income rental housing" (quoted in U.S. House of Representatives, 1983c, 12).

Nevertheless, HUD failed to implement MMFA. For over two years, HUD did not promulgate the necessary regulations. Instead, in late 1982, over a year after MMFA was enacted, HUD distributed a Draft Memorandum, "Multifamily Foreclosure and Property Disposition Policies and Issues," to its field staff (U.S. House of Representatives, 1983c, 12). The stated objectives were to return the government's inventory of properties to the private sector as quickly as possible; protect the financial interest of HUD; and protect the tenants and properties by quickly putting them under the most capable ownership and management (U.S. House of Representatives, 1983a, 131).

James Grow, attorney for the National Housing Law Project, interpreted what the new policy would mean during a congressional hearing: "Where projects are sold at foreclosure and HUD is outbid, there will be no use restrictions whatsoever. Tenants will receive certificate subsidies" (U.S. House of Representatives, 1983a, 169).

Congressman Frank described a possible scenario in which a tenant could move into a subsidized building thinking it would be available only to low-income tenants and then learn that the building was in default and about to be sold to a profit-motivated sponsor with no use restrictions. The rents would be raised substantially, and the tenant would have to move. To which Mr. Grow responded:

> That is correct. That is why Congress in the 1981 amendments to the Housing Act [of 1978] established a multifamily foreclosure policy [MMFA], a uniform procedure which would require HUD, when using its uniform foreclosure procedure, to impose the same

use restriction that existed prior to the foreclosure. Now, HUD has not been using that uniform procedure and they have been selling projects without use restrictions. (U.S. House of Representatives, 1983a, 169)

According to Congressman Frank, failure to implement the MMFA qualified as an administrative "veto by non-regulation" (quoted

---

Katherine Chavis, president of the Catharine Street Close Tenants Council, Philadelphia, describes how HUD's decision not to utilize MMFA in foreclosing her 32-unit Section 236 complex threatened her and her neighbors' security:

This complex is located in the Queen Village area of Philadelphia, which has quickly changed from a low to moderate income to a more affluent community consisting of high priced townhouses, condominiums and high rental apartments. The change in the community has caused a large displacement of many life-long residents of which many are on fixed incomes and cannot afford the high rents and taxes.

Earlier this year the tenants of Catharine Street Close learned that we could physically be put out of our housing because HUD intended to have the property at Catharine Street Close sold at a marshal sale to the highest bidder. We were not told anything by HUD. . . . We learned of this eviction through an advertisement that was in the paper

. . . a couple of weeks before the sheriff sale.

We, of course, became extremely concerned. . . . They had a lot of new housing development within the immediate area of our complex. . . .

If a new owner was to come in and purchase this property he would not be obligated to continue to rent to the subsidized tenants there and we would be simply evicted and put into the streets. . . .

Many of the existing tenants at Catharine Close have lived in deplorable conditions before moving into the development. We dread with fear the fact that we simply could be evicted and be forced to move back into deplorable living conditions that existed for many of us before moving here.

From U.S. House of Representatives, Committee on Government Operations, *HUD Is Not Adequately Preserving Subsidized Multifamily Housing*, 98th Cong., 1st sess., 1983, 6–7.

in Achtenberg, 1989). Further commenting on the MMFA, Frank continued:

> This bill . . . gave the Secretary a tool which he said he needed. It gave it to him in exactly the legal form which he requested. It simply said that if he used it . . . he would have to protect [the existing tenants]. . . . The only explanation that appears to me is that he refused to use it because it comes to him in a form which requires that subsidized tenancies be protected. (Quoted in Achtenberg, 1989)

Thus, according to Frank, the case against HUD was unequivocal.

In February 1984, HUD finally promulgated regulations for the implementation of the MMFA. But HUD interpreted the act in a way that limited its authority to impose greater restrictions on the new private-party purchaser than those imposed on the original owner. The twenty-year lock-in period, stipulated in the original mortgage, would not be extended (Johnson and the National Housing Law Project, 1985, 291–292).

A policy memorandum issued by HUD in June 1984 announced that the agency would offer only Section 8 certificates to eligible families of projects sold to a private party at the foreclosure sale. It left the attachment of project-based subsidies to the discretion of the department. The same memorandum also stated that in projects that did not meet the Section 8 Housing Quality Standards, or in projects in which rents exceeded fair-market rents, families would not be allowed to stay and use their certificates (Johnson and the National Housing Law Project, 1985, 300–302). And where the costs of the building pushed rents above fair-market levels, tenants would also be displaced. Furthermore, certificate subsidies were limited to five years, whereas project-based subsidies guaranteed that a unit would be available for at least fifteen years. Providing only certificate subsidies increased the likelihood of units being available for rental at market rates or being converted to condominiums, particularly projects located in gentrifying areas.

HUD's response to the MMFA was consistent with its overall strategy to privatize a large portion of the defaulted housing stock. At the same time, tenant interests were hurt, and an important public resource in the form of subsidized housing was undermined. Providing certificates resulted neither in guaranteed units for displaced tenants nor that once-subsidized units would stay affordable.

Both the use of the reduced bid and the failure to implement the MMFA proved contrary to the social goals of protecting tenants and properties. As indicated by Section 203 of the Housing and Community Development Act of 1978 and by the MMFA, Congress clearly intended to preserve distressed projects for use by low- and moderate-income tenants wherever possible. HUD's attempts to sell properties without use restrictions were at odds with congressional intent and, in some instances, apparently in violation of the law.

Disposition by High-Bid Auction

As a result of the congressional investigation, HUD agreed in early 1984 to go back to its earlier policy of bidding the statutory maximum at the foreclosure sale. Projects purchased by HUD are subsequently sold at a high-bid disposition auction with use restrictions. The high-bid process does not provide a forum for determining who will likely be the most capable owner and manager, however. HUD policy dictates that anyone in the private sector will do and refuses to recognize that the interests of private, for-profit owners are markedly different from those of tenants.

The sale of the TAB II project in Boston provides a good example of the problematic outcomes that often arise from the high-bid auction. TAB II, like the Granite Properties, was rehabilitated under the Boston Urban Rehabilitation Program (see Chapter 12) and suffered mortgage default in the 1970s. It was auctioned in 1984 to a company involving the city's largest commercial and residential landlord, with a record of HUD defaults and foreclosures, as well as arson-related charges (Achtenberg, 1989). Nevertheless, the record of this profit-motivated purchaser was apparently not a matter of consideration in the high-bid process. To the extent that such dispositions have been the norm, there is a good likelihood that some subsidized projects will again face a cycle of decay and financial difficulties. With the passage of the Housing and Community Development Act of 1987, however, to be discussed below, congressional intent to safeguard both tenants and subsidized projects was underscored. One hopes that the new legislation will eliminate HUD's ability to subvert the intent of the 1978 act.

Sales to Community-Based Organizations

Sophisticated community-based organizations, having developed the capability to rehabilitate and manage affordable housing—not for profit but to provide a permanent resource for the community—are rarely able to compete for HUD-foreclosed properties. The *de facto* exclusion of community-based organizations from acquiring such buildings occurs for two main reasons. First, with little up-front money, the community-based organization is at a severe disadvantage compared to more affluent private developers, who can easily outbid the community organization at a high-bid auction. Second, HUD's unwillingness both to repair properties prior to sale and commit sufficient subsidies after sale puts enormous demands on the financial capacities of both owners and tenants.

Without the intervention of Boston community groups and city and state officials, the Granite Properties likely would have been transferred to another for-profit owner. At the time of the task force's activities, project-based subsidies, not just rental certificates, had already been guaranteed by the Boston area HUD office. The task force's primary goal was to find an alternative to the high-bid auction.

Agenda for the Task Force

Early in 1984, the Task Force on HUD Distressed Properties learned of HUD's intention to auction the Granite Properties during the following summer. Concerned that community pressure alone would not halt the auction, the task force's working committee began to develop a concrete alternative to the high-bid sale. Ann Kerrey, then CEDAC's real estate specialist, called together several of Boston's Community Development Corporations (CDCs) that had a track record in affordable housing development and found that all were interested in purchasing Granite Properties.[2]

In May 1984, HUD began to foreclose on the Granite Properties, splitting the nearly 2000 units into five packages for auction. As required by law, HUD informed the Massachusetts Executive Office of Communities and Development and the city's Neighborhood Development and Employment Agency of its plans to begin advertising the packages for disposition. The heads of both agencies, Amy Anthony and Paul Grogan, wrote letters in support of an alternative sale to the CDCs. Also at that time, the working committee formally requested that HUD allow the task force to oversee and comment on the disposition process. Simultaneously, Robert Beal, executive vice-president of the Beal Companies, a private real estate development firm, lobbied influential senators and HUD officials in Washington. As a result of these initiatives, coupled with the task force's offer of a viable alternative to the auction, HUD granted a three-month moratorium on the disposition process.[3]

The moratorium allowed time to finalize the proposal for a negotiated sale of the Granite Properties to the CDCs. In this interim period, CEDAC provided technical assistance to conduct architectural and engineering studies, tenant surveys, and preliminary operating and rehabilitation cost estimates. This work formed the basis for submission to HUD a request for a negotiated sale of the Granite Properties to area community development organizations through the Boston Housing Partnership (BHP) (Morris, 1985). With the BHP's demonstration program underway (see Chapter 12), the organization was in a good position to focus on the opportunity to keep the Granite Properties off the speculative market.

On November 2, 1984, HUD received the formal request for a negotiated sale of 1171 units of the Granite Properties to eight Boston CDCs through the BHP. HUD did not respond officially to the request for over nine months. In March 1985, Silvio DeBartolomeis, HUD deputy assistant secretary for multifamily housing management, met with Robert Beal, Marvin Siflinger, executive director of the Massachusetts Housing Finance Agency (MHFA), and the staff of the BHP to discuss the negotiated sale. To some extent this meeting signaled a verbal commitment on HUD's part to enter into discussions.[4] Two months later, something occurred that cast a shadow over hopes for a negotiated sale.

John Mongan, HUD regional administrator, offered the Granite Properties to the Boston Housing Authority (BHA) for $1, contingent on HUD Secretary Pierce's approval. Sale to the BHA would in effect transfer the problem of disposition of the units to a city agency. The city was unable to assume such a large burden. And as one developer, commenting on the deterioration in the properties, said: "The City could end up in housing court fighting itself since it is responsible for code violations" (Jordan, 1985). HUD's central office did not support the BHA plan, and the negotiated sale to the CDCs was back on course. In fact, the uproar created by Mongan's offer to the BHA may have pushed HUD to make its final decision. In August 1985, HUD confirmed in writing its agreement for a negotiated sale of over half the units of the Granite Properties as a Section 8 rental assistance project.[5]

Overall, HUD made several important concessions that directly contradicted stated policies. First, their willingness to participate in negotiation was remarkable in itself. As a HUD spokeman explained: "HUD, as a government body, is required to dispose of these kinds of properties through competitive bidding. We are not in the negotiating business at HUD" (*Boston Globe*, 1985). Second, HUD agreed to provide substantial subsidy and to make repairs.

Among the property not included in the negotiated sale was a 200-unit package excluded because the participating CDCs were unable to purchase them at the time. HUD agreed to coinsure the mortgage on this package, however, with financing provided by the MHFA. The new buyer had to meet MHFA's criteria, which were designed to select the highest *responsive* bid:

1. Ability to provide sound financial management
2. Ability to provide sound physical management
3. Ability to respond to the economic and social needs of the tenants and work with resident organizations
4. Submission of a proposed ownership plan that would be responsive to the needs of the tenants and the project
5. Adequacy of the purchaser's organization, staff, and financial resources to implement the proposed ownership plan
6. Ability to satisfy the disposition requirements, particularly the bidder's experience in planning, overseeing, and implementing repairs and improvements, and a probable temporary relocation program for existing tenants
7. Experience and capabilities in successfully operating inner-city, scattered-site, subsidized rental housing[6]

The MHFA's criteria clearly provided greater security for the tenants and the properties than HUD's usual high-bid auction procedure. Unfortunately, the process still entailed a high-bid process, and it did not guarantee that the best purchaser would be chosen, only that the worst ones would be weeded out. Nevertheless, involving the MHFA brought a new measure of accountability at the local level. Moreover, the MHFA's use of HUD's coinsurance program meant that the MHFA would take an active role in overseeing the rehabilitation and management of the properties. In so doing, more emphasis was placed on management oversight at the local level and HUD was relieved of some of the burden of monitoring the projects.

The story of the Granite Properties ends on a cautiously optimistic note. On the positive side, it demonstrates that through the significant efforts of a well-organized and skillful housing community, such as the one in Boston, HUD could be pushed to bend its usual mode of operation. But despite HUD's initial agreement to the task force's plan, HUD delayed for months giving final approval to the plan, with the first phase of the project not getting under way until September 1988. Disputes over the level of subsidy that HUD would allow persisted, with HUD resisting the approval of payments based on an elevated fair-market rental level. HUD was hesitant about recognizing the costs involved in doing adequate rehabilitation and was reluctant to provide the funding to make the deal work. This final round of delays was consistent with the overall story about HUD's role in dealing with financially distressed properties—a story that reveals HUD's dismal record in protecting the public interest.

With the passage of the Housing and Community Development Act of 1987, HUD is more explicitly directed to safeguard both tenant interests and the viability of the low-income housing stock. Under the leadership of Congressmen Barney Frank and Joseph Kennedy (D-Mass.), Congress passed new provisions that attempt to close the loophole HUD used to bypass provisions of the Housing and Community Development Act of 1978. That law is now extended beyond HUD-owned projects to include projects with mortgages held by HUD that are delinquent, under a workout agreement, or being foreclosed. Further, the 1987 act clarified the overriding intent of the earlier legislation to preserve units so that they will be affordable to low- and moderate-income people. HUD's responsibility to ensure adequate management of units during the disposition period is also underscored. Finally, HUD is directed to provide Section 8 project-based contracts, to the extent that appropriations make this possible, to the new owners of disposed properties for at least fifteen years. All in all, the 1987 legislation provides significant new protections for low- and moderate-income tenants of subsidized developments and attempts to maintain the stock of affordable housing.

Another interesting aspect of the 1987 act is that Congress was apparently so persuaded by the innovative role of the MHFA, particularly in relation to the Granite Properties, that it authorized a new demonstration program, the Multifamily Housing Disposition Partnership. This program gives the selected state housing finance agencies an exclusive option to finance any HUD-disposed properties in their localities, if they so choose, with HUD providing the coinsurance. While the MHFA was named by the House version of the bill as the sole entity participating in this demonstration, the final bill deleted naming MHFA and noted only that four unspecified state housing finance agencies would be selected to participate in the demonstration.

Concluding Note

If HUD adheres to the stipulations of the Housing and Community Development of 1987, we can look forward to a substantially changed scenario concerning distressed properties. Presumably, HUD will no longer be able to subvert the intent of the Housing and Community

Development Act of 1978 and the MMFA, both of which call for the preservation of affordable housing wherever possible.

In addition, we can hope that HUD will allow more negotiated sales to community groups and tenant cooperatives. When this is not feasible, HUD should follow selection criteria such as those promulgaged by the MHFA.

Nevertheless, the case studies presented in this chapter and Chapter 6 provide substantial evidence of the potential for congressional intent to be altered by administrative negligence, incompetence, inaction, or interpretation. In addition, protections offered in the 1987 legislation depend on sufficient levels of funding, which are not guaranteed by the passage of the act itself.

In the words of former HUD Secretary Weaver, "Priority for urban development and housing as well as the image and credibility of HUD reached their nadir with the advent of the Reagan administration and the tenure of Secretary Pierce" (Weaver, 1985). Clearly, in the Reagan administration, the public sector demonstrated negligible responsibility toward protecting the public investment in subsidized housing and the rights of tenants to a decent living environment.

The remaining questions are these: Could a newly organized HUD effectively administer a low-income housing policy? Given HUD's long history, discussed in the previous chapter, and in view of HUD's problematic activities in the recent past, evidenced by this chapter, how likely is it that a new HUD can be created out of the old? Answers to these questions are offered as part of the recommendations outlined in the final chapter of this book.

A THREAT TO LOW-INCOME HOUSING

By Robert A. Jordan
Boston Globe Staff writer

At a time when Boston has a severe shortage of decent low-income housing, the federal government may allow nearly 2000 units it controls to be developed for middle- or high-income use.

The Dept. of Housing and Urban Development (HUD) seized these properties last year from a private owner, Granite Properties Inc., on charges of mismanagement and failure to pay the mortgage. Now HUD, shrinking both fiscally and physically under the Reagan Administration, is having its own management problems with the seized properties. For this reason, and because President Reagan is sharply reducing HUD's role in the housing market, the agency wants to dispose of the units.

But how it is planning to do so, and what the units could become—luxury apartments or condominiums—have aroused the concern of an activist group, the Assn. of Community Organizations for Reform Now (ACORN), and the tenants who live in most of the 1980 units. ACORN has been meeting with HUD officials in Boston to help persuade them to do the right thing. That is, ensure that the units are for low-income families after they are sold.

Ironically, the properties, located in north Dorchester and Roxbury, include nearly 200 buildings, and are mostly occupied by low-income tenants. With the exception of the Boston Housing Authority, this particular group of buildings is considered the largest single development of low-income housing in the city.

Yet, as has been shown, this HUD-subsidized housing can be developed and occupied by middle- or high-income residents. It's called gentrification.

The process that might lead to this has already begun. A HUD spokesman acknowledged this week that the agency has advertised its intention to foreclose on one group of buildings and has begun the process to foreclose on the others.

If this goes through, HUD then will be able to put the buildings out to competitive bid. Despite some HUD regulations which would still

be in effect when the buildings are sold, there is no provision guaranteeing that they remain low income.

While foreclosures are under way on these properties, HUD officials in Washington (the ones who have the final say on such matters) have before them a proposal from Denis Blackett, owner of Housing Innovations Inc., to purchase the units and maintain them as low-income housing. So far, according to ACORN, Blackett's is the only proposal thus far which guarantees moderate- and low-income status for the buildings for 20 years. This is not to say that Blackett must get these properties simply because he is the only one who has such a proposal. If others who make the same guarantee apply soon, they, too, should be considered.

It would be a better course for HUD, and the people affected by its policies, to decide on guidelines other than to sell to the highest bidder. Rather, HUD should sell to the party who expresses, through a sound proposal, the strongest concern for the plight of low-income families in Boston.

Moreover, while HUD begins its foreclosure process, some 200 of the involved units are not only vacant, but in such disrepair that they are not listed as rentable. Local HUD spokesmen said they have a proposal in Washington to rehabilitate about 70 of the units and expect a "favorable response" before Christmas. That, of course, would help.

But given the plight of low-income families in a city where more housing is becoming less affordable, it is like applying a Band-Aid to heal a serious illness that requires a major transfusion of new blood and a firm commitment of long-term care for the needy.

No doubt HUD would be on the right side of the issue if it ensured, very soon, that the properties would be under a new owner who would fix them up, maintain them properly and keep them for low-income residents.

It would be a nice time of the year for HUD to show the kind of spirit that will provide warm homes to residents who too long have been victims of cold-hearted policies.

From the *Boston Globe*, December 2, 1983

"LETTERS TO THE EDITOR"
HUD's Low-Income Housing Policies Illegal

Robert Jordan's recent column ("A threat to low-income housing," Dec. 2) pointed to an increasingly important problem: HUD's practice of disposing of subsidized housing that it owns by selling to the highest bidder and allowing the buildings to be used for market-rate housing. Although Mr. Jordan was correct when he stated that there is no provision *guaranteeing* that the buildings remain low income, there are, in fact, federal laws that are explicit on the subject.

In 1978 Congress enacted legislation which directed HUD to manage and dispose of projects "so that they can remain available to and affordable by low- and moderate-income families" . . . and minimize "the involuntary displacement of tenants." Three years later Congress passed the Multifamily Foreclo-

sure Act which also directed that, wherever possible and practicable, multi-family properties be preserved as low- or moderate-income rental housing.

The fact that federal laws are in place which render HUD's actions illegal makes Mr. Jordan's story all the more compelling. HUD is a public agency with the mandate to promote decent housing for all. Yet, it has adopted policies which are reducing the supply of low cost units.

HUD must be held accountable for its actions and it must be forced to abandon its "strictly business" approach to subsidized housing.

RACHEL G. BRATT
Asst. Professor
Tufts University
Medford

From the *Boston Globe*, December 22, 1983

Author's note: The previous letter made the error of charging HUD with illegally by-passing the Housing and Community Development Act of 1978. As discussed in this chapter, HUD subverted the intent of the act without officially violating it. By not actually taking possession of properties and therefore not having to sell them, the agency was able to avoid compliance with the legislation. Bernard Shriber's response correctly faulted my inaccuracy but attempted to absolve HUD of any wrongdoing. I did, however, manage to get the last word in the debate.

"LETTERS TO THE EDITOR"
HUD rebuts charges

In her letter to the Globe (Dec. 22), Rachel G. Bratt refers to "HUD's practice of disposing of subsidized housing that it owns by selling to the highest bidder and allowing the buildings to be used for market rate housing." The statement is incorrect. HUD follows no such practice and carefully preserves the subsidized status of all housing it sells.

Professor Bratt further charges that "HUD has adopted policies which are reducing the supply of low cost units." I know of no such policies. On the contrary, HUD has been increasing and is continuing to increase the number of low-income families it assists. The figure has grown from 3.2 million at the end of fiscal year '81 to 3.7 million at the end of fiscal year '83. These figures indicate that the number of units inhabited by low-income subsidized tenants is going up, not down.

Further, HUD has no "strictly business" approach to subsidized housing. Its only approach is to fulfill its statutory obligations. Within this constraint, HUD tries to serve as efficiently as possible the needs of low-income tenants.

BERNARD SHRIBER
State Program Coordinator,
U.S. Dept. of Housing
and Urban Development
Boston

From the *Boston Globe*, January 4, 1984

"LETTERS TO THE EDITOR"
HUD doesn't "safeguard" tenants' needs

Bernard Shriber's letter to the Globe (Jan. 4) attempted to absolve HUD's policies concerning the disposition of subsidized multifamily housing.

My view that HUD's procedures do not safeguard the needs of low-income tenants and that they do not protect the housing stock is shared by the Committee on Government Operations, U.S. House of Representatives. A Nov. 1983 report released by this committee is titled: "HUD is not adequately preserving subsidized multifamily housing."

Specifically, the report charged that, "[c]urrent Administration policies are failing to protect the existing stock of subsidized multifamily properties. . . . The Department's new policy of providing only Section 8 Existing Certificates to tenants in buildings acquired by private bidders at foreclosure fails to protect adequately the interests of the tenants involved or to preserve the housing for future use by lower income persons. . . . HUD has not adequately managed its inventory of assigned multifamily mortgages, leading to an increased likelihood that these properties may be lost from the stock of housing serving lower income persons."

From the *Boston Globe*, February 2, 1984

Recently, in Boston, we have witnessed how HUD's disposition procedures operate. In July 1983 HUD announced a foreclosure sale of the West Concord Apartments in the South End. This 74-unit fully occupied subsidized development was advertised to be sold without any low-income use restrictions. HUD had the authority to utilize a different foreclosure procedure that would have required continued low-income occupancy after the sale. However, it chose not to do so.

Unfortunately, this is not an isolated instance of HUD failing to meet the needs of low-income people. For almost two decades HUD and the Federal Housing Administration have been widely criticized for viewing government-assisted housing more as a business than as a means of meeting the shelter needs of the poor.

HUD, like other agencies, must operate within constraints. But its problematic record with regard to low-income people is indefensible.

RACHEL G. BRATT
Asst. Prof.
Medford
Tufts University

Part III

The Past, Present, and Future
of Community-Based Housing

8

An Overview and Assessment of the Community-Based Housing Strategy

PART II made clear that the record of the federal government in subsidizing multifamily housing programs is a mixed one. The key issue to be explored in this part is the potential for community-based housing organizations, with the assistance of public support, to play a significant role in a new low-income housing policy.

By 1978, there were some signs that the federal government was ready to embrace self-help and local initiative as new ingredients in its housing and community development programs. Although citizen participation had been a mandated component of federal programs for decades (see Chapter 2), President Carter's urban policy and the subsequent enactment of the Neighborhood Self-Help Development Act (NSHD) and the Neighborhood Reinvestment Corporation Act, both in 1978, seemed to guarantee a role for grass-root, community-based efforts.

The NSHD program provided $15 million in direct federal grants to neighborhood development organizations during 1979 and 1980. The Neighborhood Reinvestment Corporation Act set up a permanent structure for supporting and funding Neighborhood Housing Services (NHS) rehabilitation programs, as well as other neighborhood revitalization initiatives such as the Apartment Improvement Program. This legislation, as well as the earlier effort of the HUD–Federal Home Loan Bank Board Urban Reinvestment Task Force, were responsible for the growth of NHS programs across the country.

In announcing the first round of funding under NSHD in the spring of 1980, Monsignor Geno C. Baroni, assistant secretary of HUD's now disbanded Office of Neighborhoods, Voluntary Associations and Consumer Protection, emphasized the rationale for supporting locally based initiatives:

> We know these projects will have a major impact on their communities because they were conceived and initiated by the people in the neighborhoods they will serve. These groups are deeply rooted in their neighborhoods and they are uniquely capable of developing projects to meet the needs of their own areas. (HUD, 1980c)

Rhetoric aside, there is evidence that the Carter administration was less enthusiastic about community-based initiatives than it seemed. According to Andrew Mott, vice-president of the Center for Community Change:

> Most of us in Washington felt that the Carter administration's commitment was half-hearted. The Office of Neighborhood Development was set up as a concession to Msgr. Baroni, who was important to Carter politically. It was never a major program and it was always looked at askance by the rest of HUD, including the Secretaries who saw it as Geno's program.[1]

Despite the halfhearted support from the White House, the NSHD program managed to compile a good record, demonstrating the importance of federal funds in directly assisting local development organizations in housing and economic development projects (Mayer, 1984). But instead of signaling the beginning of federal involvement with funding community-based initiatives, however weak the presidential support may have been, in President Reagan's first term the NSHD program was swiftly removed from the federal agenda.

The outlook for community-based housing development organizations was made even bleaker by the phasing out of the deep subsidies provided by the Section 8 New Construction and Substantial Rehabilitation programs during the early 1970s. One ray of hope, however, was provided by the Neighborhood Development Demonstration (NDD) Program, created by the Housing and Urban–Rural Recovery Act of 1983. Unlike the NSHD program, which provided grants of over $100,000 and did not require community groups to match the federal funds, NDD provides grants up to $50,000 with the requirement that matching funds from individuals, businesses, and other private organizations in the neighborhoods are received before disbursement of the federal grant. In addition, NDD includes as eligible activities service delivery and neighborhood improvement projects, whereas NSHD did not. A final difference between the two programs was their overall emphases. The NSHD program focused on improving the capacity of groups to undertake neighborhood revitalization projects, while the NDD program is aimed at increasing the capacity of organizations to raise funds from local private donors and to their becoming more self-sufficient (Pratt Institute Center for Community and Environmental Development, 1988). To date, three rounds of funding—of about $2 million each—have taken place, and a fourth has been authorized by Congress. An evaluation of the first round of funding, which primarily focused on questions concerning the groups' experiences with local fund raising and their progress toward self-sufficiency, concluded that the program was "at least a modest success" (Pratt Institute for Community and Environmental Development, 1988, 208).

Clearly, the NDD program's downward shift in federal funding (compared to the NSHD program), its requirement for matching funds, and its focus on fund-raising capacity are all consistent with the kind of public–private partnership advocated by the Reagan administration—limited on the public side and substantial on the private side. Despite the program's small scale, it did provide some much needed resources and helped keep alive the promise of community-based housing in a financially constrained period.

Over the past twenty-five years, community-based housing initiatives have produced an array of diverse housing programs that are instructive for several reasons: They provide further evidence of the desperate need for decent affordable housing; they offer provocative solutions to complex housing problems; and they underscore the potential for a wider-scale community-based housing strategy.

Overview

Community-based housing programs can be defined as efforts in which members of a local group or a group of tenants join together to produce, rehabilitate, manage, or own housing. With multifamily housing, the central feature is that control and often ownership of the housing is in the hands of individuals who live in the housing or the community. Community-based housing that is rehabilitated or produced for sale, either as single-family homes or as cooperatives, is often (although not always) provided with restrictions attached concerning the amount that the owner's equity is allowed to appreciate (see Chapter 10). These efforts can be distinguished from other forms of community action that have resulted in legislative or regulatory initiatives (e.g., Community Reinvestment Act,[2] local rent control, and condominium conversion ordinances). Community-based housing programs provide housing or services or resources needed for

TABLE 4
COMMUNITY-BASED HOUSING INITIATIVES

Kind of housing	Community/tenant/resident role
Existing subsidized rental housing	Management by residents Conversion to cooperative ownership
Private rental housing	Rehabilitation/sweat equity Management by residents or community group Conversion to cooperative ownership
Homeownership	Sweat equity participation by homeowners Counseling provided by community group Reinvestment funds for financing rehabilitation provided through community group Use of community land trusts
New or rehabilitated subsidized multifamily housing	Development by community group Ownership/management by resident or community group

housing; other initiatives prompted by community action usually depend on other actors to change their mode of operation to make housing more available or affordable.

Community-based housing organizations are generally nonprofit, and their primary orientation is toward low- and moderate-income people in their neighborhoods. Although some community-based housing groups form for-profit subsidiaries, the latter operate as facilitators of the overall goals of the parent, nonprofit organization.

Community-based housing programs usually need considerable funding and technical assistance from outside sources. In this sense, they are not strictly self-help. Self-help efforts that depend on individuals helping themselves or one another in an informal context, such as through home repairs or renovations, are not considered here. Only those activities that are carried out through a formal or semiformal arrangement or organizational framework are examined (see Table 4). Finally, both in view of the outside resources provided to community-based housing initiatives and the absence of the profit motive, the net cost of the housing to renters or owners is virtually guaranteed to be below private market prices. Using the above definition, four broad kinds of community-based housing programs can be identified:

1. Management and ownership of existing subsidized rental housing
2. Rehabilitation and conversion to cooperatives of private rental housing
3. Homeownership and homeownership support programs
4. Development of new or rehabilitated subsidized multifamily housing

Strictly speaking, only the fourth category of community-based housing initiatives is directly relevant to the present study. But because the other programs have played an important role in the community-based housing movement, they are examined in the first three sections of this chapter. The fourth section presents an in-depth view of the historical and contemporary role of nonprofit and community-based groups in rehabilitating and developing new subsidized multifamily housing. The chapter concludes with an overall assessment of the strengths and weaknesses of community-based housing.

The Management and Ownership of Existing Subsidized Rental Housing

Frustrations with some public housing and other publicly subsidized housing developments, as well as the overall shortage of low-cost private housing, have stimulated a handful of tenant groups to undertake the management of their projects. The best-known example of tenant-managed public housing developments is in St. Louis: Tenant Management Corporations (TMCs) oversee the operation of more than 3000 apartments in five family developments. Robert Kolodny (1981a) has written: "An independent evaluation of the mature program has not been made, but there seems little question that the TMCs have mastered traditional real estate management. . . . [The TMCs] have overseen substantial upgrading of the projects, which they inherited in an advanced state of underoccupancy and physical deterioration" (p. 137).

Based on experiences in St. Louis, as well as TMC programs in several other cities, HUD, with the assistance of the Ford Foundation, launched a three-year demonstration of tenant management in 1976 (Struyk, 1980). The results of the national program appear to parallel those reported in St. Louis:

The National Tenant Management demonstration has shown that management by tenants is a feasible alternative to conventional public housing management under certain conditions. In the majority of the demonstration sites, the tenant participants—all long-time residents of low-income public housing, most unemployed, and the majority black and female family heads—mastered in three years the skills necessary to assume management responsibility for the housing developments in which they lived. . . .

The evaluation of tenant management on a series of measured standard performance indicators, such as rent collection and the quality and timeliness of maintenance, shows that the residents were able to manage their developments as well as prior management had and, in so doing, to provide employment for some tenants and increase the overall satisfaction of the general resident population. (Manpower Demonstration Research Corporation, 1981, 239)

Despite the many positive results, the report also indicated that several TMCs were not successful and that the additional costs of tenant management did not appear to be justified. But for most of the localities involved, tenant management was continued even after HUD's supplemental funds were exhausted; operations have continued to improve; and, over the past few years, additional TMCs have been formed (Kolodny, 1986). Robert Kolodny has concluded:

Tenant management is not an unalloyed success, but in surviving and to some extent prospering at most of the sites where it has been introduced, it shows more potential and usefulness than it is generally given credit for. [I]f the objectives . . . of low rent housing . . . include local empowerment, expanded employment opportunities for residents, leadership development, and some progress toward the revitalization of severely depressed residential districts, then tenant management would seem to have substantial if not fully realized possibilities. (1983, 68)

Although tenant management of public housing has yielded some clear benefits, it has generally been viewed as an unusual arrangement. Despite the funding authorized in the Housing and Community Development Act of 1987, tenant management probably will not, at least in the near future, become the dominant management approach in public housing (see Chapter 3).

Another community-based housing program involving subsidized multifamily housing is the conversion of developments to tenant or community ownership. Although the Boston area is rich with examples, innovation was born from necessity. Out of Boston's 14,000 units of multifamily subsidized housing, by 1980 about half were confronting serious financial difficulties, with tenants facing substantial rent increases or displacement (Citizens Housing and Planning Association, 1980). In one such development, in which HUD became the owner following foreclosure, Warren Gardens, tenants assumed control as a cooperative. The process was facilitated by the Citizens Housing and Planning Association, a local nonprofit housing advocacy group, and the availability of Section 8 rental assistance.

How a tenant cooperative is structured has important implications. If it is a limited-equity cooperative, members are guaranteed security and all other rights of homeownership, except that shares are prevented from inflating along with the private real estate market. In this way, housing units are maintained as a permanent resource for low-income households. Without this safeguard, a formerly public resource, subsidized housing, can be lost for future generations of low-income households (see Chapter 10).

There are also examples of HUD's transferring title of foreclosed multifamily developments to community groups, as opposed to tenant groups. Urban Edge, a community-based housing organization located in the Jamaica Plain section of Boston, acquired several HUD-foreclosed buildings and currently operates them as rental housing. And as discussed in Chapter 7, HUD recently disposed of a large package of foreclosed units, about two-thirds of the Granite Properties, to the Boston Housing Partnership, which is overseeing rehabilitation by community-based developers.

Rehabilitation and Conversion to Cooperatives of Private Rental Housing

In recent years, the threat of displacement resulting from neighborhood upgrading and the conversion of rental housing to high-cost condominiums has stimulated tenant and community activism. For example, in Boston, a group of tenants bought their twelve-unit building from a private owner. Sympathetic to tenant fears that purchase of the building by a private investor might force their displacement, the owner agreed to accept a lower price from the tenant group. On purchase, the tenants formed a limited-equity cooperative, the First Fenway Cooperative.

In some locales, community concerns over displacement have stimulated public action aimed at providing direct assistance to tenants. For example, in Washington, D.C., the local Department of Housing and Community Development responded to tenants whose buildings were on the verge of being sold to new investors. Between 1979 and 1983, the District government helped forty-six tenant groups convert their buildings to cooperatives (about four-fifths of which are limited equity) by providing loans and technical assistance. Although a systematic assessment of the program has not been made, one observer has reported that physical conditions have improved and the buildings are safer and cleaner than before (Black, 1984).

Despite an increase in activism surrounding displacement issues, tenants in private rental housing who have organized housing initiatives have usually done so only after the landlord has severely neglected the building and has abandoned most, if not all, management functions. Often, the city has either acquired the property for tax arrears or is in the process of doing so.

It is not surprising that New York City, with the highest number of abandoned buildings in the country, is the site of the most varied and comprehensive approaches for dealing with end-stage problems in the private rental housing stock. While some of New York's programs are now administered through the city, much of the impetus for their creation came from tenant and neighborhood organizations (Hartman et al., 1982).

New York's cooperative conversion programs emerged as a result of severe tenant frustration over buildings abandoned by the private sector and developed as part of the tenants' efforts to salvage their homes. The program emerged "primarily in response to the demands of tenants who had sustained their buildings for a period themselves but who needed the financing to upgrade the buildings and the leverage to gain permanent control of them at nominal cost" (Kolodny, 1981b, 56).

Sumka and Blackburn (1982) have estimated that fewer than fifty buildings had been converted to low-income cooperatives in the entire city. Although a formal evaluation of the program has not been done, Kolodny (1981b) has offered the following summation: "Although many projects apparently failed, others prospered in very unlikely circumstances. [In the coops that are doing well], all the basic indicators of effective management are there: low vacancy rates, limited turnover, long waiting lists, good building maintenance, and general resident satisfaction" (pp. 57–58).

The success of many of these initiatives is particularly noteworthy in view of the lack of any organized system of support for tenants. While "it was not surprising that many could not hold on and sustain what they had started . . . the potential for a large-scale mutual aid strategy represented by these efforts was impressive" (Kolodny, 1986).

In another group of cooperative conversions, *sweat equity*—community people and tenants donating their labor to rehabilitate buildings—has been an important part of the process. Here, the goals of providing housing and tenant ownership opportunities are merged with a potential for job training and employment. Despite the immediate appeal of this approach, sweat equity projects have been difficult to implement. As of 1981, between 500 and 1000 units constituted the entire sweat equity, or urban homesteading, effort (Kolodny, 1986; Sumka and Blackburn, 1982).

In yet another New York City cooperative conversion program, the emphasis is on training tenants to assume management functions. For example, the Tenant Interim Lease Program involves direct management by tenants of city-owned buildings if three-fifths of the residents sign a petition requesting it. After an eleven-month trial period, tenants are offered an opportunity to assume ownership as a cooperative (Kolodny, 1981b). The results have been encouraging: Rent collections have averaged 90 percent (compared to 63 percent for other city-managed properties), and tenant satisfaction has increased. Moreover, buildings in this program require a lower expenditure by the city than buildings managed centrally by city staff (Hurwitz, 1982). As of January 1, 1985, 130 buildings with 3470 units had been sold to tenant cooperatives. An additional 293 buildings were being managed by residents, in the hope that they would be converted to coops (Kolodny, 1986).

Another management-oriented program, the Community Management Program, involves a community group entering into a contract with the city to manage several buildings in its area. Buildings usually have fewer occupied units than in the Tenant Interim Lease Program and are more deteriorated. But the objectives of the two programs are similar: to improve management through a tenant or community-based effort and eventually to enable tenants to obtain ownership as a cooperative. A total of 27 coops, with 485 units, have already been created; another 149 properties are still in the program (Kolodny, 1986).

A nonprofit agency, the Urban Homesteading Assistance Board (UHAB), has been pivotal in sustaining New York's coop conversion programs. Established in 1974, UHAB provides tenants and community groups with technical assistance and support, in addition to acting as an intermediary with the city.

Despite the successes with these programs, problems exist. Tenant- and community-management capacity-building is often a slow, difficult process, and it is not yet known whether long-term tenant or community ownership can be achieved. At the least, however, these programs provide options for low-income people who are desperate for decent housing while enabling community residents and tenants to gain valuable experience in housing management.

The New York programs stimulated a federal demonstration. The "Section 510 demo," which derived its legal authority from 1978 amendments to the 1970 Housing Act, authorized HUD to determine the feasibility of expanding homeownership opportunities in urban areas, giving special attention to multifamily housing. Seven cities were chosen to carry out multifamily housing rehabilitation projects. Under the direct control of the city, private developers and community groups jointly rehabilitated buildings, which were then transferred to cooperative or condominium ownership. Unlike the original model pioneered in New York City, the demonstration did not include sweat equity. Instead, it depended on Section 8 or other subsidies to lower the ultimate costs to tenants.

An evaluation of the "510 demo" concluded that none of the demonstration projects was an unqualified success. Even in the most successful project, low-income cooperative ownership could be achieved only with subsidies for nearly two-thirds of the development costs and long-term Section 8 subsidies for a majority of the tenants (Sumka, 1984). Yet, on balance, the report concluded that

> the 510 demonstrations showed that a developer–community group partnership could be made to work. . . . It also showed that low-income cooperatives can be created to the benefit of the residents of inner-city neighborhoods . . . but that such projects will not bear fruit without the considerable effort and dedication of the program staff (Sumka, 1984).

In a second HUD demonstration, also based on New York City's experiences, six cities were selected to undertake sweat equity rehabilitation programs. Sumka and Blackburn (1982) found that the results of the demonstration were mixed, with only two cities establishing ongoing multifamily homesteading programs. Thus, while it is significant that HUD attempted to replicate locally initiated ideas, the multifamily sweat equity and coop conversion programs were not easily repeated in other areas.

Homeownership Programs

Two major kinds of community-based homeownership and support programs can be identified: small-scale homeownership and counseling programs, and reinvestment funds for financing home-ownership rehabilitation.

Small-scale Homeownership and Counseling Programs

Faced with no homeownership opportunities for lower-income families provided by the federal government until the late 1960s, many community groups organized their own programs. As early as 1945, an Indianapolis settlement house initiated a sweat equity housing construction program that became known as Flanner House Homes. Between 1950 and 1965, 366 families participated in the construction of their homes, with each family's work assessed at be-tween 25 and 30 percent of the total value of the house. Similarly, in 1964, Better Rochester Living offered homeownership opportunities to lower-income families, with rehabilitation work performed by the prospective owners in exchange for their downpayment. Although a total of about 500 families were helped to buy homes, it took a huge amount of administrative and other support services (much of it unpaid) to make these efforts work (Frieden and Newman, 1970).

Partly based on experiences with these early programs, the 1968 Housing Act authorized subsidies for first-time low-income home-owners (Section 235). A host of problems plagued the new program, and thousands of people eventually lost their homes through foreclo-sure. In addition to the problems discussed in Chapter 6, another rea-son for the disappointing outcome was the lack of counseling services for participants in the Section 235 program. Yet, long before prob-lems emerged, drafters of the homeownership program were well aware of the need for counseling. For example, a 1968 report issued by the U.S. House Committee on Banking and Currency offered the following rationale: "Since many of the families who would be as-sisted have had little experience in the proper care of a home and the budgeting of income to meet regular monthly payments on a mort-gage, this section [235] would authorize appropriate counseling . . . to assist these families in meeting their new responsibilities" (p. 10).

Contrary to this recommendation, counseling never became an integral part of the 235 program, and funding for counseling ser-vices was consistently omitted from HUD's budget requests (Bratt, 1976; Committee on Government Operations, 1976). Despite the lack of federal support, scores of voluntary community-based counsel-ing agencies attempted to provide needed services. A few, such as Housing Now in Hartford, Connecticut, provided cash grants to assist with downpayment and closing costs. More often, counseling agen-cies offered no direct financial assistance, concentrating on providing information (HUD, 1975a). Some counseling programs also formed because of the growing default rate in Section 235, and focused on default counseling (HUD, 1975a). Nevertheless, with no significant support from the federal government, as well as other serious problems, the voluntary counseling programs were generally insufficient. As mentioned, thousands of homes were eventually foreclosed, and since the mortgages were insured by the FHA, HUD was faced with the problem of how to dispose of the units.

In response to a landscape of boarded up HUD-owned properties, many community organizations again attempted to develop homeownership opportunities for lower-income residents. For example, Homeowners Rehab, in Cambridge, Massachusetts, and the Worcester Cooperation Council's Home Improvement Program in Worcester, Massachusetts, initiated variations on the earlier sweat equity programs. Similar to their predecessors, these programs have operated on extremely small scales: less than a dozen families a year have been assisted through each agency (Siegenthaler, 1980).

Often it took HUD months, if not years, to dispose of foreclosed properties that were piling up in its inventory at an alarming rate. In Philadelphia, community activists launched the Walk-In Urban Homesteading Program in 1977. The goal was to provide people with homes by reusing some of the 40,000 abandoned buildings, many of them belonging to HUD. HUD's opposition slowly gave way to cooperation. By February 1979, less than two years after a squatting campaign had begun, half of the 200 walk-in homesteaders had obtained legal ownership of their houses by HUD's deeding the properties to them.

Recently, two community-based homeownership initiatives have been receiving national attention. The first is the Community Land Trust (CLT) model. A CLT is a nonprofit corporation whose mission is to hold land for the benefit of a community and individuals within the community. The CLT either purchases land or receives it as a donation. In both cases, the goal is to remove the land from the private speculative market. The CLT accomplishes this by holding title to the land in perpetuity and leasing it to long-term leaseholders who use the land for a purpose consistent with the objectives of the CLT. Leaseholders, although not owners of the land, can own the buildings and other improvements. Similar to limited-equity cooperatives, however, such improvements are restricted from inflating along with the private market (Institute for Community Economics, 1982).

Although housing is only one of the possible uses of CLTs, it is probably the most prevalent. White and Matthei (1987) provide several sketches of housing-oriented CLTs. For example, in 1983 a neighborhood association in Atlanta established the South Atlanta Land Trust (SALT). Faced with disinvestment and a decline in owner occupancy, the group's first project was the acquisition of a vacant house for $5000. After rehabilitating it with the help of Community Development Block Grant funding from the city, the CLT sold the house to a young family on a limited-equity basis. A small number of additional houses have been acquired, rehabilitated, and then sold to low-income families committed to investing in the neighborhood. The role of an outside technical consultant, in this case the Institute for Community Economics, was pivotal both in launching SALT and in providing financing for acquisitions and construction through a revolving loan fund.

The second recent community-based homeownership program, Nehemiah, was started by a coalition of churches in Brooklyn, New York. Based on the success of this effort, Title VI of the Housing and Community Development Act of 1987 authorized a total of $125 million in Nehemiah Housing Opportunity Grants for fiscal years 1988 and 1989; $20 million has been appropriated. Grants will be made to nonprofit organizations that, in turn, will provide loans of no more than $15,000 to each participating lower-income homebuyer. The loans will carry no interest and will not have to be repaid until the property is sold or leased. Although a relatively small initiative, and only modest funding has been made available, it is a good reminder that many housing advocates would like to see the "American dream" of homeownership extended to a broader group of households.

Reinvestment Funds for Financing Rehabilitation

Redlining, or the unwillingness of banks to lend in certain areas of the city, has prompted some of the most widely publicized community-based housing programs. The original Neighborhood Housing Services (NHS) program, which started in a deteriorated, redlined section of Pittsburgh in 1968, was a resident-sponsored reinvestment program. Through the neighborhood's own assessment of its problems, a four-way partnership was forged between the residents, mortgage lenders, the city (which undertook a code-enforcement program and promised much-needed public services), and a foundation that provided a high-risk pool of money for potential borrowers considered ineligible by the banks.

By most accounts, NHS has enjoyed considerable success. Not only has it been credited with stabilizing the original Pittsburgh NHS neighborhood, (Ahlbrandt and Brophy, 1975), but it also has served as a model for about 200 additional NHS programs created with the assistance of the Neighborhood Reinvestment Corporation. But although the NHS concept has wide appeal, it has also been the target of criticism. For example, some of the neighborhoods selected might not have been severely deteriorated and would possibly have been rehabilitated without special assistance; programs are not under the complete control of the community; and the upgrading of NHS neighborhoods may lead to gentrification. Moreover, a bank involved with an NHS may feel justified in neglecting other inner-city areas, feeling that it has already "paid its dues" to low-income housing needs.

In addition to NHS, several locally based mortgage funds have been organized to combat disinvestment. An important example is the Bedford–Stuyvesant Restoration Corporation's mortgage pool, created in 1968. Responding to a lack of mortgage money, Restoration managed to get commitments from eighty financial institutions in New York City to lend $65 million for FHA-insured and VA-guaranteed mortgages for residents of the Bedford–Stuyvesant area of Brooklyn (Bedford–Stuyvesant Restoration Corporation, 1968).

One of the newest and largest reinvestment funds was launched in Chicago in 1984. Using the Community Reinvestment Act as a lever, a coalition of community groups, with the assistance of a nonprofit research and technical assistance agency, the Woodstock Institute, negotiated a $120 million loan commitment from the First Chicago Corporation (Swift and Pogge, 1984).

The preceding overview of community-based housing programs reveals the diversity of approaches adopted by local groups; it highlights the complexity and difficulty of pursuing a community-based housing strategy and underscores a common theme running throughout the examples: Citizens who become involved with community-based housing initiatives usually do so because they lack other viable options for attaining decent, affordable shelter.

The following section broadens the overview of community-based housing initiatives by examining past and present activities of community-based groups involved with housing rehabilitation and development.

New or Rehabilitated Subsidized Multifamily Housing

The current generation of community-based housing development groups has several ancestors: (1) early housing philanthropists; (2) nonprofits of the 1960s; and (3) community-based sponsors in the 1970s, who formed limited partnerships. Although some groups in categories 2 and 3 overlap (i.e., nonprofits also operated in the 1970s), various community-based housing groups have been dominant at different times over the past three decades.

The Early Philanthropists

Long before the formal entry of nonprofits on the housing scene in 1959, some nineteenth-century reformers saw the need to limit the amount of profit earned in housing low-income people. By the turn of the century, a small-scale movement had formed to provide model tenement houses, "philanthropy plus 5%."[3] The goals of the movement were straightforward: to provide decent housing for the poor while yielding a modest profit for investors.

The legacy of the model tenement movement is mixed. On the one hand, its efforts pioneered in providing light and air to interior rooms, an "advance that was in sharp contrast to the tenements being built by speculators" (Meyerson, Terrett, and Wheaton, 1962, 293). On the other hand, some "model" tenements turned into slums that were as bad as any produced by the private market. Moreover, according to Lawrence Veiller, a prominent housing reformer of the period, speculative builders were producing many more buildings, most of which were highly objectionable: "For every 13 people who have been provided with model tenements, 1,000 others have been condemned to live in insanitary ones" (quoted in Friedman, 1968, 86). Catherine Bauer, another key reformer, pointed out that the economics of the model tenement plan were ultimately unworkable. The model builders wanted "to provide good dwellings, on an 'economic' basis, at a price which everyone could pay, and without disturbing or even questioning any part of the current social-economic system"; it was an "impossible job" (quoted in Friedman, 1968, 87). Thus, even at the turn of the century, the goal of producing decent low-cost housing was acknowledged to run counter to the economic realities of the housing market. Housing has always been expensive to build; and, by definition, low-income households often have inadequate resources with which to pay the real cost of shelter.

The First-Generation Developers: The 1960s

From the federal government's major entry into subsidized housing in 1937 until 1959, housing for low-income households was produced and managed through local public housing authorities. But, as discussed in Chapters 2 and 4, in 1959 subsidies were made available to private sponsors of publicly supported housing through Section 202 and later Sections 221(d)(3) and 236. Although only nonprofits were eligible to sponsor Section 202 housing, the subsequent programs permitted and encouraged participation by private, for-profit as well as nonprofit developers.

Nonprofits in the Section 202 Program. Since the Section 202 program represented a major departure from the public housing program, one might have expected substantial debate in Congress concerning the advisability of nonprofit organizations sponsoring low-income housing. Yet the only groups opposed to the program's being limited to nonprofits were, as could be expected, the homebuilding and real estate lobby (see the 1959 statement by the National Association of Homebuilders, Chapter 4). More typical was the following "motherhood-and-apple pie" view, expressed by a congressman from Colorado: The nonprofit is an organization "whose interest is the well-being of the members and the persons whom it serves. . . . There is no desire to profiteer, there is no desire to cheat. There is a desire only to give the maximum service for the money available" (U.S. House of Representatives, 1959, 567).

Why did Congress limit participation in the Section 202 program to nonprofits? There is at least one possible explanation. Since the Section 202 program was modeled after the College Housing Program, and since colleges are nonprofit institutions, restricting the Section 202 program to nonprofits may have been an unquestioned assumption.

Nonprofits contributed significantly to the success of the Section 202 program. Sponsors were generally well-established religious, occupational, and fraternal groups, and they were able to raise considerable funding from their membership. They demonstrated a commitment to the project during the early phases of development and later in overseeing management functions. In addition, members of the nonprofit organization were often useful in defusing opposition to the proposed subsidized housing and formed a ready market for the completed units.

It would be convenient to attribute the positive record of the Section 202 program solely to its nonprofit sponsors, but sponsorship was only one of several important factors. First, the program primarily served white, moderate-income, elderly women—a population that presents few management problems in terms of rent arrearages and property damage. Second, HUD developed a small and highly specialized staff—in both central and regional offices—that dealt exclusively with the Section 202 program. Third, although the regulations have been called "simple, informal and flexible" (HUD, 1979b, 11), HUD staff members were tough when it came to approving sponsors' qualifications and the design, siting, and financial feasibility of the proposed project. For example, sponsors were expected to use their total resources to meet the mortgage and maintenance expenses of the project and were required to deposit 25 percent of the projected first-year operating costs before HUD would disburse the loan proceeds. Fourth, HUD's role in providing technical assistance to the nonprofit sponsors, during both development and management phases, stands in marked contrast to its more typical *laissez-faire* attitude. Fifth, the form of Section 202 financing, a direct loan from the federal government at a 3 percent interest rate, gave HUD the right and responsibility to intervene promptly if a project began to show signs of distress. In view of the high quality of HUD's Section 202 staff, this meant that projects in difficulty received needed attention and support.

In summary, nonprofits operating in the Section 202 program generally enjoyed a good reputation. Although they were only partly responsible for the program's success, they earned well-deserved praise and credibility as competent housing providers. Unfortunately, the experiences of nonprofits in the subsequent subsidized multifamily programs were not nearly as positive.

Nonprofits in Section 221(d)(3) and 236 Programs. By June 1970, nonprofits had sponsored about 28 percent of all units built under the Section 221(d)(3) BMIR and Section 236 programs (Keyes, 1971).[4] But, as discussed in Chapter 4, several major problems surfaced with the design and administration of the Section 221(d)(3) and Section 236 programs that gave them a generally negative reputation. In addition, nonprofit sponsors of housing built under these programs faced four challenges and constraints—inadequate resources, lack of experience, an unsympathetic HUD, and a desire to incorporate social goals and tackle particularly difficult problems—which are discussed in detail below. The net result was that developments sponsored by nonprofits failed at two to four times the rate experienced by their for-profit counterparts (Friedland and MacRae, 1979; GAO, 1978).

1. *Inadequate Resources.* Similar to the Section 202 program, nonprofit sponsors of Section 221(d)(3) and Section 236 housing were eligible to receive mortgages covering 100 percent of the value of the project. In addition to no equity requirements, there also were no asset requirements. According to a report by the GAO (1978), there was a general belief that asset requirements "would discriminate against groups who have a desire to provide low and moderate income housing yet lack a sound financial backing" (p. 95). As a result, many financially ill-equipped nonprofits were able to become sponsors, and according to the GAO, a lack of cash in hard times was probably the major reason for the nonprofits' higher foreclosure rate. Similarly, according to Friedland and MacRae's review of studies on default under the Section 221(d)(3) and 236 programs, since the "rates of financial difficulty are relatively close for nonprofits and limited dividends," the lower foreclosure rate of the latter's projects was probably caused by their ability to "support failing projects with cash from other sources" (1979, p. 33). Although nonprofit sponsors of Section 202 developments were expected to demonstrate considerable financial backing from their organizations, nonprofits operating under these later programs seem to have been on a much weaker financial footing.

In addition to having few, if any, assets of their own, nonprofits could not develop a financial cushion from operating the projects. Since nonprofit projects had no return built into the rents, any increase in operating costs could result in default (GAO, 1978). Another financially constraining aspect of nonprofit ownership is that these sponsors cannot raise funds through syndication, unlike for-profit or limited-dividend developers.

HUD also contributed to the nonprofits' weak financial position because of its lenient policies concerning reserves. In contrast to the Section 202 program, in which sponsors were required to set aside a significant portion of the first-year operating expenses, nonprofits participating in the Section 221(d)(3) and 236 programs were required to have only minimal reserves—a 2 percent contingency account during construction, but no operating reserves unless a project appeared to be in trouble (Plotkin, 1987).

Finally, nonprofits often had to work within a lower construction budget than if the development were being built by a limited-dividend sponsor. According to Clancy et al. (1973):

A limited dividend project with a mortgage of only 90% of the total replacement cost versus 100% for a nonprofit project has a higher maximum allowable construction cost budget than that possible for a nonprofit project, by as much as $1000–$2000 per unit. Therefore, although theoretically, there should be no difference between the construction budget allowed by HUD for a nonprofit project versus a limited dividend project, there is generally this kind of difference where a project requires mortgage financing at or near maximum mortgage limits. (P. 38)

As a result of the potentially lower per unit maximum, nonprofit projects were destined to have fewer amenities and to be inferior in quality than an equivalent limited-dividend development. Also, the need to fit into a tight construction budget probably resulted in the nonprofit's making decisions that saved money in the short run but were costly in the long run (e.g., selecting a cheaper-to-install electrical heating system in favor of a cheaper-to-operate gas or oil system) (Clancy et al., 1973).

2. *Lack of Experience.* Another key factor that contributed to the nonprofits' problems with Section 221(d)(3) and 236 programs was that most groups had only limited experience with housing development. Many well-meaning church, civic, or union groups were involved on a one-time basis and either had no intention of repeating the process or became discouraged and "burned out" after completing an initial project (Clancy et al., 1973; Keyes, 1971).

The lack of experience created a number of problems. For example, some nonprofits viewed the projects as a form of charity and thought that uneconomic rents were permissible and that rent delinquencies could be overlooked (GAO, 1978). Along with this, there was often confusion about the extent of public support and an assumption that government would be prepared to provide additional capital as needed (GAO, 1978).

Inexperience also meant that some nonprofits did not adequately oversee the construction and rehabilitation process, either in terms of monitoring costs or ensuring quality. The result often was defective workmanship and operating cost overruns. To make matters worse, HUD generally sided with the contractor on disputes related to work quality or costs (Boston Redevelopment Authority and Boston Urban Observatory, 1973).

Naiveté on the part of nonprofits provided fertile ground for unscrupulous businessmen. Some groups were used as "fronts" by developers or were lured into the projects by for-profit builders, contractors, or consultants, who often bailed out after they pocketed their fees (HUD, 1972; Keyes, 1971). Of course, there also were many honest consultants. But the maximum consultant's fee allowed by HUD under the Section 236 program was $27,500, a figure too low to guarantee top-quality assistance. According to a 1973 report prepared for HUD by a team of nonprofit consultants, most experienced and competent developers have had little interest in serving as consultants to nonprofit groups because they can make far more money working on for-profit ventures. Although some profit-motivated consultants have been willing to assist nonprofits, they have often viewed these jobs as "on-the-job training" or have placed them in a lower priority than their other work. In other situations, a well-intentioned professional, such as a lawyer or architect, may have become associated with a nonprofit's project at an early stage of development and may have provided technical advice in areas beyond his or her expertise (Clancy et al., 1973).

3. *An Unsupportive* HUD.   In addition to not requiring adequate reserves and often siding with the contractor, HUD's lack of support for nonprofits exacerbated their problems in other ways. In view of the discussions on HUD's performance discussed in Chapters 6 and 7, this should come as no surprise. Most glaring was HUD's poor record concerning the implementation of the Section 106 program.

Enacted as part of the Housing and Urban Development Act of 1968, Section 106 included two programs explicitly aimed at assisting nonprofit groups. Section 106(a) authorized funding for technical assistance for nonprofits; Section 106(b) provided "seed money" loans to nonprofit housing sponsors. Despite the need and potential of these programs, they never played a major role in assisting nonprofits. Particularly important was that HUD never actively sought funding for Section 106(a). According to Keyes (1971), this was in part because HUD assessed the Section 236 program as having sufficient activity and assumed that it did not matter whether units were produced by for-profit or nonprofit developers:

> The federal government views the 236 market as a laissez-faire situation in which it will respond to the competent sponsor—limited dividend or nonprofit. . . . There is every possibility that nonprofits [will be moved] aside in favor of the limited dividends simply because in the market place the limited dividend can move faster than the traditional nonprofit, structured as it is to deal with goals other than production. (P. 173)

In short, HUD assumed a passive role in terms of locating suitable nonprofit sponsors. According to Clancy et al. (1973), HUD probably missed many good opportunities to encourage and support a viable nonprofit group with a good record in the community, but one that had not yet become involved with housing development.

It was not until 1972 that HUD set aside $1 million for the Section 106(a) program. Thirteen grantees, mostly in rural communities, received funds. This money came from a so-called excess $6.7 million generated from the Section 106(b) revolving loan fund (HUD, 1975b). Here, too, HUD's implementation of a program designed specifically to boost the position of nonprofits was weak, although HUD may not deserve all the blame:

> Initially some confusion arose as to whether or not there would be 106(b) money allocated to FHA insuring offices. Directors were told not to build up local expectations. Those expectations were so dampened that even when funds became available there were few takers. Furthermore, there was a feeling on the part of local insuring offices that by loaning 106(b) funds to a potential sponsor, the office was thereby locked into committing 236 dollars to that project. That assumption bred further caution in administering the program. (Keyes, 1971, 174)

HUD's unsupportive attitude toward the Section 106 programs was most clearly revealed by their questioning whether Section 106(b) money was necessary "in addition to . . . private sources of funds . . . [and whether the reasons for Section 106(b) were] sufficient to justify a $150,000 a year program" (HUD, 1975b, 21).

Although HUD's unwillingness to give active support to Section 106 adds another page in the long history of the agency's nonconsumer orientation, it is noteworthy that lawmakers foresaw the need for funding and technical assistance for nonprofit housing sponsors. If Section 106 had been funded and used extensively, two key ingredients of a community-based housing system would have been put in place. As it turned out, technical assistance and funding to cover start-up costs had to be aggressively pursued by nonprofits, rather than easily obtained through federal appropriations. The lack of funding for these programs contributed to the overall impression of a fragmented nonsystem in which nonprofit community-based housing activities were forced to operate. With skimpy financial resources and few outside supports, many nonprofit groups left the housing business after finishing one development. The knowledge that the group acquired was rarely used again and new groups wanting to produce housing had to start at the beginning and "reinvent the wheel."

4. *Incorporating Social Goals and Tackling Hard Problems.* Many of the problems that faced nonprofit developers of Section 221(d)(3) and Section 236 housing can be traced to their wish to make the units as affordable and as large as possible and to build in areas that had the greatest demand for low-income housing. First, nonprofit sponsors used the Rent Supplement and leased-housing programs proportionally more frequently than did for-profit developers, thereby creating more "red tape" and a need to meet the requirements of several programs (Disario, 1969; Keyes, 1971).[5]

Second, a comparison of nonprofit and for-profit developments in Boston revealed that the former had more three-, four-, and five-bedroom apartments than the latter and that the nonprofits' tenants paid lower average rentals (Disario, 1969). This is consistent with a HUD study disclosing that projects built by nonprofit sponsors served needier families than those built by limited-dividend sponsors (HUD, 1975b).[6]

Third, a twenty-four-city evaluation revealed that nonprofit sponsors of Section 221(d)(3) housing were more likely to undertake projects in urban renewal areas than for-profit developers were (Keyes, 1971). In summary, according to Keyes (1971), many community-based sponsors openly confronted the toughest housing issues: central-city rehabilitation, utilization of minority contractors and developers, and involvement of tenants in management decisions.

The social orientation of the nonprofits, and their genuine interest in meeting tenants' needs, won them praise as managers (GAO, 1978). On the down side, however, the nonprofits' greater sensitivity put them "between a rock and a hard place" when they were confronted with rising expenditures and limited incomes. For example, the choice to either reduce maintenance or increase rents was antithetical to the goals of the nonprofit groups. As a community sponsor of subsidized housing who was fifteen months behind in mortgage payments put it: "We had to make a decision; do you let people stay cold or do you pay the mortgage? Who are we to serve, the government or the tenants?" (quoted in Urban Planning Aid, 1973a, 41).

Faced with the choice of providing housing services to tenants or paying debt service to financial institutions, some nonprofits chose to put their limited resources into the developments and allow them to default. This suggests that an important reason behind the higher financial failure rate for the nonprofits was a desire to operate the buildings as well as they could, given the shortage of funds.

Other Early Nonprofit Organizations. Several dozen community groups that focused on a broad economic development agenda had a different history from the other nonprofits. Community development corporations (CDCs) funded through the 1966 Special Impact Amendment to the Economic Opportunity Act and through Title VII of the Community Services Act of 1974 had considerably more resources than the other nonprofits had available to them. Between 1966 and 1980, over $500 million in federal dollars went to CDCs through these two programs (National Center for Economic Alternatives, 1981, 25; see also Abt Associates, 1973).

A community development corporation is a nonprofit organization committed to improving economic conditions, providing affordable housing, delivering social services to a defined geographic area, or all these things. In addition to addressing concrete needs, CDCs attempt to enhance the political position of a local community and to provide opportunities for individual empowerment. CDCs are generally under the control of the community, with a majority of the board consisting of local residents.

Interest in funding local nonprofits increased in the mid-1960s as urban problems began to capture federal attention. According to journalists Neil Peirce and Carol Steinbach (1987):

> The modern CDC movement was launched on the February day in 1966 when Senator Robert F. Kennedy toured the dilapidated streets of Bed-Stuy and planted the seeds for what would become the Bedford-Stuyvesant Restoration Corporation and the beginnings of federal involvement in CDCs. Kennedy was despondent over urban riots, just begun with Watts in 1965. . . . The idea emerged: rather than federal aid alone, rather than simply opening the doors to political participation of the poor, it was time to create new economic bases in troubled communities. (P. 20)

But the "new idea" was already being tested by the Ford Foundation. First, its Grey Areas program, which provided funding directly to local community groups, served as the prototype for the War on Poverty's community action program. Later, Ford became a major funder of CDCs and, along with the Special Impact Program and Title VII, provided millions of dollars to a small group of organizations (see Garn, Tevis, and Snead, 1976).

Many significant achievements of this early group of CDCs have been recorded in terms of jobs created, human services provided, and businesses assisted or developed. However, as discussed in Chapter 11 in the context of the Massachusetts experience, community-based economic development has proven to be very difficult to carry out. And although housing was not the primary focus of most of these organizations, several thousand units were built or rehabilitated (National Center for Economic Alternatives, 1981).

Another group of community-based organizations supported by the old Office of Economic Opportunity, as well as the Model Cities program, were the Housing Development Corporations (HDCs). Forerunners of many of the community-based housing groups that exist today, the early HDCs represented significant initial efforts to institutionalize the technical and financial resources needed to make nonprofit housing development possible (Keyes, 1971). Nevertheless, they probably revealed as much about what was wrong with the way in which community-based housing development was operating as what was right. A major evaluation of HDCs summed up the situation: "They are saddled with goals and objectives that are far beyond their resources to achieve" (quoted in Keyes, 1971, 169).

Writing from the perspective of the period, Michael Stegman (1972, 246) questioned whether nonprofits would "ever contribute significantly to improved living conditions in the inner cities via the housing production route." More optimistically, he suggested that community-based nonprofit organizations "still may become significant producers of new housing for low-income and moderate-income families" (p. 256). According to Stegman, the key to this success was to be found in nonprofits forming joint ventures with for-profit partners.

Limited Partnerships and Other Contemporary Approaches

Starting in the early 1970s, community-based housing sponsors that, up to that time, had been nonprofit groups began to form limited partnerships with for-profit developers. The push for this new form of ownership grew out of the two key problems faced by the early nonprofits: inadequate financial reserves and a lack of technical expertise.

The limited partnership was uniquely suited to address these problems. First, by entering into such an arrangement, the community sponsor could attract the participation of a for-profit developer as a general partner. The for-profit developer's experience, financial backing, and political clout were enormously helpful in negotiating the complexities of the development process. Second, the partnership could enjoy substantial financial benefits through the federal tax system, thereby creating reserves for construction overruns or future maintenance expenses.

Prior to the Tax Reform Act of 1986, and as described in Chapter 5, syndication allowed owners of a housing development to sell shares in the project to wealthy investors (limited partners), who in turn enjoyed significant tax savings. All rental property "depreciates" for tax purposes, and these paper losses could shelter portions of an owner's other income. Since nonprofits have no taxable income that needs sheltering, the depreciation losses that flow from a project are wasted as long as the housing is owned solely by a nonprofit group. If, however, the nonprofit formed a limited partnership, the limited partners could "buy into" the project and then, as partial owners, were entitled to a percentage of the depreciation generated by the project. The buy-in funds were paid to the general partners —the nonprofit group and the for-profit partner, if there was one. The latter saw the money as a key source of profit and motivation for participating in the project; the nonprofit group used the money as a cushion against increased costs, as a way to provide the project with more amenities, or as seed money with which to launch new projects. Whether a community-based housing group chose to develop housing as a nonprofit or through a limited partnership depended on the goals and particular situation facing the group.[7] Although the depreciation rules changed in 1986, community-based groups are still able to form limited partnerships and can raise equity by selling low-income-housing tax credits. However, as mentioned in Chapter 5, this program is scheduled to terminate at the end of 1989 and its demise would further reduce the ability of community-based groups to develop low-income housing.

Not all low-income housing developers have relied on limited partnerships. Jubilee Housing, a community group operating in a gentrifying neighborhood in Washington, D.C., has purchased and rehabilitated multifamily buildings depending primarily on time and money donated by private individuals and foundations. Jubilee currently owns and operates several buildings containing more than 200 units (see Chapter 13).

Mutual Housing Associations provide another approach that has recently emerged in the United States as a way to provide long-term, affordable housing through a community-based association that does not utilize limited partnerships. Section 316(a) of the Housing and Community Development Act of 1980 called for a national demonstration of the Mutual Housing Association concept. Under the leadership of the Neighborhood Reinvestment Corporation, two associations have been formed, the first in Baltimore and the second on New York City's Lower East Side, with a host of others in the planning stages.

The Neighborhood Reinvestment Corporation has developed a model based on the large-scale initiatives in West Germany and Sweden. These Mutual Housing Associations are nonprofit organizations that build, rehabilitate, or convert existing housing, as well as sustain operations at the buildings they own. Membership in the association is restricted to residents of buildings owned by the association, those on a waiting list for such a unit, and representatives of neighborhood organizations, financial institutions, businesses, local government, and others from the religious or local philanthropic communities. A majority of the board members are residents or waiting residents, and development or purchase of the buildings is accomplished through substantial up-front capital grants with as little reliance on debt financing as possible (Neighborhood Reinvestment Corporation, 1985, n.d.). Particularly important is the emphasis by Mutual Housing Associations on resident control and lifetime security of tenure. In addition to the specific association model being promoted by the Neighborhood Reinvestment Corporation, several other cities—Minneapolis, Boston, Detroit, and Madison, Wisconsin —have similar groups called Mutual Housing Associations.

Most modern community-based housing groups are very different from the great majority of the earlier nonprofit housing sponsors. For one thing, the later groups were able to take advantage of a much-improved subsidy program in the form of the Section 8 New Construction and Substantial Rehabilitation program. The financing formula of Section 8 was significantly better than the Section 221(d)(3) and 236 programs, from the developers' point of view, since it took into account increases in operating expenses. HUD pays the difference between a "fair market rental" and 30 percent of a tenant's income. Therefore, financial difficulties and operating shortfalls are virtually guaranteed not to occur as long as the "fair market rental" level set by HUD accurately reflects market conditions. Under the Reagan administration, funding for the Section 8 New Construction and Substantial Rehabilitation program was phased out, causing nonprofits to seek nonfederal sources of funding.

In comparison to their predecessors, the current generation of community-based housing groups also is less likely to quit after one development; they often launch additional housing and social service projects. Many contemporary groups have highly professional staffs that are competent in housing finance, development, and management. These groups also have been the beneficiaries of resources provided by a handful of organizations operating at national, state, and local levels. At the national level, private nonprofit groups (e.g., the Enterprise Foundation, the Local Initiatives Support Corporation, the Neighborhood Reinvestment Corporation, the Center for Community Change, and the National Housing Law Project) have been providing significant technical and financial resources to community-based housing groups. Several cities, notably Boston, New York, Chicago, and Minneapolis, also have at least one public or nonprofit agency to assist community-based housing efforts. And at the state level, agencies to assist the work of nonprofits exist in many states, including New York, Florida, and California. But Massachusetts has pioneered the most comprehensive support system for community-based housing initiatives, to be discussed in Chapter 11.

Precise figures on the accomplishments of the present generation of community-based groups involved with housing rehabilitation and new construction are not available. Several studies done in the early 1980s provided some survey information (Cohen and Kohler, 1983; Marshall, 1981). The most recent attempt to survey the achievements of community-based development organizations was carried out in 1988 by the National Congress for Community Economic Development; it was sponsored jointly with the Community Information Exchange and in cooperation with the Neighborhood Reinvestment Corporation, the Local Initiatives Support Corporation, the Enterprise Foundation, and NCB Development Corporation. The survey's 834 respondents represent about half of the existing development organizations nationwide. Eighty-seven percent were involved with housing development, with 631 groups cumulatively completing nearly 125,000 units, over 90 percent of which are for low-income occupants (National Neighborhood Coalition, 1989). In addition, research carried out by the New School for Social Research, under the direction of Mitchell Sviridoff and Avis Vidal, should provide further quantitative data on the contributions of community-based housing groups.

Although the existing data reveal that community-based housing efforts go only a very small way toward addressing overall low-income housing needs, the current generation of community-based housing developers seems to have real potential for making significant contributions in the future. The next section explores the particular attributes of community-based housing development initiatives in greater detail.

An Assessment of Community-Based Housing Programs

In presenting the following assessment, several caveats must be raised. First, the programs described earlier are only examples. They were selected solely because they constitute a typology of community-based housing initiatives. Second, they neither prove nor disprove the utility of the community-based housing strategy, in absolute terms or in comparison to other housing strategies. To do that, a controlled research design would have to be used, and comparable data for several programs—community-based and not—would have to be gathered. In contrast to such a systematic approach, the research findings for the programs described in the typology were compiled by an assortment of investigators, each of whom collected unique sets of data. In attempting to mold the available data into the criteria used in Chapters 3 and 4, I have found limited information for only three of the criteria. Additional measures, which provide insights into the community-based approach, are used in this chapter.

Despite the defects in the available research, an assessment is still appropriate. The following is offered as a way of provoking interest in the potential of the community-based housing strategy; it attempts to highlight the strengths and weaknesses, but it does not presume that what is known at the present time can be considered definitive.

Ability to Provide Direct Housing Assistance

A key attribute of community-based housing programs is their ability to address specific housing problems directly. For example, residents confronted with a lack of mortgage or rehabilitation money in their neighborhoods initiated reinvestment programs, which specifically addressed their problem. Similarly, tenants dissatisfied with conditions in their subsidized buildings formed their own management corporations, which, again, tackled the problem head-on. In these ways, people have dealt directly with the housing problems facing them, and achievements have been tangible.

Neil Mayer's 1984 landmark study of neighborhood development organizations (NDOs)[8] came to similar conclusions about their ability to achieve results: "Overall, NDOs were markedly successful in carrying out the direct project objectives they established for themselves. By the end of our study, the typical organization had already completed two-thirds of its planned tasks, and many NDOs were still at work" (p. 73).

Interestingly enough, the project area in which NDOs were most successful in meeting goals was housing, specifically rehabilitation; new housing goals were not attained as readily. Further, the benefits of NDO activities were successfully targeted to low- and moderate-income people from the NDO's own communities. According to Mayer (1984):

> What is clear is that NDOs are critical actors in targeting benefits to the people who today directly experience the problems of troubled communities. Given consistent past failures by others to direct development to serve these people . . . that role is of major consequence. . . . The level of performance, given difficult conditions and objectives, certainly seems to call for continued support for NDO work. (Pp. 88, 73)

In addition to providing direct housing assistance, community-based programs seem to deliver good-quality services. Most of the TMCs operate at least on a par with local housing authorities, and the quality of rehabilitated and newly constructed community-based housing is reported to be good or excellent. Although the information on quality is largely anecdotal, it is provocative and suggests the potential inherent in this strategy. For example, Neil Peirce (1983) has enthusiastically described the design of housing built by a leading community-based housing developer in Boston, Inquilinos Boricuas en Acción (IBA) (Puerto Rican Tenants in Action):

> Ascend to the roof of the highrise building for the elderly in Villa Victoria . . . and an astounding view awaits you. Immediately below are the Hispanic Plaza and distinctive pitched roofs, the bright yellow, orange and brown colors of the townhouses of Villa Victoria—proof that a housing project doesn't need to look like one. . . .
> The sense of territoriality is overwhelming when one walks across the central plaza, with its bright Puerto Rican mural, and strolls through the new looped streets.

Despite this glowing vignette and the directness of the approach, the limited scope and small scale of community-based housing programs raises the question whether the strategy could substantially alleviate overall housing problems. Throughout this chapter, outcomes of the programs have been described quantitatively, whenever possible, in order to underscore how much (or how little) housing has been involved. For example, although New York City has the most successful programs for dealing with abandoned multifamily housing, the number of buildings actually renovated or under tenant management or control is small. Similarly, while IBA has been praised for its magnificent housing developments in the South End, the number of units built or rehabilitated is minuscule, particularly when one considers the demand. In 1981, when IBA announced that 190 new rental units were available, literally thousands of people applied for them.[9] Subsidized developments built in the late 1980s have been deluged with applicants. Boston's Tent City, for example, received about forty applications for each available low-rent unit.

Thus, although community-based housing programs have been able to address and alleviate housing problems directly, their ability to perform on anything but a small scale has not been demonstrated. Yet it must be remembered that community-based housing groups have mostly functioned without significant financial and technical resources. On this point, Bill Jones, executive director of the Codman Square Housing Development Corporation in Boston, noted: "There are at least three other opportunities in our neighborhood that we should be working on. These opportunities will be lost if we, or someone else, don't take advantage of them soon. But we just don't have the resources, notwithstanding state and city support."[10] Not until a full-blown support system is in place, would the criticism, "they can't produce enough housing" be valid.

Another criticism of community-based housing development is less easily dismissed. If we depended on community-based groups to produce most, if not all, of the needed low-income housing, there is a real possibility that many neighborhoods that have dire housing problems but lack a strong organizational capacity would be completely left out. This would, in effect, operate as a *de facto* "triage policy" and could present serious problems for low-income households and neighborhoods. This is a key reason why a need remains for publicly produced, owned, and managed housing. The community-based housing strategy cannot and should not be expected to meet the entire low-income housing demand. These recommendations are developed more fully in Chapter 13.

Long-Term Commitment to Housing

In addition to being able to provide decent housing, one of the major attributes of community-based housing developers is their long-term commitment to meeting housing needs. Although not all community-based developers are committed to maintaining affordable housing, preferring instead to allow cooperative or homeowner-ship units to appreciate as would any privately owned unit, these instances seem to be far fewer than the long-term use restrictions imposed by most contemporary nonprofits (see Chapter 10, dilemma 1). Notwithstanding the *potential* for conflict in this area (see Chapter 10, dilemma 5), the commitment of most community-based housing developers is more similar to the long-range commitment of public housing authorities and contrasts with the relatively short-lived involvement of private, for-profit developers of subsidized housing (see Chapter 4).

Enhancing Individual Well-Being

Another important benefit of community-based housing programs is their ability to produce significant psychological benefits for the individuals involved. Although there is very little systematic evidence, community-based housing programs seem to provide participants with increased enjoyment, security, and sense of empowerment in their lives. A resident of one of Jubilee Housing's buildings described her perceptions thus: "How has the building changed since Jubilee took over? Well, I would say it is much better because we work together—we work with Jubilee to get the building in better shape. Now everybody takes their share of the work and we are getting along O.K." (Jubilee Housing, n.d. 13).

Just prior to sending this book to press, I was responsible for carrying out a survey of residents living in a mutual housing development in Baltimore, under contract to the Neighborhood Reinvestment Corporation. The survey, which was conducted by Cosmos Corporation, included thirty-nine of the forty-nine households in the Alameda Place development. It found the following:

> Mutual housing appears to be an important factor in contributing to residents' feelings about improvements in their personal lives . . . 62% of respondents indicated that their home life is better since moving into mutual housing; 69% said that their ability to rely on neighbors when unexpected problems arise is better; and a persuasive 77% reported that their hopes for the future have improved. . . . Two-thirds [of the respondents] indicated that improvements in self esteem (38%) and involvement in the community (28%) represented the biggest changes [in their lives as a result of becoming a part of Mutual Housing]. (Bratt, 1988)

Community-based housing programs can also heighten the political awareness of people as they "fight the system" to institute change and create new programs. During my research, a resident of Alameda

Place who is also an active participant in the association explained her feelings about how her participation had changed her sense of her own empowerment: "Since moving in—I guess I've become more political. I used to vote and that was it. Now I am used to going down to City Hall and asking for what I believe in. I also make speeches now. I never knew I had it in me. It makes me feel like I have more self-worth."[11] Gale Cincotta (1981), chairperson of National Peoples Action, has articulated this view: "The political leaders in this country are bankrupt. The answers, the leadership and the guts to win will come from us . . . no one who is out there organizing throughout this land expects to be rescued. . . . We know that the only way we survive is by helping ourselves."

Launching any kind of housing initiative requires participants to learn a great deal about banking and finance, federal programs, and local codes and regulations. This form of education is certainly related to building the political consciousness needed for a more fundamental agenda for change.

Producing Social Benefits

One of the most important strengths of community-based housing programs is their ability to yield positive impacts not directly related to housing that can improve overall living conditions. For example, in addition to providing good housing, IBA runs programs for the elderly, provides day-care services, and manages a closed-circuit television station for residents of the development. An IBA staff member noted: "It's not just a matter of placing bricks on top of one another to build a house. It's dealing with those who are going to live there—from all aspects. We're not dealing with buildings but people" (quoted in Sculos, 1981).

Similarly, the community relations director of the West Harlem Community Organization observed:

> Aside from community management, we provide lots of other services to tenants . . . we're putting together a manual of services that are so scattered all over the city that some people just don't know they're there—dental and health care at places other than a hospital, for instance. We're now trying to get the merchants to clean up the streets, the sidewalks, the storefronts, and to put up blood pressure mobile and polio vaccination notices, for example. (HUD, 1979a, 46)

Commenting on the expansion of tenant-management corporations into other socially oriented services, Robert Kolodny (1981a) has written:

The problems of housing a population overwhelmingly made up of welfare-dependent, female-headed households confronted the TMC's with the need to rethink their roles as managers. To a far greater extent than most other public housing in the country, the St. Louis projects have developed programs in education; recreation; health, . . . special care for children and the elderly; job training; and direct employment. (P. 137)

Based on observations such as these, Kolodny (1981a) concluded that "housing improvement may not, in itself, be the most significant results of expanded consumer roles in housing production, operation, and ownership" (p. 142).

Community-based housing development programs also have a potential for serving as an anchor in neighborhoods that are going through gentrification. As many urban neighborhoods become increasingly attractive to middle- and upper-income people, thousands of long-time residents lose their homes and businesses. As demand increases for residential and commercial space, landlords often raise rents dramatically, sell their buildings to speculators, or convert to condominiums. The net result for lower-income people is the same: Their neighborhoods outprice them, and they are forced to move. But in neighborhoods where there is community-based housing activity, residents may face a decreased risk of displacement. For example, the IBA in Boston and Jubilee Housing in Washington, D.C., both operate in areas that have become prime "gentrifying" neighborhoods and serve as important stabilizing forces by providing decent low-cost housing to community people. According to Mayer (1984), these are not isolated instances. He found that NDOs were oriented toward ensuring "control over long-term affordability [and] protecting residents against housing cost pressures that market forces might later bring to bear (or in some instances had already generated)" (p. 87).[12]

Once a community-based housing group has gained recognition for competence in housing development or management, it becomes less likely that any major program or plan can be initiated in that area without the knowledge, if not necessarily the approval, of the community group. Therefore, the housing initiative can serve as a "concrete" reminder that the group must be bargained with, considered, and consulted in the planning whenever the city or other entity begins to have designs on that area. In this way, a strong "bottom–up" group can nurture additional community-based projects and at the same time ensure that "top–down" planning or development efforts that do not take their interests into account will face considerable obstacles.

Ease of Implementation

Community-based housing programs are clearly major undertakings and are difficult to carry out. As a result, the community-based strategy has been criticized for being inefficient and slow. Housing, it has been argued, is simply too complex for novices. Groups with no experience and little expertise are pushed into a highly technical arena and often flounder as they are forced to negotiate their way through the complexities of the system. Without the necessary financial resources and technical assistance, community-based housing groups are indeed targets for criticism. Yet, where technical assistance has been available, such as in New York and Boston, community-based groups have launched many successful projects, they have not needed to "reinvent the wheel," and they have demonstrated long-term stability.

Even when funding is available, problems in implementation may still exist. Although one could argue that the limited funds provided by the Neighborhood Self-Help Development Program and the Neighborhood Development Demonstration Program would be insufficient to make a real difference, evaluators of both these programs concluded that the major reasons for a disappointing completion rate were the inexperience of groups in setting realistic targets for project milestones and the normal difficulties associated with all housing development (Mayer, 1984; The Pratt Institute Center for Community and Economic Development, 1988). Clearly, with deeper subsidies and adequate technical assistance for community-based groups, problems in implementation would be much reduced, although given the nature of housing development, they may never completely disappear.

Potential for Replication

Community-based housing programs have served as models to the federal government for national demonstrations. The most significant example of this is the Neighborhood Reinvestment Corporation, which was designed to assist locales in setting up their own Neighborhood Housing Services programs, thereby replicating the original Pittsburgh initiative. Similarly, although on much smaller scales and with somewhat less success, HUD has launched tenant-management demonstrations modeled after the St. Louis TMC, as well as demonstrations based on New York City's multifamily homesteading experiences. This indicates that locally based housing programs are not only able to address the problems of one community but are also likely to provide solutions for similar housing problems in other parts of the country. Although community-based programs *can* be replicated, the "state of the art" in duplicating successful programs is in its infancy. A great deal more needs to be understood about which programs are the best models; how these models can be adapted to other locales; whether the replicated programs, initiated in a top–down manner, can truly be labeled community-based; and the kind of agency or level of government best suited to assist in the replication of community-based housing initiatives.[13]

Ability to Address Root Causes of Housing Problems

Although community-based housing programs may heighten political awareness, critics have charged that they do relatively little toward addressing fundamental causes of housing problems (i.e., housing is built and managed on the private market only when it is profitable to do so, and the cost of shelter is a function of the need for investors to make substantial profits). By and large, they do not attempt to alter institutional relationships or change traditional business patterns within the private housing industry. While it may be a significant step for a financial institution to participate in a special mortgage-loan program launched by a community group, its involvement does not guarantee that it will assist other groups or change its overall lending practices.

Some of the most pointed criticisms of the community-based housing strategy are, in fact, based on this shortcoming. Homefront, New York's Citywide Action Group Against Neighborhood Destruction and for Low-Rent Housing, has been critical of the sweat equity cooperative-conversion programs because of their implicit acceptance of the market system. "To the extent that they [communities] believe they must learn to survive in the market, they do not demand the replacement of an exploitative market by government-provided housing" (quoted in Hartman et al., 1982, 67). According to this view, community-based housing initiatives may divert indigenous community organizations from more fundamental change and legitimate the status quo by making only incremental improvements.

Community-based housing activities also have been criticized for encouraging groups to think and act like for-profit developers. As a general partner in a limited partnership, as a landlord, or as a manager, the community-based sponsor is required to accept the basic operations of the housing and real estate systems. It is somewhat ironic that in order to do community-based housing development,

the nonprofit group usually enters into a for-profit limited partnership (see Schuman, 1986 and Chapter 10, Dilemma 2).

There are at least three responses to these criticisms. First, despite the need for community-based groups to become players in
the market economy, they still are much more likely to undertake
nonmarket projects and behave in a more socially conscious way
than strictly for-profit developers. Neighborhoods that a for-profit
developer would avoid and housing that has been abandoned by the
private market are often the targets of community-based developers.
Moreover, earlier it was discussed how community-based sponsors
have demonstrated their willingness to "break the rules" of the real
estate system by refusing to make mortgage payments rather than
reduce services.

Second, although it is possible that community-based housing
may slow down wider-scale movements for change, it is not easy for
individuals facing serious shelter problems to sit back and do nothing
to meet their immediate needs. You can "demand the replacement
of an exploitative market" all you like, but there is no guarantee
that this will result in a roof over your head. Most community-based
housing programs emerge from deep frustration and desperation, and
are launched only as a last resort.

Third, it is possible that community-based housing initiatives may
actually serve to hasten community demands for more sweeping
change. A successful community-based housing program can be a
very real symbol that socially oriented solutions are feasible. This is,
in fact, one of the key conclusions of the case study presented in the
next chapter.

A final, related criticism of the community-based housing strategy
is that groups unwittingly release the government from its responsibility for providing housing. Thus, proponents of community-based
housing underscore that the "self-help" overtones of this approach
and the actual words "community-based" do not mean that funding from other sources is unnecessary. By definition, lower-income
people require public assistance if they are to attain "a decent home
and suitable living environment for every American family." As
pointed out in Chapter 4, any high-level proclamation in support
of local initiatives is absurd as long as the phrase is equated with
self-funding. Robert Schur (1980) warned how easy it would be for
city officials to lull themselves into believing that simply allowing
people to own and manage tax-foreclosed structures is sufficient and
that, if technical support as well as financial resources are withheld,

sweat equity programs could turn into a form of "lemon socialism." Similarly, Homefront has charged that the most serious problem with the sweat equity cooperative-conversion programs

> is that they place most of the responsibility for housing improvement on individuals and local communities, which have the least resources, and get the government (which has the resources) off the hook. By working through these programs, communities implicitly accept the proposition that tenants must solve their own housing problems. (Quoted in Hartman et al., 1982, 67)

Although community-based housing can be confused with self-help and can encourage federal complacency, this need not be the case. What is needed is for the community-based housing movement to be supported by a public system of financial and technical assistance, such as the one outlined in Chapter 11. In this way, public responsibility for providing decent, affordable housing for all and for mediating problems created by the private housing market would be explicit. This system also would address the criticism that community groups are too slow and must rediscover what others already know. If we create a comprehensive technical assistance network, community groups could obtain the needed information quickly and professionally. Although housing is complex, community groups already have shown that they can master the intricacies of development, finance, and management.

In conclusion, at the present time there is insufficient information on community-based housing programs with which a systematic analysis of costs and benefits can be performed. Moreover, even with more quantitative data, a full assessment would be difficult because so many of the benefits of community-based housing are qualitative in nature. Specifically, the array of nonhousing benefits enjoyed by residents and tenants plus the positive impact on the community are key strengths of the community-based housing strategy that are not quantifiable. Taken together, community-based housing groups present a picture of productivity, increasing capacity, and a willingness to help meet the housing needs of the poor.

9

Community-Based Housing Development at the Local Level: The Challenges Facing South Holyoke, Massachusetts

THOMAS M. HARDEN, co-author

DESPITE obstacles and limited resources, community-based housing programs have shown the capability to grapple with and solve difficult housing problems. Beyond the constraints presented in Chapter 8, community-based housing development organizations face additional external challenges that warrant discussion. In this chapter, we examine how they are caught between several kinds of pressures—economic, social, and political forces that originate outside the local area, as well as problems stemming from the politics of city government. The case study of South Holyoke, Massachusetts, provides a good opportunity to view these multiple processes. In the next chapter, I examine several dilemmas that stem from the internal operations of community-based housing development organizations.

South Holyoke, Massachusetts

South Holyoke is similar to hundreds of neighborhoods in the United States. Its physical structures have deteriorated, unemployment is high, and poverty is chronic and widespread. It is a worn and battered old neighborhood. Its remaining brick tenements, survivors of arson and abandonment, stand between vacant lots, holding their ground against further destruction. Down the street and across the old canals stand the mills that once powered Holyoke, a proud and prosperous industrial city at the turn of the century.

Following World War II, the flight of industry from the old cities of the Northeast had a major impact on Holyoke. Between 1950 and 1964, the city lost thirty-four manufacturing establishments, resulting in a net loss of fourteen firms and 3128 jobs (Metcalf and Eddy, 1972). Capital flight was accompanied by the flight of many residents with skills or specialized training, and Holyoke children sought educations and job opportunities elsewhere. To a large extent, Holyoke was no longer a place of opportunity for the middle class and entrepreneurs. It became another "dying town."

Conditions in South Holyoke reflected the city's economic woes during the 1950s and 1960s. Much of the neighborhood's housing stock became vacant as population declined and jobs disappeared. Not until the late 1960s, however, did serious physical and economic deterioration become visible. By this time, the racial composition of the neighborhood had begun to change. Many Puerto Ricans who had come to the Connecticut River Valley as migrant agricultural workers settled into the inexpensive rental housing. The trickle of immigrants became a steady flow when Puerto Ricans were displaced by urban renewal in Springfield's North End, and when others came directly from Puerto Rico to rejoin their families or seek employment. As the neighborhood took on an increasingly Puerto Rican identity, both private- and public-sector investment in the neighborhood dried up. City policy exacerbated the deteriorating conditions and compounded the formidable difficulties of escaping from poverty.

During the past two decades, sharp conflicts have emerged between the city's dominant interests (seeking industrial development and economic revitalization) and the neighborhood (struggling for survival). Although much of the physical neighborhood has been destroyed, grass-roots efforts to fight displacement have successfully challenged the legitimacy of city policy and have begun to rebuild the neighborhood for those who remain there.

Nueva Esperanza (New Hope), a nonprofit Community Development Corporation (CDC), was formed in the thick of this struggle. Incorporated in 1982, Nueva Esperanza set out to marshal neighborhood, city, state, federal, and private resources for the rebuilding of South Holyoke. With a phoenix as its logo, the organization's fundamental task was to bring "new hope" to neighborhood residents. Bolstered by the Massachusetts government's support for community-based development (see Chapter 11), the CDC has become a credible voice for neighborhood needs and has taken a major role in the reversal of the downward trends.

Nueva Esperanza owns more than 100 rental units in South Holyoke, half of which have been rehabilitated. The CDC also recently completed twelve units of large-family public housing, the first new construction in the neighborhood in two decades. It has established respect and credibility with state and local governments, and with other national and local funding sources. It now operates with a full-time staff of five, and has an active, community-based board of directors. In only a few years, the CDC has indeed succeeded, against considerable odds, in bringing new hope to the neighborhood.

Yet, overall conditions remain substandard. Although the demolition of the neighborhood's structures has stopped, many residents continue to subsist at the economic margins. The statistics describing the neighborhood's population stand in sharp contrast with those of the rest of the city and metropolitan area. Per capita income, based on 1979 data adjusted for inflation, was $4445 in 1985, compared with $9272 for the city and $10,227 for the area.[1] Forty-nine percent of neighborhood households were below the poverty line in 1979. Over half the neighborhood teenagers age sixteen to nineteen were not enrolled in schools or were not high school graduates. Forty-seven percent of families in the neighborhood were headed by single women. The 1980 official unemployment rate for the neighborhood was 21.2 percent (U.S. Bureau of the Census, 1980). As is typical of underdeveloped areas, median age was significantly lower than city and area averages, while average household size was larger. The neighborhood's poor health conditions were reflected in the fact that between 1977 and 1981 Holyoke's infant mortality rate was the highest in the state (Task Force on Prevention of Low Birthweight and Infant Mortality, 1985).

Housing may be the neighborhood's most pressing problem. According to a housing development plan prepared for Nueva Esperanza (Leveille, 1985), the neighborhood needs extensive new construction and rehabilitation to meet its housing needs. Based on an inventory of the existing housing stock and projected need, the plan concluded that in order to maintain a 5 percent vacancy rate, replace substandard units, and accommodate recently displaced tenants, 223 new units would be needed over the following ten years. In addition, because 77 percent of the existing 976 neighborhood housing units were in structures at least forty years old as of 1980, and because of disinvestment in the neighborhood over the past two decades, most of the existing rental stock is in poor-to-average condition. Only a handful of units have been modernized and according to the 1980 census, the majority (64 percent) lack central heating and are heated with antiquated and inefficient room heaters. In short, the neighborhood's housing need is severe and calls for extensive rehabilitation and new construction.

Employment options for South Holyoke residents are scarce. Holyoke has been relatively unsuccessful in attracting plants to replace the old industries that went south. A Wang plant, lured to Holyoke in 1982 with tax-exempt-bond financing, reduced its workforce by more than one-third in 1985 and has not provided the employment opportunities expected. In addition, many South Holyoke residents face language and racial barriers in securing employment. The fact that many working-age women in South Holyoke are also single parents makes employment that much more difficult.

With the unveiling of Holyoke's downtown revitalization plan in 1985, it was clear that the city's official efforts to improve economic conditions arose from a very specific vision of the city's future. Documented in a full-color, twenty-six-page promotional report entitled *Holyoke on Parade: A Program for Downtown Revitalization* (Holyoke Office for Community Development, 1985), the plan emphasized creating a "new image for downtown Holyoke which will be a powerful invitation to people from the surrounding region." It created a picture of a city with an economy built around professional services, offering lucrative downtown retail opportunities because it is an attractive place for people with money to live, work, and shop. This plan represented a reasoned attempt by the city to make the change from its old industrial base to a new high-tech and service-oriented economy, but it did not address the problems of South Holyoke. Instead, it offered the indirect benefits of a stronger local economy and carried the danger that if gentrification spread to South Holyoke, displacement would occur.

The conflict between the neighborhood's and the city's interests was also illustrated when the president of the board of aldermen called for a moratorium on the production of subsidized housing, claiming that the large low-income population associated with Holyoke's public housing and rental subsidies was having a negative impact on downtown Holyoke, the private housing industry, and industrial development. "Because chronic poverty also implies an unskilled labor force," he said, "it deters high-technology industries from settling in Holyoke" (Le Blanc, 1983b).

Thus the city has been caught in a tide of change that has pushed it toward a new high-tech model of economic development that will likely lead to the displacement of its most vulnerable citizens. Are alternatives available? Reviewing the conflict between the city and South Holyoke over the past two decades, it is apparent that *both* are caught up in larger changes and are actors in a larger system; their conflict highlights a larger conflict. How far can the reversal in South Holyoke go? To what extent is the CDC attempting to deal with problems far beyond its ability to control?

To understand the underpinnings of South Holyoke's problems, it is necessary to acknowledge the roles that economic inequality, racial discrimination, and the federal government play in the larger economy. First, the neighborhood's overall condition is integrally related to the capitalist economic system, in which disparities of income and wealth serve key functions. Second, racism and patterns of racial discrimination, deeply rooted in U.S. culture, function to aggravate and legitimize economic inequality. Finally, the structural conflicts facing the federal government have placed South Holyoke, and similar neighborhoods, in a particularly difficult position.

Economic Inequality

Characteristic of the capitalist economic system is an unequal distribution of income and wealth. In the United States in 1980, ranking families according to income, the top 20 percent earned 41.6 percent of total income, while the bottom fifth earned only 5.1 percent (U.S. Bureau of the Census, 1980).

Inequality of income and wealth serves a key function in the economy, although political economists differ as to what that function is. Apologists for inequality explain that the system of unequal rewards serves as a necessary set of incentives to channel the most competent people into the most important and difficult roles and then ensure that they perform these tasks efficiently. Further, it is claimed that this system of rewards operates with the general consent of the population (Best and Connolly, 1976). An alternative explanation, informed by Marxist critique, suggests that inequality principally serves the interests of those who control the economic system, providing greater rates of profit by lowering the cost of labor. It argues that the system of inequality is reinforced by coercion more than by consent. The stability of the system is preserved because competition divides groups that would have to be united in order to change the system. In doing so, it creates an underclass of unemployed and underemployed as both a negative incentive and a way of bidding wages down.

A trend toward greater sectoral inequality and decreasing intersectoral mobility among workers has been documented in a growing body of empirical research (Gordon, 1977). The "dual labor market theory" suggests that changes in the U.S. economy toward greater service-sector concentration have coincided with changes in the labor market, so that the poor are confined to a "secondary market" characterized by low pay, lack of job security and fringe benefits, and little opportunity for advancement. Thus, increasing inequality is now accompanied by shrinking opportunities for low-income individuals to improve their situations in the economy.

Just as inequality among individuals and competing classes functions to provide better returns to capital and to reinforce the system of inequality, so inequality spatially—among neighborhoods, cities, and regions—serves a similar function. Owners of capital are able to use this differentiation to their advantage, bargaining for lower wages and bidding down the capital costs and social costs of investment. As capital shifts in search of better markets, the result is a pattern of "uneven development" wherein the logic of the capitalist system leads to a continually changing economic geography of prosperity and poverty. This effect has received widespread attention in regard to the regional shift of capital from "Snowbelt" to "Sunbelt," and the consequent boom-and-bust areas. But such a broad picture disguises "the vast and intricate mosaic of unevenness" (Walker, 1978) of economic development in the United States. As Walker (1978) points out:

> West Texas' economy is deteriorating in a fashion no less depressing
> than in the Bronx, while midtown Manhattan has an economic
> vitality which belies predictions of the demise of New York City.
> In the Midwest, fast-growing suburbs like Chicago's Schaumburg
> contrast with destitute steel-towns, while in the South, New Orleans
> contains the highest poverty rate of any big city in the country, right
> next to Delta refineries and petrochemical plants which pulse with
> economic vitality. (P. 30)

So, also, the conditions of South Holyoke stand in sharp contrast to neighborhoods "uphill" in Holyoke, to the booming economies nearby in Northampton and downtown Springfield, and to the overall economic resurgence that Massachusetts has been experiencing.

A similar analysis of the pattern of shifting pockets of prosperity and poverty refers to the phenomenon as "regional rotation" (Goodman, 1979). This explanation suggests a system analogous to agricultural management, wherein capital investment stays in an area to harvest profit until the economic surplus is used up. Then it moves elsewhere, allowing the first location to "lie fallow" until wages fall. In this way, firms keep moving to areas where there is the most surplus. As an area prospers, demand for public services increases until high taxes become a disincentive for business, and the cycle repeats itself. Thus the logic of the economic system suggests a strategy of capital mobility, wherein shifting capital from one location to another is necessary to maintain competitive rates of return.

Capital mobility has become increasingly necessary in the postwar era. Larger changes in the economic system have altered the conditions for capital investment in industry. The economic system has become increasingly global in scope as developing countries have emerged from the yoke of colonialism, attempting to participate in industry and trade on their own terms. Concurrently, the surplus generated by the boom postwar years in the U.S. economy provided the capital for foreign investment, which produced short-term profits for U.S. corporations but also provided the seeds of long-term foreign competition. As these seeds have come to fruition and the U.S. economy as a whole has lost much of its competitive edge, owners of capital have sought ways to maintain shrinking profit levels. Thus the globalization of the economy has led to increased competition, which in turn has led to new ways of managing capital.

At the same time, great advances in transportation and communication technology have made capital mobility an increasingly feasible option. As a result, the "fulcrum of bargaining power" between capital and labor has shifted "in favor of capital to an unprecedented degree," giving capital the power to exact concessions from labor, often offered in the form of a "take it or leave it" ultimatum (Bluestone and Harrison, 1982, 15–21). The management of capital, rather than the management of production, has become the key to high rates of return. Given the pressures of worldwide competition and the desire to maintain profit levels, owners of capital have become less and less willing to continue the "social contract" developed with organized labor during the boom years of the 1950s and 1960s, or to underwrite part of the costs of the "social safety net" (Bluestone and Harrison, 1982). Thus, although Holyoke achieved much of its wealth and prosperity through its use of the cheap labor of immigrants in the nineteenth century, it became decreasingly able to compete with the cheap labor of other states and nations in the twentieth century.

Accompanying these changes in capital mobility, new corporate structures have developed to handle more mobile capital. Corporations of unprecedented size and diversity have emerged, replete with their own internally generated sources of capital. Multinational corporations are able to operate with minimal legal or social bonds to any particular location, drawing off the economic surplus and moving on. While the exploitation of the poorest may be no worse at the hands of a multinational corporation than it was at the hands of the Holyoke Water Power Company, the relative consequences for the community as a whole—in terms of long-term stability and the ability of labor to bargain with capital—represent a significant change.

In short, changes in the economic system in the postwar era have served to solidify capital's advantage over labor, securing the benefits of "regional rotation" for capital and further generalizing the pattern of uneven development. Within that pattern, Holyoke now "lies fallow," waiting for new capital to bring new development. As the city's promotional literature indicates, opportunities for investors now exist. But such opportunities have not yet become sufficiently competitive to draw new capital investment for the city's "revitalization."

Yet, were such revitalization to occur, it is questionable how much the residents of South Holyoke would benefit. The ladder of economic opportunity that industrial capitalism offered to some members of the first waves of immigrants may no longer exist for those whose search for new opportunity recently brought them to South Holyoke. This change is only partially explained by economic shifts; racial issues have also contributed.

Racial Inequality

By 1980, Puerto Rican immigrants represented more than half of South Holyoke's population. Puerto Ricans shared similar characteristics with other immigrants who had come to South Holyoke. Like the groups who came before them from Ireland and Canada, the Puerto Ricans came from an agricultural, preindustrial society, many speaking little English and with minimal formal education. The new arrivals brought with them habits and customs that inevitably clashed with the dominant culture. Most were fleeing conditions of widespread and chronic poverty.

Puerto Rico's economy had deteriorated steadily since the island was annexed by the United States in 1898. The pattern of landowning changed after annexation, with U.S. corporations purchasing large tracts of land for sugar production. Displaced farmers relocated on the sugar plantations, but as agriculture became mechanized, the unemployment rate rose sharply. Attempts to bring industry to the island did not yield the jobs and income promised.

> By 1970, 10% of all Puerto Rican families had a yearly income of $250; 35% of all families had a yearly income of less than $2000. 70% of the population was eligible for food stamps, and infant mortality was 45 per thousand (compared with 25 per thousand in the U.S.). By 1970, unemployment was 40% in the urban areas and as high as 95% in the rural areas. (Vega, 1983)

Thus Puerto Ricans came to the United States and to Holyoke as victims of "uneven development." Unlike other immigrant groups who came fleeing economic conditions, however, the door of opportunity was often not open to them.

Several important differences distinguish the experience of Puerto Ricans as immigrants from that of previous groups. The first is racial. Although European immigrant groups usually suffered discrimination for language or religious differences, these barriers to assimilation could eventually be overcome. But racial discrimination has a long history in U.S. culture and represents an oppression that is not easily changed; the disparities created by racial discrimination are long-term and severe. Racial discrimination makes the experience of African, Puerto Rican, and other racial minorities in the United States qualitatively different from that of Europeans.

Second, the Puerto Ricans' arrival coincided with the decline of the economy in the Northeast and the phasing out of many manufacturing jobs that were entry-level positions for other groups. In the late 1800s and early in this century, jobs were plentiful enough to allow all family members to work. For Puerto Ricans in Holyoke over the past several decades, employment has often been difficult to obtain, temporary, and—characteristic of the "secondary labor market"— lacking opportunities for advancement. Whereas earlier immigrant groups were welcomed to the city by industrialists as a source of cheap labor, the Puerto Ricans arrived at a time when capital, not labor, was what the city's economy needed.

Not only have racial discrimination and Holyoke's economic decline been major elements in making the Puerto Rican immigration experience distinct, but they have also been key factors in the relationship between the city and the Puerto Rican community. Although Puerto Rican immigrants have contributed significantly to the city's economy—by renting vacant housing, spending for consumer goods, and drawing state and federal money for education, housing, and other urban development—they are considered by some a drain on the city and an obstacle to the city's economic development. Holyoke's Mayor Proulx commented in 1983, "A healthy town doesn't have too many rich or too many poor and we're getting an imbalance. We've got a high balance of elderly (23%) and a good size minority community (15%). We have lost the middleclass and our challenge is to bring them back" (Hundley, 1983). Holyoke's "revitalization plan, with its strategy of making the city attractive to middle-class professionals as a place to live and work, also reflected this attitude (Holyoke Office for Community Development, 1985). The inclusion of Puerto Ricans in the city's future remains an open question.

Although the city's attempt at massive displacement of Puerto Ricans may have failed, neglect and lack of support for Puerto Rican neighborhoods have helped maintain conditions of severe poverty. Were some economic revitalization to occur and employment to become available to South Holyoke residents, the neighborhood would again be a source of "cheap labor." Lacking that, many neighborhood residents are part of an underclass of displaced, migrant and unemployed citizens, described by Sternlieb and Hughes (1978) as caught in an interminable migration cycle, permanently external to the nation's economic system (1978, 8).

The fact that blacks have traditionally occupied the bottom rung of the ladder in the U.S. economic system further strengthens the link between racial discrimination and structural inequality. National unemployment figures for March 1986 showed that black unemployment was more than twice that of whites—14.6 percent compared to 6.1 percent according to the Washington-based Joint Center for Political Studies (Jordan, 1986). While the rate of unemployment in Massachusetts stands at a low 4 percent, the rate in neighborhoods such as South Holyoke or Boston's predominantly black Roxbury may be as high as 20 percent. As Massachusetts state representative Saundra Graham asked: "Why is there such a high unemployment rate among blacks and Hispanics when the state has a booming economy? Something is wrong. There's no reason for it. It appears that there are those who don't want blacks and Hispanics to participate in the state's great economy" (Jordan, 1986).

In describing the relationship between development and underdevelopment, and the role of black oppression within the system, Marable (1983) has stated that "capitalist development has occurred not in spite of the exclusion of Blacks, but because of the brutal exploitation of Blacks as workers and consumers. Blacks have never been equal partners in the American Social Contract, because the system exists not to develop, but to underdevelop Black people" (p. 2).

Underdevelopment is not simply a lack of development: it is also an active process. It is symptomatic of a deep-seated conflict of interest that plays itself out in the control of urban geography. In South Holyoke, this process has taken the form of displacement, arson, unequal distribution of public resources, redlining, and employment discrimination. The neighborhood response has included protest, advocacy, a lawsuit, and development efforts. South Holyoke not only needs to develop housing, jobs, and services; it also needs ways of intervening in this destructive process of underdevelopment.

The Role of the Federal Government

In addition to economic and racial inequality, important conflicts over the federal government's mode of operation have contributed to the problems facing neighborhoods such as South Holyoke. According to James O'Connor (1973), the conflict has centered on two key functions of government: accumulation and legitimation: "The state must try to maintain or create the conditions in which profitable capital accumulation is possible. However, the state also must try to maintain or create the conditions for social harmony" (p. 6).

Since the Great Depression, government has become increasingly responsible in the public mind for economic events. As the profit rates of big business began to fall in the late 1960s, government came under pressure to reduce its spending for social programs. Increased taxes and higher wages were in direct conflict with sustained profit levels in a slow-growth economy. The Reagan administration's assault on social programs represented a culmination of this trend. Not only was this part of a strategy to maintain falling corporate profit levels in the face of macroeconomic trends; it was also a challenge to the idea that the legitimacy of the system depends on making concessions to social movements and providing a social safety net.

The Reagan administration's success in downscaling the federal role in the public sector's legitimation function has shifted much of the responsibility for social programs to state and local governments.

Some of these governments have moved to fill the gaps left by drastic budget cuts, but their capacity is limited, particularly in areas that face a competitive disadvantage in relation to other localities, and in areas with high concentrations of poverty and unemployment. In addition, the shift to greater state and local government responsibility for social programs has served the interests of the Reagan administration and its supporters, diffusing the direct—and potentially delegitimizing—negative impacts of federal policy and undermining the political power of those most affected. As Piven (1981) states,

> Popular economic demands are thus being deflected from the national
> political arena and channelled into an increasingly competitive
> state and local politics, sparing the national government not only
> the reverberations of current discontent but also the reverberations
> of future discontent generated by the effects on working people of
> ongoing federal policies favorable to business interests. (P. 130)

Thus the regressive trend, which has prevailed through the late 1980s, represents a reversal of federal policy as it developed over the past fifty years and reflects a change in the public's expectations concerning the role of the federal government. State and local governments have been left with the consequences of this shift. Unemployment, homelessness, and urban blight are political and economic problems that demand a response. With little federal money, state and local governments are forced to rely on responses to these problems that are consistent with the logic of private-sector activity. On the local government level, demands for capital accumulation may conflict sharply with social concerns, pushing local governments toward policies that would exclude or displace victims of poverty and unemployment beyond municipal boundaries. State involvement will be limited also, by the same demands for capital accumulation that prompted the federal cutbacks. Only in states with prosperous economies, such as Massachusetts during much of the 1980s, is there likely to be enough surplus to afford the social programs needed to fill the gap left by federal cutbacks.

For neighborhoods facing poverty and unemployment, however, the existence of state programs represents a resource but not necessarily a solution to their problems. The availability of public resources does not mean that they will be used in a particular location of severe need. As has been the case in Holyoke, cities may see public spending for poor people as counterproductive to local capital accumulation, and unskilled labor may be viewed more as a liability than an asset (Schuman, 1986). Further, because subsidized housing and other public assistance may serve to institutionalize the presence of the poor in a neighborhood, cities may perceive the effects of such assistance as an impediment to their development plans.

If neighborhoods are to get what they need, the local government may have to be persuaded to lend its cooperation. For that to occur, local organization and effective advocacy may be necessary in order to create a constituency that can actively seek and obtain available public resources. But even with good organization and effective advocacy, a neighborhood may find its efforts blocked by a blatantly unsupportive local government. Holyoke's policies have been particularly troublesome in three areas: delineating South Holyoke as an industrial area, selectively enforcing building codes, and inaction related to arson.

Industrial Development Plans

For almost two decades, the city has been claiming that it needs South Holyoke's land to attract industrial development back to Holyoke. In 1968, Holyoke approved a master plan that called for the full industrialization of South Holyoke by 1990, phasing out the "aging and dilapidated housing stock" and creating larger sites more compatible with industrial needs. Also included was the phasing out of such public facilities as the neighborhood public school and library (Candeub, Fleissig, and associates, 1968). Although approval of this master plan did not create any zoning changes, condemn residential properties, or reallocate city spending, its effect was to encourage redlining of the neighborhood and initiate a period of dramatic physical and economic decline in South Holyoke. In effect, the plan signaled to the private sector that new residential investment in South Holyoke was no longer advisable. Thus, with more than 4000 people living in South Holyoke, the neighborhood was being told that it was no longer a viable residential area.

Several neighborhood organizations responded promptly to the master plan and succeeded in having an addendum to the plan approved by the city in 1969, preserving, in theory, the neighborhood's right to exist. According to community activist Carlos Vega, however, by the time the addendum was approved, the pattern of private-sector disinvestment was already set. The minority composition of the neighborhood's population increased rapidly as older white residents started to leave in large numbers.[2] Some properties were purchased by speculators seeking to make a profit on future land values under the proposed industrialization. Both new property owners who purchased for speculative reasons and existing landlords who had been watching the winds of change began to allow their properties to deteriorate, "bleeding" buildings for rental income while investing only minimally in maintenance and repairs. In short, the city's announced intention to industrialize South Holyoke, however amended, undermined the diminishing confidence of banks and landlords to invest further in the neighborhood's residential future. The results were not surprising.

Facing a future that was at best uncertain, banks refused to grant mortgages, and the flow of capital dried up. According to a local realtor, "With no money to repair deteriorating housing, landlords cannot attract tenants who can afford rents high enough to finance proper building maintenance. Landlords then abandon buildings, making the problem worse" (Hamilton, 1981). As the effects of disinvestment began to show in building code violations, properties were condemned and demolished. Other buildings were lost to fires.

In contrast to its plans for South Holyoke, Holyoke has shown its clear support of housing development and revitalization in the neighborhood known as the "Flats." Although the projects of the Olde Holyoke Development Corporation (OHDC) in the Flats have displaced large numbers of minority residents and have not produced housing affordable to most neighborhood residents, the city's unambiguous support for the activities of OHDC set a positive tone for private investment in neighborhood properties. A former South Holyoke alderman, comparing the city's commitment to the Flats to South Holyoke in 1982, said that the commitment to South Holyoke

> is not visible, not physical as the commitment the city has towards housing in the Flats. Look at the Flats. What do you see? New construction. Two family houses. New sidewalks and parks. The city was the developer. The city with federal money built homes. That's a commitment. When a landlord sees new construction going up around his building, he has no question of the city's sincerity to rehabilitating the housing in the neighborhood. (Moriarty, 1982)

South Holyoke has never had such a commitment.

Nevertheless, the city's involvement with the deterioration of South Holyoke went well beyond setting the tone for private-sector disinvestment. Through its selective enforcement of the building code and slow response to the problems of arson, the city actively participated in the destruction of South Holyoke.

Selective Enforcement of the Building Code

City officials refute charges that they selectively enforced the building code to clear land and displace tenants in South Holyoke. In the words of Mayor Proulx, "We're not picking on South Holyoke, but the most serious code violations are there" (*Holyoke/Chicopee Morning Union*, 1982). Yet there is evidence that selective enforcement was widespread. In many cases, serious violations were overlooked; in other instances, minor violations were the basis for condemnation and demolition. For example, a Holyoke Codes and Inspection Department official indicated that a round of inspections would "probably lead to minor improvements rather than to inducing landlords to give up property or have it demolished." About a month later, two buildings in South Holyoke were inspected. Although none of the conditions cited was structural, or designated as hazardous, and none required vacating the building for repairs, the inspector recommended demolition of both buildings. A tenants' union formed to oppose the condemnation and attempt to do the needed maintenance, but the group was unable to obtain assistance from any city agency. Less than four months later, the Hampden County Housing Court condemned both buildings, displacing more than forty tenants (U.S. District Court, 1980).

Given the condition of most of the housing stock in and around South Holyoke, the city can arbitrarily use code enforcement to make life very difficult for property owners. As Carlos Vega alleged in a complaint to HUD: "Landlords who do not want to be kept going to housing court for years may decide that it is easier and more profitable to evict their tenants, deed over (or sell) the property to the city, who will demolish the existing structure with CDBG funds."[3] Thus code enforcement can serve as a tool to enable the city to obtain deeds to properties it seeks for redevelopment.

The rash of arson and the negative publicity it brought to Holyoke in the early 1980s served to step up the enforcement of building codes and subsequent demolitions. Following a tragic fire in August 1981, the mayor stated, "We are not tolerating substandard buildings, but will work with landlords to improve their buildings." Proulx explained what the new, get-tough policy could mean: "And this is wild speculation, that 50 to 75 buildings could be boarded up. It could very well force people out of the city" (Laver, 1981). And as far as the city was concerned, this seems to have been the desired outcome.

The Slow Response to Arson

Holyoke's bad reputation as "arson city" seems to have been merited. Although there never has been any evidence that city officials colluded with perpetrators of arson, the city's response to the crime was slow and incomplete until the problem reached embarrassing proportions. Although arson was a serious problem by the mid-1970s, it was not until February 1982 that an Arson Squad was funded to investigate fires. Prior to this, a volunteer squad operated with an annual budget of $500 (Jones, 1981). As late as July 1981, community organizers were struggling to raise private support for an arson education program, but received little cooperation from the city. Earlier in 1981, the city was embroiled in a controversy over Proulx's attempt to cut the Fire Department from 163 to 138 members, and to underfund the arson squad as a way of cutting costs for fiscal year 1982 in the wake of Proposition 2½, Massachusetts's property tax cap initiative. "If you had 100 more firemen at that fire, they still wouldn't have been able to save the buildings," Proulx stated in the *Transcript-Telegram*, referring to a fire on June 27, 1981, that left more than 100 people homeless. In response to a suit brought by the local firefighters union, however, the city eventually received a court order to appropriate additional funds to finance 156 Fire Department positions and fully fund the arson squad.

Between 1976 and August 1981, thirty-one people died in Holyoke fires attributed to arson. The rash of arson peaked on August 24, 1981, when seven people died in a blaze on South Bridge Street (O'Hare, 1984).

The cumulative effect in South Holyoke was that more than half of the 1855 housing units existing in 1970 were destroyed by demolition or fire by 1984, displacing hundreds and pockmarking the neighborhood with vacant lots. The demolition and destruction appear to have stopped for now, but the neighborhood still has the appearance of having been through a war.

Until the arson problem became a source of bad publicity late in 1981, the city exhibited an attitude of tolerance toward the problem, as if the fires were inevitable. The city appeared willing to let South Holyoke burn. For tenants displaced by fire, relocation assistance was difficult to obtain, and attempts to provide emergency shelter for victims were resisted by the city. The burning of South Holyoke served city goals, displacing minority residents and giving the city title to land. It allowed landlords to walk away from slum properties, pocketing the insurance payments.

In its response to arson, as well as in its response to neighborhood deterioration, disinvestment, and housing abandonment, the city's overall tactic was to use its influence to effect conditions for private-sector activity and then allow "market forces" to run their course. As a set of policies toward the neighborhood, this stance closely resembles *triage,* the planned destruction of deteriorated urban areas so that public funds can be concentrated in less-deteriorated areas where marginal benefits are greater. This concept was presented and defended in 1976 by Roger Starr, a former New York City housing and community development administrator:

> If the city is to survive with a smaller population, the population must be encouraged to concentrate itself in the sections that remain alive. . . . The role of the planner is to observe and use [the trend of abandonment] so that public investment will be hoarded for those areas where it will sustain life. Federal housing subsidies can be used to encourage movement away from deteriorating areas. The stretches of empty blocks may then be knocked down, services can be stopped, subway stations closed, and the land left to lie fallow until a change in economic and demographic assumptions makes the land useful once again. (Starr, 1976)

As public policy, triage can involve public actions favoring certain areas as well as actions disfavoring them, or public inaction and neglect.

> The failure to adopt any program to deal with certain issues . . . may result in the writing off of certain areas. The failure to deal with arson for profit, for instance, or to provide for programs addressed to specific problems of new groups of immigrants may have as much effect in contributing to the decline of a geographic area as any policy formally adopted, even though it constitutes nonfeasance rather than misfeasance. (Marcuse et al., 1982)

In Holyoke, when the 1968 master plan was adopted, it appears that South Holyoke was written off. The city's community development resources were directed to the Flats and other areas, and excluded South Holyoke. Negative externalities of market conditions—arson and abandonment—were allowed to exact their toll with little intervention from the city.

Nevertheless, as discussed above, the mayor has consistently refuted charges that the city actively conspired to destroy the neighborhood, pointing instead to market forces as the cause of the destruction. But if the city is responding to market conditions, then to what do market conditions respond? The mayor has suggested that market changes represent a neutral response to physical and economic conditions. He argued in 1983, "The market value of that area is towards industrial and commercial property rather than residential. I honestly think that's the way it's going to go. It's economics" (Le Blanc, 1983a).

There is little doubt that South Holyoke has had a very depressed housing market and that these market conditions have affected the deterioration of the housing stock. But the mayor's position attempts to coat city policy with a neutrality that denies the very critical relationship between the direction of policy and private market conditions. His comments suggest that South Holyoke's deterioration was inevitable and not the result of deliberate policies.

In fact, the history of South Holyoke since 1968 suggests that city policy reinforced and accelerated deteriorating market conditions, which in turn provided demand and justification for further policy measures that adversely affected the neighborhood. Without city support for reversing the trend of deterioration, the private sector is unlikely to invest in the area. As the city's major newspaper editorialized, the mayor's statements carried the weight of a "verbal wrecker's ball":

> Mayor Proulx is no dummy. He knows that his statements have weight in the business and civic community, even though he said in the report that what he says means little on the future of the area. But South Holyoke has been a delicately balanced patchwork of partially renovated and deteriorating buildings, some of which have been a home to some residents for 50 years. What the mayor has signalled is that the business community, too, better get out while the going is good. (*Transcript-Telegram*, 1983)

The policy of triage as part of a strategy for industrial development, although questionable, might be defended as an efficient approach to a set of urban problems. But the city's consistent denial of relocation assistance and lack of planned alternatives for those displaced made this policy not only questionable but also unfair and possibly illegal. In effect, it was a policy of planned displacement. Assaulted by the effects of this policy, the neighborhood undertook to defend its turf.

The Neighborhood Response

In retrospect, no one event stopped the tide of destruction that swept through South Holyoke for more than a decade. But sometime between 1981 and 1984, it stopped. The legitimacy of the city's policy was seriously challenged, both within and outside the city. At the same time, substantive alternatives to the destruction of South Holyoke were proposed. The city's designs to industrialize the neighborhood and displace its residents were at least temporarily halted.

Several events were significant in changing the city's policy toward South Holyoke: the series of protest marches that followed the fires of summer 1981; legal action against the city for its practice of discrimination; and the formation of Nueva Esperanza and its subsequent conflict with the city over the demolition of "St. Martha's." As Nueva Esperanza established credibility and developed a working relationship with the state's community development agencies, an alternative vision for South Holyoke emerged.

It is important to note that the vision that has arisen from Nueva Esperanza's activity is rooted in the grass-roots activity and resistance that started in South Holyoke in the mid-1960s. The successes of the 1980s were built on years of organizing and struggle. Numerous organizations emerged during this time to fight displacement and discrimination, to affirm ethnic identity, and to give voice to neighborhood concerns. Most were short-lived; a few provided an ongoing presence in the neighborhood and played a major role in raising public consciousness about arson. Several organizations attempted to undertake housing development, but were unsuccessful. Nevertheless, all these efforts added to the neighborhood's collective experience, which provided the foundation for the neighborhood response in the 1980s.

The Fires in 1981

The fatal fire in August 1981 brought South Holyoke into direct confrontation with the city. Not only did it draw national attention to Holyoke and raise questions about the sincerity of the city's response to arson, it also mobilized Holyoke's Hispanic community. A series of marches to City Hall presented the mayor with neighborhood demands, such as the need for public arson investigations; the appointment of Spanish-speaking firefighters; fines or imprisonment for landlords violating fire, health, and building codes; an end to arbitrary demolitions; a commitment to affirmative action; and a fair housing plan. The mayor's response to these demands was not sympathetic: "We don't have to apologize to the Massachusetts Commission Against Discrimination. We don't have to apologize to the Hispanics. . . . They want the demolitions to stop. Who orders demolitions? Who do they think I am, God?" (*Holyoke/Chicopee Morning Union*, 1981). After the fatal fire, however, with its negative publicity and subsequent protests, the city's response to arson improved dramatically. Activity also began on other fronts.

Legal Actions

In December 1981, eight Puerto Rican residents of South Holyoke and adjacent neighborhoods filed a class-action suit against city, state, and federal officials alleging that they had been discriminated against through "systematic, official actions intended to force Hispanic and other minority residents from the city." "At no time," the complaint charged, "have Holyoke officials attempted to find less discriminatory alternatives." The lawsuit also charged the city with procedural violations for its allegedly illegal use of CDBG funds for the demolition of properties in and around South Holyoke from 1974 through 1981; its failure to have a relocation plan or provide relocation benefits for those displaced by federal highway construction, federal or state urban renewal programs, or city-ordered demolition. In addition, the city was charged with failure to "affirmatively act to remedy past discriminatory practices, and failure to affirmatively further fair housing opportunities." HUD was charged with breach of its "statutory responsibilities to adequately monitor and require compliance with federal Civil Rights statutes, anti-discrimination and anti-displacement provisions of the Housing and Community Development Act of 1974" (U.S. District Court, 1981).

As expected, the suit drew an angry response from the city. The mayor stated, "It's a nonsense suit that has no merit" (*Holyoke/Chicopee Morning Union*, 1982). But because the suit presented a coherent picture of the discriminatory impact of city policy and provided extensive documentation of city violations, the case put the city on the defensive. Although the suit may not be resolved before the end of the present decade, it has served to challenge the legitimacy of the Proulx administration's policies toward the South Holyoke area.

A second legal challenge occurred regarding city compliance with state guidelines for a fair housing plan. In order to qualify for state grants, the city is required to have a fair housing plan approved by the Massachusetts Commission Against Discrimination (MCAD). By

1983, MCAD had rejected two draft plans submitted to it by Holyoke, charging that the city failed to either describe the problem or define a solution. Nueva Esperanza added its voice to the criticism of the proposed plan: "The spirit of the plan is based on voluntary compliance. No enforcement measures are recommended. The action plan is not based on measureable objectives. Measurement of performance will be impossible."[4]

The city's plan was rejected again in 1984, but finally accepted in 1985. Although this process did not bring about major changes in city policies, it forced further public examination of their fairness.

"St. Martha's"

Perhaps the most serious challenge to the legitimacy of the city's housing policy occurred in February 1984 when the city clandestinely demolished "St. Martha's," a twenty-eight-unit, tax-delinquent apartment building that Nueva Esperanza had undertaken to rehabilitate. Nueva Esperanza, still in its first year of operation, had reached a preliminary agreement with the Massachusetts Government Land Bank to finance the project when a wrecker showed up one evening at the mayor's request. Before the organization could obtain a restraining order from the court the following morning, the contractor had taken several whacks at the building, damaging it beyond repair. The incident sparked widespread outrage. In the neighborhood, protest rallies were held at the site. City and neighborhood support was mobilized for Nueva Esperanza with the "Mayor Blasted for Ordering [the] Demolition" (Moriarty, 1984). The *Transcript-Telegram* referred to the demolition as "a lack of courtesy" and editorialized that the mayor should take "the uncharacteristic step [of] eating some distasteful, but humble pie" (Le Blanc, 1984).

An Uneasy Détente

Since the St. Martha's incident, Nueva Esperanza has continued its development activity, providing ongoing advocacy for the neighborhood. As the agency has gained credibility and respect in its dealings with state agencies, it has forced on the city an additional layer of accountability. The state has made it clear that it expects the city to work with Nueva Esperanza if Holyoke is to receive other state aid. The city has responded with a moderate level of cooperation, providing $80,000 of CDBG funds in 1985, $30,000 in 1986, and $115,000 in 1987. Further, the city worked with Nueva Esperanza in the development of twelve large-family, Chapter 705 state-funded public housing units. Thus, Nueva Esperanza's presence in South Holyoke has provided the state's community development agencies with a recognizable constituency in the neighborhood. In this way, the CDC's existence has given the state the leverage with which to exert its political muscle to force the city to assist with the housing needs of South Holyoke.

Nevertheless, there are indications that deeper changes in the city are also influencing "détente" between City Hall and South Holyoke. As happened earlier in the city's history with European immigrants, Hispanic immigrants are slowly gaining acceptance as equal citizens of Holyoke. The desegregation of Holyoke public schools by court order in 1981 was a major step in bridging the gap between different languages and cultures and undermining racist attitudes. In 1985, a Puerto Rican woman was elected to the school board, the first Hispanic to hold an elected office in Holyoke. In addition, economic interdependence between the Hispanic community and the city has become increasingly apparent as the city has come to rely on federal and state aid packages available to it because of its sizable minority population; for many professional and business people in Holyoke, Hispanics are a significant part of their clientele. Still, it would be a mistake to assume that changes in the last five years indicate that the conflicts between South Holyoke and City Hall have been resolved.

At the end of almost two decades of conflict, half the neighborhood's structures and much of its population remain. In the process, the neighborhood has gained political power and a sense of identity. But the interests that dominate Holyoke have neither changed significantly nor has the city substantially amended the goals of its economic revitalization strategy to benefit minority and low-income residents.

Although the city may no longer be able to authorize policies that have a clear discriminatory impact, there is no indication that it would intervene to prevent market changes and other public- or private-sector initiatives that would have an adverse impact on the community. For example, in 1986 the city supported the development of the Holyoke Energy Recovery Company (HERCO), a trash-burning plant on the edge of South Holyoke. The plant would bring revenues to the city, but would negatively affect the environmental quality of South Holyoke with increased truck traffic, potential pest problems, and the risk of spills, unregulated emissions, or other malfunctions. In addition, HERCO would detract from the neighborhood's ability to draw public or private investment to its residential properties. The HERCO proposal serves as a reminder to the neighborhood that the struggle for its residential future is not over.

Still another incident reveals the continuing conflict between City Hall's revitalization plans and the needs of low-income and minority residents. In March 1986, a controversy arose when the board of aldermen voted to take a downtown site by eminent domain in order to prevent the Valley Housing Development Corporation, another local nonprofit, from building eighteen units of family housing for farmworkers who work in the Connecticut River Valley. The mayor stated, "It isn't healthy for a community that is trying to revitalize its downtown to add subsidized housing to the area if it can be avoided" (Maeroff, 1986). Nevertheless, he refused to appropriate the funds required to purchase the property after taking it by eminent domain, claiming that it would "be considered a sham, designed to deny the property owners their civil rights" (Maeroff, 1986), and fearing that such action would have jeopardized the state and federal grants that Holyoke was seeking. Other than the board of aldermen's thwarted attempt to stop the project, there was no other official action to intervene, and the housing project has been completed.

One local observer explained the city's reluctance to fight the project. Although subsidized housing in the downtown area conflicted with the city's downtown revitalization plan, city officials were even more wary of presenting an image to potential outside investors of a city embroiled in racial conflict. Such an image could be the kiss of death to revitalization plans.

Based on events over the past several years, it seems that the city has a much narrower range of options available to it for displacing minorities than it did formerly. In order to attract public or private investment, it must be on good behavior and avoid at least the appearance of discriminatory policy. To some extent, the grass-roots effort that forced this increased accountability can now be used as a tool to get additional city resources for neighborhood needs.

Thus, some things may have changed. But the city's response to the farmworkers' project sounds a familiar theme, one that city officials have repeatedly used to justify policies toward South Holyoke over the past two decades. The city maintains that economic revitalization is threatened by the presence of minorities and low-income people. With a large minority population, the argument goes, the new high-tech industries and the more affluent population that would gentrify Holyoke will not be coming.

The city's assumption of conflict between economic development and minority presence deserves to be questioned. Its racist and discriminatory implications have had a severe impact on Holyoke's minority communities in the past. But while the effects of this assumption are clear, there is no conclusive disproof of the assumption's validity. The city may well be right in its assessment that with a large minority population, it will be more difficult to attract the new capital necessary to restart the wheels of prosperity in this latest high-tech era. As discussed earlier in this chapter, conditions of underdevelopment and economic blight, and the presence of a racially distinguished underclass, have been part of the pattern of capitalist development.

There is a tendency for critics of the city to view the conflict between neighborhood interests and those of the city as the product of the malfeasance of individual politicians. But evidence suggests that much of the conflict is rooted in the structure of the economy and the institutional racism that pervades the system in which the city must make its economic choices. The city has been forced to choose between "revitalization" and housing low-income minorities as a choice between development and continued decline, a no-win dilemma.

This dilemma raises questions about state development policies as they affect Holyoke. If the development of high-tech industry and accompanying service-sector growth are at the center of the state's economic development strategy, then how does the state reconcile its efforts to support low-income housing development with its attempts to create an attractive business climate for high-tech industry? If the president of the board of aldermen was right when he argued that a large minority population would keep high-tech companies from coming to Holyoke, then the state's strong stance in opposition to city displacement policies and its support of low-income housing development through Nueva Esperanza will serve to keep Holyoke deindustrialized. Without new industry in an economically depressed city such as Holyoke, what hope is there for economic development for the people of a neighborhood such as South Holyoke?

As discussed earlier, the public sector at city, state, and federal levels assumes a critical role in mediating the impacts of the larger economic system on the local economy. Public-sector influence can redirect the flow of capital into and out of specific economic sectors. Direct subsidies can determine the feasibility of a wide range of potentially beneficial economic activities. In addition, neighborhood challenges to the legitimacy of forces that threaten hardship and dislocation can bring about state intervention to forestall or prevent those impacts. As in South Holyoke, however, such intervention does not necessarily resolve the underlying conflict.

The story of the conflict between the South Holyoke neighborhoods and City Hall also reveals the importance of grass-roots mobilization and the key role played by the community-based organization in eliciting public-sector attention and support. Against considerable odds, the neighborhood was able to resist concerted efforts aimed at its destruction. But, having averted destruction and widespread displacement, Nueva Esperanza faces a conflict-ridden challenge: how to improve the economic conditions of the neighborhood through community-based development activities in a political and economic climate that is largely adverse, if not hostile, to such efforts. Beyond survival, what can Nueva Esperanza achieve for South Holyoke, given the forces that shape current conditions and opportunities?

Given the degree to which neighborhood poverty stems from broad economic trends and changes in federal policy, are efforts to address the problem at a local level really treating only the symptoms? What can community-based development achieve in the face of conditions such as those in South Holyoke without major structural changes in the economy and policy changes at the federal government level?

Based on the experience of Nueva Esperanza in South Holyoke, we conclude that addressing poverty at the local level can be a way of responding effectively to real, immediate needs in the short term and raising the larger long-term issues. Until the economic trends and other larger issues have an impact on specific local communities, they are only abstractions. When they result in displacement and unemployment in specific communities, then public- and private-sector actions can be challenged and alternative programs advanced. Thus local action represents not only a logical place to begin but also a long-term strategy for challenging the framework of the economic system.

10

Dilemmas of Community-Based Housing Development

■ CASE STUDIES

Two Community Development Corporations

ERIC BOVE, PHILLIP BROWN, PETER HOLLANDS, SARAH SNOW, and JOHN THOMA, case studies co-authors

CHAPTER 9 examined a series of economic, social, and political pressures on CDCs through a case study of South Holyoke, Massachusetts. This chapter discusses six dilemmas that all CDCs involved in housing development encounter. The sixth dilemma—the extent to which community-based organizations should market their units to local residents versus the need to provide housing on an open-occupancy basis—is explored in greater detail in case studies of two CDCs that confronted the issue.

Dilemma 1: Private Ownership and Accumulation versus Social Control and Access

Some community-based housing programs involve transferring ownership to residents as cooperative housing or assisting individuals to purchase or rehabilitate their own houses. Much of what is generally thought of as "community-based housing," however, focuses on multifamily housing and depends on long-term ownership and management by a community-based organization. In advocating for community-based housing, we are therefore implicitly supporting a collective approach, rather than one that advances private ownership and accumulation.

In this country, homeownership has been called the American dream. It is no accident that at two key points in recent history— during the economic upheavals of the 1930s and the urban riots of the 1960s—homeownership was used as a vehicle to subdue unrest. First by providing mortgage insurance to lenders through the FHA and later by offering the poor opportunities to become homeowners through the Section 235 program, the government has supported the homeownership ideal (see Chapter 6). In addition, the homeowners' deduction—the homeowning taxpayer's right to deduct from income the interest portion of mortgage payments as well as the total amount of property taxes paid when calculating tax liability—is a critical way in which the government actively reinforces the dream and reality of homeownership (see Chapter 3). Whether these initiatives have created a zeal for homeownership, thereby shaping consumer demand, or whether they simply have responded to deep-seated aspirations "to own a place of one's own," may be debatable. But particularly in the absence of competitive options to ownership, most people in the United States—two-thirds of all households—choose to own their own homes, and many of those who do not state that ownership is a dearly held goal (Tremblay and Dillman, 1983). In view of this, a policy that supports community-based ownership in favor of individual ownership would seem to be severely out of step with the preferences of most individuals. Thus the first part of this dilemma questions the grounds, if any, for advocating a community-based housing strategy instead of a homeownership approach?

First, a comprehensive policy to assist low-income households could include a homeownership component as well as other options. Proposing a community-based strategy does not mean that other alternatives should not be pursued. Public policy ought to supply alternatives that reflect the range of consumer needs and choices. For some households, whether low or moderate income, homeownership is simply not the optimal tenure. Whether because the household has no interest in home maintenance, because the desire to live in a certain location may be short-lived, or because income is so limited or unpredictable that even subsidized homeownership may be too costly, rental units are still a necessary option for many people. In addition, to the extent that homeownership is most often associated with one- to four-family houses, as opposed to cooperatives or condominiums, a physically handicapped or elderly individual may find owning a house an unwanted burden.

Second, community-based housing actually appears to offer some of the most important attributes of individual ownership, such as the feeling of control over one's immediate environment and a sense of security. For example, a community-based development can include tenants in management decisions, such as budgeting issues and determining repair and improvement priorities, and can foster a sense of shared ownership. Reporting on the feelings of tenants who live in housing built by a community-based organization in Boston, one observer noted that "because of the large role the tenants had in designing it, and because, as members of Inquilinos Boricuas en Accion [a community-based organization], they own it, there is the pride of homeownership, of keeping it attractive" (Rivas, 1982).

Although a tenant in a community-based development could face a loss of security through eviction, the reasons for this happening are likely to be limited to nonpayment of rent or extreme disruptiveness. In contrast, tenants in for-profit developments also may be evicted or have to leave if large rent increases are charged or if the building is converted to high-priced cooperatives and condominiums. Thus, although a sense of empowerment and security may be greater in a house of one's own, community-based housing does appear to offer these advantages, at least to some extent (see Chapter 8).

Third, community-based housing, in which tenants have more control than in a traditional rental situation, may provide a good opportunity to develop some of the skills in property management and budgeting that would be useful if the household assumes homeownership at some later time.

Although most housing produced by community-based housing groups is multifamily, many organizations have developed units for sale. The second aspect of the dilemma of private ownership and accumulation versus social control and access relates to the desirability of placing limitations on the amount the housing can appreciate. If the housing is owner occupied, as in a cooperative or traditional one-family house, is it appropriate to limit the return on the household's equity to some fixed standard, but in any event below what would be obtained if the unit were sold privately and not bound by any restrictions?

Arguing that it is unfair to a low- or moderate-income household that has bought a unit in which equity appreciation is limited, one could question why this household should be prohibited from enjoy-ing an inflationary housing market, while more affluent cooperators or homeowners are not? Is it fair to advocate a policy that puts a ceiling on the monetary benefits an individual can derive from hous-ing when such benefits are commonplace in the rest of the housing system?

In response, on the assumption that public subsidies were used to develop, rehabilitate, or reduce the purchase price or operating costs of the housing, it seems rational that the appreciation should not be exclusively the property of the occupant. Assuming that lower-cost housing will be needed by future households, then it would be unconscionable, as a public policy, to allow units supported with a public subsidy to disappear as a public resource. Yet advocates of equity appreciation would counter that the public subsidy should be repaid first and that any additional increase in value should be enjoyed by the individual household. Although this would be equi-table in terms of public expenditures, it would still not capture those units for future low-income households. The point of a just housing policy is not to give a windfall to households that are lucky enough to obtain a low-cost unit but to develop a stock of decent, affordable housing that can be enjoyed by present, as well as future, generations of needy households.

Both aspects of this dilemma, private ownership versus social control and private accumulation versus social access, encompass two sets of provocative arguments. Advocating a community-based housing strategy implies a willingness to accept the strong social-purpose objectives inherent in the community-based approach. But to the extent that these may clash with private goals or preferences, the dilemma is likely to be debated over and over again.

Dilemma 2: Ability to Maintain Community and Tenant Orientation versus Need to Be a Developer and Landlord

It is widely accepted that the goals of for-profit landlords in pro-ducing, owning, and managing housing differ from those of tenants. For the owner, there is a desire to reduce costs as much as possible, even if maintenance and repairs are sometimes compromised, while keeping rents as high as the market will bear. Clearly, for tenants, the reverse is true. To what extent are community-based developers and owners in the identical position as their for-profit counterparts? They, too, must be concerned with the "bottom line" and must make sure that their costs can be met by rental income. Moreover, whether as a general partner in a limited partnership, as a landlord, or as a manager, the community-based sponsor is required to accept the basic operations of the housing finance and real estate system. As mentioned in Chapter 8, it is somewhat ironic that most community-based housing has been developed by the nonprofit group entering into a for-profit limited partnership.

While there is a great deal of truth to these observations, Chapter 8 made clear that, despite the need for community-based groups to become players in the market economy, they still are much more likely to undertake nonmarket projects and behave in more socially conscious ways than strictly for-profit developers. In terms of targeting housing to low-income people, charging low rentals, being willing to undertake projects in neighborhoods that for-profit developers would avoid, and making the provision of decent housing their top priority, community-based and nonprofit developers have traditionally been much more concerned with social issues than those operating for profit.

Although a nonprofit community-based group may be more likely to assume positions that are protenant more frequently than for-profit owners, it is also clear that certain built-in conflicts between tenant and landlord are likely to persist no matter who the owner happens to be. As long as community-based organizations stay in close contact with their tenants, these conflicts are likely to be minimal. But if the community-based group loses touch with its constituency, the pressure to act like a "regular" landlord could become problematic for tenants. Whether or not community-based groups will be able to stay in tune with resident needs while still operating in a fiscally responsible manner will only become clear over time.

Dilemma 3: Advocacy versus Project Development

Many community-based development groups were originally organized around advocacy issues such as rent control, anti-arson, mortgage disinvestment, tenants rights, and displacement caused by urban renewal. After years of protest and fighting both City Hall and powerful real estate interests, many organizations went into housing development. A key reason for this shift was the frustration with the limited gains and the extent of the compromises that had to be made in order to get any change or regulation.

For example, Kathy McAfee, a Boston housing activist, explains her annoyance with the enactment of a rent-control measure sponsored by the Massachusetts Tenants Organization (MTO):

> When Boston's weak rent control ordinance was due to expire at the end of 1982, the MTO decided not to push for strong rent control or even reinstatement of the moderate, pre-1976 version. Instead, the MTO came up with a proposal for a Rent Grievance Board to which tenants could appeal rent increases. It was a measure that appeared to have a chance of passage precisely because it would not impinge significantly on the interests of most landlords and developers, and indeed, after an intensive lobbying campaign, a watered-down version of the grievance board was adopted.
>
> This pathetically weak measure has done little to stem the tide of rent increases. Most MTO members would agree, but they say they lacked the power to squeeze anything better out of the council at the time. (McAfee, 1986, 422)

Many protest organizations began to feel that this kind of watered-down victory was worse than no victory at all. Instead, they focused on ways to take direct control of the production, ownership, and management of housing. Rather than try to "change the system," they would try to leverage it to gain the resources and assistance needed to provide decent housing themselves. But herein lies a dilemma. For a protest organization, "fighting City Hall" is both expected and considered a key strategy of change. As a development organization, the group needs to cultivate good relations with City Hall and with members of the banking and development communities. A group may not find it easy to picket the mayor's office in support of a rent-control ordinance or lodge a protest against a bank for redlining when it is also applying for a Community Development Block Grant from the city or a mortgage loan from the bank. The two —protest and leveraging the system—seem to be contradictory.

But maybe the change from protest to development is fine. Maybe there is no need for a group to do both. This is plausible, but there are still persuasive reasons why a strong community group organized around protest is also likely to be essential.

First, while development is enormously satisfying, it directly benefits a relatively small number of people. In contrast, while a strong rent-control ordinance or condominium-conversion law may be difficult to enact, and problems in implementation may occur, these measures can assist thousands of households.

Second, organizing around an issue that directly affects people's lives is an extremely good way to foster resident participation. There is no way to have a mass protest movement without strong community support. A development organization, in contrast, may become so immersed in the details of housing development and finance that it may lose its grass-root support and find it impossible to engage many people in hours of technical conversations or in stacks of complex legal and financial documents.

To what extent is a community-based housing development organization able to stay representative of citizen interests and concerns while struggling through a maze that often baffles even the most seasoned real estate person? One might argue that unless a group remains active in advocacy *and* protest, it will quickly lose its base of support in the community. But unless it becomes familiar with the technicalities of development in a serious and professional way, the group will neither achieve credibility in the community nor be able to build, rehabilitate, own, or manage any housing.

It also may be possible for advocacy and development to coexist in one organization. According to Andrew Mott of the Center for Community Change:

> Recent experience has shown that it *is* possible to combine several different roles in a single organization, with great payoff for the community. It is, for instance, not inevitable that a tough organizing stance will jeopardize a group's access to essential resources and co-operation, or that building the capacity to do development or provide services will jeopardize a group's independence from city hall and powerful private institutions. In the words of one city councilman, "[There is a group that] can pack city council *and* do better housing rehab than anybody else in the city. That's why they get our cooperation." (Mott, 1985)

How to balance advocacy activities and project development therefore presents itself as a critical dilemma facing community-based housing development organizations. There are clear advantages associated with maintaining a vigorous protest agenda, but there also may be prices to be paid.

Dilemma 4: Good Staff versus Low Salaries and Few Opportunities

One of the major factors determining the success of community-based housing development organizations is the quality and expertise of its staff. In a study of ninety-nine neighborhood development organizations funded through the federal Neighborhood Self-Help

Development program, Neil Mayer cited the importance of the executive director's being skillful in a wide variety of activities: providing overall direction and leadership in the agency, maintaining good relationships with the community, and being able to raise funds for project work. In addition, Mayer underscored that the staff should have expertise in specific technical areas relevant to the development work, such as project financial feasibility and marketability (Mayer, 1984).

In short, the successful executive director of a community-based organization must be a first-rate entrepreneur. But while the private, for-profit sector pays such individuals handsomely, nonprofit salaries are usually meager. Often, a community-based organization is able to attract an individual who develops into a good executive director. But after several years, "burnout" can occur. Long hours, low pay, a constant scrambling for resources, problems with board members, and frustration in getting projects off the drawing board are some of the factors that contribute to wearing people down and finally having them resign from the agency. An executive director of a successful organization often has many job options, but they frequently involve leaving community-based development work. Often, the high salaries offered by for-profit developers or the lure of private consulting become too attractive to turn down. After years of gaining experience "in the trenches" and developing invaluable relationships, a former executive director's skills are extremely marketable.

As for staff members who want to advance in the agency, there are probably few, if any, positions they could fill. Again citing Mayer's work, most neighborhood development organizations are rather small, with a median staff size of eleven; one-quarter of the groups studied had only two to five staff members, and only about one-fifth had staffs with over thirty-five people. Similar findings come from another survey of seventy-eight neighborhood development organizations. Cohen and Kohler (1983) found that more than two-fifths of the agencies in their sample had full-time staffs of less than five people and that 87 percent had fourteen or fewer people working full-time. Less than 8 percent had more than thirty full-time employees. This means that opportunities for promotion are slim. For example, a project director probably has no place to go except to become the executive director; if that position is filled, the career path hits a dead-end, particularly if no similar organizations are in the area. If someone was willing to relocate, there would be greater opportunities, but low pay and the importance of being familiar with a given community often make this kind of move unattractive.

Thus an important dilemma facing community-based development organizations is this: In view of the critical importance of having a good staff, how can you both attract and keep well-qualified personnel when their skills can be marketed elsewhere and when there are few opportunities in your organization for advancement? Both the comparatively low wage scale of nonprofits and the lack of good career paths appear to be structurally linked to community-based development work. We never see salaries in nonprofits that are competitive with for-profit development, and the small size of most organizations precludes easy advancement.

Dilemma 5: Providing Services to Original Group versus Potential for Change and Redefinition of Objectives

The most likely reason for a community-based organization to adopt a housing development agenda is to alleviate housing problems, particularly for low- and moderate-income households living in the area. Once the housing is built or rehabilitated, and occupied by qualified households, at least some of the organization's objectives have been fulfilled. As long as the membership and board composition of the community-based group are oriented toward improving housing, the broad goals of the organization and the original target group—low- and moderate-income households—are largely consistent with one another.

As time passes, however, the neighborhood may go through a period of rejuvenation and possibly gentrification. This can result in a change in the organization's membership, its board, and, ultimately, its original objectives. It is possible, for example, for a new group of more affluent residents to assume control of the organization and change its goals to reflect the interests of the newcomers. Use restrictions that may be attached to the housing because of dependence on federal or state subsidies last for finite periods of time, usually fifteen to twenty years (see Chapter 4). Unless long-term safeguards concerning low-income occupancy are part of the original deeds, once the restrictions expire, the community-based group, like any private owner of subsidized housing, has a choice about what to do with the housing: continue operating it for low- or moderate-income households, in which event additional subsidy funds may be needed; convert it to a limited-equity cooperative or condominium with ownership targeted to existing tenants or others with low to moderate incomes; convert it to a market-rate cooperative or condominium; or sell the building to a market-rate investor who can convert the building or increase rentals to a level on a par with market-rate housing. Obviously only the first two alternatives are consistent with the needs of tenants and the original mission of the community-based organization.

Since change of some kind is virtually inevitable, and since an area in which a strong community-based group is operating stands a good chance of becoming upgraded, this dilemma may ultimately pose serious problems for low-income neighborhood residents. Although the potential for conflict is worth noting, I tend to be less concerned about the likelihood of this scenario undermining the community-based housing strategy than about other conflicts discussed in this chapter.

Dilemma 6: Neighborhood Preference versus Open Access

A large part of a community-based organization's agenda usually involves an explicit focus on improving conditions in the neighborhood, preserving existing resources for local residents, or both. Community-based development, by definition, involves a strategy of targeting improvements to the indigenous population.

At first glance, this seems both logical and straightforward. Yet the community-based approach can create some interesting conflicts, pitting two seemingly legitimate views against one another. Opposing the directing of resources to local citizens are advocates for low-income residents in general, who happen to live outside the targeted area, and for racial groups who do not constitute the dominant group in the community and have no representation in the community-based organization.

For example, several years ago when Inquilinos Boricuas en Acción (IBA), a prominent Hispanic community-based organization located in the South End of Boston, completed a federally subsidized housing development, they were charged with discriminating against eligible non-Hispanic applicants, particularly blacks. Although the units had been developed by the Hispanic organization, black community leaders argued that it was in violation of civil rights laws to limit occupancy to Hispanics. Subsequently, IBA agreed to set aside a proportion of its units for non-Hispanic tenants (Rivas, 1982).

More recently, the Massachusetts Commission against Discrimination in Housing (MCAD) issued a complaint against the Bricklayers Union, a group that had developed eighteen low-cost houses for sale on land bought from the city for $1, for limiting eligibility to existing residents in the neighborhood in which the new houses were built. Because only fifteen of the neighborhood's residents were black and there were few other minorities, the targeting would have had a discriminatory effect. As the MCAD chairman noted: "The point is access" (*Boston Globe*, 1986).

Access, in more formal terms, is called "equal opportunity," a legacy of the 1960s civil rights movement. That movement succeeded in drawing attention to historic and ongoing discrimination as a central cause of poverty in the minority community and forced the passage of legislation that sought to remove racial barriers in society. The rhetoric of the War on Poverty, which gave rise to the first CDCs, was that low-income communities of color should have greater access to and control over economic and political resources denied them for so long. So, at first glance, the CDC movement would appear to be in harmony with the goal of equal opportunity.

But what does equal opportunity mean in a neighborhood context? In a real sense, neighborhood preference is inherently exclusive. Does equal opportunity mean that CDCs must give up a certain amount of neighborhood exclusivity and a certain amount of the neighborhood empowerment it brings? In a racially mixed neighborhood, perhaps one striving to maintain integration, should the racial makeup of a CDC's housing project reflect the racial makeup of the neighborhood, or does equal opportunity mean equal access to anybody from anywhere?

When a state supports CDCs, it finds itself squarely in the middle of this dilemma. On the one hand, the state is supporting the concept of neighborhood empowerment through community-based development; on the other hand, the state must interpret and enforce equal opportunity laws. Balancing these pressures at a policy level is an exceptionally delicate feat.

Integration is the abstraction that motivates equal opportunity and affirmative action laws. Like other activists, CDC members often see integration as a desirable goal and a necessary means for breaking down racial barriers. The context in which CDCs work makes the principle of integration concrete. A single integration decision, the outcome of a wider policy, could shatter a CDC's neighborhood support, as well as cause serious problems in the neighborhood.

Conversely, state policymakers must work with abstractions: project, neighborhood, and citywide integration ratios. To make the numbers work out, the state may mandate how various processes should take place, such as where available units should be advertised and how to select applicants. Tensions between abstraction, process, and neighborhood outcome can strain the relationship between a CDC and the state. They also can strain the relationship between a CDC and a local community. These tensions are all visible in the two case studies that follow.

In addition, the cases present images of two very different CDCs. The Fields Corner Community Development Corporation (FCCDC), operating in the Dorchester section of Boston, was formed as a development agency to take advantage of a series of support programs for CDCs offered by the Massachusetts government (see Chapter 11). Although oriented to community needs, neighborhood support has been relatively weak. Finally, FCCDC's target neighborhood is made up of pockets of predominantly white and predominantly black areas.

Lowell's Coalition for a Better Acre (CBA) had its roots in organizing and advocacy work. Even after the group embarked on a development agenda, community support remained strong. CBA differed from FCCDC in two other important ways. First, CBA's target neighborhood was more integrated spatially and about 60 percent minority. Second, CBA managed to put together its development without state funding. As a result, they did not have to coordinate guidelines for selecting occupants with specific state requirements.

CASE STUDY

■

The Fields Corner
Community Development Corporation (FCCDC)

BY THE late 1970s, many buildings in the Fields Corner neighborhood of Dorchester, Massachusetts, were unoccupied and deteriorating; fires were turning many houses into brick shells. Faced with this situation, the FCCDC looked for ways to help the neighborhood help itself. Created in 1979 by a group of active, long-time residents and guided by a new neighborhood-based state housing policy, FCCDC quickly embraced the strategy of housing development. Within a few years after its start, FCCDC had successfully developed six prefabricated homes for low- and moderate-income people.

In August 1983, the Boston Housing Partnership (BHP), a local nonprofit public–private initiative (see Chapter 12), sent out its first request for proposals to community-based housing developers for the production or rehabilitation of subsidized low- and moderate-income housing. FCCDC responded with a proposal to develop 110–112 Park Street and 1396 Dorchester Avenue, along with six other buildings in the neighborhood. The two buildings noted above, plus four of the others, were chosen to receive a portion of the funding.

The Dorchester Community

For many years, the Irish dominated Dorchester's eastern and northern precincts ethnically and politically, as they came to dominate the rest of Boston. On the other side of Dorchester's hills lived most of Boston's Jews.

The 1950s and 1960s saw enormous changes in Dorchester, as Boston's economy sagged. Many of the Irish hung on in the eastern precincts, but the Jews left the western and southern precincts. Much of the "white flight" followed the arrival of blacks in the community.

The in-migration of blacks to Dorchester was speeded by local and federal programs in the late 1960s, which were designed to make homeownership possible for people of low and moderate incomes (see Chapter 6). One of the particularly negative consequences of the programs was large-scale "blockbusting." Real estate agents went into white neighborhoods such as Dorchester and convinced homeowners that the value of their property was rapidly declining because of the imminent arrival of blacks. The whites left in droves. In 1960, south Dorchester and the northern parts of neighboring Mattapan were 9.3 percent black. In 1970, the same areas were 71.7 percent black. Many neighborhoods deteriorated and abandonment skyrocketed as first-time homeowners, with as little as a few hundred dollars invested, left their homes or neglected them when expensive maintenance was required or when mortgage payments became a financial burden.

In Fields Corner, the working-class Irish suffered from Boston's decline and perceived that their needs were being neglected; blacks in similar economic circumstances were receiving attention and dollars. Separated geographically from predominantly black neighborhoods by the low hills cutting across the area, the Irish felt threatened by black encroachment.

The forced imposition of school desegregation through busing and the arrival of large numbers of Hispanics in the mid-1970s exacerbated racial tensions. As of 1980, Fields Corner was one of the most ethnically diverse neighborhoods in the city: 50 percent of the population was white, 37 percent black, 12 percent Hispanic, and 1 percent Asian.

By the early 1980s, Dorchester was starting to rebound after decades of decline. Young professionals moving into this semiurban neighborhood three to six miles south of Boston were pushing up the median income, which in 1980 was only 80 percent of the citywide median.

As Boston's economy strengthened, displacement of low-income residents became a new problem in Fields Corner. Suddenly the neighborhood was desirable, and community activists had to figure out ways to assist its low- and moderate-income people.

The Growth of FCCDC

FCCDC was launched with a phone call from a long-time Fields Corner neighborhood activist to the Massachusetts Community Development Finance Corporation (CDFC), a state agency that provides financing for community-based development. The activist, who is white, wanted to find out how Fields Corner could get more attention from state funding agencies and policymakers. CDFC directed her to the Massachusetts Executive Office of Communities and Development (EOCD), which administers state neighborhood development and housing aid programs (see Chapter 11).

EOCD helped the activist organize a racially mixed group of local merchants, civic groups, and churches; write bylaws; and get seed money. The organization's mission was to be responsive to residents of the community. Specifically, its purpose was to increase and improve housing and employment opportunities for low- and moderate-income area residents, and to stimulate development of the Fields Corner business district.

Despite its intentions to assist the community, FCCDC has had a relatively difficult time maintaining an active membership and a board of directors that matches the neighborhood's ethnic constituencies. Any neighborhood resident over age eighteen can join FCCDC by paying $3 and signing a membership certificate. As of 1984,

FCCDC could claim only 122 individual members: 87 were white (71 percent), 20 black (16 percent), and 15 Hispanic (12 percent).

The board of directors was designed for nineteen members, but often the number of active directors is around fifteen. Twelve directors are elected by the membership, and seven represent associations in the neighborhood. In 1984, the board had fourteen members: nine white, four black, and one Hispanic.

The relatively low level of community participation is probably caused, in part, by the complexity of racial power sharing in Fields Corner. In addition, it is probably the result of the FCCDC's decision to focus on housing. From the beginning, the CDC plunged into working with complicated state funding mechanisms and the technicalities of housing production. This orientation, as opposed to community advocacy and organizing, can make it difficult for a neighborhood group to rally spontaneous community support.

The BHP Demonstration and FCCDC

BHP was just what the FCCDC was looking for. It provided the kind of financial and development structure that FCCDC had positioned itself to use.

FCCDC searched the neighborhood for brick buildings that they could acquire cheaply. They found eight—four in white pockets of the neighborhood and four in minority areas—and quickly created proposals for each of them. BHP administrators selected six buildings, but the two they rejected were both "white" buildings, which FCCDC's executive director later said threw off the racial balance that the CDC had carefully planned in order to maximize neighborhood support.

For the next year, BHP and FCCDC administrators worked out the complicated details of the projects. The per unit cost of acquisition and rehabilitation was $53,709. The Fields Corner units would be subsidized by two Massachusetts programs—the State Housing Assistance for Rental Production (SHARP) program and Chapter 707 rental housing certificates. The equity for the project came from Boston's Community Development Block Grant, private foundation grants, equity partnership investments, and low-interest loans from the Commonwealth of Massachusetts and the City of Boston. Rental and occupancy of the 700 units projectwide was scheduled for the last half of 1985.

110–112 Park Street and 1396 Dorchester Avenue (1396) were the only two of FCCDC's buildings that were unoccupied, so the CDC decided to work on them first. Since BHP money was not scheduled to arrive until early 1985, however, FCCDC's executive director independently secured a bridge loan to begin construction on the two buildings in the fall of 1984. Although this bold move was a coup for FCCDC and gave it the distinction of being the first CDC in the project to complete rehabilitation and rental, it strained almost to the breaking point the bureaucratic timetables around the issue of tenant selection.

Tenant Selection

By January 1985, it was clear the rehabilitation would be complete in about four months. FCCDC's Housing Committee, with representation from the white, black, and Hispanic communities, hired a management agent, who in turn hired a consultant experienced in formulating tenant-selection plans.

BHP had set an overall project goal of 40 percent minority representation, but it had not yet developed a tenant-selection plan at the time FCCDC needed to consider its rental strategy. The Massachusetts Housing Finance Agency (MHFA), which was providing below-market-interest loans to the project, required that project participants offer for approval an affirmative fair-marketing agreement, which included efforts "directed at specific racial groups, with a specified minimal occupancy goal."[1] MHFA also required that participants advertise "in each minority newspaper" and accept MHFA recommendations to undertake further advertising and outreach.[2] EOCD also wanted to approve the tenant-selection plan.

The Housing Committee first decided it would retain current tenants who were income eligible and wanted to stay. Although some buildings were vacant, 75 percent of the units were occupied. Since all but one of the tenants were minority, FCCDC's project was slated to be overwhelmingly minority.

Members of the Housing Committee wanted the project to benefit the racially diverse Fields Corner neighborhood, as was FCCDC's mandate, yet they knew that BHP was created to serve the distressed housing population all over Boston. They further knew that this population was predominantly minority. If the committee advertised, it assumed that a large number of people would apply, most of them minority. If a minority newspaper had served only Fields Corner, FCCDC might have been able to meet MHFA's minority advertising requirement by advertising only in it, but no neighborhood newspaper fit the bill.

The Housing Committee had further dilemmas: 1396 Dorchester Avenue was in a racially mixed area, but the Park Street building was on a white and potentially violent block. The CDC received threats that if blacks or Hispanics moved there, the building would be firebombed. FCCDC obviously did not want to endanger the lives of tenants racially unacceptable to the street's other residents, but it also did not want to isolate minorities in minority projects on minority streets.

Finally, FCCDC was trying to build support throughout its complicated neighborhood: among the many poor whites, who still felt they had been neglected by government aid programs of the past, as well as among minority residents.

The Housing Committee waded through meeting after meeting as building contractors finished up the mercifully concrete details of construction. By the end of February 1985, the Housing Committee felt extreme pressure to finish the tenant-selection plan.

The committee argued about whether to advertise the units in print media at all. Most of the CDC board, as well as the executive director, did not want to do so because they thought the consequent flood of applications would overwhelm FCCDC's commitment to the neighborhood.

In the midst of the controversy, the executive director placed ads for the units in white neighborhood newspapers. At least one Housing Committee member then insisted, based on EOCD and MHFA regulations, that ads also be placed in two citywide minority newspapers. As a result, ads appeared in two local, generally white-oriented newspapers and two citywide minority newspapers.

The ads indicated that there would be only two weekdays of application taking, to occur only a few days after the ads appeared. Both provisions were contrary to MHFA guidelines, which suggested at least two weeks of marketing and at least two weeks of taking applications. After complaints from an angered Housing Committee member, MHFA required FCCDC to advertise again two weeks later, this time making applications available on a weekend, although not requiring a longer notice.

Clearly, as acknowledged by the executive director, FCCDC was trying to control the application pool, hoping to maximize the chance that the fruits of their neighborhood-motivated labor would be enjoyed by neighborhood residents.[3] Most members of the Housing Committee were also committed to a racially mixed neighborhood. Critics, however, called it loyalty to their friends, a loyalty that discriminated against needier minorities. Whatever its motivations, the Housing Committee was correct about the results of the advertising: Citywide minority advertising and the two application takings drew a total of about 1500 applications from across Boston, approximately 80 percent of them minority. FCCDC was to pick only fifteen of these applicants.

But there was still no final tenant-selection plan. Draft plans went to BHP, MHFA, or EOCD and then were returned to the Housing Committee with revisions. FCCDC Housing Committee members, the project's private management agent, and FCCDC staff felt enormously frustrated by the policy-level indecision and lack of coordination, as well as by what they felt was intrusion into their neighborhood's decision. Most identified EOCD, the agency most closely tied to overall state policy regarding CDCs, as the most difficult to work with.

Meanwhile, the buildings were completed. On April 12, the Housing Committee approved a final tenant-selection plan; tenants were to reflect the neighborhood's approximately 50–50 racial mix. "At initial rent-up, the owner will seek 46% minority representation in renting newly available units, including 20% Hispanic, 20% Black, and 6% Asian households" (Boston Housing Partnership, 1985a). FCCDC would sort the applicant pool by race and, after serving the most seriously distressed, choose by lottery from within the racially segregated categories.

But the plan for filling future vacancies proved to be more controversial. The debate focused on one sentence: "Once initial rent-up is completed, the management agent will fill vacancies at the rate of one minority to two majority occupants to the point of achieving 50% minority representation in the project" (Boston Housing Partnership, 1985a).

One member of the Housing Committee went on record opposing this policy and made a point of bringing his concern to the attention of the funding and supervising organizations, including the Massachusetts Commission against Discrimination and the Boston Fair Housing Commission. No agency raised official objection to the sentence at the time, although EOCD later promulgated much different guidelines, which eventually replaced FCCDC's.

The Housing Committee devoted virtually an entire meeting to the issue of how to fill future vacancies. The chairman noted that the plan, with the offending sentence, had been approved by EOCD and MHFA, that it could be changed in the future, and that FCCDC had a pressing practical need to tenant the buildings as soon as possible. He concluded, "For those concerned with the possibility of lawsuits over this issue, note that there is neither incentive nor standing to sue until . . . much later—when the first vacancy actually occurs. I see no malicious intent and no basis for a serious challenge."[4]

The rental went ahead, and the lottery and selection took place, followed by verifications of individual applications. The first tenants moved in during the middle of May, and both buildings were full by the end of June.

FCCDC originally filled the Park Street building's six units—on a volatile, white street—with four whites and two Hispanics, a 66–33 white-to-minority ratio. A few months later, a black family replaced a white family, bringing the white-to-minority ratio to 50–50. Five white, two black, one Hispanic, and one Vietnamese families moved into the apartments at 1396 Dorchester Avenue. The ratio of whites to minorities was 56–44.

Because EOCD ultimately withdrew support for FCCDC's tenant-selection plan, the Housing Committee had to take up the issue of future vacancies again in early July. According to a memo from the committee chair, the committee voted 3–1 to strike the reference to race/ethnicity in the sentence regarding future vacancies. The one vote to retain the sentence, possibly with a revised 1–1 ratio of majority to minority, was made "as a statement of support for integration in housing sponsored by the CDC."[5]

Meanwhile, BHP finalized its model tenant-selection plan. The BHP explicitly prohibited tenanting by race unless minority representation was too low. "In all other circumstances, tenant selection shall be carried out without regard to race" (Boston Housing Partnership, 1985b). The FCCDC board voted to adopt the standard BHP plan.

Since the initial rental of the Park Street building and 1396 Dorchester Avenue, FCCDC has tenanted its BHP units according to categories of special need, with no provision for racial goals. Aside from these two buildings, the BHP Demonstration Program buildings are almost exclusively minority.

Most of FCCDC's board and staff view the BHP project and specifically the Park Street and 1396 Dorchester buildings as very successful. On streets with substantial numbers of white households, these two buildings are over 50 percent minority. But at least a few people closely associated with FCCDC remain critical of FCCDC's original preference for tenanting the buildings with local residents.

CASE STUDY
■

The Coalition for a Better Acre (CBA)

LOWELL, MASSACHUSETTS, twenty-five miles northwest of Boston, was revitalizing. In the 1950s, many of the mills that had driven Lowell's economy had closed down, and the city had gone through a long period of decline. But high-tech industry was coming to Lowell, led by Wang Industries, and by the late 1970s, the city was embarked on a well-publicized recovery. But Lowell's revitalization was clouded by inequities.

City officials were using the revitalization to destroy downtown ethnic neighborhoods. In the predominantly Hispanic section of the city known as the Acre Triangle, municipal services were practically nonexistent. Crime and arson were rampant. Vacant buildings crumbled, and lots were strewn with rubble and garbage.

A coalition of neighborhood groups arose in protest. The coalition pursued a broad-based organizing strategy that earned it community support and significant citywide political power. The coalition, which eventually would become the Coalition for a Better Acre (CBA), focused on building community strength, not building structures, but in the early 1980s, CBA took on a housing development project within the Acre Triangle.

The Acre is an area in Lowell close to the central business district and bounded by the Merrimack and Pawtucket rivers. The Triangle section of the Acre traditionally housed immigrant families that worked the mills. Much of this area is now part of a downtown Lowell historic district.

The City of Lowell

Lowell reached its peak as an industrial mill town in the early part of the twentieth century. Families in the Acre section had always struggled financially, and after the mills closed down in the 1950s, their situation became even more desperate.

As the city rebounded in the late 1970s, many people came to believe that the City Council, the city manager, and city planners were using urban renewal to rebuild Lowell solely for the city's new white professionals. Paralleling events in South Holyoke (see Chapter 9), what had been a hidden agenda became public knowledge when the city manager announced plans to demolish the Acre Triangle. A story about bulldozing the neighborhood appeared on the front page of the *Lowell Sun*.

The story fueled the nascent CBA. Lowell's renewal had attracted national media attention, and CBA used the presence of the media to embarrass the city. CBA succeeded not only in stopping the demolition of the Acre Triangle and the removal of hundreds of families but also in registering hundreds of new voters, forcing landlords to fix up their properties and keep rents down, and securing over $1 million in state funds for new public housing.

These were heady successes for the new group, but huge problems remained. Municipal services, particularly fire and police protection, were still poor, and the rates of arson and abandonment were high. The city's earlier policies had displaced many of Lowell's blacks and French Canadians. Remaining in the Acre Triangle were many of the city's lowest-income Hispanics and Asians, a lot of neglected property, and little hope.

Following the bulldozer debacle, the city developed a plan for revitalizing the Acre based on anticipated support from Aetna Insurance Company. A few years before, Aetna had been accused in a lawsuit of practicing redlining. As part of the court settlement, the company had agreed to create the Aetna New Neighborhood Investment Plan, whose purpose would be to invest money in distressed urban areas. A block of funds was committed to Lowell.

From its corporate headquarters, Aetna did not know whether the city's plans for the money were equitable or inequitable. As a matter of fact, city officials were dealing exclusively with an all-white community organization and were ignoring Acre minorities. When the CBA president, Charles Gargiulo, found out about the city's plan, he complained to Aetna.

Aetna's representative investigated and became convinced that the Triangle had the greatest need for investment. She convinced Aetna's technical consultant—the National Training and Information Center (NTIC)—that the planning should be handed over to CBA. Aetna went along with NTIC's decision and agreed to channel their funds through CBA. If Aetna had not had an interest in supporting an equitable development model, the city's plan probably would have been implemented. At this point, in order to receive the Aetna money, the coalition incorporated as a CDC.

The Growth of CBA

CBA has a membership of over 600 households. The only requirement to join is Acre residence; there is no membership fee. Members meet annually to elect the board and plan the future course of the coalition. In 1986, a membership of more than 500 included about 70 percent Hispanics, 20 percent whites, and 10 percent Southeast Asians and other races (East Indian, French Canadian, black).

CBA's mission is to promote and support the development of decent, affordable housing for Acre residents; prevent displacement; and foster communitywide awareness of, and involvement in, the housing and economic future of the Acre. Crucial to this effort is an aggressive community organizing component. Of the six paid professional staff members, two are full-time community organizers.

Despite the largely Hispanic orientation of the coalition, many whites have been active in it, including a white president of the CBA board. Whites in the Acre do not generally have strong ethnic ties; many are single mothers who are often unable to participate in community activities. Hispanics tend to be the most active group in the CBA.

Asians have been slow to participate in CBA. Although there are a few Asian members, they have not assumed leadership positions. CBA has had two major problems in building coalitions with the Asian community. First, Asian communities tend to be insular, with kinship and national ties playing a large role in their political organization. There is often suspicion of outsiders and little knowledge on the part of the larger community (such as coalition leaders) about how to overcome this.

Second, the Asian community is itself divided along national lines. Asians identify themselves as Laotian, Cambodian, and Vietnamese, not simply as "Asian." Recently, Asians have formed self-help associations along national lines. In order to have the full backing of the Asian community, CBA will need to form alliances with all three national groups.

While the level of participation in CBA varies according to ethnic origin, CBA has the support of the whole community. Even ethnic groups that have not been active in CBA have benefited from its projects. There is little evidence of strong racial antagonisms in the

Acre, and to the extent that there have been racial difficulties, the CDC has generally been unaffected.

The Acre Triangle Homeownership Project involved the construction of both resident-owned and rental units. In all, CBA built twenty-four units for sale and thirteen rental units. Project financing came from the city, from HUD, and from private sources including Aetna, as well as other private foundations.

The for-sale units were targeted to Lowell families with incomes too low to purchase a home on the open market. Households with incomes below $18,000 were eligible for a single-family house; and those with incomes below $26,000 were eligible for a two-family house. Although there are three mortgages on the houses, only the Aetna mortgage has to be paid back. Federal Urban Development Action Grant and Community Development Block Grant loans are forgivable after ten years as long as the owner remains in the house.

Tenant Selection

Seven of the rental units were completed and marketed first. CBA obtained a list of public housing applicants from the Lowell Housing Authority. CBA sent applications to all Acre residents from that list. A Housing Committee was set up and ranked applicants based on federal Section 8 or state Chapter 707 rental certificate requirements, need, character and living habits, and residence in the Acre. State and federal rental certificate programs use the same criteria: Preference is given to families whose income does not exceed 50 percent of the median income, but families are accepted whose incomes do not exceed 80 percent of the median. All of the coalition's rehabilitated rental units had rental subsidies committed to them.

Most of the Housing Committee's work centered on questions of need and character. Evaluating the need of the applicant was the number-one priority. Housing need was a judgment based on the applicant's income, present living conditions, and ability to match available units with space needs. Members of the Housing Committee did extensive interviewing and home visits. Many Triangle residents had been displaced from their homes as a result of demolition and unfair evictions. CBA made efforts to reach these displaced families. According to Louise Costello, the assistant project manager, race was "not a factor in tenant selection." Nevertheless, the racial composition of the units reflected the diversity of the Acre: six were rented to Hispanic households, five to whites, and two to Southeast Asians.[6]

Advertising for the owner-occupied units was done through local newspapers and by distributing brochures with application guidelines to area churches. The board decided that opportunities to purchase the houses would be based on a preapplication screening and a lottery. In order to participate in the lottery, applicants had to be first-time house buyers, have good credit, be Lowell residents, and be able to afford a downpayment of $4000–$6000.

Because many Acre residents did not have the income needed to become owners, CBA had great difficulty filling its applicant pool. Finally, the Housing Committee decided to include applicants from outside Lowell. A total of sixty-three people were included in the lottery for the twenty-four spots; twenty-nine applicants were from the Acre area, twenty-nine were from Lowell generally, and five were from outside Lowell. Many applicants eventually withdrew their names from the list for various reasons, including the high crime rate in the Acre area. Ultimately, everyone on the list was offered a house: nine Hispanic, nine Southeast Asian, three white, two black, and one East Indian households became homeowners through the CBA.[7]

CBA's two main goals were to stabilize and empower the neighborhood. Both goals entailed a high level of community preference in the tenant-selection process. Since minorities were well represented in the applicant pool, CBA was free to stress local preference without fear of breaking civil rights laws.

The CBA selection process also was in compliance with state laws on affirmative action. Any affirmative action goal for the Lowell area would have been low compared to the number of minority applicants CBA expected to serve. The laws allow local preference as long as this does not cause discrimination. The final racial tally clearly shows that CBA did not discriminate against minorities. Moreover, CBA eventually offered a house to everyone in the applicant pool.

As mentioned in the case study of FCCDC, the Massachusetts Housing Finance Agency (MHFA) requires that any development it finances be marketed in a minority-targeted newspaper. While CBA received no funds from MHFA and therefore was not required to market in this way, CBA did in fact market the units in a newspaper with a large minority readership: their own newspaper. MHFA would almost certainly have accepted this form of marketing.

Did CBA neglect to market to whites? If the neighborhood had been totally minority and if CBA had received funds from MHFA, then it might have been required to set a majority goal. Neither condition held.

In selecting tenants for the rental units, CBA was more restricted;

it was given an applicant list by the Lowell Housing Authority. CBA was able to use this list in ways that did not conflict with its goals. It accepted applications only from people on the list who were Acre residents and then applied other criteria, including need, in choosing between the applications they received. CBA was able to choose Acre residents and still not discriminate in any way.

Conclusions

What lessons and observations can be drawn from these two cases? Several relate directly to the dilemma of neighborhood preference versus fair housing, while others pertain to the broader operations of CDCs.

First, the dilemma of how a CDC can be both responsive to its local community and comply with state and federal affirmative action requirements is, indeed, a complex one. But this complexity becomes more or less problematic based on the racial composition of the CDC's target neighborhood, the level of community participation in the CDC, and the number of agencies with regulatory authority over the specific project.

FCCDC operated within a racially diverse neighborhood. But its desire for the rehabilitated units to have a racial composition that mirrored this diversity did not get expressed in the final policy on tenant selection. If its base of support within the community had been stronger, or if the number of state and local agencies involved in the project had been fewer, the CDC may have been able to get its way in the tenant-selection process.

In contrast, CBA faced a much easier set of conditions, which allowed it to navigate its way through the dilemma more easily. CBA's predominantly minority population, its strong roots in the community, and the need to comply with very few external regulations made for extremely smooth sailing.

Second, the two case studies reveal the general difficulty of a CDC's adopting a strong prointegration position. FCCDC's early goal to have an integrated tenantry, although achieved in the initial rent-up, will probably be unfulfilled over the long term. State-mandated affirmative action goals, requirements to advertise all across the city, and regulations that preclude any consideration of race in tenanting the buildings will make the minority pool larger than the pool of white applicants and give the former an edge in obtaining units.

Third, actors in the community-based housing movement, along with state and federal regulatory agencies, should attempt to mediate the local preference–equal opportunity dilemma on a case-by-case basis. Given the sensitivity of the issue, inflexible state guidelines should be avoided. This approach would require more work on the part of government agencies and a high level of trust. In the case of FCCDC, if the state had been willing to relax its equal opportunity requirement, the CDC would have been permitted to address the neighborhood preference issue, create an ongoing integrated housing development in a neighborhood characterized by the spatial separation of ethnic groups, and still increase housing opportunities in the area for minorities. A greater effort by the state to understand the neighborhood from the perspective of FCCDC might have convinced it of the wisdom of such a risk. The state's role in this case, based on a commitment to equal opportunity in an isolated housing development, weakened the CDC and hurt it in its struggle to broaden community support.

Fourth, and more generally, the unique origins of each CDC will probably affect the relative ease with which it carries out development projects. In these two cases, the CDC that presented itself primarily as a political actor (CBA) generated wide acceptance for its project, while the CDC that presented itself as a housing developer (FCCDC) had to fight to have its needs respected by policymakers and to build and maintain support in the neighborhood.

Fifth, it is important to underscore the impact that the overall neighborhood setting will have on a CDC's activities and agenda. Lowell is relatively small, and its problems are more easily defined than Boston's. Moreover, the Fields Corner neighborhood is only one of many communities in Boston with a substantial need for affordable housing; FCCDC had the burden of trying to meet both neighborhood and citywide needs.

Sixth, these two cases reveal the importance of in-depth study of CDC operations. Dilemmas of community-based development, as well as insights concerning how they can be resolved, are best understood through concrete examples and analysis.

Finally, the issue of whether a CDC should have "home rule" when it comes to tenant selection remains. Should a CDC with a strong conviction, a "good" reason such as community empowerment or integration, be able to decide who gets the few available units? Or should affirmative action, which may, in fact, reduce the likelihood of integration and diminish a CDC's community support, dominate the selection process? Whether the community-based approach will be able to sustain support from neighborhood residents and still accommodate the legal and ethical demands of outsiders remains to be seen.

The six dilemmas discussed in this chapter will likely be the subject of numerous debates as local residents develop community-based housing programs and as mature organizations grapple with growth and development issues. While the dilemmas shed light on some of the conflicts facing community-based housing programs, their existence does not undermine the overall approach. In view of the significant contributions and potential of the strategy, as discussed in Chapter 8, and since, in comparison to other options for increasing the supply of low cost housing, community-based housing offers considerable advantages, public policies ought to be directed to supporting the growth of this approach.

Public Support for Community-Based Housing in Massachusetts

THIS BOOK argues that there is significant potential in the community-based housing strategy. But is it really possible to develop a comprehensive public support system for this approach that would provide the needed technical and financial resources, thereby making explicit the government's role in providing housing, yet enabling citizens to create and manage their own community-based programs? This question is a recapitulation of a dilemma raised in Chapter 2: Is it reasonable to assume that those in power will agree to empower those who are powerless? Would the public sector be willing to support a truly meaningful community-based housing system that provides initiators or participants with one of the most valuable benefits of community-based housing: control over their living environments? Since these questions relate to the politics of launching a community-based housing program, they are deferred until the final chapter.

The present chapter continues the examination of community-based housing by analyzing in some detail the only comprehensive public support system for community-based housing currently operating in the country. Although other states and cities have one or more of the pieces of such a system, the Massachusetts model is by far the most fully developed (see Barbe and Sekera, 1983; Sidor, 1982). Before assessing the Massachusetts system and the extent to which it approaches an ideal model, the first two sections of this chapter explore the growth and components of this system. The final section presents some preliminary observations drawn from the Massachusetts experience.

The Community Economic Development Movement

Ironically, the major pieces of the Massachusetts system did not start with a focus on housing; the original emphasis was on community economic development. During the late 1960s, the needs of inner-city low-income neighborhoods began to receive increased attention. First, although the federal community development programs left a mixed legacy for urban neighborhoods and their residents, they did focus attention on problems of the cities. Urban Renewal was an easy target for criticism, as thousands of low-income units were lost and whole "urban villages" demolished. In their place, luxury apartments, offices, and civic centers became the concrete symbols of the inequities of the "urban/Negro removal" program.

The federal community development programs that followed— the War on Poverty and Model Cities—although more focused on assisting low-income neighborhoods, often were viewed as token improvements, and program outcomes rarely lived up to expectations. In addition, although community control and "maximum feasible participation" became buzzwords in the mid-1960s, lawmakers gave ambiguous messages about whether neighborhood residents or the local chief executive would actually hold the reins of power (see Chapter 2). As inevitable controversies arose, the neighborhood emerged as a significant locus of activity, if not necessarily control. Whether community groups coalesced protesting urban renewal plans or vying for power with City Hall, a new generation of leaders and activists emerged, and there was a fresh awareness of the problems facing the inner city.

Consciousness about poor urban dwellers in general, and blacks in particular, also was raised by a second key factor: the civil rights movement. Although there were no geographical boundaries to inequality, the plight of blacks became synonymous with inner-city problems. This link became fixed when in the summers of 1966 and 1967, frustrations in black communities gave way to full-scale urban riots.

At about the same time, a third set of events was unfolding that also contributed to an increased awareness of the problems facing urban neighborhoods, particularly in older industrialized states such as Massachusetts. Traditional manufacturing firms began to close down and relocate in the Sunbelt, in large part as a way to employ cheaper, nonunion labor; to reduce taxes; and to utilize new, modern manufacturing facilities. The result for the cities was often disastrous, as tax bases declined and fiscal crises became a major topic of concern (see Chapter 9).

By the early 1970s, community activists, some political leaders, and a handful of academics began to see the potential in a completely new urban agenda. Two positive approaches emerged: black capitalism and community economic development. The former emphasized assisting black entrepreneurs to enter the economic mainstream; the latter focused on a collective response to poverty that viewed community control as the critical ingredient. Enthusiasm about this approach was also bolstered by the growing interest in CDCs at the national level. As discussed in Chapter 8, both the Ford Foundation and the federal government adopted CDCs as a promising vehicle for community development.

Community Development Corporations (CDCs)

Along with the few well-funded federal and foundation-supported organizations, a group of smaller CDCs became vehicles through which many community groups hoped to achieve the economic and physical revitalization of their neighborhoods. The logic and high hopes for the CDC are captured in the following passages:

> The building of a nationwide system of support for community-based economic development programs, as represented by the CDCs, is a challenge that those responsible for domestic urban policies must meet. The objectives of such a system must be to enhance the effectiveness of community development corporations and to enlarge their capacity for self-help. (Twentieth Century Fund Task Force, 1971, 12)

And,

> Breaking the vicious circle of community poverty is a matter of a coordinated attack on many levels. It is not possible to cause fundamental change in a community by working on just one of its problems—say, better education, or better roads, or new housing. When the rest of the community is deteriorating, the better educated will move away. The better roads will carry prosperity through to another location, and new housing will begin to deteriorate.
>
> Success in building a strong community is possible only when the community situation is seen as a whole, with a plan for comprehensive action laid out in step-by-step progression. Only a broad-based representative organization that responds to the community alone, because it is a creation of that community, can prepare and carry out

a comprehensive strategy for development. (Center for Community
Economic Development, 1975, 3)

Finally, the rationale for CDCs was summarized as follows:

> The corporate form appeals as a mechanism for entrepreneurship and
> investment. The local organization has the considerable advantage of
> both firsthand knowledge of the community's history, current out-
> look, and needs, and clear self-interest in the results. Its indigenous
> character helps to guard against actions imposed from outside the
> community. It also appeals to American traditions of self-help and
> the preservation of local cultural values. Finally, the CDC provides a
> mechanism for organizing professional and technical resources at the
> local level, to orchestrate all the available sources of assistance into a
> program of action that is responsible to local needs. (National Center
> for Economic Alternatives, 1981)

Although all CDCs share the broad objective of enabling residents
to exercise greater control over the local economy and improve the
quality of goods and services in their communities, the specific goals
and activities launched by a CDC can vary. The activities of CDCs
usually fall into one or more of the following categories:[1]

1. *Housing development*—rehabilitation, new development, management
   and ownership of housing as a way of providing decent, affordable
   housing to community residents
2. *Job retention*—acquiring a firm that is about to relocate to another area,
   organizing workers to assume ownership, or finding other new owners
   as a way to prevent jobs from being lost
3. *Development of new enterprises and employment opportunities*—stimulating
   new businesses or actually starting a CDC-owned venture with the main
   objective of creating new "primary sector" jobs[2]
4. *Commercial development and revitalization*—targeting resources and assistance to a local business area with the goal of enhancing its commercial
   viability, increasing the availability of goods and services to residents,
   and providing job and business ownership opportunities
5. *Providing social services*—delivering services such as day care, health care,
   and job placement and training
6. *Land assembly and development*—acquiring, assembling, or holding land
   for the immediate or future development of housing or some other retail,
   commercial, or industrial use consistent with the community's overall
   plans

Thus, the activities in which CDCs have engaged are clearly the
most critical components of community development. Reliance on
the CDC as the vehicle for change has rested on four assumptions:[3]

1. Neighborhoods are a logical focus for a comprehensive assault on the cycle of poverty.
2. Absence of equity and debt capital have thwarted spontaneous community economic development efforts; therefore, both kinds of financial resources are crucial to CDCs. Once the resources become available, demand by CDCs will flourish.
3. Control of a community's resources are central to the enhancement of its economic and social conditions; these, in turn, strengthen the community's political position.
4. Small business development is the means by which communities could turn capital into jobs and social benefits. Moreover, these businesses would be profitable despite the fact that many private enterprises had abandoned the area.

Targeted Neighborhood Strategy

During the late 1960s and early 1970s, there were major arguments over whether low-income people and minorities were best served by dispersing them throughout regions, particularly in suburbs, or maintaining separate and identifiable neighborhoods where their proximity would provide support, unity, and political strength. The latter view was articulated by Piven and Cloward (1967), who argued that the power base blacks managed to build through the 1960s was threatened by advocates of suburbanization and dispersal.

From an economic standpoint, Bennett Harrison reviewed the evidence and arguments in favor of dispersal and concluded that David Birch's assertion that "suburban Blacks are increasingly better off than their central city counterparts" was not supported by any evidence (Harrison, 1974, 103). Harrison's view was that revival of the central-city's economy is indicated by the academic research and is both technically and politically feasible. He ended his analysis by stating: "For many Americans, particularly those who are black, there is a strong presumption that the future lies in the cities, after all" (Harrison, 1974, 195).

While critics of dispersal gathered their evidence, another significant trend emerged. A new ideology of city planners was being shaped by the writings of Lewis Mumford and Jane Jacobs, who stressed the vitality of urban neighborhoods. Slowly, neighborhoods came to be recognized as the preferred focus for urban revitalization efforts. Neighborhood consciousness was raised as groups protested disruptive urban renewal and highway plans, and organized around the issue of disinvestment and redlining. As inroads were made on these problems, neighborhood groups began to realize the latent power for effecting change in their own communities.

By the late 1970s, the neighborhood movement had achieved full recognition. President Carter appointed a National Commission on Neighborhoods and a new section within HUD, the Office of Neighborhoods, Voluntary Associations, and Consumer Protection was created. Further, as mentioned in Chapter 8, in 1978 Congress passed two neighborhood-oriented pieces of legislation: the Neighborhood Reinvestment Corporation Act and the Neighborhood Self-Help Development Act.

As neighborhood initiatives were publicized, there was a prevailing feeling that if an activity was neighborhood based, it was automatically good. Thus, many came to believe that virtually any activity sponsored by a neighborhood organization was worth supporting and better than programs that did not demonstrate neighborhood involvement. While the community economic development movement emerged as an alternative to "black capitalism" and was embraced by many black leaders who espoused a separatist philosophy, it evolved into a mainstream program that was attractive to a variety of urban and proneighborhood constituencies. Interestingly enough, as the movement has matured, the goals of black capitalists have occasionally been at odds with those of community-based development. To the extent that a community group may be operating in an area that is attractive to private investment, the group may find itself competing for the same projects as for-profit developers. When these developers are minorities, there is the potential for the two strategies to come into direct conflict.

The Need for Capital

If neighborhoods were to be the basis of development, and many of them were depressed, then it was necessary to identify the roots of these conditions. The emerging analysis located fault in structural conditions in the larger society, particularly the maldistribution of wealth and power. In considering wealth, community economic development advocates argued that wealth tended to flow out of these neighborhoods not only in terms of rents, commodity purchases, and return derived from labor but also because little wealth could be retained or generated in neighborhoods that lacked locally owned or sponsored businesses, services, and housing. Not only were the channels through which most communities accumulated wealth absent or constructed in such ways that return on investment always flowed outward, but efforts to build new enterprises or develop community economic ventures were blocked by outright discrimination in capital markets that provided debt or equity financing to low-income entrepreneurs. Thus, low-income neighborhoods existed as colonies and provided cheap labor to the larger society on disadvantageous trade terms.

Proponents of community economic development also believed that once resources were made available to lower-income neighborhoods and businessmen, a demand would automatically exist. Even though residents had not developed entrepreneurial skills in the past, it was assumed that capital and technical assistance, where none had existed before, would act as an adequate incentive for neophyte businessmen.

Community Control and Power

Perhaps the most important assumption of the community economic development movement was that the revitalization of neighborhoods required control over resources and institutions. As mentioned earlier, the War on Poverty and Model Cities programs focused attention on the issue of control. In many cities, battles with City Hall gave rise to a new, community-based leadership. Service-delivery programs, such as the War on Poverty, which always promised more than they could deliver and created permanent relationships of dependency, were viewed with increasing skepticism and disfavor. Many began to think along the lines of the old Chinese proverb: "Give a man a fish and he eats for a day. Teach a man to fish and he eats for a lifetime." In the late 1960s and early 1970s, this lesson was paraphrased as "community control" and "black power." In addition, as urban residents began to understand the waves of federal funding cycles for community development programs, they began to acknowledge that reliance on the federal government ran counter to their interests. Clearly, if a community could provide the social and human services it needed by itself, it would be able to get off the federal funding roller-coaster.

Community organizations which emerged in inner-city neighborhoods in response to the civil rights movement and the threat of governmental assaults (e.g., Urban Renewal and highway construction) were eager to maintain their position of control when they turned to community development. This transition—from a protest to a development agenda—was a natural outgrowth of the struggle for community control (see Chapter 10, dilemma 3).

Business Incentives as Job Strategy

The assumption that stimulating local economic activity was an effective means of creating jobs emerged as a popular argument to make the community economic development movement acceptable to traditional policymakers. Low-income people living in inner-city neighborhoods had poor access to the labor market. As productive enterprises moved out of cities, to suburbs or other regions, those left behind were stranded without work opportunities. Job loss or unavailability led to discouragement, frustration, and unrest. Community economic development advocates reasoned that new enterprises developed in low-income communities would create jobs for local people.

Thus there was a two-pronged hope: Small businesses would be profitable in lower-income neighborhoods abandoned by the private market; and entrepreneurs would be willing to provide jobs to unemployed, low-skilled workers—individuals who had not "made it" on the job market.

As of 1979, there were about 700 community-based economic development organizations in the country, including the forty-eight CDCs that had received Title VII funding (Litvak and Daniels, 1979). Yet the high expectations of the community economic development movement have been realized only partially. An examination of one state's experience, in which community economic development received major public support, reveals some of the weaknesses in the overall assumptions, as well as the problems that CDCs all across the country have encountered.

The Massachusetts Community Economic Development Program: 1978–1983

In Massachusetts, the community economic development movement received significant support from a group of local politicians, activists, and academics. Mel King, then a state representative from Boston's South End, was probably the pivotal actor in forging the coalition that was crucial to the creation of the state program.

Community Development Finance Corporation (CDFC)

Following more than a year of negotiation and debate, a bill was signed in 1975 creating the Community Development Finance Corporation (CDFC). In exchange for giving CDFC the proceeds from the sale of $10 million in state general obligation bonds, the state received all of the agency's common stock, thereby becoming its sole owner. CDFC's mandate was to function as a development bank that would make equity investments, which are relatively risky and difficult to obtain, as well as loans that would be paid back over a period of time, by debt financing. CDFC's funds were to be targeted to CDCs operating in blighted areas.

CDFC's operation was unique because of its willingness to take equity positions in risky ventures, its explicit focus on economically distressed areas, and its restriction to working with only one client, the CDC. The requirement that CDFC channel its funds through CDCs gave clear support to the view that projects should be controlled by, and operated for, the benefit of community residents.

Because of a legal delay in the sale of CDFC's bonds, the first investments were not made until 1978. Over the next three years, CDFC found that it was enormously difficult to locate and package attractive deals. By the end of 1981, only twenty-one investments with a value of $3.6 million had been made. Despite the original assumption that lack of capital was a major deterrent to development in depressed areas, there was relatively little demand for funds. This was in part because, at the start of CDFC's operation, there were only a handful of CDCs in the state. Moreover, the CDCs that were functioning had a great deal of difficulty attracting experienced staff and locating skilled entrepreneurs who could put together sound business ventures.

Another key problem in CDFC's early years was that many of the original investments ended in failure. Of the first twenty-five ventures financed, fourteen were closed and liquidated, and two had to be reorganized. As of early 1984, the remaining nine loans had either been repaid or were current. According to Nancy Nye, then vice-president of CDFC, "This compares reasonably well to the SBA [Small Business Administration] documented 55% failure rate of small businesses, particularly considering that all the CDFC ventures are located in distressed areas and by the very nature of the investment are higher risk than a general sample" (Nye, 1984).

Along with the slowness in making investments and the high rate of failure of the early loans, CDFC also had a disappointing record in stimulating job creation. As of the end of 1983, the agency could claim that only 474 jobs had been created or retained through CDFC investments (CDFC, 1984).

Community Economic Development
Assistance Corporation (CEDAC)

The need for a new agency that would provide technical assistance to CDCs was acknowledged by Massachusetts lawmakers even before CDFC realized that demand for its capital was weak and that only a relatively small number of organizations were eligible to receive investments. The Community Economic Development Assistance Corporation (CEDAC) was created in 1978 to provide technical assistance to CDCs. CEDAC's main functions were to assist groups in becoming CDCs and then to assist them in the initial stages of economic development planning and in the preparation of business plans for CDFC financing.

In its early years, CEDAC was less financially secure than the well-capitalized CDFC. Technical assistance is a much "softer" activity than financing, and it is difficult to measure direct outcomes of such efforts. Although technical assistance may be an essential ingredient in a given project, its contribution to producing new jobs or housing often is overlooked, partly because the bulk of technical assistance usually comes early in the process. Also, technical assistance providers often choose not to take credit themselves, playing intentional "behind-the-scenes" roles, thereby enabling the CDCs to receive praise for their accomplishments.

CEDAC also faced major hurdles due to a shift in administrations. Supported by the liberal governor Michael Dukakis, CEDAC did not start its operation until early in the King administration, in 1979. Governor King's view of CEDAC went from one of direct opposition to one of tolerance, but with no active support by the state's chief executive, CEDAC was forced to seek funding from the legislature on its own. Governor King further compromised a sound working relationship between CDFC and CEDAC by requiring the former to contract for services from CEDAC, in lieu of CEDAC receiving direct state funding. According to CEDAC personnel, this damaged credibility and compromised effectiveness (CEDAC, 1983).

All these factors contributed to CEDAC's shaky funding history. Whereas CDFC was capitalized with $10 million of state-secured funds, during CEDAC's first four years of operation (1978–1982) it received only $250,000 from state appropriations. During that period, it received another $700,000 through two federal sources, the Comprehensive Employment Training Act and the Economic Development Administration, neither of which provided guarantees for future funding.

Despite these impediments, CEDAC managed to "hold on" during the lean King years, providing technical assistance to community organizations and, perhaps more important, learning from its experiences and mistakes. By the end of its first four years, CEDAC concluded:

1. For CDCs to be in a position to undertake development, they must have a clear organizational agenda, an indigenous reason for existing, and strong leadership. CEDAC's technical assistance could not replace or create these attributes.
2. The agency needed to be more aggressive in assisting CDCs to initiate developments, by identifying viable projects that could be undertaken by eligible organizations.
3. Nationally, CDCs that were involved with real estate development had been more successful than those involved with business ventures (CEDAC, 1983).

Community Enterprise Economic Development Program (CEED)

The third major component of the Massachusetts economic development system is the Community Enterprise Economic Development Program (CEED). A forerunner of this program became operational in 1976 (two years before CDFC's first loan was made). In response to a request for proposals issued by the Massachusetts Executive Office of Communities and Development (EOCD) for "production-oriented as opposed to social service—or advocacy-oriented" community development projects, forty-four applications totaling almost $1 million were filed by nonprofit groups. With only $69,000 available, only four grants were made (EOCD, 1984). Three of the awards went to community groups involved with business ventures; one was for a land-use study; none related to housing.

Despite the small size of the pilot program (or, perhaps, because of it), there was a great deal of enthusiasm for the state's creating an ongoing capital fund to help nonprofit groups finance planning and start-up activities. In 1978, the Massachusetts legislature created the CEED program, with an appropriation for fiscal 1979 of $142,450. Between 1978 and 1983, thirty-nine organizations received over $1.5 million in CEED grants. During the early years of the CEED program, staff members assisted numerous groups with the initial stages of organization, including incorporation, formulation of community development plans, and board training. Yet it was not until 1982–1983 that the "organizational efforts [began to] bear fruit, as the material outputs of CDCs began to blossom" (EOCD, 1984).

Unlike CDFC and CEDAC, during CEED's early years there was significant involvement in housing. In 1982, CEED-funded CDCs rehabilitated or created over 350 units of housing, and in 1983 the number increased by more than 50 percent, to 530 units.

Overall, by 1983, the state funded economic development program could boast several important achievements. First, the number of CDCs in the state increased from eight in 1976 to more than fifty. Second, the total state investment in CDCs leveraged $127.9 million in other public and private investments for industrial, commercial, and housing development. And third, across the state, CDC projects created or retained 4000 jobs (EOCD, 1984).

Conceptually, the state's economic development program included many of the key pieces of a support system for CDCs. First, the CEED program helped to pay start-up costs as well as provide ongoing administrative support. Next, CEDAC provided the young organization with such technical assistance as marketing analyses, economic feasibility studies, and financial packaging, as it moved toward project development. Finally, CDFC provided financing to help launch sound business ventures. Although there was sometimes overlap in providing technical assistance, particularly between CEDAC and CEED, the functions of the three agencies were, for the most part, distinct and complemented one another.

The Emergence of a Support System for Community-Based Housing

From Economic Development to Housing: 1984

As discussed in the previous section, the Massachusetts economic development system was primarily oriented toward providing technical assistance and financing to CDCs involved with business and job-creation activities. Only the CEED program included an explicit housing and real estate focus. A 1983 CEDAC progress report noted the three main reasons behind its early job-creation focus:

> Based on the earlier successes of established CDCs, it appeared that community-based groups could successfully develop housing without assistance from a support institution like CEDAC. Furthermore, CDFC, which was the primary financing target for CEDAC assisted projects, would not finance real estate. Lastly, there was a sense among board members that job creation was a primary objective for CEDAC and an overriding and inadequately addressed problem in locales that qualify as CEDAC target areas. (CEDAC, 1983)

Several factors contributed to CDFC's and CEDAC's decision to move into housing; some of them had to do with experience with economic development, while others related to the positive attributes of housing as a vehicle for community development.

First, there was enormous frustration over the difficulty in finding the right kinds of business deals to finance. An analysis of the early community economic development program in Massachusetts observed that

> technical assistance, useful in turning good venture concepts into sound business plans, could not generate good venture concepts. . . . In order to stimulate demand at CDFC, CEDAC's effort turned to finding local entrepreneurs who wanted to start businesses. Yet, it soon became apparent that it is primarily the quality of the entrepreneur, not the business plan, that makes for a good investment. CEDAC staff discovered the lessons bankers learned years ago: management experience and expertise is indispensable and very hard to find. Community zeal can achieve great things but the delicate navigation of and single-minded attention to a business' health, like the expertise acquired by surgeons or highly trained workers, cannot be found or developed easily in most communities. (Bratt and Geiser, 1982)

Second, the record of CDFC's investments was, overall, disappointing. Although this record may not have been significantly worse than the failure rate for all small businesses, given the level of support being provided through the state system one would have hoped that a much higher percentage of investments would have been successful. In order to justify state funding, CDFC's investments, while high risk, would have to be put together better than the average small business deals. Housing, it was hoped, would provide more opportunities for successful investments.

A third reason why the economic development approach was abandoned was because of constraints imposed by low-income neighborhoods. Firms that leave an area usually do so because of an inability to make a profit there; by definition, residents in low-income areas have little money with which to purchase goods and services. Thus, CDCs often sponsored ventures with inexperienced entrepreneurs in areas already abandoned by more savvy businessmen.

Fourth, the low-income nature of the neighborhoods notwithstanding, almost any business venture is faced with an uncertain market once it is operational. In contrast, a decent unit of affordable housing is virtually guaranteed to find an eager tenant.

In addition to the desire to pursue something different in view of the experiences with economic development, there were some positive pressures for the state agencies to move into housing. First, the rehabilitation and construction of housing by community-based groups were familiar and successful activities in Massachusetts. In part because of the work of Greater Boston Community Development (GBCD), the notion that good, affordable housing could be produced and managed by nonprofits was relatively well accepted throughout the state. Incorporated as a nonprofit organization, GBCD serves as a housing development consultant to community-based sponsors of housing for low- and moderate-income residents. Its primary goal is to "enable community organizations to control the development and management of housing which will best serve the needs of lower income families, elderly and handicapped people" (GBCD, 1980, 5). Although it operates in many respects like a private developer, GBCD's first priority is to help community-based groups achieve their own housing and community development goals. Since 1964, GBCD has assisted over thirty nonprofit housing sponsors to develop over 4000 units of housing.[4] In addition, GBCD manages over 1500 units of housing, some of which it also played a role in developing.

One of GBCD's most important contributions has been the way in which it has used limited partnerships and, more recently, the low-income housing tax credit, to benefit community-based housing sponsors. GBCD claims that it has "structured limited partnerships so as to maximize the financial benefits to the sponsor and the development while protecting the sponsor's tax exempt status and control over the development" (GBCD, 1984, 12; also see Chapter 5). With a staff of about ninety (including property management and maintenance personnel), the agency continues to be a vigorous advocate, initiator, and technical-assistance provider for community-based housing activities.

Second, as a community development initiative, housing is more satisfying than the often invisible "economic development." A CDC-supported venture that creates a handful of jobs does not have the same visual impact as watching a formerly vacant lot become the site of newly constructed housing or an abandoned building being renovated. Housing is always a "concrete" and visible neighborhood-oriented activity.

Third, during the early 1980s, HUD began to pursue a policy of allowing foreclosed multifamily Section 221(d)(3) and 236 developments to be sold to the highest bidder, to be used for market-rate housing. The threat of this happening in Boston mobilized an effective campaign that persuaded the local HUD office to give priority to new buyers committed to maintaining the low- and moderate-income nature of the developments. Faced with this situation and committed to preventing the possible loss of thousands of low-income units, city and state officials responded to the need to salvage the HUD-foreclosed housing (see Chapter 7).

For all these reasons, staffs of the state's economic development agencies felt the push to get into housing. According to Nancy Nye, "Housing was what the CDCs were doing or wanted to do and, to be responsive, CDFC needed to move in that direction."[5] Similarly, Carl Sussman, executive director of CEDAC, stated that they "finally became convinced that the resources to do housing development were not really available to most of the CDCs in the state."[6] The interest in housing on the part of community groups was also stimulated by the dramatic need felt in many low-income communities. Private market forces, combined with the withdrawal of the federal government from subsidized housing production, had severely affected an already limited supply of affordable units.

The shift into housing was rapid. Within a few years about half of CDFC's loans were going toward housing initiatives.

As for CEDAC, virtually all its activity is now in housing. CEDAC at present provides $1–2 million per year in interest-free development assistance loans to organizations to cover the specific costs associated with project planning. By advancing small sums of money in the early stages of the development process and larger sums as the project moves toward closing, it has effectively managed to limit its risk. Ninety percent of the funds it lends are recovered when the construction financing agreement is executed. Within the past few years, CEDAC has been directly responsible for helping CDCs rehabilitate over 2000 units of housing. In addition, through a special $3.5 million fund provided by the Massachusetts Housing Partnership program, CEDAC has provided twenty nonprofit housing developers with front-end loans, technical assistance, or both. Considering these accomplishments, most observers agree that the shift from economic development to housing development was the right decision.

Although the key pieces of the Massachusetts support system for community-based housing are rooted in the community economic development movement, several additional agencies and programs play important roles.

Massachusetts Housing Finance Agency (MHFA)

Created in 1966 through an act of the Massachusetts legislature, the Massachusetts Housing Finance Agency (MHFA) was one of the country's first state housing finance agencies. Since 1970, when construction on the first MHFA-financed housing began, the agency has made loans totaling more than $3.4 billion to finance multifamily developments as well as homeownership units (MHFA, 1988). MHFA, as well as other state housing finance agencies, operates by issuing tax-exempt securities. The proceeds are used to make below-market-interest loans to private nonprofit or for-profit developers who agree to set aside 25 percent of the units for low-income tenants, defined according to public housing limits. Unfortunately, the Tax Reform Act of 1986 reclassified housing finance as a "nonessential government function" and placed volume caps on the amount of money each state may raise through the sale of such bonds. In Massachusetts, for example, the 1987 cap was about $430 million, less than one-quarter of the 1986 dollar volume of so-called nonessential bonding; MHFA alone issued $565 million in bonds (Massachusetts Housing Finance Agency, 1987).

Although CDFC provides a much-needed source of capital that often has made the difference between a project's being launched or not, MHFA is set up to provide construction or permanent financing for large-scale housing developments. This source of financing, with its clear public purpose, is a critical component of the state's overall support system for housing, including community-based initiatives.

Massachusetts Government Land Bank

The Massachusetts Government Land Bank was created in 1975 in response to a Defense Department announcement that it would be closing five military installations in the state. The Land Bank's mandate was to "aid private enterprise or public agencies in the speedy and orderly conversion and redevelopment of certain lands formerly used for military activities to non-military uses" (Massachusetts Government Land Bank, 1985). Capital was provided by $40 million in general obligation bonds, thereby giving the Land Bank a financing capacity to cover any expenses incurred in the course of its redevelopment work. When the agency's authorization was due to expire June 30, 1980, with several conversions nearing completion, a handful of state legislators sponsored legislation that extended the Land Bank's life and broadened its powers. According to the chairman of the House Commerce and Labor Committee, a clear rationale for the Land Bank's continuance was that in the process of fulfilling its original goals, "it had acquired the skills that could be applied to other areas of development" (Massachusetts Government Land Bank, 1985, 7).

With the new state legislation, the Land Bank was empowered to acquire, develop, and sell surplus state property, as well as surplus federal property located in Massachusetts, and blighted open or substandard properties. Since its mandate was broadened, the Land Bank has financed the production or rehabilitation of over 1200 units of housing. Several projects were developed by nonprofit community-based groups.

Additional EOCD-Operated Programs

In addition to the CEED program, EOCD administers an array of programs targeted to, or that can be used by, community-based housing groups.

A particularly important program administered by EOCD is the Massachusetts Housing Partnership (MHP). Modeled loosely on the Boston Housing Partnership (discussed in the next chapter), the MHP was created in 1985. Responding to the statewide need for affordable housing, the MHP provides state support and coordinates other public and private resources for local housing initiatives undertaken by municipalities, private developers, nonprofits, and others. Local partnerships function informally on specific action-oriented initiatives and, although nonprofit groups are not the only recipients eligible for MHP funds and assistance, they do comprise a key constituency. In recent years about 10 percent of MHP's budget has been allocated to CEDAC, which, in turn, advances loans to nonprofit developers.

Massachusetts also created one of the first state rental assistance programs in the country (Chapter 707) and, as mentioned in Chapter 5, in 1983 it launched a State Housing Assistance for Rental Production program (SHARP), a shallow rental subsidy which promotes mixed-income housing. In addition, the state operates the Rental Development Action Loan Program (R-DAL), which provides various types of loans to nonprofit sponsors who are constructing or rehabilitating mixed-income rental housing or limited-equity cooperatives; a Housing Innovations Fund (HIF), which gives an initial financial commitment to projects that enables public and nonprofit sponsors to leverage funds from other public and private sources to produce innovative/alternative forms of mixed-income/affordable housing; and a Homeownership Opportunity Program (HOP), which combines low-interest mortgage rate financing with various state and local contributions in order to produce sufficient incentives to for-profit and nonprofit developers to construct mixed-income homeownership developments.

In addition, seven more programs are in operation. First, a portion of the Massachusetts Community Services Block Grant (a total of $370,000 for fiscal year 1989) is targeted to community-based nonprofit groups. This special project is targeted to innovative projects that expand the availability and affordability of existing housing for low-income households. Second, a portion of the federally funded Small Cities Community Development Block Grant is targeted to rural CDCs. Third, the Commonwealth Service Corps program pays individuals to work in community-based neighborhood development and service-delivery projects. Fourth, the Neighborhood Front Money Loan Fund is a $300,000 revolving fund that provides seed financing to CDCs to assist with real estate development projects. Fifth, the state has its own program to support the ten Neighborhood Housing Services organizations in Massachusetts. For fiscal year 1989, $835,000 was appropriated to support homeownership rehabilitation and other neighborhood revitalization projects. Sixth, the Housing Abandonment Program makes $832,000 available to community-based and tenant organizations to reimburse them for expenses associated with financing the rehabilitation of tax-delinquent, abandoned, or deteriorated residential properties. Finally, the Organizational Development Fund provides grants of up to $2500 each to help young CDC's cover some of the out-of-pocket costs associated with forming a new organization.

Outline for Evaluating the System

A thorough assessment of the Massachusetts system that supports community-based housing activities is not available at this time. Several recent reports have described the Massachusetts system of support for community-based housing, but these studies have not provided a full evaluation of that experience (Barbe and Sekera, 1983; Erdmann, 1987; Roberts et al., 1980; Seidman, 1986). Unfortunately, little data currently exist for most of the relevant measures, such as housing, neighborhood–market, social, and organizational impacts. For each of these measures, a substantial amount of information would have to be collected. Relevant data to assess housing impacts would include the number, physical quality, and cost of units produced and rehabilitated, as well as an assessment of the quality of maintenance over time. Impacts on the neighborhood or local market often are more difficult to determine. Nevertheless, researchers would want to collect information on the extent of public and private investment in housing, retail or commercial areas, and public facilities. In addition, changes in socioeconomic groups, evidence of forced displacement or gentrification, as well as indicators of neighborhood stability (e.g., homeownership rates and community perceptions) would be studied. The social impacts of community-based housing activities could be assessed by determining whether they were supplemented by social services programs; how the perceptions of residents in the buildings have changed (particularly with regard to feelings of well-being, security, and control); and whether there were evidence of an increased sense of empowerment among leaders or participants in the housing development process. Finally, the impacts on the community-based housing organizations themselves could be evaluated in terms of their ability to manage their properties, the extent to which they have been successful in launching additional production and rehabilitation projects, and their ability to act as a voice for residents in public or private controversies or development schemes.

In order to broaden our understanding of the capabilities and limitations of community-based housing, the state or an academic or research institution should launch a longitudinal project that will systematically gather this information. But since the above list of measures is, at the present, still a "wish list," we are faced with the immediate problem of evaluating how the Massachusetts system of supports for community-based housing is working. One way is to assess the extent to which the Massachusetts system incorporates the components of a hypothetical model support system for community-based housing. Another way of evaluating the system in the absence of hard facts, is to determine what the Massachusetts experience already reveals about how government can support community-based housing. Pointing out some of the areas that are likely to present future problems also is important, both for those involved in the state system and for those hoping to build similar programs. These two approaches for evaluating the Massachusetts system are presented in the following two sections.

The Massachusetts System as a Model Support System

What would an ideal community-based housing system look like? A model public support system for community-based housing could actually take many forms. At one extreme, it could include vast resources and a completely changed housing system, so that all production would be done by public and nonprofit agencies. This model would eliminate private, for-profit actors in the housing system and would, instead, have all production and management tasks coordinated through public and nonprofit development entities. But the model that follows assumes the existence of a private housing system, as we now have, and suggests "ideal" modifications to that system to support community-based housing initiatives. A model support system along these lines would provide financial resources, technical assistance, and access to land and buildings, and would create an evaluation and information-sharing network.[7]

Financial Resources

Adequate financial resources are obviously crucial to the success of community-based housing activities. Although outright grants are a cheap and direct way of subsidizing housing (see Chapter 3), the high short-term costs of this approach make it a politically difficult option (see Chapter 13). However the funding is provided, through grants, loans, or some combination of the two, four distinct types of financial resources are needed.

Seed Money for Organizational Expenses. For a community group to initiate a housing program, early funding to cover start-up costs is essential. Grants for initial operating expenses enable groups formally to establish an organization, develop specific strategies, and line up resources appropriate to the specific development to be undertaken. Seed money is needed to cover such expenses as office rental, secretarial assistance, and a director's salary.

First-Stage Funding for Project Initiation. Before a community group reaches the point where its project can go into the construction phase, it is usually necessary for a series of activities to take place. For example, legal, architectural, and engineering services probably are needed; tests on the soil may have to be done; and site options on land or buildings may have to be purchased. These costs can be substantial, and since private financing is often impossible to obtain, they may prevent a group from launching a project. A "bridge loan," which is secured by the anticipated syndication proceeds, or some other form of loan or grant that would cover these costs, is an important component of a public support system for community-based housing.

Construction and Debt Financing for Project Implementation. There are at least three distinct ways in which funds for construction loans and long-term debt financing can be obtained: (1) through a publicly capitalized bank specifically set up for this purpose; (2) from a private financial institution with or without some federal mortgage insurance or guarantee; and (3) through a special "FNMA-GNMA" tandem plan program. For the latter, the Government National Mortgage Association (GNMA) would make commitments to purchase a certain amount of below-market-interest mortgages originated by community-based housing groups. These loans would then be sold to the Federal National Mortgage Association (FMNA) at prevailing market rates, with GNMA providing a subsidy equal to the difference between the yields on the market rate and the below-market-rate transactions.

Subsidies to Reduce Costs to Households. The final component of the financial resources package is direct subsidies to individual units and households to lower the final costs, along the lines of the Section 8 Existing Housing program and the Massachusetts Chapter 707 program. In short, what is needed is a two-pronged subsidy program: one that encourages and supports the production or otherwise increases the supply of housing; and one that provides individuals with extra buying power, or effective demand, to make units affordable.

Land and Buildings

The ability of a community group to gain control of land and buildings at affordable prices is another central component of a community-based housing system. The rapidly increasing price of land and building experienced in many areas, partly the result of speculation and partly caused by inflation, and the unlikelihood that funding levels for a community-based housing system could cover these elevated costs, necessitates some form of public mechanism for controlling land and building costs.[8] A community-based housing system should provide resources both to public agencies to acquire or hold land and buildings for future use by community-based groups (land banking) and for nonprofit organizations to form community land trusts. The latter permanently removes the property from the private speculative market and guarantees that all future uses of the land or building will serve the interests of the community and its residents (see Chapter 8).

Technical Assistance

Technical assistance is the third major necessary ingredient for a comprehensive community-based housing system. Three groups of actors are in need of this assistance.

Community Groups. Community organizations are the logical first group needing technical assistance in the community-based housing system. Over the past few years, a great deal has been learned about the technical assistance needed by local organizations to launch successful neighborhood development projects. Several kinds of "hands-on" assistance are valuable to community-based development organizations, including proposal writing and negotiating with outside individuals and agencies, especially funding sources; legal assistance; accounting; defining board and staff roles and training board members; and organizational structuring (Mayer and Blake, 1981). In addition, information specifically related to housing must be available: how the housing development process works; what subsidy programs are available and how they operate; and how to relate to key actors, including financial institutions, architects, lawyers, city officials, syndication firms, contractors, and general partners.

Once a community-based housing group has successfully built or taken over the management of a housing development, it may need assistance in running the project and dealing with such issues as tenant selection, lease enforcement, and ongoing management and maintenance. As the group matures, it also may need help assessing whether or not to undertake additional developments and how it can provide nonhousing services to meet the needs of the local community better.

In order to institutionalize a high quality of technical assistance, a national technical-assistance organization could be established. One of the functions of a Community-Based Housing Support Corporation (CBHSC) would be to help locales set up statewide, citywide, or regional technical-assistance agencies modeled after CEDAC, GBCD, and UHAB (Urban Homesteading Assistance Board), for example, that would provide information, technical support, and possibly some funding to community-based housing groups. These quasi-independent organizations would serve as intermediaries, to the extent needed, between the community group and other public and private actors. For some community-based groups, technical assistance only may be needed or desired for the early projects, while staff expertise is being developed. Other groups may prefer to buy outside technical help, even after they have completed initial projects. Technical-assistance providers would have to be alert to the needs of different groups and would tailor their services to meet those needs.

CBHSCs would not replace or duplicate technical-assistance providers currently working at the national level, whose missions involve assistance in setting up a specific kind of organization, such as Neighborhood Reinvestment Corporation's focus on Neighborhood Housing Services, Mutual Housing Associations, and Apartment Improvement programs; channeling private funds to local nonprofit groups, as with the Local Initiatives Support Corporation and the Enterprise Foundation; or providing technical assistance to groups in areas where such help is not otherwise available, as with the Center for Community Change. Instead, the CBHSCs would help locales all around the country chart their own community-based housing strategies and would assist them in locating and utilizing the funds and other supports provided by the above-mentioned organizations.

Other Important Participants.   In addition to providing technical assistance to community-based housing agencies, training and educational programs would have to be launched for other important participants in the community-based housing process. Two of the most important actors are city government and the local business community, notably financial institutions.

Many aspects of community-based housing activities require a high level of commitment and support by local government. For example, buildings and land in tax arrears can either become the target of private, for-profit development interests, enormous resources to community groups, or significant blights on a neighborhood. Unless the city understands how it can quickly identify such properties and sees the benefits of allowing community-based groups to take title, usable units can quickly become extremely costly or uneconomical to repair. Cities need to be taught how early-warning systems for identifying and taking possession of properties in tax arrears operate. They must also learn from other locales about the benefits of community-based development and about how they can provide the necessary supports to such efforts. Many city governments are still uninformed about community-based development and, as discussed in Chapter 9 in reference to Holyoke, Massachusetts, the education of local officials is a critical task for an overall community-based housing strategy.

Financial institutions and other private entities also need assistance in understanding how community-based housing groups operate and how their cooperation can create affordable housing for their workforce, create new markets for their goods or services, and contribute to a worthwhile activity (see Chapter 13).

Evaluation and Information-Sharing Network

The last major component of the support system for community-based housing involves the creation of a communication and dissemination network. It is crucial that community-based groups, as well as all other actors, have opportunities to share information and experiences. Several national groups already working at disseminating information on community-based initiatives could provide the backbone for this effort, notably the Community Information Exchange and the National Congress for Community Economic Development. The final component of an information-sharing network should involve ongoing research and evaluations of community-based housing activities.

The Massachusetts system encompasses many key components of the model community-based housing system. In particular, it includes all of the necessary funding and subsidy mechanisms. But the system does not include "deep" subsidies. The subsidies, which were available through the federal Section 8 New Construction/Substantial Rehabilitation program, which guarantee tenants low rents while providing owners with adequate revenues for substantial debt and operating expenses, are not provided by the state. Although Massachusetts has several subsidy programs, none provides deep subsidies to community-based housing sponsors (or, for that matter, any private developer).[9] Without a public supply of money that can be used to lower rents substantially, the Massachusetts system, however comprehensive and exemplary, may face serious problems. The economics of housing production/substantial rehabilitation for low-income people simply does not work without significant public subsidies.

Finances aside, there are some other omissions and problems in the Massachusetts system. First, there are drawbacks to the array of programs available in Massachusetts: It is difficult to use such a complex system and it is likely that considerable overlap exists. All the programs serving nonprofits should be assessed and an effort should be made to streamline them and reduce duplication wherever possible. Second, although several agencies provide technical assistance, the system does not offer help to groups other than community organizations. Third, it does not include a land acquisition and land banking program; therefore, community-based groups must compete for land and buildings with private speculative developers.

Fourth, the Massachusetts system does not yet include a comprehensive evaluation system. A thorough assessment of the impact of the Massachusetts system should be undertaken, along the lines outlined above. Finally, more networking and sharing of information among nonprofits is needed. Although the Massachusetts Association of Community Development Corporations serves this function to some extent, there is still a need for CDCs and other nonprofit housing developers to have more opportunities to learn from each other's experiences.

Observations from the Massachusetts Experience

State Government and Community-Based Housing

The state appears to be a good level through which to administer community-based housing programs, as follows:

1. The state can pass legislation, create new programs, and put significant resources into them.
2. The power and prestige of the governor and executive departments can facilitate program development and coordination.
3. The state is in a good position to assess local needs.
4. State housing finance agencies have proven to be effective entities for channeling financial resources into housing (see Betnun, 1976).
5. State government is a manageable size through which to operate community-based housing systems.

Nevertheless, in contrasting a state system with a federal support system, the state system does reveal some weaknesses:

1. Some states would never adopt a community-based housing system, thereby leaving many people and localities without the needed resources. Only a federal support system would have the ability to reach the entire country.
2. The amount of money needed to launch and sustain a community-based housing system is substantial, and it is unlikely that any state would have the resources necessary to do the job thoroughly.
3. Not only does a state-based system have inadequate resources but it is also vulnerable to shifts in policies at the federal level that can significantly undermine its operation.

There has been little detailed work on the idea of institutionalizing a system of support for community-based housing initiatives. Although seven distinct proposals can be identified, the state generally has not been viewed as key to the overall plan.

The first, which involved a broad economic development agenda, was proposed by the Twentieth Century Fund Task Force (1971). They called for "the building of a nationwide system of support for community-based economic development programs" whose objectives would be "to enhance the effectiveness of community development corporations and to enlarge their capacity for self-help" (p. 12). Included in the proposal were seven key elements, although how they were to be administered was not discussed.

The second proposal, suggested by Keyes (1971), outlined the development of metropolitan or state-level Community Housing Corporations that would act as conduits for federal funds and provide technical assistance and financial packaging to local housing groups, similar to GBCD's present operation.

The third, presented by Egan et al. (1981), did not call for any single programmatic initiative; instead, they suggested that policy-makers and government officials change their attitudes to be more supportive toward "mediating structures": neighborhood, church, family, and voluntary associations.

The fourth, outlined by Mott (1984) and the National Low Income Housing Coalition, and introduced as legislation in 1988 by Congressman Joseph Kennedy as the Community Housing Partnership Act, calls for the creation of a new program that would target federal funds for housing production and rehabilitation to projects controlled by neighborhood residents, tenants, or both (see Chapter 13). Federal, state, and local governments would share in disbursing the subsidy money but, unlike in Keyes's proposal (1971), no new agency would be created.

A fifth suggestion to create a community-based housing supply program was first outlined by me (Bratt, 1985b); the expanded version is presented above. Similar to Keyes, in this proposal GBCD is seen as an important model for new local technical-assistance organizations. However, this proposal also calls for the creation of a coordinated group of state agencies and programs.

The sixth proposal was developed by Erdmann (1987), who advocated a key role for states in assisting community economic development initiatives. This study recommends that states examine their unique needs and tailor their programs accordingly, rather than try to replicate the system in any one state. Thus, no single model of support for community-based organizations is advocated.

Finally, the *Report of the National Housing Task Force* (1988) recommended that 10 percent of a proposed first-year $3 billion additional allocation for housing be set aside for nonprofit community-based housing organizations. The new funds, part of a "Housing Opportunity Program," would go to state and local governments with a minimum of federal regulation. HUD would be directed to administer the new program with a maximum of flexibility to enable localities to design programs to meet their own needs.

Not surprisingly, none of the proposals suggested a system of supports for community-based housing nearly as complex as the one that evolved in Massachusetts. The complexity of the Massachusetts system may be due in part to its piecemeal development and its original emphasis on community economic development, not housing.

Liberals Versus Conservatives: Support for Community-Based Housing

A progressive/liberal Democratic administration is more likely than a conservative Republican administration to support a community-based housing system. Although this may be fairly obvious, it is a reminder that some important distinctions exist between this country's two major political parties.

At the federal level, we have had ample evidence that liberal Democrats are much more likely to support housing subsidy programs than are conservative Republicans, such as Ronald Reagan, who virtually dismantled the nation's housing programs. Further, over the past twenty-five years, it has been the Democrats who have created programs that were, at least by their rhetoric, oriented toward empowering poor people. The War on Poverty and Model Cities, enacted during the Johnson administration, and despite significant weaknesses, did encompass some of the values that underlie a community-based approach to housing. President Carter's creation of a neighborhood-oriented office at HUD was another example that liberal Democrats have more aggressively explored neighborhood-based solutions to housing and community development problems.

The Massachusetts experience again demonstrates that a liberal Democrat, Governor Dukakis, has done much more to support the community-based housing agenda than his conservative predecessor, Governor King. During the King administration (1979–1982), CEDAC was almost eliminated, there was very little program development, and there were few efforts toward coordination.[10] In contrast, during Governor Dukakis's first term (1975–1978), three major community economic development initiatives—CDFC, CEDAC, and CEED—were launched. During Governor Dukakis's second and third terms (1983–present), EOCD has been staffed by individuals with extensive prior experience in community-based housing who have a genuine commitment to the approach. "A State Strategy for Neighborhood Development" (Tierney, 1984) has been developed, and a host of new programs have been launched.

Another important aspect of the emerging state system is the willingness to allocate increased funds to the various programs. Most striking is that CEED now is operating on a $2.2 million yearly budget, 50 percent more than the total CEED expenditures between 1978 and 1983 ($1.5 million).

Finally, Dukakis's EOCD is aware that coordination is a critical component of a community-based housing system. Although more work needs to be done in this area, the Dukakis administration has been alert to potential overlaps in the system. For example, EOCD staff spent much of the first six months of 1983 working out institutional links between CDFC, CEDAC, and EOCD. A key result was that CEDAC's board was reconstituted to make the agency less independent and to define its operation more explicitly as an arm of EOCD. EOCD's deputy assistant secretary for neighborhoods and economic opportunity now chairs the CEDAC board. But although the Democrats look awfully good when compared to their Republican counterparts, no federal administration has sponsored a comprehensive system of supports for community-based housing.

Questionable Replicability

Despite the growth in the number of CDCs through the 1980s, by mid-1987 only six states (Florida, Illinois, Massachusetts, Minnesota, New Hampshire, and Wisconsin) had "passed legislation authorizing community development finance programs that provide some combination of administrative support, technical assistance, and project financing to community development corporations" (Erdmann, 1987, viii). None of the other efforts, however, match the scope of the Massachusetts support system. Even in Massachusetts, it is unclear whether the system could have been launched from scratch, particularly if the original focus of the programs had been housing, not community economic development. Although the state's community economic development program was not going to compete with private entrepreneurs, since it was to provide employment and business opportunities in areas abandoned by the private market, the creation of CDFC and its capitalization were nevertheless subjects of intense legislative debates. While the community economic development program ultimately prevailed, it did so by only a slim margin.

The question is, Could a support system for community-based housing, which to many may appear to be taking business away from private, for-profit developers, get the needed support? Even though the unassisted private sector is not interested in producing low-income housing, for-profit developers are certain to be against any program of subsidies to build low-income housing that does not include them. As discussed in Chapters 3 and 4, the homebuilders and real estate associations always have been vehemently opposed to the conventional public housing program, which does not rely on private developers and owners. Conversely, these groups historically have been strong advocates of subsidized housing programs in which they had a role.

The Massachusetts support system for community-based housing may have some qualities of a "lucky accident." Community economic development was proving difficult to carry out, and there was strong support for the state to become involved with low-income housing, notwithstanding opposition by the private sector. Although it may be only coincidence, at about the same time that the state began to support community-based housing, Governor Dukakis spearheaded an initiative designed specifically to assist private developers in undertaking rental developments. The SHARP program mentioned earlier provides a significant financial incentive for all private developers—for-profit and nonprofit community groups—of predominantly market-rate rental housing. While it may be erroneous to ascribe causality, SHARP may have helped deflect opposition to the emerging community-based housing agenda. Thus, in considering how a state-supported community-based housing program could be replicated, it is important to consider who the likely opponents would be and how their objections could be handled. Aside from these political considerations, the Massachusetts state program could, conceptually at least, be replicated. Any new state initiative should, however, aim for greater simplicity and a small number of comprehensive programs.

Targeting Resources

The young and growing Massachusetts support system has pursued a strategy of deciding what programs are important and then has sought funding to implement them. This approach speaks to the debate about whether it is better to fund broad goals through block grants or to specify more explicit program guidelines and fund them through categorical grants. Massachusetts has enjoyed the flexibility provided through several federal block grant programs, but as for developing its own strategy, it has chosen to initiate new categorical programs when it felt a particular need. Nevertheless, as indicated above, it is now timely for the state to reduce the complexity of and overlap in its programs.

Will Public Support System Be Community-Based?

Experience with the state's early community economic development program revealed the difficulty inherent in government's trying to stimulate local responses to problems. If an effort is truly to be community-based, what role, if any, is appropriate for a public body? According to Annette Rubin-Casas, former director of EOCD's Office of Community Economic Development for Community Non-Profits, before CDFC became involved with housing, some CDCs were created that were not truly community-based. Local entreprenuers needing assistance to launch a business could help develop a CDC that would then serve as a conduit for state funds.[11] In pursuing a housing agenda, however, CDCs may be developing as more explicit community-based organizations. Michael Tierney, EOCD's assistant secretary for municipal government, has stated: "In venture development the CDC is dependent on entrepreneurial skills; in housing development the CDC is the entrepreneur."[12] The CDC that coalesces around housing goals and develops a project is almost certain to be responding to the needs of the community. Ulterior motives are unlikely. Nevertheless, it remains to be seen whether the state's community-based housing system will be successful in providing top–down supports to bottom–up activities (see Chapter 13).

Need for Individual Commitment and Expertise

The Massachusetts community economic development program emerged from the vision of a handful of community activists, academics, and legislators. As the program adopted a housing agenda, the commitment of many professionals to community-based housing and their willingness to work extremely hard, were essential. As one astute observer put it: "Hernandez, Edgerly, Whittlesey, and Clancy are the best in the country at making community development happen" (Robb, 1985, 65).[13] Nevertheless, a system such as the one operating in Massachusetts, is not the work of one or even a few people. While there have been some impressive leaders, the system could not work without the scores of committed and competent staff people at public and quasi-public agencies, private institutions and foundations, and the CDCs themselves.

Although the Massachusetts system of supports for community-based housing is highlighted in this chapter, the role played by the City of Boston—notably by Mayor Raymond Flynn—in advancing the agenda should be underscored. Flynn's administration has targeted city funding and vacant land to nonprofit housing groups and has played a key role in supporting the Community Housing Partnership Act (discussed in Chapter 13; see also Bratt, 1989c). The ability of the state to work so closely with its largest city has helped to strengthen its overall support system for community-based housing.

Importance of Quasi-Public Agencies

Quasi-public agencies, such as CEDAC, CDFC, and MHFA, play critical roles in the state's system. Although it is theoretically possible that many, if not all, of the functions performed by CEDAC could be carried out by EOCD, state line agencies in Massachusetts are not permitted to perform the banking functions of CDFC and MHFA. Also, the ability of these agencies to pay more than the state's maximum salaries has allowed them to be competitive with the private sector and to attract high-quality personnel and hire costly consultants when necessary. Finally, quasi-public agencies are able to move quickly and avoid some of the red tape that is an unavoidable part of a state bureaucracy.

The Need for a Flexible System

Even in the short time during which the Massachusetts system has been operating, the need for flexibility has become apparent. The shift from community economic development to housing development was a radical one, and it is a credit to the people involved that there was a willingness to change. The ability to acknowledge problems in the system and make necessary adjustments was also apparent when CEDAC became more closely controlled by EOCD.

New pressures for change are inevitable, and the system still has some important challenges facing it. For example, the overlap in the system needs to be addressed. Second, with the high cost of land and buildings in Massachusetts, many community-based housing developments that were financially feasible only a few years ago or that benefited from opportunities to acquire land cheaply through the urban renewal program, would now be impossible because site control would be too expensive. Third, a handful of older CDCs in the state are being confronted with new responsibilities, such as how to manage their services and investments. The state will have to begin to develop assistance programs to address the needs of the more seasoned CDCs.

Finally, any state system must be extremely adaptable to get through the years of minimal federal support. As discussed earlier, the Achilles heel of the Massachusetts system for community-based housing may be the lack of deep federal subsidies and the changes in the federal income tax system that have made private investment in subsidized housing less lucrative. As good as the overall program may be, the system depends on federal policies. The inability of the state to function completely on its own suggests that a comprehensive community-based housing system would have to be supported, if not necessarily implemented, by the federal government.

In summary, housing may be the most suitable vehicle for launching community-based development projects because it is highly visible and less risky than economic development initiatives. The Massachusetts system of supports for community-based housing presents an exciting model that, theoretically, could be emulated by other states. Refinements in the system should be based on a more thorough evaluation of its impacts and costs. Despite the many strengths of a state-based system, the federal government must resume a direct deep-subsidy program, as well as explore ways to launch a national support system for community-based housing.

The Massachusetts system of support for community-based housing may continue to operate only at the margins of our present housing system. If that is so, it will constantly be facing an uphill fight to sustain its programs. More optimistically, the Massachusetts model could become a centerpiece of a revived federal housing policy and a tangible symbol of a new commitment to the universal right to decent shelter.

12

Institutionalizing Community-Based Housing Development

■ CASE STUDY

The Boston Housing Partnership

WENDY PLOTKIN, co-author

THE BOSTON Housing Partnership (BHP), a public–private initiative, was established in 1983. Created jointly by the city's Neighborhood Development and Employment Agency (NDEA, now merged into the Public Facilities Department), the larger banks in the city, and neighborhood organizations, the overriding goal of the BHP is to convert deteriorating and abandoned housing into decent, affordable housing for low- and moderate-income families. Not since the late 1960s had there been such a strong interest on the part of the city in housing rehabilitation. But, this time, community-based development organizations were to be major actors in the process. Public and private resources were to be channeled to community-based groups, and the role of these entities as substantial providers of low- and moderate-income housing was to be enhanced.[1]

The partnership was a response to a number of events: the loss of affordable rental housing in Boston's neighborhoods as a result of abandonment, arson, condominium conversion, and rising rents; the increasing demand for housing in general, but particularly low-cost rental units, throughout Boston; a desire by planners at the NDEA and the Boston Redevelopment Authority (BRA) to develop a strategy for reclaiming foreclosed and tax-title properties; an increasingly strong community-based development sector in the state and city; and the success of Goals for Boston, a public–private partnership concerned with education, race relations, and jobs, created in 1980. Finally, the drastic cutbacks in federal housing subsidies during the Reagan administration, particularly the Section 8 New Construction and Substantial Rehabilitation programs, were still another major stimulus behind the creation of the partnership. Housing advocates quickly realized that no single source of funding would be able to replace the deep subsidies provided through the federal programs; creative new solutions would be needed.

Two critical elements helped bring this array of forces together to form the partnership. First, providing support from the private sector was William Edgerly, chairman of the State Street Bank and Trust Company, founder of the Goals for Boston program. As housing rose in importance as a city issue, in large part due to the leadership of Mayor Raymond Flynn, Edgerly and David Mundel, then director of the NDEA, conceived of a public–private housing partnership.

Second, the interest in community-based sponsors resulted, in large part, from the work of Greater Boston Community Development and from several successful projects that had been built. As discussed in Chapter 11, by the early 1980s GBCD had established itself as a highly professional and competent organization with an impressive track record assisting nonprofit housing sponsors. GBCD staff played key roles working out many of the major conceptual and procedural details of the partnership.

The BHP's first project was to turn 700 units of deteriorated and abandoned multifamily structures into affordable and livable housing. Known as the Demonstration Program, it was the largest coordinated rehabilitation effort in the city in fifteen years. This chapter assesses the potential of the BHP to serve as a prototype rehabilitation program and as a model for institutionalizing assistance to community-based housing organizations.

Financial Operation of the BHP Demonstration Program

In the summer of 1983, the BHP issued a request for proposals by community-based groups interested in participating in the partnership. Projects were to be 30–100 units in size and were to have acquisition and rehabilitation costs of approximately $26,000 per unit.[2] An additional $4500 per unit for other development expenses was permitted to cover architectural and engineering studies, legal fees, and consultants. Properties with tax and utility arrearages could be included, and, finally, projects had to comply with all city and state zoning, sanitary, and building codes.

The ten community groups chosen ranged from the knowledgeable to the inexperienced.[3] At one extreme was Urban Edge, which had used federal and state programs to rehabilitate nearly 300 units in the previous ten years. At the other extreme was the Quincy Geneva Housing Development Corporation, which was formed by two neighborhood organizations specifically in response to the Demonstration Program. Most of the groups selected had done a small amount of rehabilitation, usually on one- to six-family dwellings, or new construction in the form of manufactured housing. Six were receiving operating funds from the Massachusetts Community Enterprise and Economic Development (CEED) program, discussed in Chapter 11.

The community-based sponsors had a number of responsibilities: completing the paperwork required to obtain the financial resources that were arranged by the BHP; identifying and acquiring buildings; contracting with a rehabilitation contractor and overseeing the rehabilitation work; and maintaining oversight of property management. GBCD was available as a free consultant during the application stage to assist community-based applicants to identify and negotiate site control of properties and develop preliminary construction and operating budgets. Successful applicants were guaranteed development funds, which included payment to a consultant of their choice to assist in the development of the properties. The BHP staff also provided technical assistance, although its small size (initially three people) limited the resources available.

The projects ranged in size from 20 to 101 units. "Large-family" apartments—those with three or more bedrooms—constituted more than one-third of the units, with another third containing two bedrooms. Two-thirds of the buildings were of brick masonry construction; the remainder were wood frame. Approximately 25 percent of the units and 17 percent of the buildings were vacant. Two-thirds of the buildings were tax delinquent; many also owed water and sewer debts.

Prerehabilitation rents were low, ranging from $50 to $75 per month for the least-expensive one-bedroom units to $363 for the most-expensive four-bedroom unit. Four of the sponsors had significant numbers of tenants with rental subsidies in their buildings. Four sponsors also had ten or more rent-controlled units in their packages.

In order to bring the postrehabilitation costs of the units down to affordable rent levels (or those allowed by the rental subsidy programs being utilized), a complex patchwork of financing was assembled by BHP staff and GBCD. Virtually every possible federal, state, and local financing source was exploited, in addition to financing by local banks and grants and loans from private foundations, as follows:

1. *Equity/seed money*
   Community Development Block Grants awarded by the city
   Grants from the Public Welfare Foundation, the Hyams Trust, the Mabel G. Riley Foundation, and the Local Initiatives Support Corporation
   Syndication proceeds from a pooled syndication of the ten individual projects
2. *Debt financing*
   Construction loans from a consortium of four Boston banks (First National Bank of Boston, State Street Bank, Bank of New England, and Shawmut Bank)
   Below-market-interest permanent mortgages from the Massachusetts Housing Finance Agency
   FNMA guarantees of the permanent mortgages, resulting in a lower interest rate than ordinarily available on MHFA mortgages[4]
3. *Working capital*
   Loans from the Massachusetts Community Development Finance Corporation, the Local Initiatives Support Corporation, and the Program Related Investment Division of the Ford Foundation to cover construction and operating cost overruns and provide sponsoring organizations with additional operating capital
4. *Gap financing*
   Loans from the City of Boston's unspent CDBG funds (secured by a letter of credit from the banks), to be used for development purposes and repaid from later syndication payments
5. *Rental subsidies*
   Federal rental subsidies (Section 8 Existing Housing and Moderate Rehabilitation)
   State rental subsidies (Chapter 707)
6. *Interest subsidies*
   The Massachusetts SHARP program (State Housing Assistance for Rental Production): fifteen-year, interest-free loans administered by MHFA in the form of annual payments to reduce the cost of debt service on permanent financing to as low as 5 percent
7. *Abatements and writedowns*
   Property tax abatements from the city and the state (referred to as the "8 of 58" program from the legal authority in Chapter 8, Section 58 of the Massachusetts General Laws)
   Cost writedowns on tax-foreclosed properties

The sheer number of financing sources indicates that this was not a simple program. Since each provider of financing had its own rules and requirements, with which the BHP had to comply, the Demonstration Program emerged as a complex and cumbersome endeavor. From the outset, everbody viewed the financing package as far from ideal.

The BHP's Demonstration Program should be viewed in a historical context. It is one of the most recent in a series of efforts to rehabilitate housing for low-income households. More specifically, the Demonstration Program can be seen as an outgrowth of two broad types of initiatives: large-scale, public–private, for-profit rehabilitation efforts in the inner city; and production of housing by individual community-based developers. In the latter category, the Demonstration Program can be compared to the early nonprofits, those operating in the 1960s and early 1970s, and to current nonprofit development efforts that do not work through the BHP. After a brief description of Boston's only other large-scale rehabilitation program, the Boston Urban Rehabilitation Program, the ways in which the Demonstration Program differs from and improves on this as well as other initiatives are examined.

Boston Urban Rehabilitation Program (BURP): A Public–Private Initiative

Launched in 1967, BURP was an attempt by HUD to demonstrate the viability of the Section 221(d)(3) program as well as a federal–local effort to respond to the needs of low-income neighborhoods stemming from the urban riots. Providing a 3 percent mortgage to limited-dividend and nonprofit developers, the Section 221(d)(3) program had been criticized by developers for long processing times and onerous bureaucratic procedures (see Chapter 4). The recently created HUD, under its first secretary, Robert Weaver (see Chapter 6), responded to these criticisms by conceiving of a fast-track approach to rehabilitate 2000 units of housing in Roxbury, a predominantly black Boston neighborhood with much deteriorated and abandoned housing.

HUD's plan was to select experienced developers with a promise of subsidy commitments and authority to proceed in sixty days. Five well-known white developers were chosen, with the understanding that they would complete construction within six months of closing. Involvement by the black community was absent: The program lacked black sponsors or developers; the sponsors chosen were not required to hire Roxbury residents or minorities; and the relocation needs of the primarily black tenants were ignored. Black leaders were outraged.

Through pressure and threats of disrupting the program, the black community was able to extract a number of changes to the original program. In particular, an agreement was reached to hire and train more than 300 minority workers, two minority developers were added, and a $550,000 relocation plan was developed with the Boston Redevelopment Authority in charge of overseeing the plan.

The community and various evaluators were highly critical of BURP's final product. Three of the five original developers did not finish their work within the six-month deadline, taking up to a year and a half. One developer did not finish at all, and HUD foreclosed during the construction period. Change orders costing over $600,000 were submitted by another developer, and HUD was forced to approve them for fear of having to foreclose. There were also charges that the developers' work was shoddy and that there were physical problems resulting from poor management (Urban Planning Aid, 1973b). Unfortunately, the minority developers generally experienced the same difficulties as their white counterparts (Keyes, 1970).

Problems continued after rehabilitation ended. Poor management and rising operating costs generated serious financial problems; by the mid-1970s, HUD had foreclosed on over half the units, representing the parcels of four of the five original developers and both minority developers. In 1982, HUD took possession of the remaining units. Some of these buildings were resold with Section 8 subsidies to inexperienced black developers, who also failed to make ends meet. In 1986, HUD initiated plans to dispose of the BURP buildings as part of a larger package of HUD-held properties in Boston, known as the Granite Properties (see Chapter 7). Ironically, the BHP was selected to redevelop a large portion of these buildings yet again, this time with community-based sponsors.

The primary feature that BURP and the BHP Demonstration Program have in common is the attempt by a "superagency" to rehabilitate a large number of inner-city, low-income units in a relatively short time, using more than one developer. With BURP, the "superagency" was HUD, and the developers were "experienced" for-profit owners and developers. The "superagency" for the Demonstration Program was the BHP, and the developers were community-based nonprofit organizations (although they established for-profit subsidiaries for syndication purposes). For the most part, these organizations had much less tangible development experience than the BURP developers. But the BHP Demonstration Program was in a stronger position than BURP to produce and rehabilitate affordable housing successfully, as discussed below.

BHP Demonstration Program Improvements

The Demonstration Program has improved on BURP and other efforts by nonprofit developers (described in Chapter 8) in several key ways. It has generated both financial resources and jobs for the community; has been sensitive to relocation; has improved access to financing; has included technical assistance as a major component of the program; has created a highly supportive administrative structure; and has addressed how long-term affordability will likely be achieved. In some cases, the point of comparison is between the Demonstration Program and BURP, while in others it is between the Demonstration Program and either preceding or contemporary nonprofit development efforts.

Financial Resources and Jobs for the Community

One of the main criticisms of BURP was its use of for-profit developers from outside the community, which prevented local residents from enjoying the economic benefits of development, such as profits and jobs. In contrast, the Demonstration Program's hallmark has been its use of community-based, nonprofit organizations as sole developers of the properties. Syndication proceeds, the major source of residential development profit, have been divided between internal subsidies to the developments and developers' fees for the sponsoring organizations. The nonprofits have used these funds to cover operating expenses or for future development. Thus a great deal of the wealth generated from the program has remained in the local communities and can be used to produce additional affordable housing. It should be noted, however, that much of the Demonstration Program's resources still went outside the community—to downtown banks, law firms, and consultants. Also, as described below, many of the contractors chosen were neither minority nor community based.

The BHP did not initially address itself to a second issue that BURP had overlooked: targeting jobs created by its development activities to community and minority residents. No mention of job creation was made in the early descriptive material of the BHP, and no require-

ments for targeting jobs were included in the August 1983 request
for proposals. Nevertheless, a memo was sent to the sponsors two
months later and included the following recommendation:

> The Partnership is committed to affirmative action and equal employ-
> ment opportunity. It urges project sponsors to make every effort to
> involve minorities, and minority-owned businesses in their projects.
> Projects selected for funding by the Partnership will have to meet
> specific AA/EEO objectives that will be detailed once projects are
> identified; these objectives will be based upon the requirements of
> public agencies that participate in financing Partnership projects.
> Sponsors should note, for instance, that the City of Boston requires
> City-assisted development projects to hire fifty percent Boston resi-
> dents, twenty-five percent minorities and ten percent women, applied
> to each construction trade according to the hours worked in that
> trade. The Massachusetts Housing Finance Agency . . . establishes
> minority hiring goals for each project based upon the area where it is
> located.[5]

Although somewhat late in coming, this memo indicated a commitment by the BHP to economic development as a secondary goal of
the Demonstration Program.

In the end, the BHP performed quite well in terms of local and
minority hiring, primarily at the subcontractor level, with Boston
residents and minorities working a majority of hours on the job. According to one CDC executive director, contractors took the city's and
MHFA's requirements seriously. Unfortunately, the CDCs had difficulty locating general contractors who could meet the performance
bond requirments; only two of the nine general contractors chosen
were minority.[6] The tenth community-based group, Urban Edge, is
minority controlled and served as its own general contractor.

The absence of major public demands for jobs by the minority
community at the beginning of the Demonstration Program was a
striking contrast to BURP. The use of community-based sponsors,
five of whom were minority controlled, may have defused the jobs
issue somewhat. Moreover, the Demonstration Program had a significantly smaller number of units (700) than BURP, and the units
were scattered across the city, in diverse neighborhoods. BURP concentrated 2000 units in Roxbury, a black neighborhood, mobilizing
black leaders to make demands about jobs for the residents. It thus
presented an easier target for attack.

Advocates for local and minority jobs who were aware of the
BHP also may have assumed that the city's and MHFA's jobs policies

would apply, even if this was not initially stated by the BHP. Thus, a new legal climate in the 1980s, in which city and state require local and minority hiring, has removed from community-based nonprofits the need to confront this issue on their own.

Attention to Relocation

Relocation was better, although not flawlessly, handled by the BHP than by HUD and the BURP developers, who originally made virtually no provisions for relocation. In contrast, the Demonstration Program called for each sponsor to include a description of relocation needs in its application, and to outline the extent and cost of relocation.[7] The inclusion of relocation requirements indicated an increased sensitivity to the needs of the community—in this case, the residents. Yet attributing this improvement solely to the community-based groups is unjustified. As with jobs, the inclusion of relocation requirements may simply have reflected the changed legal and political environment of the 1980s, in which even profit-motivated developers from outside the community would need to address relocation.

Innovative Financing

As described in Chapter 4, community-based, nonprofit groups were not the dominant developers of subsidized housing in the 1970s. When they did participate, they often entered into joint ventures with for-profit developers, compromising control over issues such as design and use of profits.

The BHP's ability to aggregate resources in a time of scarcity and allocate them to nonprofit sponsors, providing them with a chance to develop projects independently and enhance their development skills, was one of the greatest positive attributes of the Demonstration Program. It meant that these sponsors no longer had to rely on a for-profit partner in a joint venture to obtain the MHFA mortgage or the construction loan. The BHP informally took on the role of a partner without demanding a share in the ownership or profits. Through the influence of its board and the expertise of its staff, the BHP has been able to obtain a substantial share of the development resources available, allowing many more units to be developed by community-based nonprofits in Boston than likely would have been possible if these groups had acted alone or in joint ventures. The BHP played a critical role in developing the financing package in several important ways.

First, the Demonstration Program provided sponsors with seed money, instead of requiring that they come up with these funds themselves. Approximately $4500 per unit was budgeted for initial development expenses, including staff, consultants, and architectural/engineering studies. Most of this money came from Community Development Block Grants channeled through the city and from private foundations.

As described in Chapter 11, although sources of seed money have increased, CDCs still have had to compete for them. The Demonstration Program took away the element of uncertainty in obtaining seed money, allowing the sponsor to devote attention to development issues. This was particularly important to the smaller, relatively inexperienced groups with less staff available to complete applications for funding.

Second, although the Demonstration Program's mortgage financing was enormously expensive (in terms of legal fees), the net result was that construction loans and permanent mortgages were obtained on all ten projects. It is doubtful that all of the projects would have been financed without the BHP. Many of the sponsors were new and/or young developers who could not meet the standards of MHFA, the loan servicer, or FNMA and the banks, which were carrying the risk. By packaging ten separate projects into one program, the BHP exerted pressure on the lending institutions to finance the weaker with the stronger.[8] Without the participation of influential board members and the persuasive powers of Bill Edgerly, Bob Whittlesey, executive director of the BHP, and Pat Clancy, executive director of GBCD, it is unlikely that the package could have been financed.

Third, the Demonstration Program successfully overcame the past constraints experienced by nonprofit developers wishing to syndicate their projects—the need to attract investors to the project and the need to meet the IRS's net-worth requirements. Most significantly, by pooling the projects of the ten community sponsors, the BHP created a package of a size much more appealing to potential syndication agents than any single project. This pooling had the additional benefit of reducing the per unit syndication overhead costs below what the costs would have been if each of the ten projects had been syndicated individually.[9] GBCD also assumed a number of tasks usually performed by the placement agent, such as preparing the offering, thereby further reducing overhead costs.

The program used a technique developed by GBCD on several of its individual projects to satisfy the IRS's net-worth requirements. Instead of demonstrating the needed net worth up front, the sponsors set aside 15 percent of each syndication payment in a net-worth account.[10]

Fourth, the BHP itself was included in the syndication package to supervise the projects and provide information to the investment partnership, before, during and after rehabilitation. With a $1 million reserve fund and an experienced staff, the BHP served to reassure investors about the capability of individual sponsors.

Fifth, although Section 8 Moderate Rehabilitation and Chapter 707 subsidies had generally been available to nonprofit sponsors, the role of the BHP in obtaining rental subsidies for all ten of its sponsors was significant. According to Whittlesey, HUD was initially reluctant to provide Section 8 Moderate Rehabilitation subsidies to the Demonstration Program.[11] In the end, the BHP prevailed and demonstrated its ability to secure scarce federal rental subsidies at a time when it would have been difficult for the nonprofit developers to do so on their own.

EOCD was very cooperative in awarding over 200 Chapter 707 subsidies to the BHP. Not only did it readily make these subsidies available, but it departed from its normal practice of distributing Chapter 707 funds through the Boston Housing Authority. The BHP, in turn, allocated the subsidies to sponsors according to need. EOCD also set the maximum allowable rents for Chapter 707 at 110 percent of the Section 8 Existing Fair Market Rents, thereby increasing the feasibility of the developments.

The agreement to subsidize over 200 units through the Chapter 707 program under an unusual administrative arrangement and at a higher subsidy amount was clearly a concession to the BHP's unique status. Ten community groups vying on their own for these subsidies in the same year would surely have been less successful in obtaining them. Moreover, it is likely that some of the groups would not have participated in the program without the assurance of these rental subsidies.

Altogether, 75 percent of the units in the Demonstration Program are covered by rent subsidies, compared to 20 percent required under two existing state programs involving private developers (SHARP and TELLER)[12] and the 25–40 percent more commonly achieved on other nonprofit projects done outside the BHP at about the same time.[13]

Sixth, BHP received almost $5 million in grants from the city and private foundations: $4.5 million from the city in the form of Community Development Block Grants and $430,000 from foundations, including the Local Initiatives Support Corporation. This averages $500,000 per group and $7100 per unit. While other community-based, nonprofit organizations received grant support for their projects during the same period, the average amount was generally far lower (EOCD, 1985).

The equity raised through these grants, combined with the syndication proceeds, enabled projects to reduce the amount they needed to borrow and therefore substantially lowered the debt service on the developments. This, in turn, allowed rents to fall under the maximums allowed by the Section 8 and Chapter 707 programs. If fewer subsidies had been available, the number of units affordable by low- and moderate-income households would have decreased, and sponsors would have had to market the units to a higher-income group (Edgerly, 1983). Not only would this have made the units more costly but it would have made some projects less feasible because the market does not provide the automatic rent increases offered by government rent-subsidy programs.

Seventh, the grants and syndication proceeds also allowed the BHP to set aside significant reserves to satisfy lenders of the projects' viability and to provide a financial cushion that was lacking in the past. For example, without adequate operating reserves, the substantial increases in operating costs threw the BURP buildings into a financial tailspin. Although it was expected that tenant incomes would increase over time and that additional expenses could be covered, this did not occur as fuel costs, in particular, skyrocketed in the early 1970s. In contrast, the Demonstration Program has taken into account the likelihood of rising costs and other contingencies.

The Demonstration Program's reserves consisted of a 10 percent construction contingency (included in the development costs and covered by the mortgage); a working capital reserve fund, which amounted to 8 percent of the mortgage amount (provided as loans from CDFC, LISC, and the Ford Foundation, and to be repaid from syndication proceeds); a $1 million reserve fund administered by BHP, established from the syndication proceeds; and the rest of the syndication proceeds. A total of $5 million was available in reserves. Nevertheless, less than a year after construction was completed, all but about $400,000 of it had been spent. Thus, although the Demonstration Program amassed considerable reserves, in part to prevent the problems encountered by earlier nonprofits, it is sobering that even amounts that sound fairly large can be used up very quickly.[14]

The effect of combining financing sources into a complex, unwieldy package was to allow the CDCs to rehabilitate an unusually large number of affordable scattered-site units in a short time. While the financing was highly complicated, designers of the program demonstrated their awareness of the needs of a large-scale rehabilitation program carried out by community-based sponsors.

Technical Assistance

The availability of quality technical assistance gave Demonstration Program sponsors an edge over BURP and their nonprofit predecessors. It could be argued that with the outside assistance, Demonstration sponsors were actually in a better position than the reputedly more experienced BURP developers. Clearly, BURP's choice of seasoned for-profit developers from outside the community did not in itself result in a successful program. Their experience proved to be irrelevant in some cases; they failed to anticipate community opposition or sensitively plan for the existing residents; they were initially perceived by the community as profiteers; and they delivered a poor product.

Meanwhile, the 1960s nonprofits did not have access to quality technical assistance to compensate for their inexperience as housing developers (see Chapter 11). The consultants who were available were generally considered to be ineffective at best and unscrupulous at worst. Some sponsors relied on their for-profit developer–partners, whose interests often varied from the sponsors in terms of project design, affordability, and amenities. This lack of independent, qualified technical assistance worked to the detriment of the projects, as the nonprofits were unskilled in overseeing construction or operating housing on their own.

Thus, GBCD's involvement in the Demonstration Program is a key difference between this program and earlier efforts by nonprofits. GBCD has been involved in the Demonstration Program as the early consultant to the BHP, as consultant to organizations interested in submitting applications to the Demonstration Program, and as development consultant chosen by six of the ten sponsors. In the four instances in which GBCD was not chosen, a variety of reasons were behind the decision: One sponsor believed it was sufficiently experienced to undertake the projects without a consultant; another had an association with a consultant whom it preferred. The most interesting explanation—one offered both by sponsors who did not choose GBCD and sponsors who did—was a perception that GBCD would always place the interests of the BHP as a whole over those of an individual organization. For example, if a group wanted to bargain more actively with the banks, GBCD might discourage this if it could jeopardize the relationship of the BHP with these institutions. Another reason for not choosing GBCD was the concern that it would not transfer enough skill to the CDC.

Although it is still too early to give a final evaluation on GBCD's role, we do know that GBCD was the consultant both for financially solvent projects and for at least two projects that were in the red within a few months after construction was completed. The fact that GBCD was involved with projects at both ends of the continuum underscores that technical expertise alone does not guarantee a successful project.

While contemporary nonprofits working outside BHP have much more technical assistance available to them now than in the 1960s (in the form of GBCD, CEDAC, and EOCD), the BHP's coordinated and structured delivery of technical assistance appears to have been of enormous value to participating groups.

Supportive Administering Agencies

Two agencies have the primary responsibility for overseeing the completed projects: the BHP and the MHFA. Together, they represent a significant improvement over HUD and the FHA, which were responsible for administering earlier subsidy programs.

The BHP very early demonstrated its commitment to using non-profit housing organizations to carry out its major projects. By limiting the Demonstration Program to nonprofits, BHP administrators could concentrate on the special needs of this kind of organization. With fewer financial and staff resources and less development experience than many professional, for-profit developers, Demonstration Program sponsors required special assistance if they were to bring their unique strengths—accountability, concern, and lack of financial motivation—to the development. The importance of this concentrated effort and commitment on the part of the administering agencies should not be minimized; as discussed in Chapter 11, one of the key reasons for the success of the Section 202 program was the expertise developed by the HUD staff members who administered this program.

One example of the BHP's extremely supportive attitude was its decision to provide financing to sponsors when the options on their properties were running out. The BHP drew down from its own budget to make these loans and arranged for lines of credit to be extended from the banks, with "little but faith to back them." [15]

This attitude contrasts sharply with the lack of support for nonprofit housing development within HUD when it administered the Section 221(d)(3) and 236 programs. Very little assistance was offered during development stages, and while some efforts were made to assist nonprofits, they were generally short-lived or inadequate (see Chapter 11).

As discussed in Chapter 11, MHFA was created with the primary purpose of financing mixed-income rental housing. Unlike HUD, it was not saddled with a long-standing orientation toward unsubsidized market-rate rental and owner-occupied housing. MHFA has a great deal of experience managing subsidized housing and has generally taken a more socially oriented, affirmative stance toward low-income tenants' needs than typical financial institutions. For example, all tenant-selection procedures and rent increases must be approved by MHFA, and the agency has developed support services such as alcoholism counseling for troubled tenants and a training program for minority property managers. MHFA has also established a comprehensive monitoring program to detect troubled projects and a system to attempt to bring these developments back to financial health.

Nevertheless, MHFA has not traditionally targeted its resources to nonprofit sponsors. Instead, it has encouraged them to enter into joint ventures with for-profit partners. Through its participation in the BHP, MHFA has been more involved with nonprofit groups than in the past. With MHFA in the unique position of having little or no risk in the projects, however, it will be interesting to observe how much it will choose to be involved. But, overall, the agencies administering the BHP Demonstration Program represent a stronger oversight team, in terms of professional competence, experience, and commitment to nonprofit development, than BHP's predecessors.

Long-Term Affordability

As described in Chapters 4 and 5, housing developments built by for-profit developers in the 1960s under the Section 221(d)(3) and 236 programs are quickly becoming eligible for conversion to more profitable uses such as condominiums or market rentals. Recent experience indicates that many property owners will choose this option, resulting in the loss of a significant amount of affordable housing.

The BHP has increased the chances that Demonstration Program units will remain affordable in three important ways. First, it has chosen community-based sponsors, whose interest in the housing is not primarily financial. This provides some assurance that maximizing profits will not be the primary motivation when the project's depreciation deductions have ended. Second, the terms of the syndication agreement explicitly require that the units be maintained as affordable housing, and gives investors very little power to amend this. Finally, the sponsors will have a small financial lever for increasing their power when the depreciation benefits have run out in the form of accrued interest owed them on the deferred loans they made to the limited partnerships at the start of development (from the CDBG grants received by the BHP). Although the primary purpose of making these loans was to increase the depreciation deductions for the investors, they also ensure that the sponsors are owed a significant amount at the end of the properties' depreciable lives. Thus, at the end of eighteen years, a CDC may be owed approximately $24,000 on a property worth approximately $51,000 (assuming 3 percent annual appreciation). This resource will provide the sponsors with the opportunity to buy out the investors' shares and obtain full financial control over the property, with the option to resyndicate on their own terms.

Problems in the Demonstration Program

Despite the many improvements that the Demonstration Program has made compared to the BURP program and earlier and even contemporary efforts by nonprofits, it has still faced an array of problems. These are caused by the lack of direct and deep subsidies, the fundamental difficulties of undertaking rehabilitation projects, and the tensions inherent in community-based development.

The Lack of Direct and Deep Subsidies

In the BHP Demonstration Program, multiple financing sources were a necessity, attributable to the lack of direct and deep subsidies. The resulting complexity of the financial package had a snowballing effect on the problems it caused. Compounding this, the scope of the program, the buildings targeted, and the decision to use nonprofit community-based sponsors contributed to a sense of caution among many key actors, most notably financial ones. Devising comfortable ways of participating meant trying to avoid arrangements perceived as too risky. Not surprisingly, the greater the effort to spread or share the risk among several parties, the more complex the financing package. Several plans were proposed and turned down and the BHP initiated the Demonstration Program with an incomplete financing arrangement. The lack of finality about the details of the financing—even at the point when sponsors were chosen—prompted one sponsor to note: "The diver was on the diving board but they hadn't decided where to put the pool." [16]

The financing package that ultimately emerged involved three key actors in a complex set of relationships described earlier: FNMA, the banks, and MHFA. Although FNMA was committed to the project, it was extremely cautious. After touring the individual projects, FNMA appraisers were reportedly shocked by what they had seen (McCormack, 1985); they were used to insuring lower-risk projects, and negotiations with this outside party, a relatively latecomer to the Demonstration, were time-consuming.

The banks demanded carefully worked out assurances on such issues as the stability of the CDCs, the provision of rental subsidies, the satisfaction of environmental-review requirements, and the exemption of the buildings from rent control. For example, the Bank of Boston's commitment letter for the construction loans had ten pages of additional conditions to be met and was described by one CDC's attorney as "the most sadistic commitment letter I've ever seen." [17] All this negotiating took time.

In addition, the BHP's dependence on the new state subsidy program, SHARP, created further delays for the project. When the BHP was launched, SHARP was not yet in place. Held up by the state legislature, it was not even signed into law until November 1983. Moreover, MHFA, the administering agency, needed additional time to develop guidelines. Sponsors were not invited to compete for SHARP monies until March 1984, and were not notified of the awards until late that summer. Since the financial viability of many of the projects depended on SHARP, mortgage documents could not be processed until SHARP awards were known.

The BHP originally expected the Demonstration Program to run eighteen months, from December 1983, when projects were selected, to June 1985, when rehabilitation would be completed and final closing achieved. Instead, financing was not in place and rehabilitation did not even begin until April 1985—ten months behind schedule—and was not completed until Fall 1986.

An important effect of the extended timeline was to force sponsors into buying some of their buildings before they were ready to rehabilitate and manage them. Based on the original schedule, the sponsors had arranged for most of the options to expire in June 1984. When the financing was not available at that time, the sponsors obtained option extensions where they could, but this was possible for only another five or six months. By late 1984, the sponsors had to choose between losing some buildings or purchasing them. Most often, as mentioned above, the BHP financed the acquisition of these buildings, using up to $4 million in credit from the banks. In only one instance did a CDC lose control of a building.

Although it was obviously better to acquire buildings too early than to lose them altogether, sponsors found themselves in the difficult position of owning buildings without any secure financing with which to rehabilitate them and without the funds to make immediate repairs. Boilers broke, roofs leaked, and operating expenses mounted. Again, loans from the BHP or directly from the banks proved invaluable in keeping the buildings operational.

In addition to time delays and expiring building options, sponsors had problems finding and keeping contractors. The decision to use MHFA financing meant that state prevailing wages (comparable to Davis–Bacon) would have to be paid. This was an expense that had not been anticipated: The RFP assumed that small, independent contractors would do the work at a rate of about $15 an hour. In contrast, the state prevailing wage required labor to be paid from $20 to $25 an hour. It was not until January 1984 that sponsors were told that they would have to pay prevailing wages. This meant that contractors who had bid on jobs assuming a lower wage rate would now have to pay the higher rate and still manage to complete the job at the budgeted amount. To compound the problem, MHFA's requirement that contractors be bondable for 100 percent of the contracted work excluded many firms that normally would have been interested in this kind of job.

According to Jim Luckett, the contractor dilemma was virtually unresolvable:

> The Partnership envisioned that we would use middle range contractors. They would be big enough to get a 100% performance bond and deal with all the paperwork and regulations, including minority hiring and Davis–Bacon. But at the same time they were supposed

> to be small enough to take on the trouble of doing partial rehab with tenants in place, in buildings in different locations. In the end, we found that this middle range contractor doesn't exist. (Quoted in McCormack, 1985)

The triple set of requirements eventually imposed on contractors —an ability to withstand long delays, the eleventh-hour stipulation that prevailing wages would have to be paid, and the need to find a completely bondable firm—meant that some contractors originally selected either ended up pulling out or being disqualified. For some sponsors, the task of finding a suitable contractor was nearly impossible: As late as April 1985, one CDC was still without a contractor.

For CDCs that had not enlisted a qualified contractor by December 1984, the already serious problem took on project-threatening proportions. By that time, mortgage documents had been submitted to MHFA with the sponsors' "best bid" contractor prices. The sponsors were thus locked into this amount and needed to find a contractor who would bid at or below this figure.

As a result, the Demonstration Program, like its predecessors, was forced to underestimate costs. The pressures of completing construction within the budget created incentives to compromise. Some sponsors brought in small, nonbondable contractors to complete portions of the work, or they had the work completed through their management companies as repairs, rather than as part of the rehabilitation project.

Reflecting on the inadequate rehabilitation budgets, a development director of one CDC stated:

> First, we chose some really tough buildings to be rehabilitated. We knew that one building in particular would be extremely expensive but it was an eyesore in the neighborhood and we wanted to do it. . . . But this type of building costs a lot to rehab. Second, we had to choose between a good contractor and an incomplete scope of services or a less good contractor and a more complete scope. We found a contractor who was willing to come in at the budgeted price. But he couldn't finish the job and went bankrupt. Obviously, this cost the CDC money, way beyond the budgeted price.[18]

Not surprisingly, the bottom line of the BHP Demonstration's early problems was an increase in costs. The average total cost per unit increased 45 percent from August 1983 when the RFPs were issued to the closing budgets in January 1985—from $36,844 to $53,557. Higher acquisition and rehabilitation prices, financing fees, and overhead costs were primarily responsible for the increase.

Acquisition and rehabilitation increased $7221 a unit, or 20 percent. About half this increase resulted from the need to pay prevailing wages; the other half stemmed from several causes. First, time delays resulted in building options running out and additional payments being made in order to secure the building. Second, and perhaps even more important, BHP staff and sponsors incorrectly assumed that it would be possible to cross-subsidize within a given sponsor's building.

> To get severely deteriorated buildings into the package *and* remain within the dollar limits set by the Partnership ($26,000) many tried to combine abandoned buildings with properties needing very little work. As most found out, "very little work" cost more than anticipated. The "paint and touch-up" buildings were both few and far between and had prohibitively high acquisition prices when they could be found. The result was very little cross-subsidization . . . and higher than expected rehab costs on "better buildings." (McCormack, 1985, 48)

Of greater significance than the increase in acquisition and rehabilitation costs was the more than 60 percent increase in financing fees—from $950 to $6693 a unit. One sponsor referred to this increase as a "surcharge" for complexity. The MHFA bond issue, the Bank of Boston's financing commitment, the "Build Loan" letter of credit, and the syndication process all required countless hours of lawyers' time. In all, seventeen law firms were involved in the deal. Other development costs, including sponsors' overhead, increased 46 percent as a result of the time delays.

If a direct capital grant had been available, virtually all these problems would have been prevented. The financing presumably would have been simpler, and there would have been fewer delays, lower legal and overhead costs, and an early awareness about whether or not union wages would have to be paid. But without a single subsidy program to work with and without knowing the guidelines of the subsidy sources in advance, the BHP Demonstration Program was forced to devise a patchwork financing scheme and to emerge as a reactive, rather than proactive, initiative (see Table 5).

Problems Linked to Rehabilitation

Any rehabilitation project, particularly one done on a large scale in the inner city, is certain to present difficulties for developers. The Demonstration Program was not immune from such problems.

As mentioned earlier, the Demonstration Program required spon-

TABLE 5
DEVELOPMENT PROBLEMS FACING THE BHP DEMONSTRATION PROGRAM

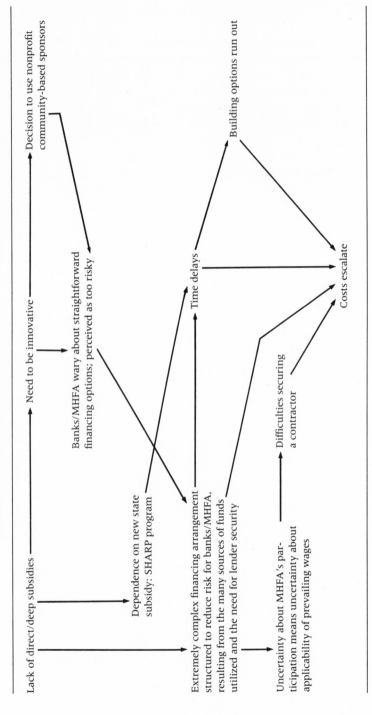

sors to include relocation plans in their initial applications. The quality of these plans was mixed. Since many sponsors did not yet own their buildings, they were unable to obtain tenant information from the existing owners. In addition, the pressure of immediate development tasks diverted the sponsors' attention from planning for future relocation, which seemed a long way off (Gillis et al., 1984).

Once the sponsors acquired the buildings, they were able to meet with tenants and assess their needs, including unit size and level of subsidy. Sometimes, the relocation problems were quite complex. An article in a local newspaper described such a situation:

> Dorchester Bay had in one of its buildings a family of nine living in a two-bedroom unit. Under regulations governing BHP which consider more than two people per bedroom overcrowding, even after renovation, there would be no apartment large enough for them; the family would have to be relocated permanently. Dorchester Bay found a five-bedroom apartment in Cambridge for them, along with a rent subsidy. (*Dorchester Community News*, 1985)

In this instance, the family was not able to stay in the community because of lack of suitable relocation housing. Should the CDC have tried to accommodate the family by creating a larger apartment? Were the tenants better off in a larger apartment in a new neighborhood, or should they have been allowed to stay in Dorchester, in their "overcrowded" situation, if they so desired? The answers are not at all clear, but the questions are familiar ones to anyone involved with rehabilitation.

In some instances, sponsors found it impossible to stick to their original relocation plans because the progress of the rehabilitation work was out of phase with the relocation timetable.

> Various tenant juggling schemes have arisen as a result of the . . . projects . . . involving more than one building. Tenants have been moved from one Partnership building to another for renovation, one that came earlier or was to come later in the construction schedule. But some of those schemes simply had to be abandoned, such as Codman Square Housing Development Corp.'s plan to renovate the vacant half of its building on Washington St., move in the tenants from the other half, and complete construction. "It turned out to be significantly cheaper to move people twice," explains director Bill Jones. (*Dorchester Community News*, 1985)

In other instances, CDCs, particularly the less experienced ones, were simply unable to cope with the pressures of relocation. At least two groups encountered problems for not giving adequate notice to existing tenants or for making inadequate relocation arrangements (*Dorchester Community News*, 1985).

Several other problems encountered by the BHP Demonstration Program are more or less predictable in any rehabilitation effort. Finding a competent and reputable contractor, staying within the construction budget, maintaining site control while the financing is being arranged, and managing unrehabilitated buildings are all integral parts of the rehabilitation process. Although the complexity of the BHP Demonstration Program may have exacerbated these concerns, they are certainly not unique to this project. Even with a direct and deep source of subsidy, these aspects of rehabilitation are likely to present problems for any sponsoring group.

Also, as discussed earlier, the final quality of the rehabilitation was a problem for the for-profit developers in BURP and for nonprofit developers in the 1960s and 1970s. Despite the BHP's, GBCD's, and MHFA's experience in working with nonprofits, the Demonstration Program did not produce a high quality of rehabilitation work on all units, in large part because of the modest initial rehabilitation standards and the lack of sufficient rehabilitation funds mentioned earlier.

Tensions in Community-Based Development

The use of community-based, nonprofit sponsors did not necessarily aim for, nor result in, widespread participation by the affected tenants. This may have been the result of tenant disinterest, as expressed by at least one CDC staff person, or CDC oversight or lack of initiative, as expressed by at least one tenant (Plotkin, 1987). But without blaming either the CDCs or the tenants, the Demonstration Program made a conscious decision to work through community-based, rather than tenant-based, organizations.

If tenants are not involved with the details of the rehabilitation process, it is easy for friction to develop between them and sponsors. As discussed above, administrative delays caused many sponsors to purchase their buildings without the financing in place to rehabilitate them. According to Kathy Weremiuk of the Fields Corner CDC, this meant that the sponsors had "to be slumlords for a period of time" (*Dorchester Community News*, 1985). This problem raises again the second dilemma discussed in Chapter 10 and is likely unavoidable when a community-based group does not explicitly include tenants. In fairness, though, even if the tenants had been more involved with the project, perhaps as cooperative owners, the only advantage would have been a greater likelihood that the tenant–owners would have been more aware and therefore more sensitive to the problems caused by unforeseen delays. The delays themselves, and the need to ask for patience on the part of those living in the soon-to-be-rehabilitated buildings, would not have disappeared.

The last dilemma presented in Chapter 10—the tension between neighborhood preference and equal opportunity goals in selecting tenants—was given a full hearing in the BHP Demonstration Program. In fact, it should be recalled that the case study on the Fields Corner CDC was based on their experience with the BHP.

One of the issues that caused concern for some sponsors was that there be a targeted level of racial integration in each project. This was to be achieved by affirmatively marketing and giving preference to the minority race in the neighborhood (*Dorchester Community News*, 1985). Although initially concern focused on how the races would mix in segregated or racially tense neighborhoods (the CDC operating in virtually all-white South Boston withdrew from the BHP for this reason), it shifted to whether the less-than-the-neediest population would be served. One critic charged that the integration goal overlooked the far greater need among minorities for affordable housing.[19] The BHP and the agencies providing rent subsidies eventually bowed to this concern and dropped the preferential renting requirements, although they continued to require affirmative marketing to whites "to give waiting lists some kind of balance" (*Dorchester Community News*, 1985).

This resolution satisfied some critics, but it raised fears among others that the weakened support for integration might result in racially segregated buildings. For example, the Fenway CDC, located in a racially diverse neighborhood with a majority of whites, expressed concern that the BHP building might end up being the only all-black building in the neighborhood, heightening the resentments of whites from the neighborhood who were not able to obtain a unit.[20]

It is sobering that even with adequate funding and subsidies, community-based rehabilitation still would be a complex process with numerous built-in obstacles and problems. In view of the BHP's ability to function *without* a simple and direct source of funding, however, its accomplishments are particularly noteworthy.

Conclusions

Should the Demonstration Program serve as a prototype for a rehabilitation program, as a model for how assistance to community-based sponsors should be institutionalized, or both? Or is it a unique product of a place and time that would be difficult to replicate in a different area and with different resources? Before answering these questions, two broad observations about the case study should be made.

First, the BHP Demonstration Program provides a rich example of how a public initiative can incorporate lessons from previous programs and experiences. The many ways in which the Demonstration Program is an improvement over earlier programs is testimony to how much has been learned about both rehabilitation and community-based housing development. Also significant is that the political atmosphere in which development now takes place has changed dramatically in the past twenty years. Although Boston may be ahead of other locales in its public consciousness about such issues as relocation and jobs for local residents, these concerns are certainly familiar to nonprofit and for-profit developers working in the inner city in many, if not most, sections of the country.

Second, a critical question that arises from this case study and, indeed, from any analysis of community-based housing development, is whether the sponsors will have the capability to operate their newly developed properties over the long term. In the case of the Demonstration Program, MHFA, the BHP, and EOCD all have oversight roles to play concerning management. Despite this multilayered structure, the sponsors, as owners, have the ultimate responsibility for their developments.

Before the Demonstration Program, only three CDCs had developed multifamily housing of more than ten units and only one, Urban Edge, was the sole owner of a large multifamily inventory. Thus, most of the sponsors are untested in their ability to take on a long-term management role, and many questions related to the organizations' staying power and viability will be answered only over time.

With limited experience in housing management, most of the sponsors will probably need technical assistance and additional funding to oversee the developments adequately. Yet in its initial program descriptions, the BHP did not indicate what kinds of assistance, if any, would be available. Fortunately, MHFA may be a crucial actor in this regard. With an impressive record in overseeing subsidized housing, it has developed methods for working with troubled developments and providing management assistance. Since it does not carry the risk on the mortgages, however, it is not clear whether MHFA will provide the same level of assistance. Even if it does, the nonprofits may still need additional resources such as staff, training, or further funding to maintain project quality and financial viability.

The BHP Demonstration Program, in its present form, would probably not be a candidate as a model rehabilitation program. Because of its incredible complexity and high administrative costs, few cities would likely want to copy the Demonstration Program's exact method of operation. Nevertheless, as both a rehabilitation program and a way of institutionalizing support to community-based sponsors, at least three distinct elements of the Demonstration Program would be worthwhile for others to emulate.

The Nonprofit–Nonprofit Partnership

The BHP presents an interesting model of a new type of partnership in which two nonprofit organizations are the two key partners. The BHP itself serves as the more experienced partner to the nonprofit sponsors without having the conflicting goals of a profit-motivated developer. In addition, the ability to hire a paid outside consultant, in most instances GBCD, provides the CDCs with another valuable partner. In short, the Demonstration Program has created a mechanism that attempts to maximize the likelihood that adequate assistance and expertise are available to the local groups.

But even in this unique partnership, there are still potential conflicts between community-based nonprofit groups and "downtown" nonprofit agencies. The staffs of both the BHP and GBCD are professional development experts rather than community activists. Although their goal is community-based development, being one step removed from the communities they are assisting may make the professional developers less sensitive to community issues than sponsors might prefer.

Also, the Demonstration Program reveals the difficulty of any agency walking the "fine line" between helper and underminer. On the one hand, technical assistance is terrific, but if it means that the consultant does all the negotiating with the banks and the CDCs have only minimal contact, the goal of helping nonprofits form their own relationships with the development community will be significantly reduced. Despite the potential for this kind of problem, the BHP and GBCD are certainly better partners and technical advisers to sponsors than for-profit developers. The interests of all the parties are not identical,[21] but they are apt to be closer than that of a community-based sponsor and a for-profit developer.

A New Public–Private Partnership

The BHP in general and the Demonstration Program in particular offer good guidelines for a new public–private partnership. Although partnerships of the 1960s and 1970s provided significant public benefits and opportunities for substantial private profits, the partnership in the BHP is based much more on the altruism or enlightened self-interest of private business people. Such leaders as Bill Edgerly of the State Street Bank and Trust Company receive no direct financial benefits for themselves or their companies. They may receive personal satisfaction and public acclaim for their hard work and generosity, but no financial gain is to be made. This allows private parties to the partnership to focus on the needs of the program, the CDCs, and the tenants. Concerns about what is most profitable are simply not relevant to those most directly involved in the partnership. Of course, to the extent that private financial institutions and limited-partner investors are involved, they are primarily concerned with their own interests.

On the public side of the partnership equation, the BHP Demonstration Program provides good models for state and local governments. Both the City of Boston and the Commonwealth of Massachusetts were strongly supportive of the Demonstration Program. With a mayor and a governor who have made housing prominent issues of their administrations, the BHP Demonstration Program was able to grow in a nurturing political environment. The array of state-subsidy programs available were critical to the overall accomplishments of the program. Specifically in support of the Demonstration Program, the state was willing to alter the operation of its rent-subsidy program. As for the city, it provided several million dollars in CDBG funds; streamlined its tax abatement and foreclosure procedures; and supported the choice to restrict the program to nonprofit sponsors, even though it would have been politically more advantageous to include for-profit developers.

To the extent that public–private partnerships are utilized to produce low-income housing, the partnership created by the BHP serves as a good model of how private initiatives can be utilized to serve the public good. This is the essence of what a public–private partnership should be (see Chapter 13).

Packaging the Projects

The case study reveals the many advantages of packaging several buildings and sponsors into a single program. Less-experienced groups that would be in a poor position competing for resources—financing, subsidies, and investors—can be brought along in a development process from which they normally are excluded. Packaging may also benefit more-experienced groups that may be less able to compete for foundation grants on the grounds that they are not the groups most in need of assistance. Ideally, the kind of packaging done by the Demonstration Program would result in economies of scale. It is theoretically far cheaper to negotiate a single mortgage and a single syndication offering than ten separate ones. Although the Demonstration Program does not seem to have benefited from such economies—in fact, it proved to be extremely costly to work out the financing arrangement—one can visualize how a simpler, more streamlined program would produce the anticipated savings.

Ultimately, there is no good replacement for simple, straightforward subsidy programs that would stimulate the production of affordable housing and provide a comprehensive support system for community-based developers. But the effort of the BHP in its Demonstration Program to rehabilitate 700 units through nonprofit groups represents an important contribution to our overall understanding of how community-based groups can become key actors in low-income housing production.

13

Rebuilding a Low-Income Housing Policy

IN 1949, Congress set forth a new national housing goal: "A decent home and suitable living environment for every American family." Since then, the goal has been reaffirmed numerous times, most recently in 1987. Although, on some measures, the housing problem has improved, we still face serious shortcomings, particularly when it comes to affordability and the availability of low-rent units.

Depending on their ideological perspective, various housing analysts advance different reasons why we have been unable to solve our housing problems. Rejecting the so-called free-market approach of conservatives, this book embraces the liberal–progressive view that more, not less, government involvement is necessary.

What follows are the major conclusions of the book; the order in which they appear follows the order in which they were discussed.

Housing evaluations should include three criteria generally omitted from such studies: the extent to which the housing program demonstrates a long-term commitment to providing decent, affordable housing; the potential for enhancing the well-being of individuals and contributing to a sense of empowerment and control; and the potential for producing social and community benefits, particularly in terms of neighborhood stability and upgrading without displacement. Also, analysts have probably overlooked the more human side of housing programs because housing policy in this country has emphasized political and economic objectives. Housing, as a human need, has not been the driving force behind housing legislation.

Citizen participation, mandated by the federal government in large-scale community development programs, has rarely resulted in a sharing of power with community residents or in substantial benefits to those affected by the programs. For resident involvement in housing programs to yield real benefits, citizens should have major roles in their design, production, and management.

Despite the conventional wisdom, which takes a negative view of public housing, the public housing program has produced a better record than is generally recognized. Although it has had substantial problems, public housing's overall accomplishments and proven ability to produce a large volume of units confirm that a revitalized public housing program should be a key component of a new low-income housing strategy. In contrast, the role of the private, for-profit development community in relation to low-income housing generally has not been a positive one. Staunch opponents of public housing, private interest groups have severely undermined its operation and can be blamed for many defects in the public housing program's design and implementation. Moreover, federally subsidized multifamily housing programs that rely on private, for-profit sponsorship and ownership have been less successful, on several criteria, than the public housing program. A case study of how a resyndication policy was formulated in Massachusetts highlights the conflicts between private, for-profit owners of subsidized housing and public goals. Although it comes as no surprise that private, for-profit developers have less altruistic interests than the public good, this case study suggests that the overwhelmingly positive rhetoric about "public–private partnerships" should be tempered substantially. The decision to include the private sector in subsidized housing programs should be made cautiously and with a clear understanding that the overall goal is to benefit the public interest, not to enhance private profit.

HUD's role as the key agency responsible for implementing federal housing programs has not been a strong one. Its activities during the 1960s and 1970s left a legacy of mismanagement and an inability to meet consumer needs that persists today. Based on a case study of HUD's property disposition policies in the 1980s, it is clear that the agency is committed neither to maintaining a high-quality stock of subsidized housing nor to protecting the low-income tenants in these buildings. These shortcomings cast considerable doubt on the advisability and, indeed, the capability of HUD, in its present form, to administer low-income housing programs.

Community-based organizations have been involved in a wide range of housing activities. There are some important weaknesses in this approach; there is also significant potential in using community-based groups to produce, rehabilitate, manage, and own low-cost housing. Some major obstacles face community-based organizations. In South Holyoke, Massachusetts, for example, the larger economic, social, and political forces put pressures and constraints on the local area. Although the root causes of a community's problems cannot be addressed by a neighborhood group, local action can be both a logical place to begin and part of a long-term strategy for challenging the economic system and federal policies. In addition to external pressures, community-based housing development organizations are virtually certain to confront a host of internal dilemmas and choices. Answers to all these problems cannot be provided, but case studies of two Massachusetts CDCs underscore that the political and social context of the CDC will have a great deal to do with how well it negotiates the problems raised by the community-based development process. From the most comprehensive state system of supports for community-based housing in the country, the one in Massachusetts, we conclude that a public support system for community-based initiatives is both logical and feasible. Although such a program might operate in a variety of ways, there are several distinct advantages in channeling funding and technical assistance through the states.

The case study of the BHP Demonstration Program reveals a new form of public–private partnership initiative. Unlike earlier partnerships, in which the private, for-profit sector's interests and those of the public sector conflicted, the BHP model places long-term affordable housing and tenant needs in central positions. Although the complexity of the BHP Demonstration Program would make it an unlikely candidate for replication in its present form, this program can pave the way for a new generation of partnership initiatives.

A Prescription for a Housing Policy

A new commitment by the federal government to subsidize housing is needed. Before presenting specific recommendations, I want to make a broad prescription concerning federal housing policy: It should be multifaceted. No single housing subsidy is appropriate for all circumstances and in all market areas. Thus the Reagan administration's almost total reliance on the Section 8 Existing Housing program and housing vouchers could not serve people who live in areas with severe shortages of affordable housing. Housing allowances, whatever the specific form, cannot provide assistance if insufficient units are available. In many cities with low vacancy rates, simply finding a unit can be an insurmountable challenge. For example, in Boston, about half of all recipients of Section 8 certificates or vouchers end up returning them unused after unsuccessful searches for decent, affordable housing. Housing vouchers can also be problematic for large families, since units with an adequate number of bedrooms are scarce on the private rental market. And, finally, discrimination on the part of private landlords is still encountered by many nonwhite households, thereby rendering the vouchers useless (Feins and Bratt, 1983; HUD, 1979c, 1979d).

Demand-side programs should be one of several vehicles for providing affordable housing; they should not be the only housing subsidy. In conjunction with programs that give housing consumers increased effective demand, or renting power, there is a need for a series of new and revised programs that will increase the supply of affordable housing.

New and Revised Programs

Public Housing

Much of this book has advocated a new, community-based housing program, but a revised public housing program is also essential to a new federal housing policy. Local housing authorities have enormous production capacity, the public housing program has proved workable, and many areas of the country do not yet have community-based development organizations. For all these reasons, public housing should be revived and the media should be enlisted to help change the public's erroneous view of the program.

At the least, a new public housing program should provide subsidies for debt service through the traditional annual contributions contracts. At the best, as discussed in Chapter 3, public housing should be constructed with "up front" capital grants from the federal government to cover construction costs, as legislated in the Housing and Community Development Act of 1987. Despite the appeal of this approach, even some strong supporters of government housing programs are critical of this method of financing. Although they acknowledge that it may be cost effective, they are quick to point out that it is also less likely to produce large quantities of housing than a strategy that depends on leveraging additional public or private investments. Unless the government was willing to appropriate substantial funds for housing, direct grants would give relatively little "bang for the buck." While proponents of this view may agree that the complexity of public–private partnership deals is unfortunate, they argue that such approaches are more likely to yield the needed units in view of the limited federal appropriations for housing.[1]

In addition to the basic funding mechanism to construct the public housing, a decision should be made on how operating budgets should be supplemented. Rather than wait until shortfalls arise or until modernization needs become acute, a new public housing program could include up-front grants that would be invested to yield sufficient income to cover such future expenses. The per unit cost of the new public housing authorized by the Housing and Community Development Act of 1987 comes to $68,857. If Congress increased the original budget authority to cover future operating and modernization costs, they would need to increase the per unit authorization some $33,000, to $102,000 (Stegman 1988).

Without such a system, a new public housing program would have to revise substantially the current mechanism for dispensing operating funds. As Stegman (1988) has pointed out, there are several ways in which "laws or regulations reward poor management or eliminate the incentives for sound and efficient management of public housing" (p. 20). Procedures should be carefully scrutinized to locate all such inconsistencies, and appropriate corrective actions should be taken.

A revised public housing program also should include new commitments to tenant participation and management. Although tenant management is not the right approach for all developments, local housing authorities should encourage tenant involvement and control, and, where appropriate, they should encourage the formation of tenant management corporations as soon after initial rent-up and occupancy as possible.

A comprehensive new public housing program should include an appropriate social services component that will meet the needs of the tenant population. Too often, such programs have been initiated as an afterthought, well after the needs became serious. Instead, all new public housing should address the social services package at the outset of the project's development.

The design of all new public housing also should be consistent with the housing in the surrounding neighborhood. Many of the earlier projects have been justifiably open to criticism because of their stark appearance. In order to reduce the possibility of stigmatization, public housing must blend into the community.

Perhaps the private, for-profit development community will be just as opposed to a revised public housing program as it has always been and will argue vehemently against it. In order not to repeat the errors of the past, lawmakers need to stand firm, not only to enact the program, but to make sure that the legislation supports good design, a decent level of amenities, social services, and adequate funding. By understanding how shortcomings in these areas harmed past public housing projects, as discussed in Chapter 3, and recognizing the significant housing needs of their constituents, one can hope that Congress would choose to overrule the private-interest opponents to public housing.

Community-Based Housing

As proposed in Chapter 11, the federal government should launch a new support system for community-based housing. In addition to providing adequate financial resources, it should also include a high-quality technical assistance component, a mechanism to acquire land and buildings, and an evaluation and information-sharing network.

There is a need for more information about how the federal government should best support community-based housing activities. Experiences with the Neighborhood Self-Help Development Program and the Neighborhood Development Demonstration program have shown that these are viable, although limited, models. Chapter 11 argued that a new kind of support program that operates through the states and Community-Based Housing Support Corporations may be another suitable approach. These organizations could actually form a partnership with the community-based group, creating a nonprofit–nonprofit partnership (as with the BHP, discussed in Chapter 12), or they could assist in the development process as consultants. In addition, two new proposals have been set forth recently at the federal level. The first was developed by the congressionally appointed Rouse Commission, under the leadership of James Rouse. Its recommendation is for a "Housing Opportunity Program" that would be channeled to states and localities, 10 percent of whose funds would be used for community-based housing development. The second initiative is Congressman Joseph Kennedy's Community Housing Partnership Act, discussed below.

Finally, the lessons learned from the array of programs that provide subsidies, assistance, or both through some centralized agency, and that rely on some form of private philanthropic or nonprofit involvement, need to be aggregated into a coherent set of recommendations about the optimum role of state and national agencies and the federal government in supporting community-based housing initiatives. The following should be included in such a study: national efforts by the Local Initiatives Support Corporation, as well as their Neighborhood Development Support Collaborative in Boston; the Enterprise Foundation; the Center for Community Change, the Neighborhood Reinvestment Corporation, and their Mutual Housing Association Demonstration program; the MacArthur Foundation's "Fund for Community Development" in Chicago; and the Massachusetts support system for community-based housing, as well as other states with significant programs.

Although one model may emerge as "the best," it is more likely that each program will reveal some unique strengths, particularly in certain situations. Thus the goal of an evaluation should be to compare various approaches and understand under what circumstances each is advisable or inadvisable. An optimum federal program in support of community-based housing should be flexible and should provide a range of services that can be adapted to the specific needs of different locales.

Whatever form a national support system for community-based housing may take, a key recommendation of this book is that such a system should be created with all the necessary components as outlined earlier. The record of community-based housing, its relative strengths in comparison to other subsidy programs, and the continuing need for decent, affordable housing presents a compelling case for a significant federal effort to support this approach.

The most recent completely formulated proposal for federal support of community-based housing is contained in Kennedy's Community Housing Partnership Act, introduced as H.R. 3891 in February 1988. Although it is significant that a support program for community-based housing is finally before Congress, the proposal does not include a decentralized structure for providing nonprofits with technical assistance, such as the one proposed in Chapter 11. Title I would, however, provide $10 million in capacity-building funds, which could be used to cover operating expenses or other technical services.

In addition to the lack of a specific technical-assistance entity, the legislation calls for HUD to be the implementing agency of the new program. As discussed in Chapters 6 and 7, HUD does not have a good record administering consumer-oriented programs. Before any new community-based housing support program goes forward, attention should be focused on whether HUD is capable of running such an effort. Finally, H.R. 3891's requirement that $1 be raised from other public or private sources for every $3 of federal funding provided may be problematic for some groups. Although this matching requirement is lenient, it may still present an obstacle in many areas of the country where community-based housing has not yet received much support.

Four final questions regarding the potential for community-based housing to become a centerpiece of a new national housing agenda need to be addressed:

1. Do community-based housing groups have the capability to supply sufficient amounts of affordable housing? This question is particularly important because in many parts of the country, there are either very few such organizations or the ones that exist do not enjoy the support of local government.
2. Is it really possible for a program aimed at empowerment to be success-ful, given that this may require those who are already holding the power to relinquish control?
3. Is it possible for resident groups that organize themselves in a bottom–up way to acquire resources through top–down channels and still retain the best features of the grass-roots initiative? Or is it more likely that once federal resources are provided, the typical features of top–down, federally prescribed citizen participation initiatives will prevail?
4. Is it politically possible to visualize the enactment of a major new federal housing program that does not include opportunities for the private development community to make a profit?

With reference to the first question, it should be underscored that I am not recommending community-based housing as the only major federal housing initiative. A revised federal housing policy must also include significant resources for public housing and should encour-age new forms of public–private partnerships, which are discussed more fully below. At the present time, community-based initiatives cannot be expected to fulfill the total need for low-income housing. As pointed out in Chapters 8 and 11, however, the establishment of a comprehensive federal support system for community-based housing would go a long way toward increasing the potential for this strategy to satisfy a significant portion of the overall demand.

The recognition that community-based housing cannot be the only component of a rebuilt federal housing policy is also based on the situation in locales that either have weak or nonexistent community-based housing groups, or in which local government is not supportive of such efforts. Only as the movement gains federal support and as local experiences start to attract widespread attention can we hope to "bring along" the slower municipalities and states. Indeed, if the federal government supported a state-based system for community-based housing, the ability to disseminate information to locales would be much improved, and the likelihood of their becoming more supportive of these efforts would be enhanced.

Concerning the second question—the potential for a program aimed at empowerment to be successful—there is ample reason to be worried, in view of the experiences with two major programs that advocated empowerment: the War on Poverty and Model Cities (see Chapter 2). Despite the rhetoric of the 1960s, empowerment of community groups was elusive. Sherry Arnstein (1969) summed up the situation: "In most cases where power has come to be shared it was *taken by the citizens*, not given by the city" (p. 222). Do we face the same circumstances today?

Probably. Nevertheless, at least some community-based groups, acutely aware that much of their strength lies in their organizing abilities, attempt to carry out advocacy work in addition to development initiatives. While it is not easy to combine the two activities, it is being done by some organizations. This might enable community groups to gain political empowerment, not so much through a new community-based program that may attempt to legislate "empowerment" but through the accompanying organizing work that at least some groups will be able to maintain.

Maybe we cannot expect too much in terms of direct political empowerment (people having greater access to the decision-making process in their communities and shaping the political process) from even the best-thought-out community-based housing program. But in terms of economic empowerment (people gaining access to goods, services, and resources) and psychological empowerment (improvements in feelings about oneself and increased power to control one's life),[2] community-based development may have a great chance at success.

Although it may be difficult for a development agenda to lead to political empowerment, it is certainly less threatening to those in power to nurture economic and psychological empowerment. Indeed, one might argue that improvements in both areas could be beneficial to the power structure, as well as to individuals and community groups. A locality with a more equitable distribution of resources and with a low-income population striving to better itself and the community could be viewed as an asset by the mayor's office. Further, to the extent that the city's elected officials can demonstrate that they participated in the success of the newly empowered community, by channeling resources or assistance to them, it may turn out to be good politics for them to support nonthreatening forms of empowerment.

It may also be possible to create a community-based program aimed at empowerment if the rhetoric is couched in terms that are less threatening to lawmakers and local chief executives and that focus more on the partnership theme. For example, the Neighborhood Reinvestment Corporation demonstrated its ability to nurture the development of hundreds of more-or-less bottom–up initiatives. Although it is unlikely that the Neighborhood Housing Services programs they helped spawn are all equally strongly rooted in their communities, it is also fair to say that many such groups are truly community based, even though their origins were a top–down program and despite the involvement of public and private, for-profit partners.

A 1981 study of the Neighborhood Housing Services program reported that about one-fifth of all NHS programs were initiated by existing community organizations. In Baltimore, for example, three community groups involved in efforts to solve problems of vacant or poorly maintained houses saw NHS as a useful vehicle for achieving objectives (Urban Systems Research and Engineering, 1981). The same study found that residents constituted the largest single group on all NHS boards and that they were an absolute majority in nearly all cases, an arrangement suggested by the Neighborhood Reinvestment Corporation. Moreover, presidents and chairpersons of NHS boards are more frequently residents than are other participants, such as lenders or city officials (Urban Systems Research and Engineering, 1981). The Neighborhood Reinvestment Corporation's commitment to a strong role for citizens is also demonstrated in its guidelines for its new Mutual Housing Association program. There, too, the Neighborhood Reinvestment Corporation calls for residents or would-be residents to constitute a majority of the association's board (Neighborhood Reinvestment Corporation, n.d.).

The view that it is possible for a top–down organization to foster empowerment among community groups also helps answer the third question, concerning the ability of groups assisted by top–down programs to retain their grass-roots orientation. The discussion presented in Chapter 2 on the ways in which the large-scale federal community development programs attempted to include citizens in the planning process, and the limited benefits arising from these top–down invitations to participate, is a reminder of how difficult it is to mandate meaningful community involvement.

Experiences with several existing programs contribute to my belief that it is possible to create centralized programs that provide top–down assistance to community-based groups without coopting or significantly altering the latter's base within the community. As mentioned, evaluations of the Neighborhood Reinvestment Corporation provide evidence that community-based initiatives can develop with top–down supports.

Also, the Neighborhood Self-Help Development (NSHD) program demonstrated that a federal program that provides funding and technical assistance to community-based groups can help them develop their organizational capacity and assist them in carrying out development projects. Neil Mayer's study of the neighborhood development organizations participating in the NSHD program revealed that although it was harder than anticipated to develop resident participation in the management of the NDO-created housing cooperatives, community support was forthcoming as groups demonstrated their ability to carry out development projects. Mayer concluded, "Many NDO leaders remain actively in touch with community concerns and problems, through direct daily contact with neighborhood citizens." And despite the difficulty of staying in close touch with the community while focusing on sophisticated development schemes (discussed in Chapter 10), "NDO's consistent delivery of results that directly benefit neighborhood residents of itself does much to generate rising community support" (Mayer, 1984, 178).

Finally, the Enterprise Foundation and the Local Initiatives Support Corporation (LISC) have both been successful in helping community-based groups without an apparent diminution of local orientation and most likely with an increase in communitywide visibility. According to Vidal et al. (1986), "It appears that LISC-assisted projects have helped the vast majority of the [community development organizations] in the evaluation to establish wider or more intense relationships with their neighborhoods" (p. VI–34). Although the evaluation team did not gather direct evidence, the report notes that beyond gaining the attention of the direct beneficiaries of the community-based development work, they considered it "likely that most of the projects have enhanced the public reputations and visibility of the sponsoring community groups" (1986, VI–35).

Despite these apparent successes, the central administering agency must be very careful to make sure that their preferences do not dominate the community-based organization. Some ways for the administering agency to do this include the following:

1. Be clear that the goals of the support program are to assist community-based development. The history of federal involvement with community development underscores that multiple objectives are invariably trans-

lated into a confused program with a lack of clarity about the role of the community in planning and implementation.
2. Issue broad guidelines for projects, yet allow the community-based organizations flexibility to develop their own programs.
3. Provide technical assistance, financial resources or access to financial resources, and feedback through a monitoring process, but do not assume control or ownership of the projects.
4. Develop a professional relationship with the community-based organization, not one based on the latter's dependency.

Not only is it possible for bottom–up initiatives to be nurtured by sensitive and well-thought-out top–down projects, but it is also possible for community-based organizations to maintain advocacy roots in the community. Indeed, as the comparison between the Coalition for a Better Acre (CBA) and the Fields Corner Community Development Corporation (FCCDC) revealed in Chapter 10, CBA, with a significant base of support in the community, had an easier time than FCCDC in navigating the tenant-selection process and balancing the dual goals of integration and neighborhood preference. Nevertheless, it is important to remind ourselves of the difficulty of any organization's combining the two roles of developer and advocate.

The fourth question—the potential for a major new piece of housing legislation to be enacted that does not include a profit-making role for the development community—is equally complex. Experience with public housing provides a critical example of the power of the homebuilding and real estate lobbies. Moreover, the precedent for private-sector participation in subsidized housing programs was set in the 1960s and 1970s with the Section 221(d)(3), Section 236, and Section 8 programs. And, finally, federal cutbacks in housing have in a few locales prompted state and local governments to create their own public–private partnership programs. Programs such as SHARP in Massachusetts rely heavily on for-profit developers, and reinforce and keep alive the notion that the private development community is, and can continue to be, a key player in subsidized housing production. Thus the precedent for including the private, for-profit sector is substantial.

I am guardedly optimistic about the ability of Congress to carve a new role for the private sector that does not jeopardize the viability of the housing programs. This optimism is based on the hope that a significant and influential segment of the private development community will choose to support new kinds of public–private partnerships, discussed below. Until this involvement is forthcoming, however, policymakers will need to plan for and work with private interest groups in an attempt to soften opposition to the new subsidy programs.

Such effort would be well spent. Not only must we create a new federal support system for community-based housing but obstacles to the success of the program must be acknowledged and removed. Community-based housing has an enormous potential for becoming the centerpiece of a new federal low-income housing policy. It should be given an optimum chance at success.

Public–Private Partnerships

The case study presented in Chapter 5 and the growing problem of expiring use restrictions, discussed in Chapter 4, make clear that all is far from well with the earlier public–private partnership programs. As recommended in Chapter 5, any involvement by the private, for-profit sector, in any housing program in which profit is a motive, must include a full analysis of the ways in which their short-term and long-term goals and objectives conflict with those of the public and tenants. These conflicts must be articulated and resolved before the programs are enacted. Waiting until the problems surface, when in many instances they were known in advance, runs counter to the housing agenda being proposed here.

Probably the most important issue that demands early resolution is that of how long-term affordability will be maintained. If a public–private partnership can be fashioned that provides the private developer with front-end profits but with little or no residual interest in the housing, so that it can be converted to limited-equity cooperatives or public or nonprofit ownership, the partnership might be workable. But, in general, as long as long-term profit is the motivation for private-sector participation in low-income housing programs, conflicts between the goals of private partners and those of the public and tenants are virtually inevitable.

There are many political and practical reasons why the federal government should include the private, for-profit development community in any new production programs. First, the private sector has expertise, capital, and a proven track record in producing significant quantities of subsidized housing. In view of the need for affordable housing, one might argue that it would be misguided to ignore any available production capacity or resources.

Second, any new federal housing program would probably be enacted in an atmosphere of financial austerity. In view of current budget deficits and caps on federal spending, it is very unlikely that such programs could be passed without a significant reliance on leveraging. In real terms, this means that a role for the private, for-profit sector is almost inevitable.

Third, as discussed above, in view of the lobbying strength of key private-interest groups—the National Association of Home Builders, the National Association of Real Estate Boards, and the Mortgage Bankers Association among others—Congress would probably encounter opposition to any new housing programs that did not include a major role for these organizations.

In view of the significant reasons why it is rational to include the private development community, Congress should consider launching a new public–private partnership program. The theme of it could be "partnerships with shared interests," and the intent would be for private, for-profit partners to participate in ventures clearly aimed at benefiting low-income housing needs. The quest for profit would have no direct role in such initiatives. Federal matching funds could be provided to projects that include a certain level of private-sector participation in such a partnership.

State Street Bank and Trust Company's involvement with the Boston Housing Partnership, discussed in Chapter 12, is a good example of how such a new partnership could operate. The Enterprise Foundation, funded in part by the for-profit Rouse Company, as well as other private corporations, is perhaps the most intriguing example of what appears to be private-sector altruism in the face of serious low-income housing needs.

While most earlier public–private partnerships emphasized that it was "good business" for the private sector to locate new and profitable markets, whether in low-income housing projects or elsewhere, these new partnerships should not be based on direct monetary returns. Instead, rewards to the private sector should be in the knowledge that humanitarian actions aimed at helping the poor will yield returns to society that cannot be measured in dollars. This rationale clearly will not appeal to all businesspeople. But a sizable number of socially minded entrepreneurs may welcome participating in this new partnership.

It is encouraging that the Franklin Research and Development Corporation, in their Advisory Letter for Concerned Investors, strongly advocated a corporate support role for affordable housing. Three means of support are described, including cash contributions, in-kind gifts of service or expertise, and direct investments or loans. Only the latter provides opportunities for private profit in more-or-less traditional terms, although such loans are usually provided at below-market interest. Moreover, the Advisory Letter points out that it is most impressed by "initiatives that keep control at a local level and encourage self-help and self-reliance among community organizations [since] these are the projects that . . . will carry the longest term benefit to the community" (Lydenberg, 1988, 3).

Although this role for the private sector may not assuage a disappointed homebuilding and real estate lobby, since direct profit from low-income housing would be removed, it could be supported by a significant cadre of committed and powerful representatives from the private sector, who could prove crucial in gaining passage of new housing legislation.

Jubilee Housing, the program that served as a model for the Enterprise Foundation, presents a good example of extensive involvement by concerned businesses. Because it represents a "partnership with shared interests," it is worthwhile taking a brief digression to examine the case in more detail.[3]

Jubilee Housing.   Starting in the early 1970s, several groups, or missions, of the Church of the Saviour began addressing the needs of the poor in the neighborhood, the Adams–Morgan section of Washington, D.C. Housing was one of the issues that surfaced as being particularly problematic. Church members estimated that about 70,000 families in Washington were in need of housing assistance. Their goal was to provide decent, safe, affordable, permanent housing for very-low-income people.

In 1973, Jubilee Housing was incorporated as a nonprofit group. After leasing its first two buildings, it began a massive rehabilitation program. By 1979, Jubilee had acquired six buildings with a total of 213 units. The only federal money Jubilee received was a $1.8 million HUD grant that, along with private donations, supported much of the rehabilitation costs.

Jubilee involves a complex set of relationships with the private sector including loans, grants, and donations of labor. James Rouse, developer of Columbia, Maryland, and scores of other major projects, including Boston's Quincy Market, Baltimore's Harbor Place, and, most recently, the Enterprise Foundation, was the cornerstone of the private-sector's involvement with Jubilee. Although not an official member of the Church of the Saviour, he had been a long-time friend of its minister, Gordon Cosby. When the housing mission started to make plans for undertaking a development project, Cosby suggested that Rouse be contacted. Rouse's first response was: "You can't do anything. The problems are too massive." He later changed his mind as church members went ahead and made commitments to buy the first two buildings. Rouse was instrumental in arranging mortgages, and from that time on, Rouse and Jubilee have been closely connected.

In 1978, Rouse organized a private-sector support group. Its purpose was to provide technical assistance and advice to Jubilee whenever necessary. In addition, as more and more people became aware of Jubilee and Rouse's commitment to private/neighborhood-based revitalization, Rouse decided to spend his "retirement years" devoted to implementing this process elsewhere. Hence the birth of the Enterprise Foundation.

Establishing a local private-sector support group is an essential ingredient of the Jubilee model. Once such a group has been organized, the community can draw on a variety of supports, including grants, low-interest loans, and in-kind services. In Washington, Rouse was instrumental in assembling the original support group, which consisted of six prestigious local firms. It has since grown to include more than twenty private entities, including the Wilmer, Cutler and Pickering law firm; Skidmore, Owens and Merrill, an architectural firm; George Hyman Construction; Price-Waterhouse, an accounting firm; and the Rouse Company.

The way in which the support group coalesces may not be the same in each new Enterprise City, but a basic ingredient appears to be the "old-boy/word-of-mouth" network. In Washington, Rouse solicited the support of a friend, Jim Clark, president of Hyman Construction, the largest building firm in the city. Clark in turn engaged the support of large mechanical and electrical contracting firms. Similarly, an individual volunteer knew a partner at Wilmer, Cutler and Pickering who, after becoming involved with the support group, convinced Price-Waterhouse to join in.

Some principals of large corporations who donate funds, services, or both to the Enterprise Foundation or Jubilee clearly become involved because of their personal connection to Rouse. Other individuals decide to participate because they know somebody who has already joined. A "domino effect" is brought into play. Once the first major corporate figure, someone who has the respect of others in the community, becomes committed, others are likely to follow. In a sense, participation becomes the fashionable thing to do.

James Rouse describes how new private partners enlist in the Enterprise Foundation. "As a process, it operates by itself. It gathers its own momentum. If things begin to work, others will follow. Many people are capable of walking to a higher mountain top than they may have experienced in their business careers."[4]

Initial contacts by a respected peer are important, but participation may be more likely if the endeavor appears logical and seems to fulfill some important objectives of the business, aside from direct monetary gain. This "enlightened self-interest" can have several meanings. First, if a goal is to live in a relatively tranquil environment, impoverished, dilapidated areas may threaten this stability. It may follow that potential sources of unrest should be removed in order to ensure personal security. Doing something to revitalize a neighborhood may help guarantee social tranquility.

The private sector may also view involvement in community development activities as a way to promote business. It can be argued that to the extent that a population is better housed, has better health care, and is employed, they will be better consumers. With a more stable population, the overall business environment is apt to be improved.

A third aspect of the enlightened self-interest line of thinking responds to the conservative ideology of the federal government through the 1980s. One argument that Rouse used when addressing business associations to encourage participation in the Enterprise Foundation or try to promote the idea of a local support group was to emphasize that President Reagan was giving the private sector a chance to show that it could operate efficiently. Corporate America consistently asks for less government involvement in local affairs and for reduced regulation. To the extent that President Reagan delivered in these areas, Rouse challenged his colleagues to show that they, too, could come through. The assumption is that if this is not to be a third-rate civilization, then the private sector has to play its part. If the private sector wants to show that the marketplace *can* operate with less regulation and fewer controls, it follows that it must be prepared to do more for local communities than it has done before.

Fourth, enlightened self-interest may be expressed by businesses that become aware that if they do not get involved in providing low-cost housing, the viability of their workforce may be threatened. In areas known for having a particularly expensive housing stock, there is a real possibility that businesses will either lose out or be unable to attract workers, thereby threatening their firms.

Finally, enlightened self-interest may also mean that if a company sponsors a local and highly visible activity, then any publicity flowing out of that involvement will essentially provide free advertising. The firm's reputation is apt to be enhanced, and more people may be inclined to buy its product or service.

In spite of the logic inherent in some of these positions, Rouse is quick to point out that he does not like the notion of enlightened self-interest: "I never use the phrase 'enlightened self-interest.' It's a magnification of selfishness. I talk about the responsibilities of businessmen. Business is too focused on profit. It should, instead, be focused on providing good services or products. If it does its job well, then the reward is profit."[5]

Some individuals became involved with helping Jubilee because of a firm belief that neighborhood-based revitalization was the right approach, and that it was appropriate and necessary for those with resources to assist those who had less. In this sense, participation with Jubilee came out of a moral, ethical, political, or religious conviction that helping one's fellow citizens is the charitable and correct thing to do. According to Bob Boulter, vice-president of Jubilee, many who contributed services or money reported a feeling of genuine delight in helping Jubilee.[6]

Does this sound too idealistic and impractical? Perhaps. But in view of the enormous resources of the private sector and the continuing need for housing that may go unmet if we rely only on direct federal appropriations, it is worth pursuing new ways of involving the private sector. Several public–private and private–private partnerships are feasible. With Jubilee, the partnership was actually between a private nonprofit entity and several private, for-profit businesses. But in all instances, the goal must be benefiting the public and the occupants of the housing. Private profit, in traditional monetary terms, has no place in this new generation of ventures.

Additional Policy Recommendations

In addition to, or as a part of, the new and revised production programs discussed above, a new housing policy should: (1) address the existing stock of affordable housing, (2) end the stigma of low-income housing, (3) focus on nonspeculative uses of land, (4) be gender-sensitive, and (5) resolve the role of HUD.

The Existing Stock of Affordable Housing

A new housing policy should provide incentives to private owners of unsubsidized housing to maintain their units as affordable or to contribute their units to the public or nonprofit stock of "permanent" low-rent housing. One such program would enable local public housing authorities to acquire existing privately owned units and, in so doing, provide long-term security of tenure to occupants who relinquish some or all of their equity in their home. This proposal was first articulated by Hartman and Stone (1986) as part of a larger set of "socialist housing alternatives":

> Homeowners facing foreclosure, as well as other owners unable to afford current housing costs, would have the option of converting their homes to social ownership and getting relief from further mortgage payments. The residents could remain, with full security of tenure, but they would no longer have the right to sell their homes. The government would assume the mortgage debt and make monthly payments to the lending institution until the debt was paid off. (Pp. 495–496)

Although this may appear to be an unlikely choice, it could, in fact, appeal to many homeowners in serious financial difficulties. Interestingly enough, when the Houston Housing Authority launched a program that involved the purchase of foreclosed single-family homes for subsequent rental by low-income households on its waiting list, some homeowners indicated that they "wanted to sell their house to the housing authority and rent it back" (*New York Times,* 1987). Although Houston's program did not assist homeowners to stay in their homes, thereby avoiding foreclosure, it would be a relatively short step from their initiative to one that offered the kind of protection outlined by Hartman and Stone (1986).

A new housing policy also must be committed to maintaining and preserving the existing subsidized housing stock. Potential losses of subsidized units, which, as mentioned in Chapter 4, could reach the hundreds of thousands, is an enormous problem. The protections in the Housing and Community Development Act of 1987 could help reduce the actual loss of the subsidized inventory. Nevertheless, this situation will have to be monitored closely to ensure that possible loopholes in the legislation or inadequate implementation by HUD do not undermine the intent of the act. At the same time, local government officials and housing advocates will have to work vigorously to protect the existing federally subsidized units through whatever creative solutions they can muster.

Ending the Low-Income Housing Stigma

In recommending ways for rebuilding a low-income housing policy, I am aware that many believe that low-income housing, per se, is undesirable. This view maintains that if the government is going to subsidize new production, low-income units should be mixed in with moderate-income and market-rate housing. Among the advocates of the mixed-income approach are private, for-profit housing developers who have participated in past public–private partnership programs that have utilized such mixing and state housing finance agencies whose developments may be occupied by as few as 25 percent low-income households. In supporting their views, they are likely to point to the failure of low-income public housing and the success of mixed-income housing as proof that government should permanently abandon housing targeted strictly for low-income households.

For example, a well-respected Boston-based housing developer, Corcoran-Jennison, produced a film on the redevelopment of an old, terribly dilapidated public housing project in Lynn, Massachusetts, known as America Park, into a new, mixed-income project, Kings Lynne. The film contrasts the poor conditions in the old public housing with the manicured lawns, attractive landscaping, tennis courts, and swimming pools in the redeveloped project. Statements by satisfied tenants provide "evidence" that mixed-income housing works better than concentrating the poor in public housing.

Indeed, there is much that is provocative in this position. The lack of stigma associated with living in a "project" and the possibility of the middle-income tenants serving as role models are two of the most compelling arguments for mixed-income housing. Yet, I am unconvinced that this is the only desirable approach. It may be what some people would choose, but it should not be the only strategy for tenanting subsidized developments. Some low-income tenants may find living with the more affluent uncomfortable because of disparities in material possessions. This can be particularly troublesome to parents who are unable to provide their children with toys, clothes, and vacations comparable to their higher-income neighbors. Also, mixed-income housing may be considerably less cost effective than fully subsidized developments. Specifically, the tax-exempt status of bonds issued by state housing finance agencies translates into a subsidy in the form of a lowered interest rate on the total development, not just the below-market-rate units.

Comparisons between poor-quality public housing and high-quality mixed-income housing do not provide a sound basis for concluding that the latter are superior. If, for example, low-income developments were equipped with the same amenities as mixed-income ones, and were better or as good as other housing in the neighborhood, I suspect that there would be virtually no stigma associated with living in the "project." Evidence that the quality of the buildings are more important contributors to tenant satisfaction than the income mix comes from a 1974 study of mixed-income housing:

> Income mix, surely, and racial mix, very probably, have no significant effect on satisfaction; whatever conceivable effect they *might* have is overwhelmed and completely overshadowed by more basic factors of design, construction, space, facilities, location, maintenance and management. [Further], broad income mix "works," . . . producing higher levels of satisfaction and dissatisfaction at all levels—market, moderate-income, and low-income—principally because these developments are superior in design, construction and management. (Ryan et al., 1974, 23–24)

Finally, if low-income housing is community based, the pride and sense of autonomy that would result would contribute to feelings of being special, in a positive sense, because of residence in a project. Thus stigma associated with low-income projects is a problem that could probably be eliminated if the quality and management of the buildings made people feel proud, rather than embarrassed, about where they live.

Nonspeculative Uses of Land

Fundamental to a new housing policy must be a new commitment to programs aimed at helping localities and nonprofit organizations acquire and hold land and buildings for subsidized housing development. In many urban areas, where the demand for housing is acute, the availability and affordability of land are of paramount concern. If local housing authorities and community-based groups are forced to compete with private developers, there is little chance that they will outbid their for-profit counterparts.

Ironically, the old Urban Renewal program, which gained notoriety for displacing thousands of poor and nonwhite citizens from their homes, turned out to be a major benefit to some community-based groups. Boston's Inquilinos Boricuas en Acción, which spent years protesting the anticipated use of a parcel of Urban Renewal land, ultimately was designated as the developer and was able to launch an impressive housing development. But without that significant subsidy for the land, its attempt to gain a foothold in the South End, a rapidly gentrifying community, would probably have failed.

Although it is perhaps not desirable to revive the Urban Renewal program, its positive lessons should not be lost. Through public action, private land that would have been automatically subject to the private speculative market was, in many instances, removed from such use. But we must also remind ourselves that in addition to displacement, Urban Renewal disposed of land to numerous private, for-profit developers, who were free to use it for speculative purposes.

The idea that land should be used for the common good and that speculation should be limited or nonexistent comes from the Bible, the Book of Leviticus. According to the Reverend Stephen Ayres, several significant laws concern land use (see also Ayres, 1988b):

> The first is the law of jubilee. The jubilee year occurred every fifty years. Since its purpose was to limit speculation on the value of the land, the law prohibited the permanent transfer of land from person to person or family to family. . . . Once distributed, ownership of the land remained within the family and was handed down from generation to generation. Property rights could only be *leased* outside the family. The lease was made in relation to the fifty year jubilee. In hard times, the owner could sell the production value of the family's land up to the next jubilee. At the jubilee, property rights would revert back to the original owner. (Ayres, 1988a)

Thus land could neither be sold nor accumulated in the hands of a few individuals. In addition to the jubilee, the Book of Leviticus details the law of redemption. Again, according to Ayres (1988a):

> [The law of redemption] asserts that no one should be denied their God-given property rights just because of economic hardship. . . . If a person was forced to lease away property because of economic hardship, that person's family would be obligated to redeem the property as soon as possible. The economically secure were obliged to transfer their excess funds to their poorer kin, so that the disadvantaged would not be denied access to the land for an extended period of time.

A little more than 100 years ago, Henry George revived many of the themes in the Old Testament and argued that land should be used for the common good and that many contemporary social problems, including poverty, could be traced to inequities in the distribution of land (George, 1880). Some of the most recent views on the need to end the speculative treatment of land and housing come from Achtenberg and Marcuse (1983). Arguing that under the capitalist system, housing is treated as a commodity, an item bought and sold for profit, they advocate social ownership of housing and an end to its speculative uses (see also Institute for Policy Studies Working Group on Housing, 1987).

Public policy needs to address the speculation issue in two ways. First, a new housing program should include guidelines and funding for localities or nonprofit developers to acquire and hold land and buildings for extended periods of time, until they are able to initiate development projects. Land banking and taxes on the transfer of properties, with the proceeds set aside for purchasing parcels earmarked for affordable housing, present two viable models.

Second, research is needed to assist developers of affordable housing to decide which of the various mechanisms for limiting the appreciation of property over time are most advantageous, and under what circumstances. Chapter 8 includes discussions of several initiatives, including limited-equity cooperatives, mutual housing associations, and community land trusts. It should also be recalled from Chapter 10 that a key dilemma facing community-based housing developers is whether and how to place such limitations on units produced for sale to low- and moderate-income households.

Thus, both before launching a new development and once the units are ready to be marketed, strategies are needed for acquiring land and buildings, and for maintaining them on a nonspeculative basis over the long term. Again citing the Book of Leviticus (25:23), "And the land shall not be sold in perpetuity; for the land is Mine; for ye are strangers and settlers with Me."

A Gender-Sensitive Housing Policy

Housing problems are generally more severe for lower-income and nonwhite households than for those who have higher incomes and are white. In addition, it is important to recognize that gender is an important factor in housing. More than half the family housing units in public housing are occupied by women heads of households. Nationally, 43 percent of households with children that are headed by women live in poverty. This is more than five times the rate of poverty among households headed by a man or a married couple (Women's Economic Agenda Working Group, 1985).

This disparity has implications for housing policy. Much of the eligible population for subsidized housing is not the two-parent family, equivalent to the somewhat mythical image of the "average American family," only poorer. Many consumers of subsidized housing programs, who are frequently single female heads of households, face particular stresses, such as how to manage both jobs and families.

The design of housing could be far more responsive to the needs of such families. Rather than reinforce a sense of separateness, as does the typical apartment or detached house, new and innovative designs and support services could help with difficulties associated with raising children alone. For example, the architect Dolores Hayden has observed:

> The woman who does leave the isolated, single-family house or apartment finds very few real housing alternatives available to her. The typical divorced or battered woman currently seeks housing, employment, and child care simultaneously. She finds that matching her complex family requirements with the various available offerings by landlords, employers, and social services is impossible. One environment that unites housing, services, and jobs could resolve many difficulties. (Hayden, 1986, 234)

Hayden has proposed the establishment of experimental communities that would share such facilities as a day-care center, laundromat, communal kitchen, grocery, dial-a-ride service, and an emergency service providing helpers for elderly residents or sick children. Jacqueline Levitt (1988) has also proposed new housing designs that combine both private and shared spaces, as better equipped to serving the needs of single parents.

The potential for housing design to support female heads of households is a relatively new area of concern. Although it has not yet received the attention of many housing advocates or policymakers, a new federal housing policy offers an opportunity to examine the issue closely and pioneer new forms of housing. This kind of federal leadership is critical to creating alternatives to our virtually homogenous housing stock.

Maintaining the status quo is consistent with the goals of the homebuilding, banking, and real estate industries. It is generally considered far easier and desirable to build, finance, and sell housing that fits the conventional mold, as opposed to units that are unique and innovative. But with strong signals from the federal government, and with experimental designs that could prove marketable, we might see a new interest on the part of the private sector and a willingness to venture into innovative housing designs for a wide range of income groups.

To HUD or Not to HUD?

One of the most difficult questions about a new housing policy involves the role of HUD. Should HUD be in charge of the new kinds of housing programs being recommended here? A quick answer would be yes. In creating HUD in 1965, Congress vested it with responsibility for administering "the principal programs of the Federal Government which provide assistance for housing for the development of the Nation's communities [and] . . . for achieving maximum coordination of the various Federal activities which have a major effect upon urban community, suburban, or metropolitan development."[7] HUD's mandate clearly includes administration of the programs discussed above.

Yet HUD's historical proindustry orientation hampered the administration of the new homeownership programs enacted in 1968 and resulted in a disregard for consumer needs (see Chapter 6). As a 1973 law review article put it: "It is clear that HUD's dealings and concerns are with the mortgage companies and builders and that little attention is given the homeowner [in the 235 program]" (Traxler et al., 1973, 131). Moreover, the case study presented in Chapter 7 demonstrated how HUD has continued to compromise on consumer needs, as well as on the goal of preserving an affordable stock of housing. Finally, after two terms of Ronald Reagan and a HUD secretary, Samuel Pierce, who seemed to have relatively little interest in the programs he was administering, HUD has been significantly undermined.

Unless HUD can be rejuvenated, it would be inadvisable for it to implement the new programs recommended here—a community-based support program and a new series of partnership initiatives. The changes being recommended here go way beyond the assignment of a new secretary or hiring some new personnel. The needed reorganization of HUD would involve a careful management plan and a shift in its administrative structure to reflect a new set of consumer- and public-oriented goals. The resulting agency would look and "feel" substantially different from the old HUD; indeed, it may even be advisable for the name of the agency to be changed.

If this reorganization is not done, responsibility for administering the new programs should be assigned to a new or existing, congressionally created public agency, such as the Neighborhood Reinvestment Corporation. Even assuming a major overhaul by HUD, it may still be desirable for new programs to be administered by a new agency. This issue deserves a thorough congressional investigation.

While it may be feasible to create a new agency to administer new programs, HUD, whether in its present or revised form, will almost certainly be placed in charge of any old programs that resurface, such as the public housing program. This is cause for concern and provides further justification for a thorough overhaul of HUD.

Most likely, some HUD employees would resist sweeping changes in its structure as well as the creation of a new agency. But others would probably welcome such a move and would embrace the ideals of a new, consumer-oriented HUD. In fact, it may be easier than it seems to undertake a major revamping. With the ranks of HUD personnel substantially reduced, and with morale among those who have stayed at a low, there may be less opposition to change than one might assume. The fact that HUD has not had a real mission for so long might make it easier for workers to adapt to a new set of expectations and responsibilities.

Decent, affordable housing for all should be more than rhetoric. It is a worthwhile goal; it is a humanitarian goal; it is an attainable goal. Housing is central to how people live and how they feel about themselves; it is also a necessity. The dramatic increase in homelessness has brought the housing crisis to new levels of public consciousness. Perhaps this social concern will help stimulate the passage of new legislation and the appropriation of significant federal resources. But it is also important to see housing reform as part of a larger set of domestic initiatives in health care, education, nutrition, economic development, and job training. Ideally, new efforts in housing will be accompanied by a new dedication to the many serious problems facing Americans.

The programs outlined in this chapter could go a long way toward rebuilding a housing policy for low-income households. But they require a President who is an advocate for the poor, a Congress that will appropriate the necessary funding, and an administrative structure that is supportive and capable of carrying out initiatives. Our housing programs and policies must, once and for all, be geared to those who most need assistance. Anything short of that perpetuates a national disgrace and a waste of human resources.

Notes
References
Index

Notes

Chapter 1

1. For a history of the 25-percent-of-income rule of thumb, see Feins and Lane (1981). Since 1981, households in federally assisted housing have been required to pay 30 percent of income for rent, instead of 25 percent. Also see Chapter 2, note 1.
2. "Very low income" is generally defined as households with incomes at 50 percent or less of area median family income. "Low income" includes households with incomes from 50 to 80 percent of area median family income.
3. Interestingly, just a page earlier, Lowry argued that it was actually not possible to establish rental surpluses or shortages. He stated, "We are presently unable to assess supply–demand balance in rental housing markets, either nationally or locally, so we cannot evaluate arguments about rental housing surpluses or shortages. It is likely that we have enough data for such assessments, but we lack a coherent model of market processes that would allow us to interpret the data we have" (Lowry, 1981, 34).
4. Author's interview with William Apgar, associate professor, John F. Kennedy School of Government, Harvard University, August 1983.
5. Specific regulations viewed as detrimental to the private market were rent control, restrictions on conversion to condominiums and cooperatives, and certain zoning and land-use controls and building codes. For example, rent control was called "the most evident interference in the ability of the private market to supply rental housing" (Report of the President's Commission on Housing, 1982, 91). Appelbaum and Gilderbloom (1983), however, have shown that there is no difference in the rate of multifamily housing construction between rent-controlled and non-rent-controlled communities. Therefore, simply eliminating rent control would not stimulate multifamily construction activity.
6. Housing and Community Development Act of 1987, Sec. 2(a)(1).
7. Ibid., Sec. 2(b)(1).

Chapter 2

1. Under present HUD regulations, rentals are based on 30 percent of income for new tenants. This income limit, increased from 25 percent, was

set in the Omnibus Budget Reconciliation Act of 1981. In July 1983, the House passed a bill that would have reinstated the 25 percent of income formula for all subsidized housing programs. The final legislation enacted by Congress, the Housing and Urban–Rural Recovery Act of 1983, did not reinstate the 25 percent of income formula. It did, however, modify deductions on which income is based, thereby reducing rents for many households.

A proposal to assess tenant rent contributions more equitably has been made by Michael Stone (1983). He has argued that "any attempt to reduce affordability of housing to a single percentage of income—no matter how low or high—simply does not correspond to the reality of fundamental and obvious differences among households." That is, "a small household with a given income can afford to spend more than a large household of the same income; while a household of a given size can afford a higher proportion of income for shelter as its income rises." Therefore, according to Stone, "an appropriate standard of affordability for housing is a sliding scale, with household size and income as the principal variables" (pp. 102–103).

2. For Marxist critiques of Turner's views of self-help housing, see Burgess, 1977, 1982; and Conway, 1982. For a general critique of the self-help strategy, primarily as it has been used in Third World countries, see Ward, 1982.

3. Comment by Pat Nichols during a cable television show produced by Continental Cable (Wayland, Mass.), "A Home of My Own."

4. For a comparison of tenants in two types of housing developments, public housing and Section 221(d)(3), interviewed both before and after the move into their new housing, see Feagin, Tilly, and Williams, 1972. This study is also unique because it attempts to examine the impact of housing on individuals' well-being. A sample of 35 residents of subsidized housing and 24 residents of public housing were surveyed on "a few attitudinal items." The researchers concluded that those moving into the subsidized housing "tended to become somewhat more optimistic about life in general and less anxious after their move . . . while the public housing group tended to remain as uneasy as, and became somewhat more pessimistic than, before the move" (P. 123).

5. Housing and Community Development Act of 1974, P.L. 93-383, Title I, Sec. 104(a)(6).

Chapter 3

Acknowledgment. This chapter is revised from Rachel G. Bratt, "Public Housing: The Controversy and Contribution," in *Critical Perspectives on Housing*, ed. Rachel G. Bratt, Chester Hartman, and Ann Meyerson. © 1984 by Temple University. Reprinted by permission of Temple University

Press. A shortened version of this chapter appeared in Rachel G. Bratt, "Controversy and Contributions: A Public Housing Critique," *Journal of Housing*, Vol. 42, No. 5, September/October 1985, pp. 165–173; reprinted with permission.

1. U.S. Housing Act of 1937, Public Law 412, 75th Congress, 50 Stat. 888; 42 U.S.C. 1401.
2. Some early public housing (pre-World War II) had less differentiated architecture and more amenities than subsequent developments. This has been attributed, in part, to the work of housing reformers such as Edith Elmer Wood and Catherine Bauer Wurster, women who stressed the importance of including community facilities such as meeting rooms and playgrounds in public housing developments (Birch, 1978; Wood, 1919).
3. The major legal reason for a decentralized program was that a court decision "cast grave doubt upon the right of the Federal government to condemn property for housing purposes" (Abrams, 1946, 255–256).
4. Additions to the public housing stock during the 1970s were not predominantly in central cities; in 1976, only 22 percent of new public housing units were located in central cities (Kolodny, 1979). This trend is both the result of HUD regulations (enacted in 1967), which required dispersion of public housing outside "racially impacted areas" (Kolodny, 1979), as well as legislative amendments, beginning in 1956, which made single older people eligible for public housing and authorized the construction of housing specifically designed for the elderly (Olson, 1982). While many communities have avoided building public housing for families, they have been willing to build such housing for the elderly. Nearly half the public housing units completed in fiscal year 1979 were designated for the elderly (HUD, 1980); 46 percent of all public housing units are at present occupied by elderly households (President's Commission on Housing, 1982).
5. Even this fell far short of congressional authorizations. The 1949 Housing Act authorized funding for 810,000 units—135,000 units per year over a six-year period. Through the 1950s and 1960s, whether there was a Republican or Democratic administration, completions lagged well behind congressional authorizations.
6. Four surveys of specific housing projects, while less generalizable, are also worth mentioning. Rainwater (1970) found that even in the Pruitt-Igoe project, in which most tenants showed little attachment to the project community and indicated an interest in moving, the great majority felt that their apartments were better than their previous dwellings. A 1964 survey of Easter Hill Village in Richmond, California, found that 75 percent of the tenants liked their house either "a lot" or "quite a bit." Despite these high satisfaction levels with their particular unit, a considerably smaller percentage of tenants (40 percent) reported that they felt positive about living in public housing, while another 25 per-

cent said that they were indifferent (Cooper, 1975). And a 1980 survey of a public housing project in Decatur, Illinois, disclosed that 43 percent of the adult residents reported positive feelings toward their environment; 40 percent gave negative responses; 17 percent were neutral (Weidemann et al., 1982). A fourth study of why people were leaving public housing projects in Puerto Rico found that only a small percentage (5 percent) of those moving away had cited dissatisfaction with living in public housing as their main reason for moving (Hartman, 1960).

7. But Paul Warren (1982), citing *Annual Housing Survey* data, notes that tenant satisfaction is lower among Boston Housing Authority nonelderly residents than among nonelderly renters of private housing with incomes below 50 percent of the median. Levels of satisfaction for elderly renters were almost identical. These findings might be tempered somewhat, if we knew the answer to the following question: If public housing residents had to find units in the private market, would they be able to rent dwellings comparable to those occupied by existing private-market residents?

8. Although their definitions varied, both the Jones et al. and Perkins and Will and the Ehrenkrantz Group's estimates of the number of troubled or chronic-problem projects are reasonably close. Nevertheless, it is surprising that the two studies found the number of units involved to be quite different. Since we know that the larger projects tend to have more problems than the overall public housing stock, Jones's estimate of 15 percent of public housing units being troubled seems more plausible than Perkins and Will and the Ehrenkrantz Group's estimate of only 7 percent.

9. According to the Perkins and Will and the Ehrenkrantz Group's study, however, large, high-rise projects accounted for more than half (54 percent) of the projected modernization cost for chronic-problem projects. Small, family, low-rise projects accounted for only 14 percent of these costs.

10. In addition to managing and owning these federally supported public housing units, the New York City Housing Authority administers about 24,000 city and state subsidized public housing units. Several other states besides New York (e.g., Massachusetts and Connecticut) also have their own public housing programs.

11. Abt, the research and consulting firm cited earlier, also received a HUD contract to study the Section 8 program. See Wallace et al., 1981.

12. Letter to Rachel Bratt from Joseph Riley, HUD economist, April 8, 1983.

13. In its response to Urban Systems Research and Engineering's report, the National Association of Housing and Redevelopment Officials has argued that the findings were misinterpreted and methodologically imperfect (Maffin, 1983b).

14. Evaluations of both the Section 8 Existing Housing program and the

housing allowance experiments also have demonstrated that the population currently living in public housing is inadequately served by these newer programs. Summarizing the available data on the housing allowance experiments and the Section 8 Existing program, the President's Commission on Housing (1982) reported: "Persons starting out in housing that does not meet the quality standards of the program are less likely to participate in a Housing Payments Program than those who start out in units meeting the program standards. . . . Large families, single-parent households, and minority families are more likely than other groups to live in substandard housing. Therefore, these households are less likely to become program participants" (pp. 26–27).

Chapter 4

1. The most important reason for the federal government's major entry into housing, which occurred during the Great Depression, was to revive the faltering financial system and help stimulate the economy. The need for low-income housing was acute, but it almost certainly would not have been sufficient to stimulate federal involvement without the other economic and political pressures. But if the private market had been providing the needed low-rent housing on its own, it is unlikely that housing would have been chosen as a key vehicle to alleviate the broader problems stemming from the Great Depression. Although the Depression signaled the federal government's first significant involvement with housing, several small-scale emergency housing programs were implemented during World War I to accommodate workers involved with the war effort.
2. See Report of the President's Commission on Housing, 1982 (pp. xix–xx).
3. Housing Act of 1949, P.L. 171, 63 Stat. 413, 42 U.S.C. 1441, Sec. 2.
4. The position of the committee was not surprising: Twelve of the eighteen members were corporate officials.
5. Housing and Urban Development Act of 1968, P.L. 90-448, 82 Stat. 476, 601, 12 U.S.C. 1701t and 42 U.S.C. 1441a, Sec. 2.
6. One small bit of information about accessibility has been found. A study of sixty-two Section 236 developments revealed that sixteen of the sites were inaccessible. Tenants in these projects were not adequately served by convenient shopping and social services (HUD, 1972).
7. For an exception, see Feagin, Tilly, and Williams, 1972. Also see Chapter 2, note 4.

Chapter 5

Acknowledgment. This chapter, with minor modifications, was originally published in the *Journal of the American Planning Association*. It is reprinted by permission of the *Journal of the American Planning Association*, vol. 53, no. 3, Summer 1987.

1. The 1981 tax law also reduced the top marginal tax bracket from 70 to 50 percent, reducing the tax savings per dollar of tax deduction for the wealthiest investors. But ERTA provided "substantially more tax shelter benefits to high-tax-bracket investors" (Rumpf, 1983, 8).

2. Besides the decreased tax-shelter value of the property, a key incentive for selling a subsidized property within a few years of the crossover point was that an owner's income tax liability was substantially reduced at this time. Both before ERTA and under ERTA, if owners of low-rent developments retained their property for at least fifteen years, they avoided paying a special tax under the Internal Revenue Service "recapture" provisions. Recapture discouraged owners from taking huge write-offs for a few years, thereby reaping the benefits of accelerated forms of depreciation, and then selling the project. The IRS stipulated that the difference between the amount of accelerated depreciation taken and what would have been deducted if the "straight-line" method had been used must be taxed, or recaptured, as ordinary income. ERTA left the recapture provisions for low-cost housing unchanged. Depreciation recapture is eliminated for properties subject to the Tax Reform Act of 1986, however.

3. Not surprisingly, when ERTA went into effect, there was a rush to resyndicate. HUD estimated that ERTA's tax incentives stimulated 3000 to 4000 resyndications—a tenfold increase from pre-ERTA days (GAO 1985b). The Deficit Reduction Act of 1984 made resyndication somewhat less financially advantageous by changing various provisions for accounting interest payments and deductions on secondary loans provided by the seller. For a detailed description of these changes, see GAO, 1985b.

4. Owners of residential property who actively participate in its operation may use up to $25,000 in losses resulting from depreciation to offset ordinary income and reduce taxes. The full $25,000 deduction is available only to taxpayers with less than $100,000 in adjusted gross income. The amount of the passive loss deduction gradually phases out between $100,000 and $150,000 of adjusted gross income. In contrast, investors utilizing low-income tax credits may make full use of the credits if their adjusted gross incomes are below $200,000; use of the tax credit is gradually phased out for incomes between $200,000 and $250,000.

5. Newly constructed or substantially rehabilitated Section 8 developments not bound by other regulatory requirements are under five-year con-

tracts, during which occupancy is restricted for low-income use. At the end of the five-year period owners can choose not to renew the contract, thereby forfeiting the Section 8 subsidy and removing the use restriction. HUD, however, has committed a Section 8 subsidy for these projects for periods of twenty to forty years.

6. The audit concluded that the transfer process had been "ineffective in improving the condition of projects" (HUD, 1982).
7. The author is a member of the MHFA Multifamily Advisory Committee and was a participant in the debates on resyndication.
8. Early MHFA developments carried a twenty-year use restriction. An MHFA board ruling in 1973 increased the use restriction to forty years.
9. Reasonable plans included such alternatives as "a provision for conversion to tenant cooperatives; extended notices for particular classes of tenants; special discounts for purchase of a converted unit; continued subsidy options for the original lock-in term; donations of secondary notes to a non-profit advocacy organization; etc." (Kuehn and Finch, 1984).
10. Drafters of the SHARP legislation were concerned about this limited use-restriction period and wrote the bill with certain characteristics that, they hoped, would encourage low-income occupancy after the fifteen years. There are no guarantees that these provisions will work, however, and tenants still may face unwanted displacement, and affordable units may be lost.
11. Projects financed with tax credits must have a minimum of either 20 percent of the units occupied by households with incomes under 50 percent of area median income or 40 percent of the units occupied by households with incomes under 60 percent of area median income.

Chapter 6

Acknowledgment. Portions of this chapter are revised from previously unpublished material in Rachel G. Bratt, "Federal Homeownership Policy and Home Finance: A Study of Program Operations and Impacts on the Consumer," Ph.D. dissertation, MIT, 1976.

1. For a good account of problems that the Veterans Administration caused for consumers, see Keats, 1957.
2. P.L. 91-609, December 31, 1970, 4 Stat. 1770, 1771, Sec. 104.
3. Ibid.
4. Letter from George O. Hipps Jr., acting director, Office of Underwriting Standards, HUD, to Rachel G. Bratt, June 10, 1975.
5. Author's interview with Rose Strickland, housing counselor/community services advisor, Phoenix HUD Insuring Office, 1974.

Chapter 7

Acknowledgment. Rachel G. Bratt wrote this chapter based on the master's thesis of Emily J. Morris, which was written under Bratt's supervision. See Morris, 1986.

1. Emily J. Morris's interview with Dan Manning, Greater Boston Legal Services, Boston, March 1986.
2. Emily J. Morris's interview with Ann Kerrey, Boston Housing Partnership, Boston, 1986.
3. Ibid.
4. Ibid.
5. Ibid.
6. Letter from Marvin Siflinger, MHFA director, to Janet Hale, HUD acting general deputy assistant for housing, Boston, September 18, 1985.

Chapter 8

Acknowledgments. Portions of this chapter are revised from Rachel G. Bratt, "Community-Based Housing Programs: Overview, Assessment, and Agenda for the Future," *Journal of Planning Education and Research* 5, no. 3 (Spring 1986): 164–177. Reprinted by permission of the Association of Collegiate Schools of Planning. And from Rachel G. Bratt, "The Role of Citizen-Initiated Programs in the Formulation of National Housing Policies," originally published in *Citizen Participation in Public Decision Making*, Jack DeSario & Stuart Langton, Eds. (Greenwood Press, Inc., Westport, CT, 1987), pp. 153–176. Prepared under the auspices of the Policy Studies Organization. Copyright © 1987 by the Policy Studies Organization. Reprinted with permission of the publisher.

1. Letter from Andrew Mott to Michael Ames, editor-in-chief, Temple University Press, March 1988.
2. Enacted in 1977, the Community Reinvestment Act authorizes federal financial regulatory agencies to reject applications for bank mergers and branch openings if the bank is not meeting the credit needs of the local community. Passage of the act was stimulated by citizen activism.
3. Model tenements produced for no profit, rather than limited profit, were extremely rare. Edith Wood, writing in 1919, knew of only two such instances (Friedman, 1968, 76).
4. Keyes (1971) provided the following data, from which the 28 percent figure was derived:

	Nonprofit Units	Total Units
221 BMIR		
Insurance in force	45,669	160,594
Commitments outstanding	2,458	8,834

236

Insurance in force	9,799		32,830
Commitments outstanding	7,364		27,428
TOTAL	65,290	of	229,686 (28%)

5. Clancy et al. (1973) pointed out that "a high level of rent supplement or leased housing units in a Section 236 project, create a more difficult management situation requiring much greater input of management staff time" (p. 49).
6. However, the same report also noted that "limited dividend sponsored units serve minorities more than nonprofit sponsored units do" and that "no plausible explanation can be suggested by this situation" (HUD, 1975b, 7).
7. For a thorough evaluation of the various form of ownership available to a community-based housing sponsor, see National Housing Law Project, 1982.
8. NDOs are equivalent to community-based housing organizations, with the exception that some NDOs also engage in nonhousing activities.
9. Another concrete example of the extent to which community-based housing activity is overwhelmed by the overall need was revealed by Mayer (1984, 89). He found that the average number of units rehabilitated by the NDOs in his study was 25, while neighborhoods in which these organizations were located reported that the number of units needing repair averaged over 1500.
10. Remark made at the Housing Roundtable meeting, Boston, November 5, 1987.
11. Author's interview with Shirley Allen, April 1988.
12. However, Mayer (1984) has also noted that "unfortunately, an unintended impact of NDO work in a few cases has been to encourage such behavior [non-NDO investment designed for gentrification] by improving the most blighted properties that discouraged other neighborhood investment" (p. 88).
13. For further discussion of the issues surrounding replication of locally based programs, see Bratt, 1986c.

Chapter 9

Acknowledgment. Rachel G. Bratt wrote this chapter based on the master's thesis of Thomas M. Harden, which was written under Bratt's supervision. See Harden, 1986.
1. According to the 1980 census, per capita incomes were $2942 for tract 8115 (approximates the boundaries of South Holyoke), $6137 for Holyoke, and $6769 for the SMSA. The 1985 figures are based on an average 7.1 percent inflation rate.

2. According to the 1980 census, for tract 8115, minority population was 64 percent in 1980, compared to 23 percent in 1970.
3. Letter from Carlos Vega to the U.S. Department of Housing and Urban Development, April 18, 1984.
4. Letter from Miguel Arce, director of Nueva Esperanza, to the Massachusetts Commission against Discrimination, October 26, 1983.

Chapter 10

Acknowledgments. Four of the six dilemmas discussed in this chapter were first presented in Rachel G. Bratt, "Dilemmas of Community-Based Housing," *Policy Studies Journal* 16, no. 2 (Winter 1987–1988): 324–334; these four dilemmas and two additional ones are presented in Rachel G. Bratt, "Community-Based Housing: Strengths of the Strategy Amid Dilemmas That Won't Go Away," in *Neighborhood Policy and Programs: Past and Present*, edited by Naomi Carmon (London: Macmillan Press, 1989).

The case studies of the two CDCs were originally written by a team of students at Tufts University as part of a field project exercise. I rewrote the case studies for inclusion in this chapter. The project was carried out under the supervision of Professor Ken Geiser and me.

1. Peter Hollands's interview with Kathy Gannett, former board member, FCCDC, March 1987.
2. Peter Hollands's interview with Lynn Whipple, Abrams Management Co., March 1987.
3. Phillip Brown's interview with Kathy Weremiuk, former executive director, FCCDC, March 1987.
4. Memo from Bill Sketchley, chair, FCCDC Housing Committee, to members of the committee, May 1985.
5. Memo from Bill Sketchley to Pat Egan, chairman of the board, FCCDC, July 1985.
6. Rachel Bratt's interview with Mara Benitez, project coordinator, CBA, February 1988.
7. Ibid.

Chapter 11

Acknowledgment. Portions of this chapter are revised from Rachel G. Bratt, "Community-Based Housing in Massachusetts: Lessons and Limits of the State's Support System." Originally written for *Housing Issues of the 1990's*, ed. Sara Rosenberry and Chester Hartman (Praeger Publishers, New York, a division of Greenwood Press, Inc., 1989). Copyright © 1989 by Sara Rosenberry and Chester Hartman. Used with permission.

1. The list of CDC activities is adapted from Counsel for Community Development, 1982.
2. Dual labor-market theorists divide the labor market into "primary" and "secondary" sectors. According to Bennett Harrison, "The primary labor market is characterized by employers who offer jobs that pay relatively decent wages, provide relatively good opportunities for mobility, some degree of control over the job and stability in employment." In contrast, "a secondary labor market job is one with low wages, high instability, and frequent turnover. For the employee, there is a high risk of job loss which is not a function of the person's skills, capabilities or motivation. Rather, the vulnerability stems from the nature of the job itself" (Harrison, n.d., c. 1978, 35).
3. These assumptions were originally presented in Bratt and Geiser, 1982.
4. These data include the accomplishments of GBCD's predecessor, South End Community Development. GBCD was formed in 1970.
5. Author's interview, April 1985.
6. Author's interview, May 1985.
7. A briefer version of this proposal originally appeared in Bratt, "Housing for Low-Income People: A Preliminary Comparison of Existing and Potential Supply Strategies," *Journal of Urban Affairs*, vol. 7, no. 3 (Summer 1985), pp. 1–18, and is used here with permission.
8. It has been estimated that the cost of land acquisition and improvements, along with related transaction costs for development, are significant contributors to the sharp increase in the cost of housing. These costs have increased from 31 percent of total capital costs in 1949 to over 55 percent in 1986, an escalation of over 75 percent (Kuehn, 1988). But despite the increases in the cost of land, the major factor in the high cost of housing for the consumer is finance costs. Kuehn (1988) has estimated that 67 percent of housing costs are finance costs, compared to 33 percent for capital costs. This compares to 66 percent for capital costs and 34 percent for finance costs in 1949.
9. Massachusetts has a well-funded public housing program, Chapter 705, which usually operates through local housing authorities. In fiscal year 1984, some Chapter 705 funds began to be channeled to nonprofit sponsors in areas where development was not occurring through the LHAs.
10. There also may be other reasons for Governor King's antipathy toward these programs, such as a desire to destroy anything associated with his predecessor, Governor Dukakis.
11. Author's interview, April 1985.
12. Ibid.
13. Until his death in 1986, Jorge Hernandez was the long-time executive director of IBA, a CDC; William Edgerly is chairman of the board of State Street Bank and Trust Company and was pivotal in the creation of the Boston Housing Partnership, a public–private venture with a major

emphasis on the role of community-based groups (see Chapter 12); Bob Whittlesey was the founder of GBCD and currently is the executive director of the Boston Housing Partnership; Pat Clancy is the executive director of GBCD. Statement was made by Mitchell Sviridoff, former president of the Local Initiatives Support Corporation, an organization that channels private foundation and corporate funds to community-based programs.

Chapter 12

Acknowledgment. An earlier draft of this chapter was titled "The Boston Housing Partnership: A Prototype Rehabilitation Program?" It was presented at the Annual Conference of the Association of Collegiate Schools of Planning, Atlanta, Georgia, November 1–3, 1985 and was co-authored with Wendy Plotkin. The work is based on Plotkin's master's thesis (1987), which was written under Bratt's supervision.

1. Another goal of the BHP was to promote institutional change in the city's foreclosure and tax-abatement procedures, thereby salvaging units that otherwise would have been lost from the housing stock.

2. Per unit acquisition and rehabilitation costs were raised to $29,000 when it was learned that prevailing wages would have to be paid.

3. Twelve groups were originally selected, but two dropped out early in the process.

4. FNMA's role is a complicated one. MHFA issues bonds. Rather than use the proceeds to make the mortgage, the money is used to buy mortgage-backed securities from FNMA, which actually is giving the mortgage.

5. Letter from Boston Housing Partnership to nonprofit community organizations in Boston, October 21, 1983.

6. According to Mat Thall, executive director of the Fenway CDC, one of the organizations participating in the Demonstration Program, one of the minority contractors was chosen at the last minute when an agreement could not be reached between the CDC and the previously chosen white contractor. A key difficulty in enlisting minority participation was that there are only a few minority contractors in Boston; of these, many are small and not bondable. Small contractors are generally unable to put up with the delays, paperwork, and additional requirements involved in a program such as the BHP Demonstration. Wendy Plotkin's interviews with Mat Thall, Boston, April and November 1986.

7. Boston Housing Partnership, "Request for Proposals," August 18, 1983.

8. The pressure also worked the other way. Without some guarantee of financing, which many sponsors perceived the Demonstration Program offered them, it is likely that several groups would not have participated. Thus, if the BHP had not arranged the financing, some nonprofits likely

would not have been interested, and the number of units rehabilitated would have been smaller.

9. Wendy Plotkin's interview with Peter Munkenbeck, GBCD, April 1984.
10. Wendy Plotkin's interview with Louise Elving, GBCD, September 1985.
11. Wendy Plotkin's interview with Robert Whittlesey, executive director, BHP, September 1985.
12. The SHARP program is discussed in Chapters 5 and 11. TELLER stands for Tax Exempt Loans to Encourage Rental Housing. Created in 1984, it permits local housing authorities to issue bonds to finance mixed-income housing. Prior to TELLER, local housing authorities had been restricted to using bond proceeds to produce housing available only to low- and moderate-income tenants.
13. For example, only 25 percent of the units developed by for-profits through the 1984 round of the SHARP program were affordable by low-income tenants (MHFA, 1984).
14. According to Jim Luckett, currently managing director of the BHP, and formerly the director of development of one of the CDCs that participated in the Demonstration Program, there were several reasons why the reserves were depleted rapidly. By the fall of 1986, which was toward the end of construction, there was an "avalanche of costs." Most CDCs left many "small" aspects of the work out of the general contractor's scope of services in order to get the budgeted price down as low as possible. By doing this, sponsors also could bypass the requirement that union wages be paid. But, as it turned out, many repairs were either much larger than anticipated or these costs, incurred some two years after the original estimates were made, had gone up significantly. As of late 1987, five of the CDCs were on the verge of getting mortgage increases. After paying outstanding debts, as much of the reserves were to be paid back as possible, although, according to Luckett, one half of the BHP's original $1 million reserve fund was "gone for good." Rachel Bratt's and Wendy Plotkin's interview with Jim Luckett, November 1987.
15. Wendy Plotkin's interview with Robert Whittlesey, September 1985.
16. Wendy Plotkin's interview with Edward Burke, president of the Fenway Civic Association, March 1985.
17. Memo from Galen Gilbert, attorney for the Fenway CDC and board member, to the executive director.
18. Rachel Bratt's and Wendy Plotkin's interview with Jim Luckett, November 1987.
19. Letter from Kathy Gannett to the community, April 1985. Printed in "What Is the B.H.P.?: Fact Sheet on Boston Housing Partnership," sponsored by the Fields Corner CDC.
20. Conversation between Wendy Plotkin, Galen Gilbert, and Mat Thall, 1986.
21. The potential for conflict between the BHP and the sponsors exists in

the former's authority over release of the reserves and its supervisory role in behalf of the investment partners. Theoretically, the BHP could refuse to release the reserves if it decided that a group was unfit to continue to manage the housing, and could force the project to seek funds elsewhere or default. Meanwhile, the BHP would identify another community group to take over management. In such a case, the original sponsor could charge that the BHP was overriding the decisions of the community. The procedures to be followed in case of disagreement between the BHP and the sponsors are not clearly laid out.

MHFA's involvement is again crucial. MHFA will be responsible for monitoring the health of the developments and trying to resolve the situation should problems emerge. If MHFA believes the sponsor is no longer capable of overseeing the development, it may use its own authority as mortgagee. It may also bring in the BHP with its control over the reserve funds and syndication proceeds. MHFA's experience with community-based groups has mostly been in joint ventures between these groups and for-profit partners. It is unclear how MHFA would deal with a floundering nonprofit, particularly in the unique situation in which it holds no risk.

Chapter 13

1. This view was articulated in a conversation with Patrick Clancy, executive director, Greater Boston Community Development, March 1988. Also see Clancy's comments in Focer, 1987.
2. I am grateful to Janet Howley (1987), a former student of mine, for her work in defining the different kinds of empowerment.
3. The discussion on Jubilee, with some minor changes, originally appeared in Bratt, 1984.
4. Author's interview with James Rouse, executive director, Enterprise Foundation, December 1982.
5. Ibid.
6. Author's interview with Bob Boulter, vice-president of Jubilee Housing, November 1982.
7. Housing and Urban Development Act of 1965, Public Law 89–174, Sec. 2, 79 Stat. 667, 5 U.S.C. 624.

References

Aaron, Henry J. 1972. *Shelter and Subsidies*. Washington, D.C.: Brookings Institution.

Abrams, Charles. 1946. *The Future of Housing*. New York: Harper & Bros.

———. 1955. *Forbidden Neighbors*. New York: Harper & Bros.

———. 1965. *The City Is the Frontier*. New York: Harper & Row.

Abt Associates, Inc. 1973. *An Evaluation of the Special Impact Program Final Report*. Vol. 1, *Summary*. Report prepared for the Office of Economic Opportunity, Contract No. BOO-5181. Cambridge, Mass.

Achtenberg, Emily P. 1982. *The Need for Rent Eviction and Condominium Conversion Control in a Revitalized Boston*. Report prepared for the Episcopal City Mission, Boston.

———. 1989. "Subsidized Housing at Risk: The Social Costs of Private Ownership." In *Housing Issues of the 1990s*, edited by Sara Rosenberry and Chester Hartman. New York: Praeger.

Achtenberg, Emily Paradise, and Peter Marcuse. 1983. "Towards the Decommodification of Housing: A Political Analysis and a Progressive Program." In *America's Housing Crisis: What Is to Be Done?* edited by Chester Hartman, 202–231. Boston: Routledge & Kegan Paul.

Advisory Group. 1983. *Report to the Mayor on the Linkage between Downtown Development and Neighborhood Housing*. Boston: City of Boston.

Ahlbrandt, Roger S., and Paul C. Brophy. 1975. *Neighborhood Revitalization*. Lexington, Mass.: Lexington Books.

Apgar, William C., Jr. 1982. *The Changing Utilization of the Housing Inventory: Past Trends and Future Prospects*. Cambridge, Mass.: Joint Center for Urban Studies of MIT and Harvard University (now known as Joint Center for Housing Studies).

———. 1985. *Recent Trends in Housing Quality and Affordability: A Reassessment*. Working Paper No. W85-1. Cambridge, Mass.: Joint Center for Housing Studies of MIT and Harvard University.

———. 1988. *The Nation's Housing: A Review of Past Trends and Future Prospects for Housing in America*. Working Paper No. HP 1. Cambridge, Mass.: Center for Real Estate Development, MIT.

Appelbaum, Richard P., and John I. Gilderbloom. 1983. "Housing Supply and Regulation: A Study of the Rental Housing Market." *Journal of Applied Behavioral Science*, Winter.

Arnstein, Sherry. 1969. "A Ladder of Citizen Participation." *Journal of the American Institute of Planners* 35, no. 7 (July): 216–224.

Ayres, Stephen. 1988a. "Theological Reflections of Affordable Housing." *City Issues* (Episcopal City Mission, Boston) 8, no. 1.

———. 1988b. "In My Father's House: Church Perspectives on Affordable Housing." Master's thesis, Department of Urban and Environmental Policy, Tufts University.

Bain, Dixon, Michael Battaglia, Sally Merrill, Vince Scardino, and James E. Wallace. 1988. *Study of the Modernization Needs of the Public and Indian Housing Stock.* Report prepared for U.S. Department of Housing and Urban Development, Contract No. HC-5685, by Abt Associates, Inc., Cambridge, Mass.

Barbe, Nancy, and June Sekera. 1983. *States and Communities: The Challenge for Economic Action.* Washington, D.C.: National Congress for Community Economic Development.

Bazan, Horace B. 1974. *The Fragmentation of FHA.* Washington, D.C.: Mortgage Bankers Association of America.

Bedford-Stuyvesant Restoration Corporation. 1968. *Annual Report.*

Best, Michael H., and William E. Connolly. 1976. *The Politicized Economy.* Lexington, Mass.: D.C. Heath.

Betnun, Nathan S. 1976. *Housing Finance Agencies: A Comparison Between States and HUD.* New York: Praeger.

Birch, Eugenie Ladner. 1978. "Woman-Made America: The Case of Early Public Housing Policy." *Journal of the American Institute of Planners* 44, no. 2 (April): 130–144.

Black, Bill. 1984. "Limited-Equity Cooperatives: An Option for Low- and Moderate-Income People?" Manuscript.

Bluestone, Barry, and Bennett Harrison. 1982. *The Deindustrialization of America.* New York: Basic Books.

Boston Globe. 1984. "Unrest Seen Ripe in Five Massachusetts Cities." August 23.

———. 1985. "HUD Rejected Deal of $1 for Housing." June 20.

———. 1986. "A Housing Success." Editorial, March 12.

Boston Housing Authority. 1983. Unpublished results from the Tenant Survey.

Boston Housing Partnership. 1985a. Draft Tenant Selection Plan for BHP 1. April 12.

———. 1985b. Model Tenant Selection Plan. November.

Boston Redevelopment Authority and Boston Urban Observatory. 1973. *Subsidized Multi-Family Rental Housing in the Boston Metropolitan Area.* Boston: The Authority.

Bove, Eric, Phillip Brown, Peter Hollands, Sarah Snow, and John Thoma. 1987. "Grey Areas: CDCs, Integration and State Policy." Student field project, Department of Urban and Environmental Policy, Tufts University.

Bowly, Devereux, Jr. 1978. *The Poorhouse: Subsidized Housing in Chicago, 1895–1976.* Carbondale: Southern Illinois University Press.

Bratt, Rachel G. 1976. "Federal Homeownership Policy and Home Finance: A Study of Program Operations and Impacts on the Consumer." Ph.D. dissertation, MIT.

————. 1984. "Partnerships Assist Housing Developments." *Public/Private* 2, no. 2 (Winter): 37–59.

————. 1985a. "Controversy and Contributions: A Public Housing Critique." *Journal of Housing* 42, no. 1 (September–October): 165–173.

————. 1985b. "Housing for Low Income People: A Preliminary Comparison of Existing and Potential Supply Strategies." *Journal of Urban Affairs* 7, no. 3 (Summer): 1–18.

————. 1985c. "The Neighborhood Movement: A Blip on the Landscape or a Blueprint for Action?" *Community Development Journal* 20, no. 2: 80–88.

————. 1986a. "Public Housing: The Controversy and Contribution." In *Critical Perspectives on Housing*, edited by Rachel G. Bratt, Chester Hartman, and Ann Meyerson, 335–361. Philadelphia: Temple University Press.

————. 1986b. "Community-Based Housing Programs: Overview, Assessment, and Agenda for the Future." *Journal of Planning Education and Research* 5, no. 3 (Spring): 164–177.

————. 1987a. "Private Owners of Subsidized Housing versus Public Goals: Conflicting Interests in Resyndication." *Journal of the American Planning Association* 6, no. 4 (Summer): 328–336.

————. 1987b. "The Role of Citizen-Initiated Programs in the Formulation of National Housing Policies." In *Citizen Participation in Public Decision Making*, edited by Jack DeSario and Stuart Langton. Westport, Conn.: Greenwood Press.

————. 1987–1988. "Dilemmas of Community-Based Housing." *Policy Studies Journal* 16, no. 2 (Winter): 324–334.

————. 1988. *Mutual Housing Associations*. Report prepared under contract to the Neighborhood Reinvestment Corporation, Washington, D.C.

————. 1989a. "Community-Based Housing: Strengths of the Strategy Amid Dilemmas That Won't Go Away." In *Neighborhood Policy and Programs: Past and Present*, edited by Naomi Carmon. London: Macmillan.

————. 1989b. "Community-Based Housing in Massachusetts: Lessons and Limits of the State's Support System." In *Housing Issues of the 1990's*, edited by Sara Rosenberry and Chester Hartman. New York: Praeger.

————. 1989c. "Nonprofit Housing Development: Boston." Prepared under contract to Phillip L. Clay, M.I.T., as part of a Ford Foundation project.

Bratt, Rachel G., and Kenneth Geiser. 1982. "Community-Based Economic Development: The Massachusetts Experience." Manuscript, Tufts University.

Break, George F., and Jack Guttentag et al. 1963. *Federal Credit Agencies*. Report prepared for Commission on Money and Credit. Englewood Cliffs, N.J.: Prentice-Hall.

Burns, Leland S. 1983. "Self-Help Housing: An Evaluation of Outcomes." *Urban Studies* 20, no. 3 (August): 299–309.

Burns, Leland S., and Donald C. Shoup. 1981. "Effects of Resident Control and Ownership in Self-Help Housing." *Land Economics* 57, no. 1 (February): 106–114.

Candeub, Flessig, and associates. 1968. *Master Plan for the City of Holyoke, Massachusetts.* Holyoke: City Planning Board.

Carnegie, Christa. 1970. "Homeownership for the Poor: Running the Washington Gauntlet." *Journal of the American Institute of Planners* 36, no. 3 (May): 160–167.

Center for Community Economic Development. 1975. *Community Development Corporations.* Cambridge, Mass.: The Center.

Checkoway, Barry. 1980. "Large Builders, Federal Housing Programs, and Postwar Suburbanization." Reprinted in 1986 in *Critical Perspectives on Housing,* edited by Rachel G. Bratt, Chester Hartman, and Ann Meyerson, 119–136. Philadelphia: Temple University Press.

———. 1985. "Neighborhood Planning Organizations: Perspectives and Choices." *Journal of Applied Behavioral Science* 21, no. 4: 471–486.

Cincotta, Gale. 1981. *Disclosure,* no. 62 (April).

Citizens Housing and Planning Association. 1980. *Planning for the Future of HUD-Owned Housing. A Residents' Guide.* Boston: The Association.

———. 1986. "Tenants and Costs in Public Housing—Policies, Attitudes and Case Studies." Boston: The Association.

Clancy, Patrick. 1984. "Proposed Alternative Approach to Resyndication of MHFA Developments." Memorandum to MHFA Multi-Family Advisory Committee. January 9.

Clancy, Patrick E., Langley C. Keyes, Jr., Edward H. Marchant, and Robert B. Whittlesey. 1973. "The Role of Nonprofit Organizations in the Housing Process." Mimeographed report to HUD.

Clay, Phillip L. 1987. *At Risk of Loss: The Endangered Future of Low-Income Rental Housing Resources.* Washington, D.C.: Neighborhood Reinvestment Corporation.

Cohen, Rick, and Miriam Kohler. 1983. *Neighborhood Development Organizations After the Federal Funding Cutbacks: Current Conditions and Future Directions.* Report prepared for the U.S. Department of Housing and Urban Development, Office of Policy Development and Research. Contract Order No. HUD 7177-82.

Cole, Richard L. 1974. *Citizen Participation and the Urban Policy Process.* Lexington, Mass.: D.C. Heath.

Colean, Miles L. 1944. *American Housing.* New York: Twentieth Century Fund.

Community Development Finance Corporation, 1984. *Annual Report.* Boston: The Corporation.

Community Economic Development Assistance Corporation. 1983. *A CEDAC*

Progress Report: Its Past Experience and Its New Directions. Boston: The Corporation.

Congressional Budget Office. *See* U.S. Congressional Budget Office.

Congressional Research Service. 1973. *The Central City Problem and Urban Renewal Policy.* Washington, D.C.: Government Printing Office.

Connerly, Charles E. 1986. "What Should Be Done with the Public Housing Program?" *Journal of the American Planning Association* 52, no. 2 (Spring): 142–155.

Cooper, Claire C. 1975. *Easter Hill Village.* New York: Free Press.

Council of Large Public Housing Authorities. 1986. *Public Housing Today.* Boston: The Council.

———. 1988. "CLPHA Modernization Survey." Boston, January 29.

Counsel for Community Development, Inc. 1982. *The Experience and Potential of Community-Based Development.* Cambridge, Mass.: The Counsel.

Dean, John. 1945. *Home Ownership: Is It Sound?* New York: Harper & Row.

deLeeuw, Frank. 1981. "A Synthesis of Views on Rental Housing." In *Rental Housing: Is There a Crisis?* edited by John C. Weicher, Kevin E. Villani, and Elizabeth A. Roistacher, 61–64. Washington, D.C.: Urban Institute.

Demery, Thomas T. 1987. Testimony. *Hearing on Preservation of Subsidized Housing, U.S. Department of Housing and Urban Development for the Subcommittee on Housing and Community Development of the Committee on Banking, Finance and Urban Affairs,* March 26.

Disario, Rita Michele. 1969. "Nonprofit Housing Sponsors: An Evaluative Study." Master's thesis, MIT.

Dolbeare, Cushing. 1983. "The Low-Income Housing Crisis." In *America's Housing Crisis: What Is to Be Done?* edited by Chester Hartman, 29–75. Boston: Routledge & Kegan Paul.

———. 1986. "How the Income Tax System Subsidizes Housing for the Affluent." In *Critical Perspectives on Housing,* edited by Rachel G. Bratt, Chester Hartman and Ann Meyerson, 264–271. Philadelphia: Temple University Press.

Dommel, Paul R., Victor E. Bach, Sarah F. Liebschutz, Leonard S. Rubinowitz, and associates. 1980. *Targeting Community Development.* Third report prepared by the Brookings Institution Monitoring Study of the Community Development Block Grant Program. Contract Order No. HUD H-2323R.

Dommel, Paul R., James C. Musselwhite, Jr., Sarah F. Liebschutz, and associates. 1982. *Implementing Community Development.* Study of the Community Development Block Grant prepared by the Brookings Institution. Contract Order No. HUD H-2323R.

Dommel, Paul R., Michael J. Rich, Leonard S. Rubinowitz, and associates. 1983. *Deregulating Community Development.* Report prepared by the Cleveland State University Field Study of the Community Development Block Grant Program. Contract Order No. HUD HC-5547.

Dorchester Community News. 1985. "CDCs Grow With Partnership." November 19.

Downs, Anthony. 1972. *Federal Housing Subsidies: Their Nature and Effectiveness and What We Should Do about Them.* Washington, D.C.: National Association of Home Builders.

———. 1973. *Federal Housing Subsidies: How Are They Working?* Lexington, Mass.: D.C. Heath.

———. 1983. *Rental Housing in the 1980's.* Washington, D.C.: Brookings Institution.

Edgerly, William S. 1983. "Boston Housing Partnership." In *Pending Tax Reform Proposals.* Washington, D.C.: Committee on Ways and Means, U.S. House of Representatives. July 17.

Egan, John J., John Carr, Andrew Mott, and John Roos. 1981. *Housing and Public Policy: A Role for Mediating Structures.* Cambridge, Mass.: Ballinger.

Erdmann, Robin J., ed. 1987. *States and Communities: The Challenge for Economic Action.* Vol. 2. Washington, D.C.: National Congress for Community Economic Development.

Executive Office of Communities and Development. 1984. *The Community Enterprise Economic Development Program. A Survey of CEED Funded CDC Activities, 1979–1983.* Boston: EOCD.

———. 1985a. "Community Services Block Grant Special Project Fund, Request for Proposals, FY 1985." Mimeographed.

———. 1985b. *CDC Project Survey, 1984–85: Preliminary Data.* Boston: EOCD.

Feagin, Joe R., Charles Tilly, and Constance W. Williams. 1972. *Subsidizing the Poor: A Boston Housing Experiment.* Lexington, Mass.: D.C. Heath.

Federal Housing Administration. 1938. *Underwriting and Valuation Procedures under Title II of the National Housing Act.* Washington, D.C.: Government Printing Office.

Federal Register. 1984. "Public Housing Homeownership Demonstration" 49, no. 208 (October 25): 43, 028–43, 034.

Feins, Judith D., and Rachel G. Bratt. 1983. "Barred in Boston: Racial Discrimination in Housing." *Journal of the American Planning Association* 49, no. 3 (Summer): 344–355.

Feins, Judith D., and Terry Saunders Lane. 1981. *How Much for Housing?* Cambridge, Mass.: Abt Books.

Finch, Wesley. 1984. "Recommendations for Reunderwriting Policy." Draft proposal, Massachusetts Housing Finance Agency, Boston. January 10.

Fisher, Robert Moore. 1959. *Twenty Years of Public Housing.* New York: Harper & Bros.

Focer, Ada. 1987. "Safe Haven?" *Boston Business Journal,* September/October.

Francescato, Guido, Sue Weidemann, James R. Anderson, and Richard Chenoweth. 1979. *Residents' Satisfaction in HUD-Assisted Housing: Design and Management Factors.* Report prepared for the U.S. Department of

Housing and Urban Development, Office of Policy Development and Research.

Freedman, Leonard. 1969. *Public Housing: The Politics of Poverty*. New York: Holt, Rinehart and Winston.

Fried, Marc. 1963. "Grieving for a Lost Home." In *The Urban Condition*, edited by Leonard J. Duhl. New York: Basic Books.

Frieden, Bernard J., and Jo-Ann Newman. 1970. "Home Ownership for the Poor?" *Trans-Action*, October.

Frieden, Bernard J., and Marshall Kaplan. 1975. *The Politics of Neglect: Urban Aid from Model Cities to Revenue Sharing*. Cambridge: MIT Press.

Friedland, J. Eric, and C. Duncan MacRae. 1979. "FHA Multifamily Financial Failure: A Review of Empirical Studies." *Journal of American Real Estate and Urban Economics Association* 7, no. 2 (Spring): 95–122.

Friedman, Lawrence. 1968. *Government and Slum Housing*. Chicago: Rand McNally.

GAO. *See* U.S. General Accounting Office.

Gans, Herbert. 1962. *The Urban Villagers*. Updated and expanded ed. New York: Free Press.

Garn, Harvey A., Nancy L. Tevis, and Carl E. Snead. 1976. *Evaluating Community Development Corporations—A Summary Report*. Washington, D.C.: Urban Institute.

Genung, George R., Jr. 1971. "Public Housing—Success or Failure?" *George Washington Law Review* 39, no. 4 (May): 734–763.

George, Henry. 1880. *Progress and Poverty*. 1929 ed. New York: Modern Library.

Gibbs, Kay. 1985. "Slumming It." *Boston Observer*, March.

Gillis, Brian, Frank Hornstein, Wendy Plotkin, and Bryan Wyatt. 1984. "The Boston Housing Partnership Demonstration Program: A Reconnaissance Report." Student field project, Department of Urban and Environmental Policy, Tufts University.

Gittell, Marilyn. 1980. *The Limits of Citizen Participation*. Beverly Hills, Calif.: Sage.

Goetze, Rolf. 1983. *Rescuing the American Dream*. New York: Holmes and Meier.

Goodman, Robert. 1979. *The Last Entrepreneurs*. New York: Simon and Schuster.

Gordon, David, ed. 1977. *Problems in Political Economy—An Urban Perspective*. Lexington, Mass.: D.C. Heath.

Greater Boston Community Development, Inc. 1980. *A Decade of Housing Services: 1970–1980*. Boston: GBCD.

———. 1984. *Building Communities*. Boston: GBCD.

Greer, Scott. 1965. *Urban Renewal and American Cities*. Indianapolis: Bobbs-Merrill.

Hamilton, Walter. 1981. "Realtor Claims Banks Contribute to Decline." *Holyoke/Chicopee Morning Union*, November 6.

Harden, Thomas M. 1986. "Uphill All the Way: The Potential of Community-Based Development in South Holyoke." Master's thesis, Department of Urban and Environmental Policy, Tufts University.

Harrison, Bennett. 1974. *Urban Economic Development*. Washington, D.C.: Urban Institute.

———. n.d. (ca. 1978). "Jobs: What Kind, for Whom and Where?" In *Developing the Public Economy: Models From Massachusetts*, edited by Pat McGuigan and Bob Schaeffer. Cambridge, Mass.: Policy Training Center.

Hartman, Chester. 1960. *Family Turnover in Public Housing*. San Juan, Puerto Rico: Office of Research, Urban Renewal and Housing Administration.

———. 1983. "Housing Allowances: A Critical Look." *Journal of Urban Affairs* 5, no. 1: 41–55.

———, ed. 1983. *The Housing Crisis: What Is to Be Done?* Boston: Routledge & Kegan Paul.

Hartman, Chester W., and Gregg Carr. 1969. "Housing Authorities Reconsidered." *Journal of the American Institute of Planners* 35, no. 1 (January): 10–21.

Hartman, Chester, Dennis Keating, and Richard LeGates. 1982. *Displacement: How to Fight It*. Berkeley, Calif.: National Housing Law Project.

Hartman, Chester W., and Margaret Levi. 1973. "Public Housing Managers: An Appraisal." *Journal of the American Institute of Planners* 39, no. 2 (March): 125–137.

Hartman, Chester, and Michael E. Stone. 1986. "A Socialist Housing Alternative for the United States." In *Critical Perspectives on Housing*, edited by Rachel G. Bratt, Chester Hartman, and Ann Meyerson, 484–513. Philadelphia: Temple University Press.

Hayden, Dolores. 1986. "What Would a Non-Sexist City Look Like? Speculations on Housing, Urban Design, and Human Work." In *Critical Perspectives on Housing*, edited by Rachel G. Bratt, Chester Hartman, and Ann Meyerson. Philadelphia: Temple University Press.

Healy, Robert G. 1971. "Effects of Improved Housing on Worker Performance." *Journal of Human Resources* 6, no. 3: 297–308.

Hipshman, May. 1967. *Public Housing at the Crossroads: The Boston Housing Authority*. Boston: Citizens Housing and Planning Association.

Hodes, Laurent, Donald Bradley, Stevenson Weitz, and James Hoben. 1987. HUD/FHA *Insured Rental Housing: Physical and Financial Condition of Multifamily Properties Insured Before 1975*. Washington, D.C.: U.S. Department of Housing and Urban Development, Office of Policy Development and Research.

Holyoke/Chicopee Morning Union. 1981. October 28.

Holyoke/Chicopee Morning Union. 1982. "Area Low on Mayor's List," October 27.

Holyoke Office for Community Development. 1985. *Holyoke on Parade: A*

Program for Downtown Revitalization. Holyoke, Mass.: Greater Holyoke, Inc., with assistance from the *Holyoke Transcript-Telegram.*

Holyoke Transcript-Telegram. 1980. "Building Code Inspections Pushed," August 22.

———. 1981. "Mayor Standing Tough on Minimum Fire Staff," June 29.

———. 1983. "Verbal Wrecker's Ball," July 1.

Hopper, Kim, and Jill Hamberg. 1986. "The Making of America's Homeless: From Skid Row to New Poor, 1945–1984." In *Critical Perspectives on Housing*, edited by Rachel G. Bratt, Chester Hartman, and Ann Meyerson, 12–40. Philadelphia: Temple University Press.

Housing and Development Reporter. 1975. 2, no. 24 (April 21).

Howley, Janet M. 1987. "Community Development Corporations and Empowerment of Low-Income People: Have They Been Successful?" Manuscript, Department of Urban and Environmental Policy, Tufts University.

HUD. *See* U.S. Department of Housing and Urban Development.

Hundley, Kristen. 1983. "A Clash of Interests in Holyoke." *Boston Globe Magazine*, October 2.

Hurwitz, Ani. 1982. "New Alternatives for City-Owned Property." *City Limits*, February.

Institute for Community Economics. 1982. *The Community Land Trust Handbook.* Emmaus, Pa.: Rodale Press.

Institute for Policy Studies' Working Group on Housing. 1987. *A Progressive Housing Program for America.* Washington, D.C.: The Institute.

Johnson, Sara Elizabeth, and the National Housing Law Project. 1985. *Preserving HUD-Assisted Housing for Use by Low-Income Tenants: An Advocate's Guide.* Berkeley, Calif.: National Housing Law Project.

Jones, Cynthia. 1981. "As Holyoke Burns." *Valley Advocate*, July 15.

Jones, Ronald, David Kaminsky, and Michael Roanhouse. 1979. *Problems Affecting Low-Rent Public Housing Projects.* Report prepared for the U.S. Department of Housing and Urban Development, Office of Policy Development and Research.

Jordan, Robert. 1985. "An Offer They Could Refuse." *Boston Globe*, June 22.

———. 1986. "Overlooked in the Boom." *Boston Globe*, May 31.

Journal of Housing. 1973. "Myths/Realities of Public Housing," April, 179–191.

Jubilee Housing, Inc. n.d. *The Making of a Jubilee Coop: The Ontario Court.* Washington, D.C.: Jubilee Housing.

Keats, John. 1957. *The Crack in the Picture Window.* Boston: Houghton Mifflin.

Keith, Nathaniel S. 1973. *Politics and the Housing Crisis Since 1930.* New York: Universe Books.

Keyes, Langley C., Jr. 1970. *The Boston Rehabilitation Program: An Independent Analysis.* Cambridge, Mass.: Joint Center for Urban Studies of MIT and Harvard University.

———. 1971. "The Role of Nonprofit Sponsors in the Production of Housing." In *Papers Submitted to U.S. House Committee on Banking and Currency, Subcommittee on Housing Panels on Housing Production, Housing Demand, and Developing a Suitable Living Environment*, 92d Cong., 1st sess, pt. 1, 159–181.

Kolodny, Robert. 1979. *Exploring New Strategies for Improving Public Housing Management*. Report prepared for the U.S. Department of Housing and Urban Development, Office of Policy Development and Research.

———. 1981a. "Self-Help Can Be an Effective Tool in Housing the Urban Poor." *Journal of Housing*, March, 135–142.

———. 1981b. *Multi-Family Housing: Treating the Existing Stock*. Washington, D.C.: National Association of Housing and Redevelopment Officials.

———. 1983. *What Happens When Tenants Manage Their Own Public Housing?* Report prepared for the U.S. Department of Housing and Urban Development, Office of Policy Development and Research.

———. 1986. "The Emergence of Self-Help as a Housing Strategy for the Urban Poor." In *Critical Perspectives on Housing*, edited by Rachel G. Bratt, Chester Hartman, and Ann Meyerson, 447–462. Philadelphia: Temple University Press.

Kuehn, Robert H., Jr. 1988. *The Homebuilding Industry: What Will It Take to Produce More Affordable Housing?* HP6. Cambridge, Mass.: Center for Real Estate Development, M.I.T.

Kuehn, Robert, and Wesley Finch. 1984. Memorandum on Final Resyndication Recommendations to the MHFA Advisory Committee. Massachusetts Housing Finance Agency, Boston. February 9.

Langton, Stuart. 1978. "What Is Citizen Participation?" In *Citizen Participation in America*, edited by Stuart Langton. Lexington, Mass.: Lexington Books.

Lauer, Martin J. 1981. "Inspector Orders Thirty Families Out of South Holyoke Block." *Holyoke/Chicopee Morning Union*, October 1.

Leavitt, Jacqueline. 1988. "Two Prototypical Designs for Single Parents: The Congregate House and the New American House." In *Alternative to the Single Family House*, edited by Karen Franck and Sherry Ahrentzen. New York: Van Nostrand Reinhold.

LeBlanc, Barbara. 1983a. "Proulx Wants Housing Razed." *Holyoke Transcript-Telegram*, June 30.

———. 1983b. "Housing Aid Blamed for Economic Woe." *Holyoke Transcript-Telegram*, November 18.

———. 1984. "Minorities Slap Proulx on Demolition." *Holyoke Transcript-Telegram*, February 15.

Leveille, Karen. 1985. *South Holyoke Housing Development Plan*. Report prepared for Nueva Esperanza.

Liebert, Larry. 1983. "San Francisco's No. 1 Headache, A Chronic Shortage of Affordable Housing." *Boston Globe*, August 14.

Lilley, William III. 1973. "The Homebuilders' Lobby." In *Housing Urban America*, edited by Jon Pynoos, Robert Schafer, and Chester W. Hartman. Chicago: Aldine.

Lineberry, Robert L., and Ira Sharkansky. 1971. *Urban Politics and Public Policy.* New York: Harper & Row.

Lipsky, Michael, Donald Dickson, John Mollenkopf, and Jon Pynoos. 1971. "Citizen Participation in Federal Housing Policies." In *Papers Submitted to U.S. House Committee on Banking and Currency, Subcommittee on Housing Panels on Housing Production, Housing Demand, and Developing a Suitable Living Environment*, 92d Cong., 1st sess., pt. 2, 895–925.

Litvak, Lawrence, and Belden Daniels. 1979. *Innovations in Development Finance.* Washington, D.C.: Council of State Planning Agencies.

Long, May. 1977. "Community Groups, Banks Work Together to Fight Neighborhood Disinvestment." *Journal of Housing*, January.

Low Income Housing Information Service. 1987. *The 1988 Low Income Housing Budget.* Special Memorandum. Washington, D.C.: The Service.

———. 1988a. *Distribution of Tax Benefits for Real Estate Taxes and Mortgage Interest Deductions.* Report prepared for the Low Income Housing Service, Washington, D.C., by Barry Zigas.

———. 1988b. *The 1989 Low Income Housing Budget.* Special Memorandum. Washington, D.C.: The Service.

Lowry, Ira S. 1981. "Rental Housing in the 1970s: Searching for the Crisis." In *Rental Housing: Is There a Crisis?* edited by John C. Weicher, Kevin E. Villani, and Elizabeth A. Roistacher, 23–38. Washington, D.C.: Urban Institute.

Lydenberg, Steven, D. 1988. *Room for Improvement: The Franklin's Insight Study of Corporate Support for Affordable Housing.* Boston: Franklin's Insight: An Affiliate of Franklin Research and Development Corporation.

McAfee, Kathy. 1986. "Socialism and the Housing Movement: Lessons from Boston." In *Critical Perspectives on Housing*, edited by Rachel G. Bratt, Chester Hartman, and Ann Meyerson, 405–427. Philadelphia: Temple University Press.

Maeroff, Gene I. 1986. "Housing Project Sets off Dispute in Old Milltown." *New York Times*, March 24.

Maffin, Robert. 1983a. "Failure to Enact Major Housing Legislation Would Be an Expensive Lapse of Leadership." *NAHRO Monitor* 5, no. 12 (June 30).

———. 1983b. Letter to Honorable William L. Armstrong, U.S. Senate, January 25.

Mallach, Allan. 1984. *Inclusionary Housing Programs: Policies and Practices.* New Brunswick, N.J.: Center for Urban Policy Research, Rutgers University.

Manpower Demonstration Research Corporation. 1981. *Tenant Management, Findings from a Three-Year Experiment in Public Housing.* Cambridge, Mass.: Ballinger.

Marable, Manning. 1983. *How Capitalism Underdeveloped Black America*. Boston: South End Press.

Marcuse, Peter. 1981. *Housing Abandonment: Does Rent Control Make a Difference?* Washington, D.C.: Conference on Alternative State and Local Policies.

―――. 1986. "A Useful Installment of Socialist Work: Red Vienna." In *Critical Perspectives on Housing*, edited by Rachel G. Bratt, Chester Hartman, and Ann Meyerson, 558–585. Philadelphia: Temple University Press.

Marcuse, Peter, Peter Medoff, and Andrea Periera. 1982. "Triage as Urban Policy." *Social Policy* 12, no. 3 (Winter): 33.

Marris, Peter, and Martin Rein. 1967. *Dilemmas of Social Reform*. New York: Atherton Press.

Marshall, Sue. 1981. *A Profile of Revitalization Projects Being Implemented by Neighborhood Development Organizations*. Working Paper 1457-01 (prepared with the assistance of Jennifer Blake). Washington, D.C.: Urban Institute.

Massachusetts Government Land Bank. 1985. *Tenth Anniversary Report*.

Massachusetts Housing Finance Agency. 1984a. *Policy Regarding the Resyndication of Housing Developments*. Boston: The Agency. April.

―――. 1984b. *Developments Selected for SHARP Funding*. Boston: The Agency.

―――. 1987. *The Housing Environment in Massachusetts*. Boston: The Agency. July.

―――. 1988. *Annual Report*.

Massachusetts Tenants Organization. 1984a. "Resyndication." Memorandum to the MHFA Advisory Committee, Massachusetts Housing Finance Agency, Boston, January 12.

―――. 1984b. "Proposed Resyndication Policy." Memorandum to MHFA Advisory Committee, Massachusetts Housing Finance Agency, from Emily Achtenberg, consultant. Boston, February 2.

―――. 1984c. "Alternative Resyndication Recommendations." Memorandum to MHFA Advisory Committee, Massachusetts Housing Finance Agency, from Emily Achtenberg, consultant. Boston, February 9.

Matulef, Mark L. 1987. "This Is Public Housing." *Journal of Housing* 44. no. 5 (September/October): 175–181.

Mayer, Neil S. 1984. *Neighborhood Organizations and Community Development*. Washington, D.C.: Urban Institute.

Mayer, Neil S., and Jennifer Blake. 1981. *Keys to the Growth of Neighborhood Development Organizations*. Washington, D.C.: Urban Institute.

Mayo, Stephen K., Shirley Mansfield, David Warner, and Richard Zwetchkenbaum. 1980. *Housing Allowances and Other Rental Housing Assistance Programs—A Comparison Based on the Housing Allowance Demand Experiment*, pt. 2, *Costs and Efficiency*. Report prepared for the U.S. Department of Housing and Urban Development, Office of Policy Development and Research, by Abt Associates, Inc.

Mayor's Office. 1983. *Mayor's Management Report, Preliminary*. New York: Mayor's Office.

Meehan, Eugene J. 1975. *Public Housing Policy: Myth Versus Reality*. New Brunswick, N.J.: Center for Urban Policy Research, Rutgers University.

————. 1979. *The Quality of Federal Policy Making: Programmed Failure in Public Housing*. Columbia: University of Missouri Press.

————. 1983. "Is There a Future for Public Housing?" *Journal of Housing* 40, no. 3 (May–June): 73–76.

Metcalf and Eddy, Inc. 1972. *Planning Report—Community Renewal Program*. Holyoke, Mass.: Metcalf and Eddy.

Metropolitan Area Planning Council. 1986. *Inclusionary Housing and Linkage Programs in Metropolitan Boston*. Boston: The Council.

Meyerson, Martin, and Edward C. Banfield. 1955. *Politics, Planning and the Public Interest: The Case of Public Housing in Chicago*. Glencoe, Ill.: Free Press.

Meyerson, Martin, Barbara Terrett, and William L. C. Wheaton. 1962. *Housing, People and Cities*. New York: McGraw-Hill.

Moriarty, Jo-Ann. 1982. "Housing Commitment Urged for South Holyoke." *Holyoke/Chicopee Morning Union*, October 26.

————. 1984. "Mayor Blasted for Ordering Demolition." *Holyoke/Chicopee Morning Union*, February 16.

Morris, Emily J. 1985. "Granite Properties: Deteriorated but Affordable Housing Worth Saving." CEDAC *Newsletter* (Boston), Summer.

————. 1986. "HUD Policy and the Granite Properties: Who Is Representing the Public Interest?" Master's thesis, Department of Urban and Environmental Policy, Tufts University.

Mott, Andrew H. 1984. "Making Affordable Housing a Reality." *Testimony before the U.S. House Committee on Banking, Finance, and Urban Affairs, Subcommittee on Housing and Community Development*, 98th Cong., 2d sess., June 28, 211–227.

————. 1985. *The Decades Ahead for Community Organizations*. Report prepared for the National Neighborhood Coalition by the Center for Community Change, Washington, D.C.

Moynihan, Daniel Patrick. 1969. *Maximum Feasible Misunderstanding*. New York: Free Press.

Muth, Richard F. 1973. *Public Housing: An Economic Evaluation*. Washington, D.C.: American Enterprise Institute for Public Policy Research.

NAHRO *Monitor*. 1988. "Cranston Outlines Prospects for Future National Housing Policy," February 15.

National Center for Economic Alternatives. 1981. *Federal Assistance to Community Development Corporations: An Evaluation of Title VII of the Community Services Act of 1974*. Report prepared for the U.S. Community Services Administration, Washington, D.C.

National Center for Housing Management, Inc. n.d. (ca. 1973). *Public Hous-*

ing. Vol. 2, *Report of the Task Force on Improving the Operation of Federally Insured or Financed Housing Programs*. Washington, D.C.: The Center.

National Commission on Neighborhoods. Joseph F. Timilty, chair. 1979. *People Building Neighborhoods. Final Report to the President and the Congress of the United States*. Washington, D.C.: The Commission.

National Housing Law Project. 1982. *The Subsidized Housing Handbook*. Berkeley, Calif.: The Project.

————. 1987. *Housing Law Bulletin* (Berkeley, Calif.) 17 (November/December).

————. 1988. *Housing Law Bulletin* (Berkeley, Calif.) 18 (January/February).

National Low Income Housing Coalition. 1987. "A Community-Based Housing Supply Program." *Low Income Housing Round-Up*, May, 108.

National Neighborhood Coalition. 1989. Monthly Information Report.

Neighborhood Reinvestment Corporation. 1985. *The Mutual Housing Association: An American Demonstration of a Proven European Concept. Proceedings of a Meeting Held in Baltimore, Maryland, October 9–10*. Meeting convened by the Neighborhood Reinvestment Corporation, Washington, D.C.

————. n.d. *A Progress Report to the United States Congress on the Mutual Housing Association National Demonstration*. Washington, D.C.: The Corporation.

New York Times. 1987. "Houston Is Buying Homes for Low-Income Tenants," April 28.

Nuveen Research Comment. 1984. "Survey of State Multi-Family Programs Reveals Low Delinquency Rate." March 15.

Nye, Nancy. 1984. "Six Years Later: The Experience of the Massachusetts CDFC." *Entrepreneurial Economy* 2, no. 9 (March): 11–12.

O'Connor, James. 1973. *The Fiscal Crisis of the State*. New York: St. Martin's.

O'Hare, Kevin. 1984. "Arson City Tag Is Erased, Proulx Says." *Holyoke/Chicopee Morning Union*, September 6.

Olson, Laura Katz. 1982. *The Political Economy of Aging*. New York: Columbia University Press.

Organization for Social and Technical Innovation. 1969. *Self-Help Housing in the U.S.* Report prepared under contract to the U.S. Department of Housing and Urban Development.

————. 1974. *A Study of the Effectiveness of Voluntary Counseling Programs for Lower Income Home Ownership*. Newton, Mass.: The Organization.

Pearlman, Janice. 1978. "Grassroots Participation from Neighborhood to Nation," In *Citizen Participation in America*, edited by Stuart Langton. Lexington, Mass.: Lexington Books.

Peattie, Lisa R. 1969. "Social Issues in Housing." In *Shaping an Urban Future: Essays in Memory of Catherine Bauer Wurster*, edited by Bernard J. Frieden and William W. Nash. Cambridge: MIT Press.

Peirce, Neal R. 1983. "In South End, a Housing Project That Works." *Boston Globe*, August 8.

Peirce, Neil R., and Carol F. Steinbach. 1987. *Corrective Capitalism: The Rise of America's Community Development Corporations.* New York: Ford Foundation.

Perkins and Will and The Ehrenkrantz Group. 1980. *An Evaluation of the Physical Condition of Public Housing Stock.* Final report prepared for the U.S. Department of Housing and Urban Development, Office of Policy Development and Research.

Peroff, Kathleen A., Cloteal L. Davis, and Ronald Jones. 1979. *Gautreaux Housing Demonstration: An Evaluation of Its Impact on Participating Households.* Report prepared for the U.S. Department of Housing and Urban Development, Office of Policy Development and Research.

Pickman, James, Benson F. Roberts, Mindy Leiterman, and Robert N. Mittle. 1986. *Producing Lower Income Housing: Local Initiatives.* Washington, D.C.: Bureau of National Affairs.

Piven, Frances Fox. 1981. *The New Class War.* New York: Pantheon Books.

Piven, Frances Fox, and Richard A. Cloward. 1967. "Black Control of Cities." *New Republic,* September 30 and October 7.

———. 1971. *Regulating the Poor.* New York: Vintage Books.

Plotkin, Wendy. 1987. "The Boston Housing Partnership Demonstration Program: Non-Profit Housing Revisited." Master's thesis, Department of Urban and Environmental Policy, Tufts University.

Portnoy, Fern C., and James Pickman. 1984. "Innovative Approaches to Low-Income Housing." *Public/Private* 2, no. 2 (Winter): 27–35.

Pratt Institute Center for Community and Environmental Development. 1988. *An Evaluation of the Neighborhood Development Demonstration.* Report prepared under contract to HUD, No. 1146-PDR.

Pynoos, Jonathon Morris. 1974. "Breaking the Rules: The Failure to Select and Assign Public Housing Tenants Equitably." Ph.D. dissertation, Harvard University.

Rabushka, Alvin, and William G. Weissert. 1977. *Caseworkers or Police? How Tenants See Public Housing.* Stanford, Calif.: Hoover Institution Press.

Rainwater, Lee. 1970. *Behind Ghetto Walls.* Chicago: Aldine.

Ratcliff, Richard U., Daniel B. Rathbun, and Junia Honnold. 1957. *Residential Finance.* New York: Wiley.

Report of the National Commission on Urban Problems. Paul H. Douglas, chair. 1968. *Building the American City.* 1968. Washington, D.C.: Government Printing Office.

Report by the National Housing Preservation Task Force. G. Lindsay Crump, chair. 1988. *The Preservation of Low and Moderate Income Housing in the United States of America.* Washington, D.C.: National Advisory Council of HUD Management Agents.

Report of the National Housing Task Force. James W. Rouse, chair. 1988. *A Decent Place to Live.* Washington, D.C.: The Task Force.

Report of the National Low Income Housing Preservation Commission.

Carla A. Hills and Henry S. Reuss, co-chairs. 1988. *Preventing the Disappearance of Low Income Housing.* Report prepared for the House Subcommittee on Housing and Community Development and the Senate Subcommittee on Housing and Urban Affairs, U.S. Congress. Sponsored by the National Corporation for Housing Partnerships, Washington, D.C.

Report of the President's Commission on Housing. William F. McKenna, chair. 1982. Washington, D.C.: Government Printing Office.

Report of the President's Committee on Urban Housing. Edgar F. Kaiser, chair. 1968. Washington, D.C.: Government Printing Office.

Rivas, Maggie. 1982. "Villa Victoria: Where Families Stay." *Boston Globe,* April.

Robb, Christina. 1985. "Rehabbing the American Dream." *Boston Globe Magazine,* March 31.

Roberts, Benson F., with Robert O. Zdenek and William E. Bivens III. 1980. *Community Development Corporations and State Development Policy: Potential for Partnership.* Washington, D.C.: National Congress for Community Economic Development.

Rossi, Peter H., and Robert A. Dentler. 1961. *The Politics of Urban Renewal: The Chicago Findings.* New York: Free Press of Glencoe.

Rumpf, William N. 1983. *Developing State Policies on the Sale and Resyndication of Subsidized Housing.* Working Paper No. W83-8, Cambridge, Mass.: Joint Center for Urban Studies of MIT and Harvard University.

Ryan, William, Alan Sloan, Mania Seferi, and Elaine Werby. 1974. *All in Together: An Evaluation of Mixed-Income Multi-Family Housing.* Boston: Massachusetts Housing Finance Agency.

Saulnier, R. J., Harold G. Halcrow, and Neil H. Jacoby. 1958. *Federal Lending and Loan Insurance.* Princeton: Princeton University Press.

Schifferes, Steve. 1986. "The Dilemmas of British Housing Policy." In *Critical Perspectives on Housing,* edited by Rachel G. Bratt, Chester Hartman, and Ann Meyerson, 514–534. Philadelphia: Temple University Press.

Schorr, Alvin L. 1963. *Slums and Social Insecurity.* Washington, D.C., Government Printing Office.

Schuman, Tony. 1986. "The Agony and the Equity: A Critique of Self-Help Housing." In *Critical Perspectives on Housing,* edited by Rachel G. Bratt, Chester Hartman, and Ann Meyerson, 463–473. Philadelphia: Temple University Press.

Schur, Robert. 1980. "Growing Lemons in the Bronx." *Working Papers,* July–August.

Scobie, Richard S. 1975. *Problem Tenants in Public Housing: Who, Where and Why Are They?* New York: Praeger.

Sculos, Marianne. 1981. "Viva Villa Victoria." Manuscript, Tufts University.

Seidman, Karl. 1987. "A New Role for Government: Supporting a Democratic Economy." In *Beyond the Market and the State,* edited by Severyn T. Bruyn and James Meehan, 185–216. Philadelphia: Temple University Press.

Sherman, Michael, and Wayne Sherwood. 1984. "CLPHA Preliminary Analysis of the Office of Inspector General's Report on PHA Income Projections: 1977–1982." Unpublished report of the Council of Large Public Housing Authorities, Boston.

Sherwood, Wayne, and Elizabeth March. 1983. *Operating Subsidies for Public Housing: Problems and Options.* Boston: Citizens Housing and Planning Association.

Sidor, John. 1982. *State Assistance for Community Economic Development.* Boston: Council of the State Community Affairs Agencies.

Siegenthaler, Mark. 1980. "Work Equity and Housing Assistance Projects." Master's thesis, Department of Urban and Environmental Policy, Tufts University.

Smith, Wallace, ed. 1983. "Housing in America." *Annals of the American Academy of Political and Social Science* 465 (January).

Smolensky, Eugene. 1968. "Public Housing or Income Supplements—The Economics of Housing for the Poor." *Journal of the American Institute of Planners* 34, no. 2 (March): 94–101.

Solomon, Arthur P. 1974. *Housing the Urban Poor.* Cambridge: MIT Press.

Spence, Harry. 1981. "An Interview with Harry Spence." *Working Papers,* November–December, 42–49.

Staats, Elmer B. 1972. "Housing Subsidies and Housing Policies." *Testimony Before the U.S. Senate, Subcommittee on Priorities and Economy in Government of the Joint Economic Committee,* 92nd Cong., 2d sess., December 4, 5, 7.

Starr, Roger. 1976. "Making New York Smaller." *New York Times Magazine,* November 14.

Stegman, Michael A. 1972. *Housing Investment in the Inner City.* Cambridge, Mass.: MIT Press.

———. 1988. *The Role of Public Housing in a Revitalized National Housing Policy.* Working Paper No. HP 19. Cambridge, Mass.: Center for Real Estate Development, MIT.

Stein, Rose. 1932. "More Homes or More Mortgages." *New Republic,* September 7.

Sternlieb, George. 1966. *The Tenement Landlord.* New Brunswick, N.J.: Rutgers University Press.

———. 1972. *The Urban Housing Dilemma: The Dynamics of New York City's Rent Controlled Housing.* New York City: New York Housing and Development Administration, Department of Rent and Housing Maintenance, Office of Rent Control.

Sternlieb, George, and James W. Hughes. 1978. *Revitalizing the Northeast.* New Brunswick, N.J.: Rutgers University Press.

———. 1981. *The Future of Rental Housing.* New Brunswick, N.J.: Center for Urban Policy Research, Rutgers University.

Stokes, Charles J. 1962. "A Theory of Slums." *Land Economics* 38, no. 3: 187–197.

Stone, Michael E. 1983. "Housing and the Economic Crisis: An Analysis and Emergency Program." In *America's Housing Crisis: What Is to Be Done?* edited by Chester Hartman, 99–150. Boston: Routledge & Kegan Paul.

Struyk, Raymond J. 1980. *A New System for Public Housing: Salvaging a National Resource*. Washington, D.C.: Urban Institute.

Sumka, Howard. 1984. "Factors Influencing the Success of Low-Income Co-operatives." Paper presented at the annual meeting of the Association of Collegiate Schools of Planning, New York City.

Sumka, Howard J., and Anthony J. Blackburn. 1982. "Multifamily Urban Homesteading: A Key Approach to Low-Income Housing." *Journal of Housing*, July–August.

Swift, Larry D., and Jean Pogge. 1984. *Neighborhood Reinvestment Partnership*. Chicago: Woodstock Institute.

Taggart, Robert, III. 1970. *Low-Income Housing: A Critique of Federal Aid*. Baltimore: Johns Hopkins University Press.

Task Force on Prevention of Low Birthweight and Infant Mortality. 1985. *Closing the Gaps: Strategies for Improving the Health of Massachusetts Infants*. Report to the Massachusetts Department of Public Health. Boston: The Task Force.

Taylor, Terry. 1981. "190 Housing Units—and 5000 Applicants." *Boston Globe*, April 29.

Tierney, Michael. 1984. "A State Strategy for Neighborhood Development." Massachusetts Executive Office of Communities and Development. Mimeographed.

Traxler, William B., Jr., Jefferson Boone Aiken, III, John E. Carbaugh, Jr., James M. Griffin, and John Milling. 1973. "The 235 Housing Program in Action: An Empirical Examination of its Administration and Effect on the Homeowner–Participant in the Columbia, South Carolina Area." *South Carolina Law Review* 25, no. 1.

Tremblay, Kenneth R., Jr., and Don A. Dillman. 1983. *Beyond the American Dream: Accommodation to the 1980s*. Lanham, Md.: University Press of America.

Turner, John F. C. 1976. *Housing by People: Towards Autonomy in Building Environments*. New York: Pantheon Books.

Twentieth Century Fund. 1971. *CDC's: New Hope for the Inner City*. New York: Twentieth Century Fund.

U.S. Bureau of the Census. 1980. *Census of Population and Housing. Census Tracts: Springfield-Chicopee-Holyoke, Mass.-Conn. SMSA*. PHC 80-2-341. Washington, D.C.: U.S. Department of Commerce. Issued July 1983.

——. 1982. *Annual Housing Survey: 1979*. Part B: "Indicators of Housing and Neighborhood Quality by Financial Characteristics, U.S. and Regions." Ser. H 150-179. Washington, D.C.: Government Printing Office.

——. 1983. *Annual Housing Survey: 1983*. Part C: "Financial Characteristics of the Housing Inventory, U.S. and Regions." Ser. H 150-183. Washington, D.C.: Government Printing Office.

U.S. Commission on Civil Rights. 1975. *Twenty Years After Brown: Equal Opportunity in Housing.* Washington, D.C.: Government Printing Office.

U.S. Congress. Joint Committee on Taxation. 1988. *Estimates of Federal Tax Expenditures for Fiscal Years 1989–1993.* Report prepared for the Committee on Ways and Means and the Committee on Finance. Washington, D.C.: Government Printing Office.

U.S. Congress. Joint Economic Committee, Subcommittee on Priorities and Economy in Government. 1972. *Hearings on Housing Subsidies and Housing Policies,* 92nd Cong., 2d sess., December.

———. 1973. *Hearings on Housing Subsidies and Housing Policy,* 93rd Cong., 1st sess., March.

U.S. Congressional Budget Office. 1983. *Federal Subsidies for Public Housing: Issues and Options.* Washington, D.C.: Government Printing Office.

U.S. Congressional Research Service. 1976. *Comparative Costs and Estimated Households Eligible for Participation in Federally Assisted Low Income Housing Programs.* Washington, D.C.: Government Printing Office.

U.S. Department of Housing and Urban Development. 1971. Office of Audit. *Audit Review of Section 235 Single Family Housing.* Report No. 05-2-2001-4900. Washington, D.C.: Government Printing Office.

———. 1972. Office of Audit. *Report on Audit of Section 236 Multifamily Housing Program.* Report No. 05-02-2001-5000. Washington, D.C.: Government Printing Office.

———. 1973a. *Housing in the Seventies.* Washington, D.C.: Government Printing Office.

———. 1973b. Office of Audit. *Report on Internal Audit of HUD Single Family Appraisal/Inspection Procedures and Mortgagees' Loan Processing Activities.* Report No. 05-2-4001-000. Washington, D.C.: Government Printing Office.

———. 1975a. Office of Policy Development and Research. *Neighborhood Preservation, A Catalog of Local Programs.* Washington, D.C.: Government Printing Office.

———. 1975b. *Housing Production with Nonprofit Sponsors: A Staff Study.* Washington, D.C.: Government Printing Office.

———. 1975c. *Multifamily Property Disposition: A Staff Study.* Washington, D.C.: Government Printing Office.

———. 1977. Boston Area Office. *Assisted Multi-Family Projects, City of Boston.* Washington, D.C.: Government Printing Office.

———. 1978a. *Programs of HUD.* Washington, D.C.: Government Printing Office.

———. 1978b. *Final Report of the HUD Multifamily Property Utilization Task Force.* Washington, D.C.: Government Printing Office.

———. 1979a. Office of Neighborhoods, Voluntary Associations and Consumer Protection. *Neighborhoods: A Self-Help Sampler.* Washington, D.C.: Government Printing Office.

————. 1979b. Office of Policy Development and Research. *Housing for the Elderly and Handicapped: The Experience of the Section 202 Program from 1959 to 1977.* HUD PDR-301-(2). Washington, D.C.: Government Printing Office.

————. 1979c. *Discrimination Against Chicanos in the Dallas Rental Market.* Washington, D.C.: Government Printing Office.

————. 1979d. *Measuring Racial Discrimination in American Housing Markets: The Housing Market Practices Survey.* Washington, D.C.: Government Printing Office.

————. 1980a. Office of Policy Development and Research. *Experimental Housing Allowance Program: Conclusions, the 1980 Report.* Washington, D.C.: Government Printing Office.

————. 1980b. *1979 Statistical Yearbook.* Washington, D.C.: Government Printing Office.

————. 1980c. Office of Neighborhoods, Voluntary Associations and Consumer Protection. *Neighborhood Self-Help Case Studies.* Washington, D.C.: Government Printing Office.

————. 1981. Office of Policy Development and Research. *Rental Housing: Condition and Outlook.* Washington, D.C.: Government Printing Office.

————. 1982. Office of Inspector General. *National Report on the Transfer of Physical Assets in the Sale of Multifamily Projects.* No. 82-TS-113-0013. Washington, D.C.: Government Printing Office.

————. 1983. Office of Inspector General. *Report to the Congress.* No. 10. Washington, D.C.: Government Printing Office.

————. 1984. Office of Inspector General. *Internal Audit of Income Projections Used by Public Housing Agencies under the Performance Funding System.* Washington, D.C.: Government Printing Office.

————. 1988. *HUD Perspective on Public Housing Modernization.* No. 1142-PDR. March.

U.S. District Court. 1981. Civil Action Complaint No. 82-0422-F. District of Massachusetts, Western Division.

U.S. General Accounting Office. 1978. *Section 236 Rental Housing: An Evaluation with Lessons for the Future.* Report to the Congress of the United States by the Comptroller General. PAD 78-13. Washington, D.C.: Government Printing Office.

————. 1979a. *Rental Housing: A National Problem That Needs Immediate Attention.* Report to the Congress of the United States by the Comptroller General. LED-80-11. Washington, D.C.: Government Printing Office.

————. 1979b. *HUD Should Improve Its Management of Acquired Formerly-Subsidized Multifamily Projects.* Report to the Congress of the United States by the Comptroller General. Washington, D.C.: Government Printing Office.

———. 1980. *Evaluation of Alternatives for Financing Low and Moderate Income Rental Housing*. Report to the Congress of the United States by the Comptroller General. PAD 80-13. Washington, D.C.: Government Printing Office.

———. 1985a. *Changes in Rent Burdens and Housing Conditions of Lower Income Households*. Report prepared by the Division of Resources, Community, and Economic Development for Senator Donald W. Riegle, Jr. Washington, D.C.: Government Printing Office.

———. 1985b. *Impact of Federal Tax Provisions on Resyndication of Federally Assisted Rental Housing*. Report to the Honorable Donald W. Riegle, Jr., U.S. Senate. GAO/RCED-85-112. Washington, D.C.: Government Printing Office. July 10.

———. 1986. *Public Housing: Proposed Sale of the Allen Parkway Village Project in Houston, Texas*. Report to the Chairman, Subcommittee on Housing and Community Development, Committee on Banking Finance and Urban Affairs, U.S. House of Representatives. GAO/RCED-86-160. Washington, D.C.: Government Printing Office.

U.S. House of Representatives. Committee on Banking and Currency. 1952. *Hearings Before the Subcommittee on Housing*, 82nd Cong., 2d sess.

———. 1959. *Hearings*, 86th Cong., 1st sess., January 28–February 3.

———. 1961. *Hearings*, 87th Cong., 1st sess., April 24–May 5.

———. 1968. *House Committee Report on the 1968 Act*. Washington, D.C.: Government Printing Office.

———. 1970. *Investigation and Hearing of Abuses in Federal Low- and Moderate-Income Housing Programs*, 91st Cong., 2d sess., December.

U.S. House of Representatives. Committee on Banking, Finance, and Urban Affairs. 1987. *Housing, Community Development, and Homelessness Prevention Act of 1987*. With Minority, Supplemental, and Additional Views, 100th Cong., 1st sess. Report 100-122. June 2.

U.S. House of Representatives. Committee on Government Operations. 1971. *Hearings on Defaults on FHA-Insured Mortgages (Detroit)*, 91st Cong., 1st sess., December.

———. 1972a. *Hearings on Defaults on FHA-Insured Mortgages*, 92nd Cong., 2d sess., February and May.

———. 1972b. *Fifteenth Report: Defaults on FHA-Insured Home Mortgages, Detroit, Michigan*, 92nd Cong., 2d sess., June 20.

———. 1973. *Review of Federal Housing Administration*, pt. 1, *The Financial Status of FHA Mortgage Insurance Funds*, 93rd Cong., 1st sess., July 10, 11, 12.

———. 1974. *Review of Federal Housing Administration*, pt. 2, *Update of FHA Mortgage Insurance Funds Deficits*, 93rd Cong., 2d sess., March.

———. 1976. *Nineteenth Report: HUD's Responsiveness to Previous Recommendations for Corrective Action*, 94th Cong., 2d sess., March 29.

———. 1983a. *Hearings on HUD Multifamily Property Disposition Programs*, 98th Cong., 1st sess., May 24, 25.

————. 1983b. *Hearings on HUD Multifamily Repair and Foreclosure Policies,* 98th Cong., 1st sess., July 26.

————. 1983c. *Eleventh Report: HUD Is Not Adequately Preserving Subsidized Multifamily Housing,* 98th Cong., 1st sess.

U.S. Senate. 1955. *Hearings Before the Committee on Banking and Currency,* 84th Cong., 1st sess.

————. 1965. *Hearings Before the Committee on Banking and Currency,* 89th Cong., 1st sess., March 29–April 9.

————. 1968. *Hearings Before the Committee on Banking and Currency,* 90th Cong., 2d sess., March 5–20.

————. 1972. *Hearings Before the Subcommittee on Antitrust and Monopoly of the Committee on the Judiciary, Competition in Real Estate and Mortgage Lending,* parts 2A and 2B, 92nd Cong., 2d sess., May and June.

————. 1980. *Hearings on Management of HUD's Multifamily Properties: The Clifton Terrace Case,* 96th Cong., 1st sess.

Urban Planning Aid. 1973a. *Community Development Corporations: The Empty Promise.* Cambridge, Mass.: Urban Planning Aid.

————. 1973b. "An Evaluation of the Boston Urban Rehabilitation Program." In *Housing Urban America,* edited by Jon Pynoos, Robert Schafer, and Chester W. Hartman. Chicago: Aldine.

Urban Systems Research and Engineering, Inc. 1981. *Neighborhood Housing Services and the Neighborhood Reinvestment Corporation.* Report prepared for the U.S. Department of Housing and Urban Development, Office of Policy Development and Research.

————. 1982. *The Costs of HUD Multifamily Housing Programs.* Report prepared for the U.S. Department of Housing and Urban Development, Office of Policy Development and Research.

Vega, Carlos, ed. 1983. *Puerto Ricans in Holyoke: The Last Wave.* Holyoke, Mass.: Holyoke Public History Project.

Vidal, Avis C., Arnold M. Howitt, Kathleen P. Foster, et al. 1986. *Stimulating Community Development: An Assessment of the Local Initiatives Support Corporation.* Report submitted to the Local Initiatives Support Corporation by the State, Local, and Intergovernmental Center, John F. Kennedy School of Government, Harvard University.

Walker, Richard A. 1978. "Two Sources of Uneven Development under Advance Capitalism: Spatial Differentiation and Capital Mobility." *Review of Radical Political Economics* 10, No. 3: 28–37.

Wallace, James E., Susan Philipson Bloom, and William L. Holshauser. 1981. *Participation and Benefits in the Urban Section 8 Program: New Construction and Existing Housing.* Report prepared for the U.S. Department of Housing and Urban Development, Office of Policy Development and Research, by Abt Associates, Inc.

Ward, Barbara. 1976. *The Home of Man.* New York: Norton.

Warren, Paul. 1982. *The Effect of Voucher-Based Subsidies on Urban Public*

Housing Authorities. Policy analysis exercise prepared for the Kennedy School of Government, Harvard University.

Weaver, Robert. 1985. "Looking Back at HUD." *Journal Forum* 469 (Fall).

Weicher, John C. 1981. "Comments on Anthony Downs, 'Some Aspects of the Future of Rental Housing.'" In *Rental Housing: Is There a Crisis?* edited by John C. Weicher, Kevin E. Villani and Elizabeth A. Roistacher, 95–98. Washington, D.C.: Urban Institute.

Weidemann, Sue, James R. Anderson, Dorothy I. Butterfield, and Patricia M. O'Donnell. 1982. "Residents' Perceptions of Satisfaction and Safety: A Basis for Change in Multifamily Housing." *Environment and Behavior* 12, no. 6: 695–724.

White, Kirby, and Charles Matthei. 1987. "Community Land Trusts." In *Beyond the Market and the State*, edited by Severyn T. Bruyn and James Meehan, 41–64. Philadelphia: Temple University Press.

Whiteside, William A. 1983. "Administration's Housing Authorization Proposals for Fiscal Year 1984." Statement submitted to the House Banking, Finance and Urban Affairs Subcommittee on Housing and Community Development. February 23 and March 1.

Will, Herbert L. 1974. *Community Planning Report* (Washington, D.C.) 1, no. 14 (October 31).

Wilner, Daniel M., Rosabelle Price Walkey, Thomas C. Pinkerton, and Matthew Tayback. 1962. *The Housing Environment and Family Life.* Baltimore: Johns Hopkins University Press.

Wilson, James Q. 1966. "Planning and Politics: Citizen Participation in Urban Renewal." In *Urban Renewal: The Record and the Controversy*, edited by James Q. Wilson, 407–421. Cambridge: MIT Press.

Wolfe, Tom. 1970. *Radical Chic and Mau-Mauing the Flak Catchers.* New York: Bantam.

Women's Economic Agenda Working Group. 1985. *Toward Economic Justice for Women: A National Agenda for Change.* Washington, D.C.: Institute for Policy Studies.

Wood, Edith Elmer. 1919. *The Housing of the Unskilled Wage Earner.* New York: Macmillan.

Wurster, Catherine Bauer. 1957. "The Dreary Deadlock of Public Housing." *Architectural Forum* 106, no. 5 (May): 140–142, 219, 221.

Yates, Douglas. 1977. *The Ungovernable City: The Politics of Urban Problems and Policy Making.* Cambridge: MIT Press.

Index

Low-income housing (*continued*)
(*see* Homeownership); scarcity of,
10–13. *See also* Community-based
housing; Public housing; Publicly
subsidized private housing
Low-income housing, evaluation of:
community-based programs, 196–
205; contributions/limitations of, 24–
26; and multiple goals of programs at
cost to human impacts, 33–35; and
need to broaden evaluation criteria,
26–33, 318; public housing, 63–80;
publicly subsidized private housing,
95–103
Low-income housing, federal policy on,
3–6, 318–343; call for new federal
commitment to, 320–343; ending
land speculation in, 338–340; ending
stigmas against, 336–338; gender
sensitivity in, 340–341; maintaining
affordable housing, 335–336; new and
revised programs in, 321–335; role of
HUD in, 341–343; scarcity of housing
and trend toward noninvolvement
in, 10–13; strategies for encouraging
construction of, 18–24
Low Income Housing Information
Service, 8, 74
Low-income housing production
strategy, 18–24; capital grants for, 21;
direct production subsidies for, 22–24;
FHA and HUD's, 140–142; private
market regulation of, 21; private–
public partnerships in, 87–94, 102,
104–105, 117–119, 121, 171, 290–317,
321, 329–335, 337; and supports to
financial institutions, 18–20; and tax
incentives for (*see* Tax incentives for
low-income housing)
Low-income housing tax credit, 3, 20–
21, 105, 107–108, 193, 271, 352 n.4,
353 n.11
Luckett, Jim, 307–308, 359 n.14
Lynn, Mass., 78, 337

McAfee, Kathy, 235–236
MacArthur Foundation, Fund for Community Development, 324

Madison, Wis., 194
Marable, Manning, 216
Marcuse, Peter, 339–340
Marris, Peter, 41
Marxist critiques, 210–211, 348 n.2
Massachusetts: case study of Holyoke,
206–230; proposition 2½, 221; public
housing in, 71
Massachusetts Association of Com-
munity Development Corporations,
282
Massachusetts Chapter 705 program,
227, 357 n.9
Massachusetts Chapter 707 program,
245, 253, 274, 278, 293, 300, 301
Massachusetts Commission Against
Discrimination (MCAD), 225–226,
241, 248
Massachusetts Commonwealth Service
Corps, 275
Massachusetts Community Development
Finance Corporation (CDFC), 244,
265–276, 284, 285, 287, 288, 293,
301; moves into housing, 269–272
Massachusetts Community Economic
Development Assistance Corporation
(CEDAC), 149, 157–158, 266–269,
274, 284, 285, 288, 303; moves into
housing, 269–272
Massachusetts Community Enterprise
Economic Development (CEED),
268–269, 284, 285, 292
Massachusetts Community Services
Block Grant, 274
Massachusetts Executive Office of Com-
munities and Development, 157, 244,
248–249, 268, 274, 285, 287, 288,
303, 314
Massachusetts Government Land Bank,
226; support for community-based
housing through, 273–274
Massachusetts Homeownership Oppor-
tunity Program, 274
Massachusetts Housing Abandonment
Program, 275
Massachusetts Housing Finance Agency
(MHFA), 159–161, 248–249, 254;
support for community-based housing

developers' position on resyndication in MHFA case study, 111–113; federal strategies to encourage low-income construction in, 18–24; federal subsidies for housing production/ownership by, 22–24 (see also Publicly subsidized private housing); nonprofits' limited partnership with for-profits, 192–196; nonprofits' sponsorship of multifamily housing using Section 202 program, 184–185; nonprofits' sponsorship of multifamily housing using Section 221(d)(3) and 236 programs, 185–191, 354 n.4; public–private housing partnerships, 87–94, 102, 104–105, 117–119, 121, 171, 290–317, 319, 321, 329–335, 337; and recommendations on federal policy toward public–private partnerships, 334–336; regulation of, 21, 347 n.5; role of, in low-income housing shortages, 7–10, 11, 347 n.5; tax incentives for (see Tax incentives for low-income housing)
Privatization of public housing, 54–55, 79, 81–82
Proulx, Ernest, 215, 220, 221, 223, 225, 226
Proxmire, William, 92, 150
Pruitt–Igoe, St. Louis, 53, 54, 71, 78, 349–350 n.6
Psychological factors related to housing, 26–33; as enhancing well-being of tenants, 79–80, 104, 200–201; little attention to, by policymakers, 33–35
Public housing, 53–85, 319; ability to accommodate neediest in, 78–79; accessibility of, to public services, 70; administration/management of, 59–60, 67–70, 348 n.4; community-based management and ownership of, 173–175; costs of, to federal government, 72–77; and federal government commitment to housing with, 79; financial viability of, 77–78; financing and operating subsidies for, 22, 57–59; future policy considerations in, 80–85; historical overview of, 55–

62, 349 n.2; leased-housing program in, 61, 73, 81, 91; modernization of, 59; negative image of, 53; negative image vs. reality in, 63–80; physical characteristics, condition, and design of, 65–67, 350 n.8; production/location of, 56, 57, 60–61, 349 nn.4,5; racial integration of, 70–72; Reagan administration Privatization Commission's policy toward, 54–55; recommendations for a new federal policy on, 321–323; sale of, to tenants, 54, 79, 82–83; tenants in (see Tenants); turnkey program in, 61–62, 81, 91, 93
Public Housing Administration, 58
Public Housing Homeownership Demonstration Program, 82
Publicly subsidized private housing, 86–103; ability of, to accommodate the neediest, 100; assessment of, 95–103; federal housing policy toward, from 1930s to 1980s, 87–94; financial viability of, 97–100; leased housing program in, 61, 73, 81, 91; physical characteristics, condition, and design of, 96; racial integration impacts on, 96–97; tenants in (see Tenants)
Public sector: federal subsidies for housing ownership/production by private partnerships, 22, 87–94, 102, 104–105, 117–119, 121, 171, 290–317, 321 (see also Tax incentives for low-income housing); recommendations on federal policy toward public–private partnerships, 329–335, 337; support for community-based housing (see Community-based housing, public support for, in Mass.). See also Federal government; Local government; State government
Public services: cutbacks in, for low-income residents', 221; public housing's accessibility to, 70
Puerto Ricans, 207, 213–215, 227
Puerto Rico, 29, 207, 213–214, 349–350 n.6. See also Inquilinos Boricuas en Acción (IBA), Boston

Weremiuk, Kathy, 312
West Germany, 194
West Harlem Community Organization, 200
White, Kirby, 181
Whittlesey, Robert, 287, 299, 300, 357–358 n.13
Wilmington, Delaware, 63–64
Wilner, Daniel N., 26
Wilson, James Q., 36, 38–39
Winn, Philip D., 147; memorandum, 147
Wisconsin, public housing in, 71
Wolfe, Tom, 43

Women, housing for, 15, 340–341
Wood, Edith, 349 n.2, 354 n.3
Wood, Robert, 122
Woodstock Institute, 182
Worcester Cooperation Council Home Improvement Program, Worcester, Mass., 180
Workable Program, 37
World War II, 56, 58, 207, 349 n.2
Wurster, Catherine Bauer, 60, 183, 349 n.2

Zigas, Barry, 74
Zoning codes, 347 n.5; inclusionary, 21